Counter-terrorism Networks in the European Union

Counter-terrorism Networks in the European Union

Maintaining Democratic Legitimacy after 9/11

Claudia Hillebrand

OXFORD
UNIVERSITY PRESS

OXFORD
UNIVERSITY PRESS

Great Clarendon Street, Oxford, OX2 6DP,
United Kingdom

Oxford University Press is a department of the University of Oxford.
It furthers the University's objective of excellence in research, scholarship,
and education by publishing worldwide. Oxford is a registered trade mark of
Oxford University Press in the UK and in certain other countries

First Edition published in 2012

Published in the United States of America by Oxford University Press
198 Madison Avenue, New York, NY 10016, United States of America

British Library Cataloguing in Publication Data
Data available

Library of Congress Cataloging in Publication Data
Data available

ISBN 978–0–19–965505–2

Acknowledgements

Writing this book has been a journey during which I have acquired many intellectual debts. First, I thank my colleagues Alistair Shepherd and Len Scott who have been incredibly supportive.

I am grateful to all the public officials and counter-terrorism experts who took off some time from their busy schedules to talk to me about my project. My interviewees requested to remain anonymous, which is completely understandable given the sensitive field of the research.

A number of people provided insights and support at various stages on the way. I would like to express my gratitude to Peter Gill, Peter Jackson, Thierry Balzacq, Christopher Harding, Monica Den Boer, Christian Kaunert, Marco König, John Occhipinti, Sarah Leonard, Andreas Nölke, Jörg Monar, Roger Scully, and Wolfgang Wagner. For what I have made of their advice I alone am responsible.

As this book engages with network-like structures, it might come as little surprise to the reader that I believe in the importance of social networks. My personal one provided me with the comfort and freedom to work on this project and, when necessary, offered distraction and fun to free my head. Many will have to go unnamed here, but I want to highlight Jay and Mari, Davide, Zeynep, and Nils for offering their couches during my field trips, Sebastian for opening the doors to the policy world of Washington, DC for me, and Ross, Ed, Rich, and Soumita for their advice. Special thanks go to my family for their unconditional support and great patience.

During the course of this research, I was supported by the European Community under the Marie Curie Host Fellowship for Early Stage Research Training, which also allowed me to conduct interviews both in Europe and the US. Without this Fellowship, this book would not have been written. I am also indebted to the Netherlands Institute for International Relations—Clingendael, The Hague, which hosted me as a visiting researcher for three months in 2008.

This book is for you, Huw. Thank you for reminding me that there is more to life than counter-terrorism and the EU.

Claudia Hillebrand
Aberystwyth, February 2012

Contents

List of Abbreviations

ACLU	American Civil Liberties Union
AFP	Agence France-Press
AFSJ	Area of Freedom, Security and Justice
AWF	Analysis Work File
BfV	Federal Office for the Protection of the Constitution
BIBE	Bank of Spain Investigation Unit
BKA	Federal Police Office
BND	Federal Intelligence Service
BR	Red Brigades
CAT	(UN) Convention against Torture
CBP	Bureau of Customs and Border Protection
CEPOL	European Police College
CEPS	Centre for European Policy Studies
CFI	Court of First Instance
CIA	Central Intelligence Agency
CNCA	National Centre of Anti-terrorist Coordination
CoE	Council of Europe
COSAC	Conference of Parliamentary Committees for Union Affairs of Parliaments of the European Union
COSI	Standing Committee on operational cooperation on internal security
COSPOL	Comprehensive Operational Strategic Planning for the Police
CPS	Crown Prosecution Service
CSDP	Common Security and Defence Policy
CSI	Container Security Initiative
CT	Counter-terrorism
CTA	Clandestine Transnational Actor
CTG	Counter-terrorism Group
CTIU	Counter-terrorism intelligence unit
CTN	Counter-terrorism network
CTP	Counter-terrorism policing
C-TPAT	Customs-Trade Partnership against Terrorism
CTTF	Counter-terrorism Task Force
CTU	Counter-terrorism unit
DG	Director General
DHS	Department of Homeland Security
DPD	Data Protection Directive
DPFD	Data Protection Framework Directive
DPO	Data Protection Officer

EAW	European Arrest Warrant
EBDS	European Bomb Data System
ECCHR	European Center for Constitutional and Human Rights
ECD	Europol Council Decision
ECHR	European Convention on Human Rights
ECJ	European Court of Justice
ECRIS	European Criminal Records Information System
ECtHR	European Court of Human Rights
EDIU/EDU	European Drugs Intelligence Unit
EEAS	European External Action Service
EEODN	European Explosive Ordnance Disposal Network
EEW	European Evidence Warrant
EIS	Europol Information System
ELB	Europol Liaison Bureau
ELO	Europol Liaison Officer
ENU	Europol National Unit
EP	European Parliament
EPE	Europol Platform for Experts
ESDP	European Security and Defence Policy
ESETF	Explosives Security Experts Task Force
ESS	European Security Strategy
ETA	*Euskadi Ta Askatasuna*
EU	European Union
EULEC	European Institute for Freedom, Security and Justice
EuNAT	European Network of Advisory Teams
Eurodac	European Fingerprint Database
EWS	Early Warning System
FATF	Financial Action Task Force
FBI	Federal Bureau of Investigation
FIU	Finance Intelligence Unit
FRN	First Response Network
Frontex	The European Agency for the Management of Operational Cooperation at the External Borders of the Member States of the European Union
GTAZ	Joint Counter-terrorism Centre
GWOT	Global War on Terrorism
HENU	Head of National Unit
HUMINT	Human intelligence
HVD	High Value Detainee
ICPO	International Criminal Police Organization
iOCTA	Threat Assessment on Internet Facilitated Organised Crime
IRA	Irish Republican Army
JCHR	Joint Committee on Human Rights
JHA	Justice and Home Affairs
JIT	Joint Investigation Team
JSB	Europol Joint Supervisory Body

JTAC	Joint Terrorism Analysis Centre
LIBE	Committee on Civil Liberties, Justice and Home Affairs
LTTE	Liberation Tigers of Tamil Eelam
MAD	Military Counterintelligence Agency
MEP	Member of the European Parliament
MI5	Security Service
MP	Member of Parliament
MS	Member State(s)
NATO	North Atlantic Treaty Organization
NCTC	National Counterterrorism Center
NIAS	Intelligence analysis and information point
NP	National Parliament
NSB	National data protection supervisory body
NTA	New Transatlantic Agenda
NYPD	New York Police Department
OCAM	*Organe de Coordination pour l'Analyse de la Menace*
OCTA	Organized Crime Threat Assessment
OLAF	European Anti-Fraud Office
OSCE	Organization for Security and Cooperation in Europe
PACE	Council of Europe Parliamentary Assembly
PCTF	Police Chiefs Task Force
PIAS	Police analysis and information point
PJCC	Police and judicial cooperation in criminal matters
PKGr	German Parliamentary Control Panel concerning intelligence
PNR	Passenger Name Record
PWGT	Police Working Group on Terrorism
RAF	Red Army Faction
SCDEA	Scottish Crime and Drug Enforcement Agency
SIRENE	Supplementary Information Request at National Entry
SIS	Schengen Information System
SIS	Secret Intelligence Service
SISMI	*Servizio per le Informazioni e la Sicurezza Militare* (Military Intelligence and Security Service)
SitCen	Joint Situation Centre
SOCA	Serious Organised Crime Agency
SSI	State Security Investigations Service
SUPO	Security Intelligence Service
SWIFT	Society for Worldwide Interbank Financial Telecommunication
TDIP	Temporary Committee on the alleged use of European countries by the CIA for the transport and illegal detention of prisoners
TEC	Treaty establishing the European Community
TECS	Europol Computer System
TE-SAT EU	Terrorism Situation and Trend Report
TEU	Treaty on European Union

TFEU	Treaty on the Functioning of the European Union
TFTP	Terrorist Finance Tracking Programme
TSDB	Terrorist Screening Database
TREVI	*Terrorisme, Radicalisme, Extrémisme et Violence Internationale*
TWP	Terrorism Working Party
UK	United Kingdom
UN	United Nations
UNHCR	United Nations High Commissioner for Refugees
US	United States
VIS	Visa Information System
VWP	Visa Waiver Programme
WEU	Western European Union

Introduction

> *Many of today's security challenges are cross-border and cross-sectoral in nature. No single Member State is able to respond to these threats on its own.*
>
> (Commission, 2010a: 2)

> *Practices of transnational policing unfold in opaque governmental settings that empower a new coterie of security actors. Each, in different ways, obscures lines of transparency and accountability and gives a new twist to long-standing problems of democratic authorization and legitimation.*
>
> (Loader and Walker, 2007: 21–2)

Terrorism is now widely perceived as an 'international problem with domestic implications' (Hennessy, 2007: 25).[1] As a consequence, counter-terrorism policing (CTP) increasingly stretches across the globe. Cooperation in network-like structures between security authorities of different countries has become a crucial feature of efforts in the fight against terrorism since the attacks on New York and Washington on 11 September 2001 (hereafter 9/11 attacks).[2] At the domestic level, European counter-terrorism (CT) actors have experienced a considerable increase in budgets, a widening of their mandates, and broadening of their

---

[1] Much has been written about the lack of an international definition of terrorism and the struggle of scholars to agree on a common vocabulary (Guillaume, 2004; Schmid and Jongman, 1988). The label 'terrorist' is so emotionally charged and widely used in a pejorative manner that some have suggested not using it at all. Given those challenges, it was widely understood as a remarkable achievement of the Member States (MS) of the European Union (EU) to agree on a legal definition of terrorism in 2002 (Council, 2002a). This book will refer to terrorism as defined in that Council Framework Decision.

[2] The terms cooperation and collaboration will be used interchangeably in this book.

functions. At the global level, international organizations—most notably the United Nations (UN)—have set up CT units or expanded their existing capacity to fight terrorism.

Located between the domestic and the global level, the European Union (EU) has emerged as a CT actor in the aftermath of 9/11. This book is concerned with the ways in which the EU established and fostered cooperation in this field. It approaches the EU as an emerging networking security actor in the fight against terrorism. It will outline how the EU spins network-like structures between European institutions involved in CTP and provides a framework for such bodies to set up communication networks under its umbrella. Most of these efforts focus on the sharing of information and, in its processed form, intelligence.

The term CTP refers to measures intended to *prevent* terrorism, aiming at the intervention in processes that—potentially—lead to criminal behaviour. CT activities range from investigations and surveillance by police and intelligence authorities to intelligence gathering, strengthened border security, and so on.[3] They also include activities which inform decision-makers' strategic efforts to anticipate threats and target preventive action (Verfaillie and Vander Beken, 2008: 534). Intervention at an early stage is understood to be of particular relevance concerning contemporary transnational terrorism, as one successful attack might cause a high number of casualties (Treverton, 2009). Yet, given the emphasis on pre-emption, this type of policing is 'more likely to interfere with the rights of the individual than conventional police powers' (Privy Counsellor Review Committee, 2003: point 86).

A focus on early intervention implies that many CT practices, including those of the EU, concern terrorist *suspects*, or *potential* terrorists. While the criteria of who constitutes a suspect are vague and often not legally defined, the CT measures can be harsh.[4] Usama Nasr, better known as Abu Omar, had to experience this when he was kidnapped by officials of the American Central Intelligence Agency (CIA) on the streets of Milan, Italy on 17 February 2003 and brought by plane to Egypt. Officials of Italy's military intelligence service (then SISMI) were involved in the abduction. In the fourteen months of Abu Omar's detention by the Egyptian State Security Investigations Service (SSI), he was allegedly subject to torture (Hendricks, 2010). He was never charged for a crime. Abu Omar had become subject to one of the most notorious CT measures in the aftermath of the 9/11 attacks—the 'extraordinary rendition' campaign run by the CIA. While the term lacks a definition in international law, it refers to the transportation of

---

[3] The term 'intelligence services' refers to both domestic secret services and foreign intelligence services, unless stated otherwise.

[4] A British Privy Counsellor Review Committee (2003) pointed out that such suspicion can be based on intelligence material which is either inadmissible as evidence in a criminal court or material which the authorities do not wish to disclose for fear of compromising sources or methods. In Germany, security authorities categorize terrorist suspects as 'endangerers' (*Gefährder*)—a category which has no basis in law (Deutscher Bundestag, Wissenschaftliche Dienste, 2008).

terrorist suspects from one country to another without legal proceedings (European Parliament, TDIP Committee, 2007).

International cooperation is widely understood to strengthen proactive efforts of policing. Terrorism can be seen as one of the 'policy issues that cut across territorial jurisdictions and existing political alignments, and which require international cooperation for their satisfactory resolution' (Held, 2004: 366). In the EU, and the transatlantic arena more broadly, most security actors had already some collaborative experience before the 9/11 attacks, but they are now said to cooperate more intensely, regularly, and in more network-like structures than ever before, in particular with respect to data sharing (Gill and Phythian, 2006; Andreas and Nadelmann, 2006; Aldrich, 2009a).

This book is concerned with the question of whether international networking and the emphasis on proactive CTP are sufficiently subject to forms of democratic scrutiny. It will focus on the EU as a regional political entity comprising national, transnational, and integrated supranational policing bodies and actions. The networks explored in the following chapters aim to provide security to the EU and its citizens, or the transatlantic sphere more broadly. Terrorism is conceived as a key threat to the safety of EU citizens and, as a consequence, it is deemed as justified that CT bodies have wide-ranging powers and instruments to ensure the provision of security (eg, Council, 2004b; UK Prime Minister's Office, 2005). Yet it is the concern of this book to explore how far such cooperation is democratically legitimized.

The term democratic legitimacy involves mechanisms which link a political entity's governance structures—in this case, the EU—to its citizenry. The relationship between policing bodies and the citizenry has always been complicated given the coercive means involved, and this is in particular the case concerning the increased used of proactive CT measures. The EU is striving for an Area of Freedom, Security and Justice (AFSJ), first announced in the 1997 Treaty of Amsterdam amending the Treaty on European Union, The Treaties Establishing the European Communities and certain related Acts (Amsterdam Treaty) and reemphasized in the Treaty of Lisbon amending the Treaty on European Union and the Treaty establishing the European Community (Lisbon Treaty), which entered into force on 1 December 2009, as well as the EU Internal Security Strategy (ISS) of 2010 (Council, 2010a).[5] Drawing on social contract theory, societies grant powers to executive bodies, but mechanisms of scrutiny are meant to ensure that the bodies are limited in their activities and can be held responsible for them at the same time. As a consequence, in European policing the 'need for protection *by* the police has always been accompanied by the need for protection

[5] The Lisbon Treaty amends the EU's previous core treaties, the Treaty on European Union (TEU) and the Treaty establishing the European Community (TEC), which is now renamed Treaty on the Functioning of the European Union (TFEU). It brought, and—due to periods of transition—will continue to bring, institutional reforms.

against the police' (Van Sluis and Cachet, 2007: 107; emphasis in original). Given the EU's increasing efforts at providing security, the question arises of what is the nature of the relationship between this security provider and the citizens.

Focus of Research

The EU continues to challenge traditional ideas of sovereignty as it increasingly takes over tasks that were territorially organized within state borders, including core aspects of a state's sovereignty. This is a well-known transfer in several policy fields, such as economics (the 'common market'). In the field of internal security provision, the EU is only meant to get involved where/when it can provide an 'added value' to the national policies and actions—in other words, if it can deliver a service or good that the MS cannot, or less well, provide on an individual basis (Monar, 2005a).[6] In those fields, the MS keep most of their sovereignty—though they might pool it—and might conduct actions parallel to the EU. One of this book's aims is therefore to describe and analyse which CT tasks have been transferred to the transnational level and how CTP is conducted in this framework.

The focus of the analysis will be on network-like CTP structures. Though little explored in the academic literature so far, networks tend to raise normative concerns with respect to democratic legitimacy, even more so in an international context (for exceptions see Sørensen and Torfing, 2005; Gill and Phythian, 2006; Aldrich, 2009b). The network concept is a useful methodological tool to embrace the structural particularities of EU-wide CT activities. Executive network structures can pose a threat to democratic governance (O'Toole, 1997). Ironically, their structural advantages and therefore the causes of their existence—flexibility, adaptability, and their decentralized nature—are problematic with respect to mechanisms of democratic legitimacy (Gerspacher and Dupont, 2007: 348; Sørensen and Torfing, 2005).

Security institutions and practices are traditionally embedded, guided, controlled, and overseen in a domestic framework. The forms of CT cooperation analysed in this research include a mix of national and transnational, public and private network participants. This creates further problems with regard to scrutiny. In addition, practices of fighting transnational terrorism blur the realm of internal and external security. Some authors imagine an emerging EU 'homeland security policy' (Davis Cross, 2007). To what extent do those forms of security provision challenge mechanisms of scrutiny, and democratic legitimacy more broadly? To study this in more depth, the research focuses on the question of what are the particular challenges for arrangements for parliamentary and judicial scrutiny of EU-wide CT cooperation.

---

[6] 'Maintaining law and order and safeguarding national security' are two of the 'essential State functions', which the EU has to 'respect', according to art 4(2) TEU. The Justice and Home Affairs (JHA) provisions shall not affect the exercise of national responsibilities in these fields.

External scrutiny ought to ensure democratic accountability and oversight as well as the protection of fundamental rights and compliance with the rule of law. Yet, the following chapters will show that the EU provides for forms of CTP that do not (always) meet these political ideals. Two key features to ensure democratic legitimacy in this field can be identified: parliamentary scrutiny—to ensure democratic accountability and oversight—and instruments to ensure the protection of human rights and compliance with the rule of law through judicial scrutiny. Concerning the latter, the focus of the analysis will be on mechanisms and instruments established to protect individuals against harm by transnational policing activities at the EU level. Both parliamentary and judicial scrutiny used to be conceptualized within a domestic framework, but the development of transnational policing structures requires reconsidering the current arrangements and judging their appropriateness in this emerging environment. In particular, hurdles are posed by the increasing, loose, and sometimes ad hoc cooperation, the number of actors involved, and the overall secrecy surrounding CT practices. It is in this complex context that the monograph will discuss the relationship between democratic legitimacy and networked security provision in the field of EU-wide CTP.

Operationalization and Methodology

The research focuses on European-wide networks with a strong CTP agenda. Networks in this field vary in their membership, degree of institutionalization, purpose, mandate, and access for the academic researcher. Yet they are all information-sharing networks with a semi-operational character and CT as one of their priority tasks. Moreover, all of them involve European actors and are (partly) operational on European territory.[7]

The study of the network of the European Police Office (Europol) will provide the empirical anchorage of the research. Europol is widely understood as the EU's central law enforcement authority and its activities illustrate the changes in policing in general, and the focus on information exchange in transnational policing networks in particular. So far, there is 'a dearth of empirical research on Europol' (Busuioc et al, 2011: 849). Post-9/11, Europol struggled to define its role in the field of CT and it is illuminating to study the evolution of its efforts since. The analysis through a network lens facilitates the exploration of Europol's wider international contacts. In comparison to the other networks briefly mentioned earlier, it is a very formalized body accompanied by mechanisms of parliamentary and judicial scrutiny. Those mechanisms will be explored in depth in this book.

Yet many of the EU's CT actions are of a rather administrative and regulative manner. Prominent examples concern the EU–US exchange of Passenger Name

[7] That the geographical boundaries of the EU's security governance remain unclear will become obvious, for example with respect to the transatlantic dimension and several networks.

Record (PNR) data as well as the creation of terrorist lists and the subsequent freezing of financial assets of listed terrorist suspects or 'donors'. The inclusion of these instruments into the analysis provides a broader picture of the manifold ways in which the EU establishes networks, also with non-EU partners. It also allows scrutiny mechanisms to be discussed against a background of different settings.

Data Collection: Challenges

The research topic poses immediate challenges to any researcher interested in its empirical aspects. CTP is a secretive field and therefore access to information and individuals is restricted. This is even more so the case concerning cooperation with foreign partners. Also, the EU's policy area of police and judicial cooperation in criminal matters (PJCC) is well known for its lack of transparency and opaque decision-making structures (Monar, 2005b).

The primary data collection included a review of official documents by various EU and national bodies, some of which only became available through the work of civil society groups, such as Statewatch. This includes legislative documents and reports by inquiry bodies. In addition, I exploited court judgments, parliamentary reports, and media coverage. The primary sources are used in combination with relevant academic literatures, deriving from disciplines, such as international relations, sociology, criminology, policing as well as intelligence studies.

The book is also based on interviews conducted between December 2006 and August 2009 with personnel involved in, or with knowledge of, the networks under research. Interviews with individuals with a particular professional or political expertise or those 'with close proximity to power' (Lilleker, 2003: 207) are usually referred to as elite interviews in the academic literature. I conducted thirty-two interviews with, for example, personnel of Europol, other EU bodies, and national security authorities, including liaison officers stationed abroad. I also spoke with individuals involved in CT policy-making as well as its scrutiny (eg, through parliamentary committees and data protection bodies). The focus is on countries which feel threatened by current terrorism and have developed extensive CT policies and capabilities, such as Germany, the UK, the Netherlands, France, Belgium, and the US (Van Leeuwen, 2003; Brady, 2009: 7). While I also spoke to interviewees from Lithuania, Sweden, and Portugal, for example, the perspective of some MS is barely reflected in the interviews. The great majority of interviewees only agreed to being interviewed under the condition of anonymity.

Researching a 'Moving Target'

By its nature, this is a project bound to the contemporary moment. Concepts such as democracy, legitimacy, and accountability emerge within a particular historical context and do not carry a fixed meaning. Public perceptions of the necessity of certain CT measures depend on the particular time and space. Moreover, the EU itself constitutes a political realm which is difficult to classify as a political community and which has been struggling for reforms for some time. Finally, networks are, by definition, fluid entities and the researcher can only provide a momentary snapshot. This book focuses on the EU's CT activities between 11 September 2001 and 1 December 2009. Where applicable, the analysis will include an exploration of recent changes. The domestic structures are only touched upon insofar as they are of relevance for cross-border cooperation; otherwise the research will concentrate on the EU level.

Structure

The EU's network-like structures grow within a broader 'context of new nodes and networks of security delivery' (Fleming and Wood, 2006b: 2). The first chapter will place the EU's efforts into a wider context of security networks and transnational policing. An understanding of networks will be put forward which sees networks as actors with a common intention and shared aims. The chapter will conclude by introducing key CT efforts of, or related to, the EU.

Based on this, the second chapter will provide an overview of the discussion about democratic legitimacy in the context of transnational, and in particular EU policing. The chapter approaches democratic legitimacy from a liberal democratic governance perspective. The EU understands itself as a democratic political entity: it comprises twenty-seven MS with a democratic constitution, or constitutional tradition, and it refers to democracy and the protection of human rights as key values in its founding treaties and official documents. Leaning on such an understanding of representative democracy, the chapter generates two criteria as key elements of democratic legitimacy: parliamentary and judicial scrutiny.

In the third chapter, the focus will be on Europol, as the main example of a counter-terrorism network (CTN). It will provide a picture of Europol's wide network, including international contacts, and will analyse its CT activities. The network lens allows for not only mapping the variety of actors involved in the setting, but also for bringing various policy levels into the analysis, which is of crucial importance when studying the EU and scrutiny issues.

The fourth chapter will carefully open the space for a wider discussion about current trends in European CTP. It will explore current shifts in CTP, such as increased cooperation with foreign partners and the move towards increased proactive policing. Those techniques, partly encouraged and/or facilitated by the EU, touch on normative questions, which are of immediate relevance to the debate about the democratic legitimacy of CTP. The identified trends pose new questions to the old problems of the nexus between democracy and security provision.

Chapter 5 analyses the EU's unique CT cooperation with one particular state—the US. It outlines the emergence of increased transatlantic CT collaboration, drawing on several empirical examples. In a second step, it critically examines the power dynamics within the transatlantic CT relationships. The chapter suggests that the US has a particularly strong position in the existing networks and examines the challenges this poses to the democratic legitimacy of the EU's CT efforts.

Chapters 6 and 7 will respectively explore existing mechanisms and instruments of parliamentary and judicial scrutiny with respect to CTNs. The available scrutiny mechanisms concerning networked EU policing and their shortcomings will be analysed in depth in these chapters. Chapter 6 will focus on the role of the European Parliament (EP) and National Parliaments (NPs) in scrutinizing EU-wide CT cooperation. Based on a variety of exemplary cases, it will critically examine the ways and means by which parliamentary bodies can monitor and hold policing actors to account. The analysis in Chapter 7 will draw on examples of judicial scrutiny concerning current CT networking to ensure compliance with human rights and the rule of law. Particular attention will be paid to the so-called terrorist lists established by the EU. The cases explored will illustrate that those at the wrong end of CT activities through networking find that the procedures for redress are cumbersome and, at times, inadequate.

1

Towards a Transnationalization of European (Counter-terrorism) Policing

Western security authorities have intensified and expanded their cooperation considerably since the 9/11 attacks, often creating network-like structures. To investigate the potential problems that collaborative networks cause for democratic legitimacy in the field of EU-wide CT cooperation, this chapter will draw a picture of the complex environment in which European efforts in CTP take place. This way, it will become clearer as to why European actors in this field tend to cooperate in network-like structures. It provides an understanding of EU-wide CTP as a particular type of transnational policing.

Most of the EU's CTNs are part of the EU's policy field of JHA, which was formally established with the Treaty on European Union (TEU) of 7 February 1992. Yet, the phenomenon of terrorism and the fight against it had already brought European CT actors together on an informal basis in 1975. Moreover, EU CT actions partially overlap with other forms of police and intelligence work and it is therefore necessary to explore the broader development of the EU's internal security policy before focusing on CTP only. This chapter will trace recent developments in this field with regard to their significance for policing matters. To do so, the EU's internal security policies ought to be put into a wider context, in particular with respect to three global issues: the emergence of new types of criminal actors and activities; the perceived need to address this problem through forms of international security governance; and the merging of internal and external realms of security. The way in which European states tried to make sense of those developments will be described and the evolution of transnational policing is understood to be a key reaction. Those developments stimulated the creation of 'networks of security', which will be explored in the subsequent section, focusing on the conceptual framework of security governance and networks and providing a definition of CTNs. The chapter then turns to the peculiar internal security governance of the EU, traces the emergence of EU-wide efforts to combat terrorism, and introduces some of the policing networks involved in CT.

Transnational Crime Actors and State Responses after the End of the Cold War

The emergence of 'new' transnational security challenges for the transatlantic community since the end of the Cold War has been described in depth by several academic scholars. The term 'transnational' refers to social activities across state boundaries or, in other words, social interactions which are deterritorialized or only loosely coupled to a certain territory (Nye and Keohane, 1971: xii). Those security challenges have existed before, of course, but both qualitative and quantitative changes have been argued to justify the claim of the proliferation of new threats, or 'new wars' (Kaldor, 1999; Münkler, 2002). Particular attention has been paid to Clandestine Transnational Actors (CTAs) in the field of terrorism and organized crime (Andreas, 2003; Allum and Siebert, 2003).

Clandestine transnational actors

Clandestine Transnational Actors are individuals or groups planning, preparing, and committing criminal offences in at least two states. Those CTAs are understood to have motivation, capacities, and resources which enable them to be active beyond their own state's border (D'Appollonia and Reich, 2008: 2). For actors such as al Qaeda, the groups and individuals inspired by it as well as Colombian drug cartels, cross-border activities constitute an advantage to purely domestic activities (Gunaratna, 2002; Kenney, 2005, 2007).

There have always been, of course, clandestine actors, which have benefited from the simple fact that state borders exist. Smuggling, for instance, was one of the crimes that the oldest global police association—the International Criminal Police Organization (ICPO-Interpol)—was meant to address when founded in 1923 (Bowling, 2009: 149).[1] Other clandestine actors have used the international arena to gain wider public attention for their political cause, such as Black September during the Olympic Games in September 1972 in Munich, or to ensure financial or material support for their domestic fights (Reeve, 2006; Neumann, 2009). Yet, both the number of CTAs taking advantage of international activities

---

[1] Interpol is 'a non-governmental collaborative network' (Deflem, 2009: 179), currently comprising policing bodies of 190 nations, with a secretariat in Lyon, France (Interpol website).

and activities conducted across borders has increased since the end of the Cold War. One indicator of this is the increasing number of court cases in European countries that deal with terrorism and, at the same time, have international links. For the United Kingdom (UK), Peter Neumann (2009: 155–56) has pointed out that while 'the number of jurisdictions involved in IRA [ie, Irish Republican Army] investigations rarely exceeded three (typically the UK, the Republic of Ireland and sometimes another European country or the United States), Al Qaeda-related cases routinely involve up to ten different countries.' Similarly, high-ranking governmental authorities have stated that '(a)ll the most serious plots and attacks in the UK in this decade have had significant links abroad' (Johnson and Miliband, 2009).

The increased appearance of CTAs led to claims that international security is increasingly challenged by those non-military and non-state threats. According to the 2003 European Security Strategy (ESS), for example, the EU understands the activities of CTAs as the most pressing security issue which needs to be addressed jointly by its MS (Council, 2003d). Terrorism is listed as the first of threats posed by those actors to the EU. Current terrorist actors are understood to use political violence in a more indiscriminate manner than groups which were active on European territory during the 1970s and 1980s, such as the Red Army Faction (RAF), the Red Brigades (BR), and the IRA.

To conceive of those criminal actors as threats to (both national and international) security means to broaden the traditionally narrow international security agenda with its particular focus on state-based military issues. So far, the internal security apparatus used to be responsible for tackling criminal activities. While there have been attempts by security actors to tackle crime problems through international cooperation before (as will be shown on pages 20ff, the EU's internal security policy is actually built upon early informal cooperation in the field of CT), there has been a qualitative step in the last decade or so with respect to the intensity and variety of cooperation (see also Andreas and Nadelmann, 2006: 4). Internal security is no longer exclusively organized within a domestic framework but interwoven with regional and international issues, partly through the cooperation of security agencies (Bigo, 2000a: 184).

To facilitate such cooperation, a common understanding of security threats is now regularly promoted at the European, transatlantic, and, to a lesser extent, at the global level. Contemporary threats are widely understood to be transnational, asymmetric, driven by non-state actors, and complex (Neumann, 2009). This includes jihadist terrorism, a term which refers to 'the variety of international terrorism that draws on extreme interpretations of Islam for its rationale, its ideology, and to varying degrees its motivation, and whose focus is not limited to any one national or ethnic milieu or that revolves around any one national conflict or campaign' (Pillar, 2006). This form of terrorism is widely understood as an international problem with domestic implications, as it 'threatens public safety in novel ways, particularly because of its nongeographically based membership and operational base, strategy of attacking targets on a global basis, and expressed primary intent to inflict injury to civilians' (D'Appollonia and Reich, 2008: 2). The network-like, loose structures of terrorist groups appear to present an unprecedented challenge to the security authorities (Treverton, 2009). The following sub-section will explore the rationale of state responses in more depth.

State responses

State actors are inclined to be vigilant about CTAs since the latter's activities tend to 'put into question the foundations of a security system based on the norms of national sovereignty and a state monopoly of the legitimate use of violence' (Krahmann, 2005: 204). One of the key pillars of sovereign statehood is the maintenance of public order by ensuring obedience to the laws. Yet, CTAs are able to use this system in their favour: while they can cross borders without great difficulties, the law enforcement and criminal proceedings are grounded within a domestic framework and are severely hampered in the international arena (Kenney, 2005). As Howorth (2008: 96) has stated, jihadist terrorism was thought of as 'a form of terrorism that crossed borders more easily than did European public authorities themselves'. As a corollary, state security actors have tried to align with their new environment and find ways to address jointly those changes since the end of the Cold War (Krahmann, 2005: 3). At the same time, they strive to prevent international cooperation from impinging too much on their national sovereignty in this field.

To overcome this dilemma, security strategies, structural and institutional changes have emerged that can be summarized as security governance. The term *governance* refers to patterns of governing which are characterized by network like structures of interactions and relationships among a variety of actors, and the key governance function is the regulation of social and political risk (Van Waarden, 2003: 4). The concept maintains that states are neither any longer independent from other actors nor from each other, but that they are closely interwoven with other actors in the policy field in question (Krahmann, 2005: 203). The increasing role that non-state actors—such as civil society groups, private security actors, the media, but also international organizations and regional institutions—have in policy decision-making is highlighted.

The field of security policies is no exception. States are accompanied by a variety of security providers, both from beyond and below the nation-state. Emphasizing the growing importance of transnational security providers, Ian Loader and Neil Walker (2007: 235) describe the current status quo as follows: '(w)e inhabit a world of multilevel, multicentred security governance, in which states are joined, criss-crossed and contested by an array of transnational organizations and actors.' In addition to that, local security actors are adding another layer to the complex pattern. Sullivan (2008) pointed out the example of 'global metropolitan policing'. Most prominently, the New York Police Department's (NYPD) liaison programme is based on the slogan: 'The war on terrorism has no national boundaries and now the NYPD doesn't either' (Sullivan, 2008). In 2008, the

NYPD had liaison officers posted in London, Paris, Lyon, Madrid, Toronto, Montreal, Santo Domingo, Tel Aviv, Amman, and Singapore (NYC Police Foundation website). Thus, state governments do not vanish as actors and keep the central position in security governance for the time being, but they are 'joined, criss-crossed and contested' by other security providers.

This development leads to a third challenge posed by CTAs to the sovereign state system. While a key feature of the Westphalian system of states was the clear distinction between a domestic and a foreign sphere, or in other words, an internal and an external realm, examples such as the one of the NYPD suggest that this distinction is increasingly blurred.

Merging the internal and the external?

Traditionally, *internal* security refers to the territory within the boundaries demarcated by a border, while *external* security refers to the territory beyond that border. In security practice, one often finds this distinction reflected by the separation of internal and external security bodies: the military are responsible for threats from outside, while the police are in charge of internal security; and several countries run both an internal security service and a foreign intelligence service, respectively responsible for addressing internal and foreign security threats. In the post-Cold War era however, the understanding of joint European security problems has led to a remarkable permeability of the two realms. This development has two dimensions.

Firstly, the blurring refers to an increasing cooperation beyond the national level. As a strategy paper of the French government on *domestic* security put it: '(a) characteristic of global terrorism is to refuse to recognize any territorial limits. Any attempt to deal with a movement that disregards borders without the help of others [ie, international partners] would be doomed to failure' (De Villepin, 2006: 62). Jonathan Evans (2009), the current head of the Security Service (MI5), stated likewise for the British case: '(g)lobalisation has operated in this area as in many others, so that our domestic security is now dependent as much on events in Pakistan, Afghanistan and Somalia as it is on events in London, Manchester or indeed Bristol.' Finally, for the context of European policing, a senior police officer at the London Metropolitan Police argued that '(b)y making Europe a safer place, we add to the safety and security of this country.... Our security starts not just at our own borders, but at the Greek islands or the Finnish frontier' (as quoted in Brady, 2007a: 4). These examples point to an understanding that domestic security in European countries depends on international security cooperation.

Secondly, the French sociologist Didier Bigo (2000a: 173) has suggested that security authorities, such as police, intelligence, and military institutions, overlap more and more in their threat assessments, focusing on the same opponents. His argument proves to be convincing in the field of CT. While in liberal democratic societies the police and judiciary are traditionally the key CT actors, the other actors mentioned have gained an increasing role since the emergence of the 'new' terrorism. National CT strategies, for example, refer to such a variety of actors. Many intelligence services have experienced an increase in their powers and the extension of their functions based on recent terrorist legislation. Even the involvement of the military became an option—most visibly in the 'war on terror' in Afghanistan, but military personnel of the Special Reconnaissance Regiment of the British Armed Forces were also providing 'technical support' in the context of the shooting of Jean Charles de Menezes at Stockwell tube station in July 2005 in London (McDonald, 2009).

To anticipate the section later in the chapter on the EU's internal security governance: the EU is now establishing an AFSJ which covers internal policies, including asylum and immigration policy as well as cooperation in police, customs, and judicial matters, and thus by its nature encapsulates an external dimension to traditionally domestic politics. In other words, one can speak of an externalization of the (transnational) internal security agenda (see also Bigo, 2000a: 190). European state governments, law enforcement authorities, and other security providers continue to increase their cooperation efforts with foreign authorities in the field of internal security. This has been described as not being a strictly formal feature only, but as a broader process towards a pan-European ideology of an internal security field (Bigo, 2006a, 2000a; Walker, 2004: 25). Terrorism, organized crime, illegal immigration and asylum, border control, and, more generally, public order are components in this field. The involved security actors tend to merge those categories both in ideological and practical terms (Anderson, 2002: 229; Bigo, 2000a: 174).

All three developments explored in this section—the increasing importance of CTAs and the challenges they pose to the traditional understanding of state security, the involvement of a variety of security providers next to the typical state actors, and the increasing merger of an internal and external realm—initiated the emergence of new structures of security provision, sometimes referred to as *security networks*.

Networks of Security

Basically, the term network refers to a set of actors and the interactions between them. In the academic literature, early network approaches related to social science questions were to be found primarily in the literature of public policy, sociology, and management studies (eg, Rhodes, 1990; Castells, 1996; O'Toole, 1997). More recently, a network lens has been used by academic scholars to analyse issues of international security (eg, Arquilla and Ronfeldt, 2001; Johnston and Shearing, 2003; Raab and Milward, 2003; Slaughter, 2004a; Krahmann, 2005; Kenney, 2007; Gill, 2006; Gill and Phythian, 2006; Wood and Dupont, 2006; Eilstrup-Sangiovanni, 2009). While the authors agree about the increasing relevance of network structures in contemporary globalized societies with increasingly integrated political and social structures, there is a considerable lack of agreement on a coherent conceptual approach. This is hardly surprising given the different natures of the networks being researched, yet is challenging for applying a network lens to one's own research. However, the advantage of learning from a range of perspectives on the phenomenon of networks outweighs the danger of providing an assorted framework. The following sub-section therefore draws on insights of a variety of literatures on networks.

Public administration scholar Laurence O'Toole (1997: 445) provides a useful starting point for a conceptual exploration of networks, referring to them as:

> structures of interdependence involving multiple organizations. They exhibit some structural stability and include, but extend beyond, formal linkages alone. The term is meant to capture a broad range of structural types. And the institutional 'glue' congealing networked ties may include authority bonds, exchange relations, and common-interest based coalitions.

One useful distinction is the one between two ideal-types of network analysis, namely networks-as-structures and networks-as-actors (Kahler, 2009: 4ff). The first category of network approaches focuses on relational linkages between actors, or the *nodes*, the density and strength of the individual relationships. It understands networks in particular as random, unintentional groupings. In contrast to that, the networks-as-actors approach understands networks as actors with a common intention, or an interest in a particular issue, which led to the creation, or joining, of the network in the first place (Kahler, 2009: 5–6; Krahmann, 2005: 14). This approach acknowledges the structural particularities of each network, but focuses on *what is going on* within them. Given the focus of this research, the latter path of network approaches will be followed.

Ideal-type networks are understood to be non-hierarchical, ie power is distributed equally. In practice, the distribution of power in networks varies immensely. For security authorities, networks are convenient tools of cooperation, as a network structure ensures that they keep their autonomy while collaborating with other members. Moreover, they can participate in several networks at the same time. Given the sensitivity of security matters and their closeness to issues of sovereignty, networks in the security sector are usually—and may remain—at a rudimentary stage. For example, secure data transfer is difficult and, in international networks, language problems might appear. Information tends to be jealously guarded (De Laat, 1999: 211). In addition, police and intelligence cooperation is restricted by various legal obligations and moral concerns.

In the conception of *nodal security governance* by Les Johnston and Clifford Shearing, governance is understood as the 'relationship contained within a shifting network of alliances' (Johnston, 2006: 34). Studies of networks in different fields of security highlight a pluralization of security governance and have identified four key network participants: state agencies, corporate actors, non-governmental organizations, as well as the voluntary sector (Johnston and Shearing, 2003: 147; Gill and Phythian, 2006: 39). Those nodes are connected via network structures, which enable them to interact with, and relate to, each other (for ideal-types of security networks see Dupont, 2004: 79ff). Yet, the key purpose of Johnston and Shearing's approach is to pinpoint the increasing involvement of private actors in such networks. They argued that although state actors keep an important role in the governance process, they are only participants *among others* in networks of institutions that govern security (Johnston, 2006: 34). But is such a description correct for networks in the field of *high* policing?

The distinction between high and low policing refers, according to criminologist Jean-Paul Brodeur, to a French distinction reaching back to Napoleon's times. The term 'high policing' implies the police measures provided by the intelligence community to protect the state apparatus, while 'low policing' refers to day-to-day community policing (Brodeur, 1983, 2007). Undercover operations and the use of human sources are identified as typical measures of high policing; and high policing conflates the spheres of the judiciary and the executive. Brodeur has argued that the two spheres of high and low policing have been slowly merging after the end of the Cold War, but he suggests that the old categories were reinforced after the 9/11 attacks. According to him, 'the higher the stakes in security the more will the responsibilities of public government be (re)asserted' (Brodeur, 2007: 32), ie the impact of private actors in issues of high policing is expected to be less intense than in those of low policing. The author has justified this assumption by referring to two features. Firstly, he assumes a 'need for *legitimacy* in the provision of security' (Brodeur, 2007; emphasis in original), which he understands to originate mainly from public institutions, or the state in more general terms.

Secondly, Brodeur refers to the feature of *symbolic power* inherent to state actors rather than private ones. While authors like Shearing and Clifford assume the same power footing for all actors—both private and public—in security networks, Brodeur understands the private actors to be less powerful in this field. Yet, private actors are also involved in the fight against terrorism: bankers and accountants support the fight against terrorist financing and money-laundering; experts of ID-related technologies ensure border security; private security companies might be involved in surveillance or provide technical equipment; and scientific experts are needed for the identification and handling of chemical, biological or nuclear materials. Brodeur appears to be correct in suggesting that the power is not distributed equally between public and private actors, yet the involvement of private actors even in the field of high policing is nowadays substantial.

Overall, it appears that the network lens provides a useful analytical tool to conceptualize recent security cooperation in the fight against terrorism, also because of the variety of institutions and policy-levels involved (see also Gill, 2006: 28). This research is engaged with issues of 'high policing' and therefore public actors will be at the centre of the research, but the role of private ones is by no means neglected. Benoît Dupont (2004: 78) provided a definition of security networks broad enough to be suitable for issues of high policing, and CT more specifically. Based on his definition, CTNs are referred to in the following as *sets of expert institutional nodes or individual agents from at least two countries that are interconnected in order to authorize and/or provide security with regard to CT to the benefit of the network participants or external 'clients'.*

Referring to the al Qaeda group, which has often been described as a network, it has been argued it 'takes networks to fight networks' (Arquilla and Ronfeldt, 2001: 15), implying that security authorities ought to interact more intensely to bring together information from various sources to identify terrorist suspects and potential plots. This has been argued both for the national as well as the international level (National Commission on Terrorist Attacks upon the United States, 2004; Andreas and Nadelmann, 2006; Treverton, 2009). However, tackling terrorism is a difficult objective for security authorities. Apart from private actors as described on page 16, the endeavour involves multiple agencies, such as police and intelligence services as well as immigration authorities. Even within the domestic framework, the coordination of those agencies is difficult to achieve but this is even more complicated across borders (Anderson, 2002: 233). One key reason for the emergence of security networks is that network-like structures allow actors to pool and distribute information and other resources. The recent escalation of fusion centres and joint task forces, both in the field of intelligence and law enforcement, is an obvious example of this (Gill and Phythian, 2006: 58). Such fusion centres can be described as a continuous 'collaborative effort of two or more agencies that provide resources, expertise, and information to the center with the goal of maximizing their ability to detect, prevent, investigate, and respond to criminal and terrorist activity' (US Department of Justice, Office of Justice Programs, n.d.: 2). Examples of this are Spain's National Centre of Antiterrorist Coordination (CNCA), the British Joint Terrorism Analysis Centre (JTAC), and the German Joint Counter-Terrorism Centre (GTAZ) (cf Chapter 6). In contrast to such centres, joint task forces are ad hoc constructions of units that are brought together to tackle a single issue, such as terrorism.

Having established the wider context of current security provision, the following section aims to focus more narrowly on transnational policing. The section will provide a categorization of policing which will subsequently facilitate a classification of EU-wide CTP.

Transnational Policing

Traditionally, the police are the responsible governmental institution to ensure 'law and order' within a nation-state. For this purpose, its competences include the exercise of coercive power (Sheptycki, 2000: 9). From the perspective of social contract theory, citizens agreed to monopolize the physical exercise of power in the hands of the state as long as this arrangement would protect them from physical violence and grant them personal freedom. Though the functions of the police are not clearly defined and differ from state to state, common police functions are crime control, the enforcement of law and order maintenance (Bowling, 2006: 2). The literature on police studies and criminology has recognized enormous changes with respect both to the functions of the police and the spatial reach of its practices over time. Moreover, the provision of traditional police tasks is increasingly supported or even taken over by other actors, such as intelligence analysts and private security companies. While there has been, of course, some overlap in terms of functions and mandates between several actors before, the term *policing* encapsulates such qualitative changes and the widened range of policing actors and will be used throughout this book.

As a consequence of those developments, a 'transformation of the architectures of policing' (Sheptycki, 2007: 71) has been described. The term *transnational policing* encapsulates 'those organized forms of order maintenance, peacekeeping, law enforcement, crime investigation and prevention, surveillance of suspect populations and information-brokering that transcend national boundaries' (Bowling, 2006: 6). In Europe, the forms of transnational police cooperation that have emerged are best described as crowded, institutionally complex, and fragmented (Anderson, 1995: 266; Sheptycki, 2001: 149ff.). They include the domestic police activities within the EU's MS and other European countries, an increasing level of cooperation between security authorities and their counterparts abroad, and, sometimes, this has led to the creation of policing networks across national borders (Loader, 2002; Bigo, 2000b). Some of the more institutionalized networks are located at the EU level itself, such as Europol (see page 30 and Chapter 3).

Most transnational policing activities concern information sharing. Information is crucial for policing work in various ways. For instance, information is needed to put together the picture of a criminal organization. The collection of information is based on a variety of sources, including human sources, such as informants and infiltrators, and methods, such as surveillance of phone communications (Den Boer, 2003). Disrupting terrorist networks often depends on 'low-level, factual and fragmented' (Gibson, 2009: 923) information and intelligence, including foreign phone numbers, travel records, or credit card transactions.

The emphasis on information collection and sharing has brought a new dimension to policing: next to the provision of physical security, security providers 'increasingly produce and disseminate security intelligence' (Lippert and O'Connor, 2006: 50). This fits into the early observation by Richard Ericson (1994: 151) that police officers ought to be understood as 'knowledge brokers' who produce and distribute knowledge. Such a shift of activities includes the increasing amount of information collection *prior* to a crime and the decreasing importance of reactive law enforcement approaches. While reactive policing approaches rely on the reporting of a crime which has already occurred, proactive models of policing focus on the prevention, or disruption, of crime (cf Chapter 4). Informants, intelligence, and surveillance are crucial instruments of this approach (Ratcliffe, 2008; Treverton, 2009).

Proactive policing is intimately linked with network-like structures, as they allow for a flow of information from various sources. Indeed, Peter Andreas and

Ethan Nadelmann (2006: 9) argued that the emphasis on information and intelligence brokerage has led to the establishment of a 'transnational criminal law enforcement community based on expanding cross-border governmental networks with shared technical and investigative expertise'. Yet the description of a *community* appears to be misleading insofar as it suggests a homogenous group of policing actors, which is currently not the case. Instead, one can distinguish between five ideal types of transnational policing (Bowling, 2009):

- *local* policing exercised by local domestic agencies working with foreign policing counterparts;
- *national* policing bodies which enable cooperation within the domestic framework and provide for cooperation with foreign partners;
- *regional* policing through national agencies working within regional structures;
- *international* policing which might be exercised through cross-border legal arrangements, cross-border coordination mechanisms, cross-border systems of information sharing, and cross-border operations; and
- *global* policing through extra-territorial policing bodies with a global reach.

Drawing on Bowling's five types of transnational policing, European policing can be described as a mixture of domestic policing—both *local* and *national*—with impact abroad, policing through regional networks, such as Europol, and bi- as well as multilateral *international* cooperation through national liaison officers. To link the individual efforts and capacities of European security agencies and EU institutions, security networks were created. Concerning CT, 'police institutions across the globe have proliferated their counterterrorism strategies, both domestically and abroad, while international police have likewise stepped up their campaigns against terrorism' (Deflem, 2006b: 241). Similarly, intelligence services felt, despite favouring bilateral cooperation, that it has 'become necessary to expand cooperation in a multilateral framework, given the convergence of interests and risks with our partners' (De Villepin, 2006: 51).

This stated emphasis on cooperation needs some clarification. Authors, such as James Sheptycki (2002, 2007), suggest that transnational policing is a reaction to the increasing threats posed by CTAs. It is important not to over-emphasize the functional necessity of this move, though. Organization theory provides a deeper understanding of institutions as learning organizations. From this perspective, the development is understood as a process of 'organizational sensemaking' (Weick, 1995), suggesting that all institutions are, at least in principle, able to 'learn' in the sense that they are making an effort to understand their complex environment and interpret what is relevant to the organization's goals and needs. Such a reading of the state reactions to the 'new' terrorism is convincing. In contrast to the hypothesis about functional necessity, the approach of institutional learning suggests that the security authorities provide a particular understanding—*their* understanding—of their environment or a particular situation. A purely functional approach would suggest that there was only one potential way of reacting to the new developments. The ideas of institutional learning promoted by Weick and others allow for a more careful reading. Depending on an organization's interpretation of 'an uncertain situation' (Weick, 1995: 9), it will identify the issues, or events, it pays attention to and decide 'in what directions the situation needs to be changed' (Weick, 1995: 9) and by which means.

Weick's perspective includes the notion of *choice*, a feature, which tends to be neglected in the police and intelligence literature post-9/11. Several authors focus on increased international cooperation and better information sharing as the only suitable ways of addressing jihadist terrorism, which leaves little room for a discussion about alternatives. Similarly, EU policy-makers argue that only actions at the EU level can ensure an effective response to cross-border crime (Commission, 2009f). Yet, the literature on organizational learning suggests that the paths chosen to tackle a particular type of crime depend on the interpretation of the events or situation in question.

Closely related to this aspect is the point that functional explanations tend to overlook the fact that policing actors can be *drivers* of international policing (Bowling, 2009: 151). As bureaucratic entities, policing bodies are competing with other institutions and have their own interests to promote, not least their own survival (Deflem, 2002). Finally, to understand policing bodies as organizations that continuously learn explains better why policing actors are not harmonious actors. Bigo (2006a: 387–88; 394) has shown that the security actors in the EU's internal security field do not necessarily agree with each other and have different ideas about defining security in general, and threats in particular and, consequently, do not necessarily agree on the measures to approach them. Although they might agree on certain definitions, ideas, strategies, or tactics, the approaches they adopt to reach agreed-upon goals vary immensely. This is, of course, partly because of their different mandates, but the various procedures of learning also provide a potential explanation.

Having explored key aspects of transnational networked policing, it appears that one excellent realm to study the complicated structures of security governance is the EU. As Wyn Rees (2003: 115) has rightly pointed out, the EU-wide recognition of transnational crime forced 'an acknowledgement of a set of shared security concerns that necessitate transcontinental solutions'. To its MS, the EU seems to offer a suitable political framework for finding those 'solutions.' The following section will therefore trace the EU's efforts at policing terrorism.

The EU's Internal Security

As stated earlier in the chapter, various European countries have longstanding experiences with terrorism, and the origins of the EU's internal security policies are related to the aim of combating the phenomenon. In the late 1960s and during the 1970s, this became a particular concern for some Western European countries, such as Germany, Italy, France, and the UK, which put high pressure on the individual state governments and stimulated improved coordination between law enforcement authorities in Europe (Friedrichs, 2007: ch 4). Crucially, the then members of the intergovernmental European Economic Community (EEC) agreed at a Council meeting in Rome in 1975 on the creation of the *Terrorisme, Radicalisme, Extrémisme et Violence Internationale* (TREVI) group, which provided an informal framework for cooperation in matters of policing and criminal justice, including CT cooperation.[2] TREVI was an intergovernmental forum comprising justice and interior ministers, policy experts from the respective ministries, as well as police officers; all arranged in five working groups (Occhipinti, 2003: 31). Peter Katzenstein (2005: 135) argued that the 'institutionalization of European police cooperation under TREVI's auspices surpassed all previous efforts'. Indeed, the creation of TREVI must be understood as the trigger for increasing European cooperation in the fields of policing, judicial cooperation, and mutual assistance in civil and criminal law—yet, in an informal, intergovernmental, and non-binding manner.

It was only on 1 November 1993 that this cooperation was formalized when the TEU was fully ratified. The TEU introduced for the first time explicit provisions on cooperation regarding JHA matters (Title VI of the TEU). The TEU established the so-called three-pillar system of the EU. The communitarized first pillar comprised the European Communities policies where MS share their sovereignty via the EU institutions. The second pillar encompassed the common foreign and security as well as security and defence policy, and the third pillar covered matters of JHA. The second and third pillars were organized intergovernmentally, ie the EU's MS remained the decisive policy-makers. The 1997 Treaty of Amsterdam revised some of the arrangements. Crucially, it 'moved' several aspects of JHA—in particular, asylum and immigration policies—to the first pillar, so that the third pillar's focus was narrowed to PJCC only.

Already the original TEU identified nine areas of 'common interest' shared by the EU MS in the field of JHA. One of these was police cooperation, in which it provides for EU-wide 'police cooperation for the purposes of prevention and combating terrorism, unlawful drug trafficking and other serious forms of international crime... in connection with the organization of a Union-wide system of exchanging information within a European Police Office (Europol)' (Article K.1(9) TEU). Thus, the fight against terrorism through police cooperation is already stated as a key aim in the 1992 Treaty. Yet the decision-making processes in the third pillar were of an intergovernmental nature, with the JHA Council of the European Union, comprising the national Ministers of Home Affairs and Justice, as the decision-making body, and several preparative bodies.

The Lisbon Treaty is bringing considerable changes to the JHA policy field's structure, including the introduction of a Standing Committee on operational cooperation on internal security (COSI) within the Council to:

[2] Members of the EEC at that time were Belgium, France, Germany, Italy, the Netherlands, Luxembourg, Denmark, the UK, and Ireland.

> ensure that operational cooperation on internal security is promoted and strengthened within the Union.... (I)t shall facilitate coordination of the action of Member States' competent authorities. Representatives of the Union bodies, offices and agencies concerned may be involved in the proceedings of this committee (Article 71 TFEU).

However, several changes regarding JHA bodies will only apply after a transition period. William Shapcott, Director of the EU's Joint Situation Centre (SitCen, cf page 30), referred to the existing JHA bodies as an 'alphabet soup' (House of Lords (HL), EU Select Committee, 2011: para 173) and details regarding mandates and functions continue to lack clarity (House of Lords (HL), EU Select Committee, 2011: ch 6; for an early proposal concerning the changing structure of the JHA working parties see Council, 2009i).

It is foreseeable that the EU's institutional security structure will retain a unique and complicated pattern. The majority of the EU's CT efforts are part of the area of PJCC. Some aspects relate to external aspects which were previously covered under pillar two, such as foreign intelligence cooperation, the freezing of terrorist assets, and the CT agreements with international parties. Also, a few efforts used to be regulated under the first pillar, in particular those related to immigration and visa regulations, but also the exchange of PNR data with the US. Given the involvement of all EU pillars in CT cooperation, the increasing merger of internal and external security realms in Europe becomes very obvious. In addition, the pillar system was never entirely fixed, as the transfer of policies related to immigration and asylum to the first pillar and the recent abolishment of the system has shown. Yet, the pillar structure symbolized the different decision-making procedures and political sensitivities for the various policy fields. This is unlikely to change in the foreseeable future.

As a consequence of this complex pattern, Francesca Bignami (2007: 680) has argued that in the field of EU internal security 'European integration has proceeded not through the transfer of national sovereignty to a federal center, but through the sharing and pooling of sovereignty in the network form of governance'. The political importance of police cooperation is often overlooked, despite the fact that it touches on those core features of the state system (see also Katzenstein, 2005: 134). As established earlier, networking is an ideal tool to ensure the autonomy of the participating nodes. As sovereignty is closely related to autonomy in international politics, network structures allow state actors to cooperate with little costs, but the potential added value of cooperation. As a consequence of those possibilities in the EU's third pillar, the developments in that field have been driven by a 'restless institutional dynamic' (Walker, 2004: 14) since its creation. This institutional growth is mirrored by the speedy development of legislation in this field (Monar 2008, 2009).

The EU's commitment in matters of JHA has been legally established in the European treaties at various points. Notably, Article 29 TEU maintained that the EU aims to 'provide citizens with a high level of safety' and Article 61(e) of TEC included 'an explicit mandate as a provider of internal security' for the EU. The

EU's broader vision of its internal security policy became apparent at the 1999 EU Summit in Tampere, when it was agreed to establish an AFSJ across the Union. This AFSJ would comprise police and justice cooperation, the fight against organized crime and terrorism, but also the free movement of persons and migration and asylum policy (Council, 1999b). The idea was formally provided in the Treaty of Amsterdam and was confirmed and outlined in the so-called Hague Programme, a five-year programme setting out the priorities of the EU for closer cooperation in JHA matters between 2005 and 2010 (Council, 2004c). The Stockholm Programme for the period of 2010 to 2014, which succeeded the Hague Programme, outlines further AFSJ provisions (Council, 2009f).

Certainly, the AFSJ is not only meant to be a compilation of existing policies. Rather, as Neil Walker (2004, 7; emphasis in original) stated,

> (t)he new internal security domain may lack any precise and singular objective, may lack a common national pedigree of distinctive and coherent treatment, and may be institutionally diversified, yet the post-Amsterdam era is clearly marked by an attempt to *construct* a new kind of policy whole out of diverse parts.

Andreas and Nadelmann (2006: 186) have argued that the AFSJ made police cooperation 'much more supranational in its aspirations'. Indeed, since 1999, matters of JHA must be described as the EU's 'most dynamic policy domain' (Apap and Carrera, 2004: 1). Correspondingly, the TFEU as of 1 December 2009 provides for improved cooperation and coordination between MS 'as they deem appropriate between the competent departments of their administrations responsible for safeguarding national security' (Article 73 TFEU).

From a functional perspective, this has been described as a spill-over effect in the EU from the cooperation in economics to the cooperation in the field of internal security (Huysmans, 2006). The JHA area grew unevenly and impressively quickly, both in terms of functions and institutional capacity. The arrangements in the AFSJ have been widely described as being complex, ambiguous, and opaque (Guild and Carrera, 2005: 2). Moreover, intergovernmentalism includes a certain lack of parliamentary control owing to its fixation on executive cooperation and lack of transparency (Glaeßner and Lorenz, 2005a: 27). Overall, the 'EU suffers from weak legitimacy in this area, making the cooperation of governments and citizens less than reliable' (Apap and Carrera, 2004: 10). This is partly because '(t)he division of competence... between European and national competences is far from clear-cut' (De Hert, 2004: 93). Moreover, as will be discussed in more detail in Chapters 6 and 7, the EU has been criticized for not providing sufficient safeguards of human rights in that sensitive area.

Some authors have argued that the growing internal EU security governance is an indicator that the EU is taking on more characteristics of a territorial state (Andreas, 2003: 101). The powers of the police in Western states have long been justified as necessary to maintain the public order. Arguably, there is now a tendency to describe police work as shifting from the production of state security to the provision of individual or human security (Aden, 2001). Such a move towards a focus on human security—as opposed to a state-centred one—opens space for EU actions in the field of CT. For example, the EU's Counter-Terrorism Strategy maintains a 'strong commitment' of the EU 'to combat terrorism . . . and make Europe safer, allowing its citizens to live in an area of freedom, security and justice' (Council, 2005b).

Yet, while state borders do not provide the absolute framework for the provision of security anymore, the EU is not a territorially demarcated institution with a single administrative space (Walters, 2002: 567). There is not a single security policy for the 'European space'. While Bruggeman (2004: 152) has argued that European police cooperation is, 'in an increasingly pressing way, demanding the handing over of state sovereignty to European institutions and instances in all areas, including police powers', this is a slightly incorrect description of the field of policing, which is instead pooling sovereignty—ie, sharing decision-making powers—rather than taking it away from nation-states to a supranational level (as described by Bignami, 2007). It seems more correct to describe the EU as an inter-linking, or networking actor in the field of internal security. In a similar vein, Walters (2002: 568) has argued that, '(r)ather than replacing national systems, the tactic is one of finding ways of linking them, of "harmonising" their operations and rules'.

Developing and ratifying multilateral common policies or legislation in such a sensitive policy field is a time-consuming process, however, which is partly why the majority of actors still prefer informal and often bilateral forms of cooperation in the field of law enforcement and intelligence. Some of those arrangements have evolved over a long period of time, usually as cross-border inter-agency cooperation between two or more neighbouring countries. The policing of the Channel and the longstanding cooperation between France and Spain to fight the Basque *Euskadi Ta Askatasuna* (ETA) are two striking examples of this (Sheptycki, 2002; AFP, 2008; Morgan and Newburn, 1997: 57ff).

Cooperation in the field often started as a rather informal process, but since the early 1990s there has been an increasing process of 'formalization' of such arrangements in Europe. Many European countries have concluded wide-ranging police agreements with their neighbouring countries. For instance, Germany and the Netherlands agreed on a revamped Police Agreement, which entered into force on 1 September 2006 (Deutscher Bundestag, 2005). Since January 2008, the governments of Spain and France have established both a permanent joint police unit to investigate ETA and a joint security committee to fight terrorism, drug trafficking, and illegal immigration (AFP, 2008, 2009). Yet, there are also bilateral agreements between non-neighbouring states, such as the Agreement on the Mutual Protection of Classified Information between the UK and Poland, which has applied since 1 August 2007 to British and Polish law enforcement agencies and government departments. It allows them 'to exchange classified information and intelligence including on organised crime and terrorism' (British Embassy, Warsaw, 2007). The Agreement also explicitly provides for the exchange of 'operational intelligence' (British Embassy, Warsaw, 2007).

To summarize, it appears that cooperation in this field is increasingly institutionalized in the sense that it is based on bi- or multilateral agreements and possibly includes the establishment of channels for communication, information sharing, or joint investigation teams. According to Didier Bigo (2006a: 397), some of the most informal networks in Europe are institutionalized today. One field in which this development can be seen clearly is CT, on which the following section will focus.

Counter-terrorism as a Policy Objective of the EU

Despite the fact that the TREVI group was founded in 1975 to fight terrorism jointly, an EU CT policy which is worthy of the name only started to emerge in the aftermath of the 9/11 attacks. Andreas and Nadelmann (2006: 211) rightly argued that 'terrorism made a dramatic comeback as the priority policing issue in Europe' after 9/11. In the aftermath of the events in New York and Washington, the Council of the EU stated that the fight against terrorism would become a policy objective of the EU (Council, 2001a). By now, the EU's CT policy is manifold and only the most relevant provisions will be described in the following.[3]

Immediately after the 9/11 attacks in the US, the EU showed unanimous support for the US. At two extraordinary meetings—one of the JHA Council on 20 September 2001 and one of the European Council the following day—the governments of the EU MS agreed to prioritize the fight against terrorism on their common political agenda. They adopted a series of CT measures, which focused on 'intelligence, judicial and police cooperation, and measures against terrorism financing' (Howorth, 2008: 98), including the establishment of a common list of terrorist organizations; closer cooperation between police and intelligence and easier access to data for European security authorities; improved data exchange via Europol and the creation of a Counter-terrorism Task Force at Europol's headquarters; improved joint fight against money-laundering and terrorist financing; the introduction of a European arrest warrant (EAW); further harmonization of law enforcement regulations and EU-wide criminal frameworks for terrorist acts; and improved cooperation between EU and US security authorities including, for example, the 2004 EU-US Declaration on Combating Terrorism, a new Extradition and Mutual Legal Assistance Agreement of 2003, an agreement on the exchange of PNR data, the Container Security Initiative, and a Policy Dialogue on Border and Transport Security (cf Chapter 5; for an overview on the transatlantic dimension see Rees, 2011).

[3] For overviews as well as more specific accounts of certain aspects of the EU's CT policy see, among others, Argomaniz, 2011; O'Neill, 2012; Bures, 2011; Kaunert, 2010a, 2010b; Coolsaet, 2010; the 2008 Special Issue on the EU and Counter-Terrorism of the *Journal of Common Market Studies*; Howorth, 2008; Wiegand, 2008; Monar, 2007; Spence, 2007a; Balzacq et al, 2006; and Den Boer and Monar, 2002.

The majority of these instruments built on previous crime-fighting instruments (eg, the EU's money-laundering directive, originally focusing on drug trafficking only, now also includes terrorism and other serious crime). Others, such as the EAW, which replaces previously existing extradition procedures, had been long prepared and were quickly 'redefined' as crucial instruments for combating terrorism after the 9/11 attacks (Den Boer and Monar, 2002; Bossong, 2008). In addition, CT efforts concerning relationships with third countries ('external relations') were discussed. On the one hand it was agreed to evaluate existing external relationships with a view on 'the support which those countries might give to terrorism' (Presidency of the Council of the EU, 2001a). On the other hand, political dialogue and financial cooperation were strengthened with countries such as Pakistan, Iran, India, the Central Asian countries, and the Gulf Cooperation States (Bretherton and Vogler, 2006: 182). In addition, the EU regularly establishes threat analyses on countries and regions, which are used to determine the CT clauses included in external agreements and the assistance provided by the EU (Council, 2003c: 43).

Crucially for the integration of CT efforts, the Framework Decision of 13 June 2002 on Combating Terrorism, agreed on 6/7 December 2001, provides a common definition of the term 'terrorism' (Council, 2002a). A first European-wide attempt to refer to a spectrum of terrorist acts, accompanied by a list of terrorist actions, had already been made in the Council of Europe's (CoE) Convention on the Suppression of Terrorism of 27 January 1977 (Glaeßner and Lorenz, 2005a: 37).

Yet it was only after the Madrid bombings that the EU's CT efforts really 'began to come together' (Howorth, 2008: 96). The bombings were followed by a Declaration on Combating Terrorism of 15 March 2004 which provides for a long-term EU strategy to combat terrorism with a particular focus on the root causes of terrorism. This included the creation of the post of Counter-terrorism Coordinator with the key responsibility to coordinate the efforts between EU Ministries of Interior and Justice, but without any funding or rights to propose legislation. The Declaration also, for example, provided for the expansion of Europol's as well as SitCen's competences. Based on this Declaration, an EU Action Plan on Terrorism was accepted by the European Council on 17/18 June 2004 with the aim to intensify the existing measures to fight terrorism and organized crime.[4] In a meeting right after the Madrid bombings, Belgium, the Netherlands, and Austria suggested the establishment of a European intelligence service, but were turned down quickly by the EU's major intelligence-gathering countries: the UK, France, Germany, Italy, and Spain (Glaeßner/Lorenz, 2005a: 40).

To strengthen and streamline the various EU activities, mainly based on the Action Plan, the JHA Council adopted the European Union Counter-terrorism Strategy in December 2005 (Council, 2005b). According to the Strategy, the EU

[4] EU Action Plans outline concerted measures to achieve previously accepted objectives.

MS aim is 'to combat terrorism globally while respecting human rights, and to make Europe safer, allowing its citizens to live in an area of freedom, security and justice'. Referring to the European, national, and international level, the strategy comprises four pillars—Prevent, Protect, Pursue, and Respond (Figure 1.1).

Figure 1.1 The European Union Counter-terrorism Strategy

Source: The European Union Counter-Terrorism Strategy, <http:/www.consilium.europa.eu>
© European Union, 2004–2012.

The four key objectives all relate to policing, but in particular the three P's ('Response' refers to disaster- and crisis-management efforts). The EU claims to provide an added value concerning the following features: strengthening the existing national capabilities; facilitating European cooperation; developing collective capability; and promoting international partnership. One of the crucial components of the EU's CT approach is information sharing, also including the exchange of best practices and skills.

That the EU's Counter-terrorism Strategy puts considerable emphasis on information sharing, among national security authorities as well as with and among EU bodies, fits with earlier observations in this chapter concerning trends towards increased transnationalization and the importance of information sharing for police networks. This will be explored further in the following section.

Information Exchange at the Heart of EU Police Cooperation

One of the key benefits of many forms of cooperation is information transmission (Heath, 2006: 327). As has been stated at several points previously in the chapter, information exchange is also a key reason for the existence of European transnational policing. This is widely acknowledged in official EU documents since the Schengen Convention of 1990.[5] However, the events of 9/11, and in particular the Madrid bombings, led to new efforts in projects concerning information sharing. In a proposed Council Framework Decision on the Principle of Availability, the Council maintained the 'central role of information exchange in the security gambit of the Union' (Council, 2005a: 2). The Stockholm Programme states that 'developments over the past years in the EU have led to a wide choice and created an extensive toolbox for collecting, processing and sharing information between national authorities and other European players in the area of freedom, security and justice' (Council, 2009f: 16).

A plethora of EU legislation, and institutional (re)structuring in this area is focusing on the creation, fostering, and expansion of information sharing networks. The overall aim is to overcome structures of information and intelligence sharing in Europe which are thought to be insufficiently integrated and too bureaucratic. The current channels of information sharing provided for by the EU and those loosely connected to the EU are numerous, including virtual databases and (human) liaison networks, some of which are very informal while others are highly institutionalized and formal. A Council Decision on the exchange of information and cooperation concerning terrorist offences obliges MS to share information with Europol and the EU's Judicial Cooperation Unit (Eurojust), as well as with each other, on data relating to pending investigations and prosecutions in the field of terrorism (Council, 2005h).[6]

Inter-agency networks in the EU are composed of staff of very diverse institutional backgrounds, such as law-enforcement agencies, Ministries of the Interior or Justice, intelligence services, as well as judicial bodies (Bigo, 2006a: 398). Bigo's study on European liaison officers offers crucial insight into their work. Liaison

[5] The Convention of 19 June 1990 Implementing the Schengen Agreement of 14 June 1985 between the Governments of the States of the Benelux Economic Union, the Federal Republic of Germany and the French Republic on the Gradual Abolition of Checks at their Common Borders established the Schengen Area and provided for the removal of systematic border controls between the participating countries. The Treaty of Amsterdam incorporated the Convention into EU law. All MS participate apart from Ireland and the UK, which opted out of the border control arrangements, but participate in certain policies concerning PJCC. In addition, Norway, Iceland, and Switzerland joined the Schengen Area.

[6] Set up in 2002, Eurojust's overall purpose is to foster the cooperation among judicial authorities within the MS concerning cross-border investigations and prosecutions. Europol's work will be outlined later in this chapter and, in particular, in Chapter 3.

officers are affiliated with a national agency, but are sent to a foreign agency in order to facilitate and/or foster information exchange between the agencies. Engaged in tasks of high policing, they work at EU or other regional or international levels (Bigo, 2000a: 172; Bigo, 2000b). Liaison officers are not a new phenomenon in policing practice, but it seems that they are used in an increasingly strategic manner to establish relationships between agencies. They are also frequently used by ministries—for instance, in 2009 the German Ministry of Interior based a high-ranking liaison official in the French Ministry of Interior and one in the US Department of Homeland Security (DHS). Liaison arrangements between EU countries are encouraged by EU politics, such as the 2003 JHA Council decision on the common use of liaison officers posted abroad which recommends the increased networking of liaison officers (Council, 2003a). Liaison officers based in the same host country or at the same international organization are asked to constitute 'liaison officers networks' with the aim to provide each other with information and mutual assistance. They are meant to pass on information concerning serious criminal threats to other MS through such a liaison network.

Those inter-agency networks, in particular in their capacity as distributors of information, and those practices of transnational CTP can have a direct effect on citizens. Citizens interact with policing networks in very 'different ways and at differing points' (Goldsmith and Eggers, 2004: 149). For example, citizens can be subject to surveillance or they might be arrested based on information shared through a network. Yet the bonding between the EU's internal security realm and the European citizenry appears to be fragile and barely existing with respect to accountability and legitimacy more widely.

To investigate this claim, this study focuses on the cooperation of police and, to a lesser extent, intelligence, thus policing actors mainly working under the umbrella of the EU's third pillar. Problems of democratic legitimacy can be illustrated in an illuminating way by focusing on the network-like nature of transnational CT cooperation.

Such a mapping of CT activities within, or loosely coupled with, the EU enables the researcher to explore potential dilemmas presented by those networks regarding democratic legitimacy. One advantage of a network approach is that it allows thinking beyond traditional analytical *boxes*, which seems necessary in order to understand not only the unique nature of EU CT structures, but also the challenges this poses to a concept of democratic legitimacy. It has been established (page 15) that the networks vary in their degree of institutionalization. This needs to be taken into account as well as, for instance, their membership, structure, and mandate, when making judgments about their democratic legitimacy. To sharpen the argument and allow an in-depth analysis, the focus will be on Europol as the 'central hub' of EU information and intelligence exchange (Europol, 2008a: 5). However, the following sub-section will provide a more complete picture by briefly introducing, in addition to Europol, five other key networks: SitCen, the Counter Terrorism Group (CTG), the network based on the so-called Prüm Provisions, the European Police Chiefs Task Force (now integrated in the COSI), and the Police Working Group on Terrorism (PWGT).

Europol

As Chapter 3 will show in depth, Europol is best understood as a very institutionalized network due to its extensive liaison system and its task to coordinate the activities of the national police units (Deflem, 2006a). While it is now a formal organ of the EU, Europol was originally set up as an independent organization based on an international treaty (Article 26 Europol Convention). It focuses on criminal and analytical intelligence, collects and analyses data from intelligence services and law enforcement authorities, and transfers information to those national agencies or EU bodies, if necessary. Europol's databases are a common investigative tool for national authorities. Fighting terrorism became part of Europol's mandate in 2000 and it now has a Counter-terrorism Unit, composed of specialized officials. Europol can start an investigation into issues of serious crime the moment this is related to at least two MS. It does not have 'true executive policing authority' (Occhipinti, 2003: 35) but, despite such severe operational limits, Europol has nevertheless established 'a fluent, multinational network of law-enforcement professionals' (Stevenson, J., 2005: 211) and, to a much lesser extent, intelligence authorities. There is also an external dimension to Europol's network. Several non-EU countries as well as international organizations, such as Interpol, have representatives at Europol and, in December 2001, Europol opened a liaison office in Washington.

Joint Situation Centre

The police initiatives are accompanied by arrangements in the field of intelligence. The crucial EU institution in this respect is SitCen which is located in the European External Action Service (EEAS), under the supervision of the High Representative of the Union for Foreign Affairs and Security Policy. While it started as a small analytical cell under the EU's former second pillar, it currently comprises more than 100 staff members, roughly 70 per cent of them being intelligence officials seconded from EU MS, such as France, the UK, Germany, Finland, Poland, Spain, and Hungary (Rettman, 2011; Schmid, 2009: 336). SitCen's intelligence work covers all aspects of crisis management. For example, the group produces threat analyses, which 'provide a basis for the operational measures of the European Union, for counter-terrorism elements in contractual relations with third countries, and for technical assistance projects to third countries in the field of counter-terrorism' (Szyszkowitz, 2005: 179). On 1 February 2005, a special analytical capacity was created for strategic intelligence-based assessments on CT matters (Müller-Wille, 2008). SitCen is largely dependent on voluntary contributions from MS' sources, including intelligence agencies, military, diplomats, and the police (De Villepin, 2006: 52). Yet, it sometimes sends staff for fact-finding missions to crisis regions, such as Georgia in 2008, Haiti in 2010, and Libya in 2011 (Norheim-Martinsen and Ravndal, 2011: 464; EU Institute for Security Studies, 2010: 24–5; Rettman, 2011). According to a French Strategy Paper, SitCen

> can also make useful contributions to operational issues, such as the terrorists' destinations, motives and movements, in order to sensitize all MS and help them to take appropriate measures. Experience shows that Member States have different threat perceptions and that their harmonization is highly useful (De Villepin, 2006: 52).

Counter-terrorism Group

The importance of the CTG for multilateral intelligence exchange in the field of CT was pointed out during several interviews conducted in the framework of this research (Interviews M, P, Q, Z). Immediately after the 9/11 attacks, the CTG was established as a sub-group of the so-called Club of Berne comprising the heads of the security and foreign intelligence services in Europe. The CTG brings together terrorism experts of the participating agencies who come regularly together in working groups. These groups are aimed at supporting the analytical work of the participating agencies and to provide EU bodies with intelligence evaluations in the terrorism field (Bergenstrand, 2004: 85–8). Though it is said to be set up 'in line with the position of the Justice and Home Affairs Council of 20 September [2001]' (Bergenstrand, 2004: 88), there is no official legal arrangement known to the public and it should be described as an 'independent body' (Lefebvre, 2003: 530) with loose connections to the EU (Bossong, 2008). Europol (2004a) has described the CTG as the 'Security Services counterpart to the Police Working Group on Terrorism (PWGT)'. There are links to Europol, SitCen, and US agencies with regard to information exchange (Bergenstrand, 2004: 88). Group meetings are chaired in rotation with the EU Presidency but practitioners emphasize the informal character, or the 'easy atmosphere' (Bergenstrand, 2004: 85).

European Police Chiefs Task Force (now integrated in the COSI)

The PCTF was set up in the aftermath of the 1999 Tampere Council and held its first meeting on 4 April 2000 (European Council, 1999). It comprised high-ranking national police commissioners. The fight against terrorism was one of the main issues on its agenda and it organized, for example, high-level meetings between the heads of EU CT units (Bergenstrand, 2004: 87; Den Boer, 2003: 202). While the PCTF started as an informal discussion forum for senior EU law enforcement officers, the group was increasingly taking over semi-operational tasks since 2005 (Brady, 2007a: 13–14; Nilsson, 2004: 18). Together with Europol and Interpol, joint operations were planned against organized crime networks. After 9/11, US authorities were allowed to sit in the meetings as well (Szyszkowitz, 2005: 181). In multilateral policing teams and with a clear division of responsibility through the planning system called COSPOL ('Comprehensive Operational Strategic Planning for the Police'), investigations were conducted under the guidance of a 'driver' country, often being the country directly affected by the criminal actors in question. However, responsibility could be shared with other countries or Europol (Brady, 2007a: 14). The PCTF's role and COSPOL have recently been transferred to the COSI (House of Lords, 2011: ch 6).

Prüm

The Convention on the stepping up of cross-border cooperation, particularly in combating terrorism, cross-border crime and illegal immigration (often referred to as the Treaty of Prüm) was signed on 27 May 2005 by the heads of government of Austria, Belgium, France, Germany, Luxembourg, the Netherlands, and Spain (Council, 2005j). It establishes a network of national police units involved in cross-border cooperation on terrorism and other forms of crime. The crucial aim is to improve the exchange of information for law enforcement purposes among the participating countries by granting reciprocal access to national databases on deoxyribonucleic acid (DNA) profiles, fingerprints, and vehicle registration data (ch 2 of the Treaty). The Convention was quickly adopted into EU law, with only minor amendments (Council, 2007b, 2008i, 2008j; see Chapter 6 for an extensive discussion).

Police Working Group on Terrorism

A comparatively old instrument of police cooperation is the PWGT which has brought together terrorism experts of European police forces since 1979. While focusing on the fight against terrorism, the PWGT's tasks are multiple ranging from the promotion of information exchange to criminal intelligence gathering and operational cooperation (Salgó, 2004: 98; Chalk, 1996: 124). The group is only loosely connected to the EU. Membership is not publicly disclosed but comprises of CT experts from the MS, plus Norway and Switzerland (House of Lords, 2011: ch 6). The representatives meet twice a year in a plenary meeting in which they provide information about the situation in their country. For the day-to-day work, the communication system Elcrodat is used between the MS' relevant agencies. A Hungarian officer commented that '(t)he co-operation is close, daily and due to the established personal contacts, the information flow is fast and efficient' (Salgó, 2004: 99). The PWGT also enables 'liaison officers to be deployed quickly to the scene of incidents in other countries' (Chalk, 1996: 124).

These networks have some characteristics in common. They are all policing networks in a broad sense, including intelligence or intelligence-led agencies, and all have CT as one of their priority tasks. They are all information-sharing networks with a semi-operational character. Moreover, they are all multilateral networks. Finally, all of them involve European actors and are (mainly) operational on European territory. Those 'networks of information exchange' (Monar, 2006: 503) often have only limited capacities to gather information on their own but need to be provided with data from the national nodes.

Some of the networks described in this chapter are more deeply interwoven with EU structures than others, and in the case of intelligence services it is not easy to tell the degree of EU-wide interactions at all (for the challenges of conducting research on current international intelligence cooperation see, for example, Svendsen, 2008). The loose structure of the EU's AFSJ allows groups of MS to move ahead in certain political projects and also allows 'the participation of non-EU actors, and justifying their existence on the basis of their non-bureaucratic, professional and informational character' (Den Boer et al, 2008). The concept of *variable geometry*, ie, regulations set up by a group of EU MS outside the EU framework, reinforces the pattern of the field of JHA. One crucial example for such a network is the Prüm Group which was originally established outside the EU framework but was quickly integrated within EU law.

The intelligence networks are clearly less developed than the police ones. For the time being, there remain considerable limits to intelligence sharing, in particular multilateral sharing. The EU's role in this field is so far marginal (eg, Müller-Wille, 2008, 2002). As Bossong (2008) has argued,

> (t)he defence of sovereignty in matters of 'national security' is buttressed by a culture of secrecy and independence of these services. Confidential sources and methods of work could be compromised if intelligence was widely shared.... Therefore, it is not appealing to share it on the basis of general rules with all EU member states.

Yet, others have understood the creation of SitCen, for example, as a proof that EU-wide intelligence cooperation must be taken more seriously (Nomikos, 2005).

The aim of this chapter was to provide a picture of the complex environment in which European efforts in CTP currently take place. The main trends towards the increased transnationalization of policing were identified. The proliferation of CTAs, including the emergence of jihadist terrorism, caused a strong reaction by European security authorities towards intensified police cooperation. This degree of cooperation led to an increasing merging of the internal and the external, or the domestic and foreign realm. The chapter illustrated that cooperation in this field often takes place through network-like structures. Networks are meant to be of beneficial value in comparison to hierarchical structures, as they offer loose relations with other actors while retaining their autonomy. This also means that the same actor can participate in various networks. It has been shown that, in particular, the EU's field of internal security provides an excellent arena for such networks to emerge.

Having explored how the EU has become a networking actor in the field of transnational policing, and CT in particular, the following chapter will provide the theoretical ground for an in-depth analysis of the dilemma between network-like structures of governance and democratic legitimacy in the context of EU-wide CTP. Some of the aspects widely seen as the advantages of networks, such as their flexibility and loose linkages, raise concerns with respect to democratic scrutiny, and the relationship between the networks and citizens in particular.

2

The Democratic Legitimacy of European Counter-terrorism Policing: Parliamentary and Judicial Scrutiny

Democracy dies behind closed doors.

(Judge Damon Keith, US Court of Appeals for the Sixth Circuit, *Detroit Free Press v Ashcroft* (2002))

The rule of law is not to be turned on and off like a tap.

(Paul Hunt, UN special rapporteur, as quoted in Strange, 2005)

The previous chapter outlined the institutional and legislative growth of JHA matters of the EU, and the area emerged as a collaborative space for European actors in policing and CT. The emergence of a variety of policing networks under this umbrella fits well with more general descriptions about the EU's governance being a complex web of cross-border interactions of a great variety of actors (Borrás, 2007: 235). Others have described the EU as a 'networked polity' (Ansell, 2000). However, how do such regional, network-like forms of cooperation between security bodies fit with the longstanding relationship between citizens and policing bodies in European liberal democratic societies? Though primarily intergovernmentally organized and limited in its executive powers, it has become clear in the previous chapter that the EU's cooperation in policing matters requires, at least to some extent, a 'pooling of sovereignty' within European institutions. The EU can therefore be described as one actor to challenge the individual state's monopoly on policing—though often rather in an indirect manner, as an 'activator and partner' (Borrás, 2007: 232) providing a framework for policing networks.

Yet, matters of security—security policies, actors, and instruments—are deeply interwoven with the political community in question. The modern liberal democratic state is based on the assumption that the state is the key provider of security for its citizens. Terrorism is understood to pose a particular threat to liberal democratic societies, as it poses a 'basic attack... to the right of the individual to exist in a setting that is free from the arbitrary coercion and violence of others' (Chalk, 1996: 91). From the perspective of contractual theory, there is an overall consensus in liberal democratic societies that the work of police, intelligence, and other law enforcement bodies is necessary and justified: security provision as a service *for* the people. This consensus is reflected in international human rights law which maintains the positive obligation of states 'to take preventive measures in order to protect individuals whose life or security is known or suspected to be at risk from the criminal acts of another individual, including terrorists' (Scheinin, 2009: point 26). Yet, to avoid arbitrary acts and an overly powerful role for security institutions, the mandates and work of security authorities are restricted—most notably by the law—and democratically scrutinized.

The increasing interconnectedness of security providers, as described in the previous chapter, challenges this system of legitimization which emerged, and is institutionalized, at the national level. This chapter therefore seeks to provide a theoretical framework in which to study the democratic legitimacy of EU CTP. The overarching question is whether EU policing actors and their work are adequately and sufficiently accompanied by mechanisms that ensure their democratic legitimacy. Can, or do, such forms of cooperation have a negative impact on the concept of democratic legitimacy? The EU provides a particularly interesting case to study such challenges owing to the considerable degree of cooperation and integration in the internal security sector. Moreover, the EU as a whole has been criticized for serious democratic deficits for a long time (Schmitter, 2000).

This chapter draws on literatures of democratic theory, international governance, police and intelligence accountability. While the literature on policing has discussed the loss of control and challenges to accountability in an international setting for some time, important lessons can also be learnt from studies on intelligence accountability. EU-wide networked policing has little in common with conventional policing and focuses instead on information and intelligence sharing, as maintained in Chapter 1. Therefore, new, or so far little considered, features of scrutiny might become more important and the literature on intelligence is likely to provide ideas. Moreover, fighting terrorism includes both aspects of police and intelligence cooperation, and the mandates and functions overlap, or merge, more and more. In the long run, there might even be a scrutiny mechanism necessary which can cover both features.[1]

The chapter is structured as follows: the first section will explore concepts of democratic legitimacy, with a particular focus on the international membership, network-like structure, and secretive nature of EU CTP. Based on this, two key features of democratic legitimacy will be identified in this context: parliamentary and judicial scrutiny. The second section will explore the dimension of parliamentary scrutiny, in particular with respect to the practice of external democratic accountability. This will be followed by an exploration of mechanisms of judicial scrutiny. The final section will briefly discuss the relevance of sound access to information and transparency to scrutiny mechanisms.

Conceptions of Democratic Legitimacy

In the academic literature, legitimacy is approached from various angles but remains, despite extensive studies, a contested concept. Political scientists and IR scholars often distinguish between empirical and normative approaches to legitimacy. According to this distinction, empirical theories focus on the 'societal acceptance' (Zürn, 2005: 136) of political decisions and governance activities, while more normative-oriented theories generate 'general criteria in terms of which the right to rule can be appraised' (Clark, 2005: 18). This distinction between empirical and normative approaches is somewhat misleading, however. Normative theories do not generate a pure 'abstract set of values' (Clark, 2005: 23), but tend to include empirical evidence as well—it matters what is conceived as right and legitimate in a certain political community. In this sense, rules and norms are a reflection of the assumptions of the community's members. The strength of a more normative-oriented approach is to allow assumptions about the quality of an institution and its activities with respect to legitimacy or, in other words, to generate criteria which can be used as a yardstick for judging legitimacy. Obviously, this can be a time-bound conception only, as it is related to a certain political order and period of time.

'Critical' and 'affirmative' approaches to democracy

In a domestic setting, legitimacy usually refers to the notion of 'the right to rule' (Clark, 2005: 11). In the context of modern liberal democratic states, this implies that the citizenry provides for 'popular consent' (Rees, 2003: 115). Usually, citizens authorize representatives to approve the actions of executives who then

[1] In Belgium, for example, the intelligence review committee already reviews the Anti-Terrorism Centre (OCAM) whose key purpose is the evaluation of terrorist threats in and to Belgium based on information obtained from governmental bodies, including the General Intelligence and Security Service and the federal and local police (Vande Walle, 2008; website of the Belgian Standing Intelligence Agencies Review Committee).

conduct their work. In a second step, 'decision-makers and decision-takers create processes and institutions' (Held, 2004: 372) to ensure legitimacy. As a consequence, in contemporary European societies 'laws, rules, and policies appear justified when they are "democratic"' (Held, 1995: 1; see also Zürn, 2005).

When can a political system be called democratic? The term is used indiscriminately in the academic literature (Dahl, 1999: 19). For example, democracy is often referred to in terms of *institutions*, such as elections and parliaments, which provide for 'democratic' procedures. Democracy then means the responsive rule according to the principles of popular control and political equality (Lord, 1998: 12). But those institutions, as well as the society as a whole, are based on democratic *values* and principles. Beetham (2008a: 4) therefore suggested that 'democracy is to be defined, in the first instance, by its underlying principle or principles, and only secondarily in terms of the institutions which embody them'.

For the purpose of this book it is helpful to draw on the distinction between critical, or liberal, and affirmative features of democracy (Harden, 1996). An affirmative approach refers to the notions of identity and belonging, emphasizing 'that popular sovereignty is the positive source of legitimacy of public power and of collective choices about goals and purposes' (Harden, 1996: 134–35). In other words, people are supportive of their government and its policies because they conceive of themselves collectively as a *demos*. Such a notion of democracy is widely agreed not to work at an international level (yet), however. For Europe, it has been convincingly argued that there is neither a singular European *demos* nor a singular public sphere in whose frame such a *demos* could develop any time soon (Scharpf, 1999: 187; Weiler, 1995).

As opposed to the affirmative approach to democracy, liberal democracy approaches do not need an existing singular *demos* as a pre-condition, but take the individual as their point of origin. They refer to a sceptical notion towards the government, highlighting the importance of limiting and constraining public power to ensure that life does not depend exclusively on the goodwill of a society's leader (De Greiff, 1999). Public 'checks' are important in order to allow people to be 'in control of decisions about one's life' (Beetham, 2008a: 7). The basic understanding is that individuals 'have rights that cannot legitimately be taken away' (Harden, 1996: 134) by any governing body, which enable them to participate in a democratic system and to conduct the popular control mentioned previously. Consequently, individual rights are thought of as an essential and intrinsic part of democracy itself (Beetham, 2008c: 92; Harden, 1996: 134). Similarly, Guillermo O'Donnell (2004: 32) has emphasized that 'a truly democratic rule of law [is needed] that ensures political rights, civil liberties, and mechanisms of accountability which in turn affirm the political equality of all citizens and constrain potential abuses of state power'.

To prevent the misuse of power, democratic legitimacy understood in this way 'requires constant scrutiny and debate of the conduct of those exercising public power' (Harden, 1996: 134). For police and other security authorities this appears to be crucial as those institutions exercise power over others. Their actions have potential consequences for individuals who can be deprived of liberty or reputation, for example. Thorough scrutiny mechanisms, eg of parliamentary bodies, provide the 'information needed for judging the propriety and effectiveness of the [executive's] conduct' (Bovens, 2007a: 463). Also, as institutions with a learning capacity, as established in the previous chapter, policing bodies can gain from a scrutiny procedure. They are meant to deliver high-quality work and the process of accountability might push them towards finding better solutions (Bovens, 2007a: 464). In this sense, procedures of democratic scrutiny can bring benefit not only to the democratic quality of a society but also to the performance of security bodies (for intelligence services, see Müller-Wille, 2006). The EU's MS are widely understood to agree on many of these principles: '(a)lthough there are differences of interpretation, all the Member States of the Union acknowledge the rule of law, the existence of fundamental rights and freedoms and the role of Parliaments in scrutinising and criticising the exercise of public power.' (Harden, 1996: 137–38.)

To summarize, from the perspective of critical democratic governance, democratic legitimacy refers to mechanisms which link a political entity's governance structures, including the executive, to the citizenry. A policy, or institution, is understood to be legitimate if it fulfils certain democratic criteria. Scrutiny mechanisms to ensure public control and the protection of human rights are widely understood to be of crucial importance.

To be sure, such a critical approach to democracy does not mean to ignore the idea of legitimacy as a function of public expectation. Rather, scrutiny bodies ought to be understood as the citizenry's 'proxy' (Peirce, 2009). Those bodies work (ideally) on the basis of certain public expectations or, at least, take them into account. Moreover, the mixture of scrutiny mechanisms will, to some extent, depend on the overall political consensus on what is felt as right and justified in a society. As those details of scrutiny appear to vary within European countries, it is important to acknowledge that scrutiny can take place in a variety of social mechanisms.

To ensure adherence with the two principles of public scrutiny and the protection of human rights, various mechanisms ought to be considered. While internal forms of scrutiny (eg through managerial accountability mechanisms) might be necessary to ensure internal democratic procedures of institutions, the requirement of public control refers first and foremost to the notion of *external* scrutiny. Typical forms of external examination in representative democracies are *parliamentary* and *judicial* scrutiny. Parliaments represent the citizens and ensure a certain degree of monitoring of the executive. They can hold those governmental actors to account and provide overall guidance for them. In addition, an independent judiciary ought to examine the legality of regulations and actions and ensure the compliance with the rule of law. Before these instruments are discussed in more depth, the following section will explore briefly whether the concept of democratic legitimacy developed previously is applicable for the international sphere in which European CTP takes place.

Democratic Legitimacy in an International Setting? The Case of the EU

In the international arena, political authority is increasingly claimed by actors other than national governments. In particular, actors beyond the nation-state, such as the EU, international organizations, and transnational networks, are increasingly calling for a share of authority. If legitimacy is required for national governments, it is also required for other political entities which claim political authority. As a consequence, the struggle for political authority is intimately linked with the struggle for legitimacy and actors such as the EU can be understood as 'legitimacy entrepreneurs' (Finnemore, 2005: 205) in international relations: the various actors claim authority on a particular issue in order to ensure legitimacy for their activities. They are often not authorized through elections, but gain authority through expertise or social capital, as epistemic communities (Haas, 1992). For example, human rights organizations, such as Amnesty International or Human Rights Watch, have, since their creation, successfully claimed and gained a high level of authority concerning issues of human rights. Of particular importance for this research, however, are those EU institutions which 'exercise authority over individuals and over the governments of member states that those individuals elect' (Harden, 1996: 132).

What has been observed is that the increasing diffusion of political authority at the international level is not accompanied by a proper system of legitimacy.[2] Similar to the debate about legitimacy in the domestic setting, the legitimacy deficit in international relations is usually understood as a democratic deficit (Benner, Reinicke, and Witte, 2004). Processes of internationalization challenge democratic principles and mechanisms, as it becomes more difficult to find effective 'means for holding political and bureaucratic elites accountable for their decisions' (Dahl, 2000: 183; see also Kaiser, 1971). International organizations remain to be widely understood as having a democracy deficit (Zweifel, 2006; Dahl, 1999). Overall, there is a disagreement about whether democracy can be extended to the international realm (for a positive answer see Archibugi and Held, 1995; Held, 1995; for a sceptical perspective see Dahl, 1999). Dahl (2000: 183) has pointed out that:

> the challenge posed by internationalization is to make sure that the costs to democracy are fully taken into account when decisions are shifted to international levels, and to strengthen the means for holding political and bureaucratic elites accountable for their decisions. Whether and how these may be accomplished is, alas, far from clear.

The EU has a particular role in this discussion. On the one hand, the EU has maintained an explicit commitment to 'democracy as political ideal' (O'Toole,

[2] See Moravcsik (2002) for a critical stance on this.

1997: 447) and understands it as one feature contributing to the Union's identity (Bretherton and Vogler, 2006: 30). On the other hand, the EU claims a substantial amount of authority in various policy fields. Perhaps most notably for the individual, every citizen of a MS is also an EU citizen. Less visible, the EU's legal and political system has a substantial impact on the domestic politics of the MS (Wincott, 2002: 491). As in many other policy fields, in the fight against terrorism the EU positions itself as an actor that provides instruments to solve problems that the states cannot deal with sufficiently on their own. Given this claim of authority, the institutional structures and policies of the EU require close scrutiny.

There remains considerable disagreement in the literature about how to judge the democratic legitimacy of the EU's system of governance, however. Authors involved use a variety of terminologies, interpretations, and yardsticks to explore democratic legitimacy and the (potential) lack of it at the EU level (Wimmel, 2008: 48–49).[3] This book is following the more sceptical line of arguments stating that there is currently a democratic deficit of the EU polity. This is usually attributed to the EU's inherent multilateral characteristics (Beetham and Lord, 1998: 6–9). More precisely, it has been argued, for example, that the EU's 'democratic deficit' refers to features such as 1) the large distance between the citizenry and the EU's institutions; 2) the powerful role of the European Commission; 3) the limited role for parliamentary bodies in the process of governing; and 4) decisions made behind closed doors which are therefore opaque and difficult to trace (eg, Craig, 1999: 23–24; Pollack, 2003: 407–414; Harden, 1996: 133). The EP itself warned as early as 1992 about the democracy deficit of the EU institutions. At least up to the entry into force of the Lisbon Treaty, the following description of the EU machinery was valid:

> (c)rucial decisions mainly come about through bargaining among political and bureaucratic elites. Limits are set not by democratic processes but mainly by what negotiators can get others to agree to and by considering the likely consequences for national and international markets. Bargaining, hierarchy, and markets determine the outcomes. Except to ratify the results, democratic processes hardly play a role (Dahl, 2000: 115).

The EU nevertheless puts great emphasis on democracy and the protection of human rights in its legal treaties and public documents. Given this promoted emphasis, it is fair to use features of parliamentary and judicial scrutiny as yardsticks for the democratic legitimacy of the EU's policing activities and CTNs. Yet before discussing these two features in depth, the following section will briefly discuss the insufficiencies of internal scrutiny mechanisms for European CTP.

---

[3] Compare, for example, Scharpf, 1999; Moravcsik, 2002; Schmitter, 2000; Føllesdal and Hix, 2006; and Kohler-Koch and Rittberger, 2007.

The Insufficiency of (Purely) Internal Accountability for Transnational Counter-terrorism Policing

Internal accountability refers to the individual day-to-day control of authorities (Lord, 1998: 80). Key formal instruments are internal organizational control and supervision through (ministerial) guidelines, specific statutes, and prescribed legal norms (Bovens, 2007a: 456).

At the national level, the political authorization of the work of police and intelligence services is usually provided at the ministerial level, for example in cases of high-impact operations or concerning certain types of surveillance. Legal legitimacy is ensured by means of a (court) warrant which might be needed for operations like phone tapping (Edwards, 2005: 137f). In addition, there are informal mechanisms of internal accountability, which refer to non-legal notions of responsibility, loyalty, and an ethos of transparency for the working conditions (Den Boer, 2002: 280–281). Those norms are implemented in various ways, for example through police leaders who 'set an example by complying with and enforcing the ethical code' (Eijkman, 2006: 421) of the respective police body. A good system of internal accountability is important in this field, as any misconduct could harm an individual, but also the overall reputation and legitimacy of the agency. Perhaps even more important, a damaged reputation and a lack of trust in security authorities by the citizens can harm operational activities—the police might not be able to gather the information necessary for their work.

Yet there are serious shortcomings of a purely internal accountability structure. It is first and foremost a model of self-regulation and as such there are clear limits to the system: failures in internal investigations could be made; and citizens have no channels to give their concerns and critique a public voice (Goldsmith, 1999: 35, 64). Crucially, a purely internal accountability system is insufficient for EU CTP owing to the network-like structure of such cooperation. Within an international network, the internal accountability of the individual nodes usually follows (national) hierarchical lines. Formal networks, such as Europol, have developed their own internal accountability mechanisms, thus adding an extra layer of responsiveness and responsibility. Indeed, Europol's Management Board was the first European institution to conduct, at least to a certain extent, internal accountability functions with respect to a transgovernmental police body (Anderson, 1995: 254). More informal networks do not provide such an extra layer of accountability, however, and the—nationally organized—internal accountability mechanisms appear to be inadequate to scrutinize the work, members, output, and effectiveness of such networks. Thus, internal accountability leaves the question open to whom the networks are responsible as a whole.

To be sure, internal accountability is also closely related to executive accountability. The security sector is supervised and directed by the executive. As stated previously, security authorities are responsible to certain ministries, and are guided and steered by them. Respectively, the ministers have to justify the work to parliamentary committees. This can happen through a variety of parliamentary mechanisms and the ministers might report to various committees, such as those covering home affairs, constitutional law, EU scrutiny, or foreign affairs. This fragmentation might actually hamper the possibility for the parliament to gain an overall picture of the policing activities in question. The overall scrutiny is further weakened through the fact that those committees might deal with classified information or generally meet behind closed doors. This is not to say that executive accountability cannot be a powerful tool. For example, when then British Foreign Minister David Miliband had to apologize in the context of the extraordinary rendition campaign relating to the government's misinformation of the public concerning Diego Garcia, his apology before Parliament provoked an embarrassing moment for the government (Pavia, 2008).[4] Indeed, legitimacy of policing actors and their actions provided through executive accountability is a well-established system in European democracies.

Yet again, executive accountability does not provide for an independent, external form of scrutiny. To maintain public confidence in the executive's willingness to do what is in the best public interest, it is sometimes necessary to provide for a broad political debate—which mechanisms of internal and executive accountability are less likely to do than external scrutiny mechanisms. In the post-9/11 climate, it has been argued that current CTP is of 'such moral seriousness and public importance' (Peirce, 2009) that it needs proper external inquiry and scrutiny. Just three examples of contested issues shall be given. Firstly, improvements in surveillance technologies provide for an increasing use of 'data mining' by policing bodies, whereby databases are matched with each other. Scheinin (2009: point 32) warned that this 'blurs the boundary between permissible targeted surveillance and problematic mass surveillance which potentially amounts to arbitrary or unlawful interference with privacy'. Similarly, the use of undercover agents and human sources, while being thought of as a crucial means to fight transnational terrorism, raises 'serious ethical problems about what limits the state should respect when suppressing crime' (Van den Wyngaert, 1997: 170). Finally, the toleration of mistreatment and torture of terrorist suspects, or the use of information likely to be gathered through mistreatment, in particular by foreign security authorities, is contested. While torture is forbidden by international law, there currently seems to be a grey area which calls for thorough political debate (cf Chapters 4 to 6).

Given those serious limitations of internal and executive accountability, external scrutiny mechanisms are necessary to ensure democratic legitimacy. The following section will explore parliamentary scrutiny followed by a section on scrutiny through the judiciary.

---

[4] Both former Prime Minister Tony Blair and former Foreign Secretary Jack Straw had repeatedly stated between 2005 and 2007 that there had been no evidence for rendition flights stopping on British territory. On 21 February 2008, Miliband had to admit that US planes had indeed been refuelled on Diego Garcia, the UK's dependent territory, on two occasions.

Parliamentary Scrutiny

It has emerged from the previous sections that parliamentary scrutiny is widely understood to be an important tool to ensure democratic legitimacy. In modern representative democracies, the parliament is understood as the 'watchdog of liberty' (Held, 1996: 108), aiming to control executive powers and prevent their abuse (Van Kersbergen and Van Waarden, 2004: 7). As democratically elected bodies, parliaments are mandated to check the executive, debate policy directions, and pass laws. Doing so, they also discuss and decide what kinds of conduct a society wishes 'to declare off-limits' (Peirce, 2009). Overall, this process 'confer[s] democratic legitimacy upon the binding rules that govern the demos' (Tsakatika, 2007: 549). Parliamentary debates about aspects of CT can also promote and inform a public debate about a contested feature. For example, the inquiries which the British Joint Committee on Human Rights (JCHR) conducted into extraordinary renditions and torture allegations appear to have been driving debates about these issues to a considerable extent (House of Lords/House of Commons Joint Committee on Human Rights, 2009b).[5]

Concerning the realm of intelligence, Hans Born (2004: 5) has argued that parliamentary oversight provides a 'security check' to prevent abuse of intelligence by 1) intelligence officers and 2) the executive branch. In this sense, parliaments ought to keep 'the services in line with their legally defined mandate' (Born and Johnson, 2005: 225). Moreover, parliaments ensure the supervision of the intelligence budget and thus the spending of taxpayers' money. Finally, 'parliament, on behalf of the people it represents, has to check whether human rights are respected' (Born, 2004: 5). One aspect not mentioned very often is that part of the accountability system is the justification of *in*action (Omand, 2007: 164). The 9/11 Commission, for example, has analysed in great depth why the responsible intelligence and law enforcement agencies did *not* act on the basis of certain information, which opened up a discussion about intelligence failures (National Commission on Terrorist Attacks upon the United States, 2004).

How can a parliament fulfil such a demanding role with respect to the secretive field of CT? Above, it has been explained that the details of scrutiny mandates and procedures vary, depending on the national context. Typical mechanisms are open and closed meetings, hearings, and parliamentary enquiries as well as the analysis of reports provided by the institutions. The aims of parliamentary scrutiny are multifold as well: key purposes might be a 'legality' check, financial scrutiny, the adherence to human rights provisions, the exploration of necessity and effectiveness of the security institution and/or its activities, the proper use of technology, and so on. The performance of policing bodies can be measured, for example, 'by their efficiency, outcome, competition,

[5] The JCHR is a permanent committee comprising six members of each House which met for the first time on 31 January 2001. It is to examine matters relating to human rights in the UK on a topical basis.

value-for-money, their partnership, customer orientation and so on' (Den Boer, 2002: 281). By providing organizational feedback on the bodies' behaviour, scrutiny bodies can add to the overall effectiveness of an institution (Goldsmith, 1999: 37). Finally, parliaments could be a place to identify whether there is a common public interest in this transnational field of security provision and whether this form of provision of security is oriented towards the 'common good' (Wood and Dupont, 2006: 2).

To fulfil their mandate, parliamentary committees may be granted budgetary powers or oversight rights, the right to ask questions to ministries and executives, the right to set up an inquiry committee, and a no-confidence vote (Schmidt-Radefeldt, 2005: 39). In addition, further criteria need to be fulfilled so the committees can actually meet their demanding task. They need a sufficient supply of resources (assistant staff and budget, for example), the 'willingness to hold the executive to account' (Born, 2004: 213), and they need to have access to sufficient and reliable information.

While all parliamentary scrutiny bodies work differently, a description by a member of the Belgian intelligence review committee appears to be a good example:

> Our Committee carries out investigations. These investigations can be either descriptive or assume the form of an audit; they can be reactive or prospective; they can be extensive or very brief. But the exercise always comes down to describing the situation 'as is' as accurately as possible. The Committee's investigations are fact-finding missions.
>
> The next step is consequently to compare this current situation 'as is' with 'what should be' by checking compliance with the law in the widest sense of the word, the effectiveness and efficiency of the services' operations, the way they coordinate their activities, and last but not least, the respect for 'the rights which the Constitution and the law confer on individuals' (Vande Walle, 2008).

The literature on intelligence oversight provides some arguments against parliamentary scrutiny and, in particular, security officials tend to be sceptical towards too much involvement by external bodies, such as parliaments (eg, Glees and Davies, 2006). There appears to be an overall consensus, however, that, within a democratic entity, 'no area of state activity should be a "no-go" zone for the legislature' (Leigh, 2005: 8). For the police, Morgan and Newburn (1997: 196) have argued that a parliamentary body's involvement is necessary—it is 'both a principle and a requirement for long-term public confidence'. External scrutiny is not meant to replace internal control mechanisms. For example, certain operational details about ongoing investigations ought not to be accessible to a parliamentary body for reasons of ensuring the safety of informants or undercover agents on the ground (Chalk, 2000). Yet parliaments can provide added value of scrutiny as stated previously. The following subsection will explore the roles of the EP and National Parliaments (NPs) in the field of policing.

The roles of the European Parliament and National Parliaments

With respect to the EU, the EP is *the* parliamentary actor. Yet when the EU was incrementally developing substantial parts of its CT legislation—between 9/11 and the coming into force of the Lisbon Treaty—its measures of monitoring, control, and supervision were strictly limited concerning matters of PJCC. Chapter 6 will describe and analyse the EP's role in depth, but a striking example is the implementation process of the EU's CT policy in which the EP had merely consultative powers (Monar, 2005a: 450). Also, the Parliament was completely excluded from the two agreements between the EU and the US on extradition and mutual legal assistance in criminal matters signed in 2003 (Monar, 2004: 406).

Similar to the EP, the NPs had a limited role concerning the scrutiny of CT policies and institutions, as will be outlined in Chapter 6. Scrutiny through the NPs is important as it directly links the elected parliaments with the EU system (Guild and Carrera, 2005: 4). Some authors have argued that the crucial problems regarding democratic legitimacy remain at the nation-state level and should therefore be tackled at that level as well (eg, Müller-Wille, 2006). Yet, there are situations imaginable in which NPs are resistant to or not capable of performing their role as accountability forums. The parliamentary investigations in the CIA's extraordinary rendition campaign have shown, for example, that in such extraordinary cases a transnational body might actually work as a 'substitute', or 'fire brigade', in case the NPs do not adequately conduct their role as accountability holders (Hillebrand, 2009).

In addition, one further positive aspect of an increasingly Europeanized system of scrutiny bodies needs brief mentioning. The EU environment might push NPs towards better scrutiny mechanisms owing to mechanisms of peer pressure. When, for example, the head of the Constitutional Law Committee of the Finnish Parliament, Kimmo Sasi, suggested in 2004 to create a parliamentary scrutiny body concerning the Security Police (SUPO) in Finland, he explicitly emphasized that parliamentary and ministerial supervision of the SUPO are 'among the weakest in Europe, if not the weakest of all EU countries' (Helsingin Sanomat, 2004).

Yet there arise problems for parliamentary scrutiny through the international, networked nature of EU CTP. One serious problem for parliamentary scrutiny arises through the EU's overall structure. As Monar (2005a: 450) has warned: '(n)ational governments can actually use the European level for reducing... parliamentary scrutiny.' This refers to a well-known practice of the national governments to introduce legislation by the 'backdoor'. If a government experiences resistance within its domestic political framework concerning the introduction of a certain piece of legislation, then it might want to convince other governments in the Council to introduce a common, EU-wide legislation. Depending on the resulting piece of EU legislation, it might then be obligatory to implement the legislation at the national level. As a consequence, the national government can refer to its international commitments and obligations and/or 'blame Brussels' for the legislation. This way, it managed to avoid political opposition in its own country (see also Wagner, 2004: 14). Thus, the move towards a 'European internal security' implies that the debate about fundamental directions of home and security politics, the balance of repressive and preventive executive measures, as well as the necessity and adequacy of measures moved more and more towards an international level of political—and executive—debate (Bukow, 2005: 60–61).

Moreover, in contrast to (some forms of) internal accountability, parliaments tend to deal with an incident only *ex post facto*, ie *after* the incident has happened. The case of a parliamentary hearing concerning a CT police operation in Brussels in 2007 suggests some typical lines of *ex post facto* enquiry (Jozwiak, 2008). On 11 December 2008, Belgian police conducted a big operation, involving 242 officers and large-scale street barriers, in which the police arrested fourteen suspects in overnight house raids in the cities of Brussels and Liège (Erlanger, 2008). After the operation, the parliament asked the responsible security authorities to justify their intense operation.

Yet some parliamentary scrutiny bodies have more proactive mandates which, according to Born (2004: 8), allow 'the oversight body to veto or alter the policy or functioning of the services before the policy or operation is put into practice'. This includes powers of budget control which would enable the body 'to alter the policy priorities' (Born, 2004) of the policing bodies in question. This is an important aspect of parliamentary scrutiny, which will be discussed later concerning Europol. Here it is sufficient to say that this is one of the crucial changes under Europol's new legal mandate: as an EU agency, its budget is now part of the overall EU budget, which is partly controlled by the EP.

Challenges for parliamentary scrutiny

Apart from the need for information, or transparency, for effective parliamentary scrutiny—an aspect, which will be discussed on pages 51ff in combination with challenges for judicial scrutiny—authors have mentioned a variety of concerns related to parliamentary scrutiny. For example, the problem of who is competent and responsible not only becomes apparent in the struggle between the EP and NPs. In the field of CTP, the challenge is that often various parliamentary bodies are involved in the scrutiny procedures—even within *one* state. Scheinin (2009: point 46) warned that

> compartmentalized oversight, whereby oversight bodies are assigned to examine just one part of the intelligence community, cross-cutting problems fall through the gaps between oversight bodies. Oversight bodies with a thematic mandate are therefore generally better equipped to address the increasing overlap of functions, cooperation and the sharing of information between various governmental agencies.

Similarly, a former member of the German Parliamentary Control Panel concerning intelligence (PKGr), pointed to difficulties of control arising from the increased use of intelligence material by the police—a means of proactive policing, as explained in the previous chapter (Neumann, 2007: 49). This would pose challenges to the scrutiny of police and intelligence—Germany's PKGr, for example, does not supervise the police executive. Indeed, this consequence of proactive policing is currently not covered by intelligence oversight bodies in Europe (Smidt, 2007: 249).

Finally, Ian Leigh has pointed out the unusual way that many parliamentary committees in this field are constructed and the powers they have. Leigh (2005: 8) suggested that members of parliamentary committees with a 'privileged access to secret material' might cause jealousy and distrust amongst the wider group of parliamentarians. Moreover, such 'an immature approach by parliamentarians may lead to sensationalism in public debate and to wild accusations and conspiracy theories being aired under parliamentary privilege' (Leigh, 2005: 8). Similarly, the extensive involvement of parliaments in matters of CT is that such matters of 'law and order' might become party-politicized (Morgan and Newburn, 1997: 104ff; see also Glees and Davies, 2006, 2004). To prevent those scenarios, independence and robustness against political pressure must be a key element of any scrutiny committee (cf the five criteria of strong oversight identified by Born and Johnson (2005: 235–238)).

One potential shortcoming of parliamentary scrutiny mechanisms is that they can be quite 'toothless' instruments when it comes to sanctioning powers. Moreover, the complexity of the EU structure including the complicated legal framework makes it difficult for parliamentarians to monitor and control compliance with the rule of law and the respect and protection of human rights, which have been established as cornerstones of democratic legitimacy. One crucial example relating to the EP's scrutinizing actions concerning the first EU-US agreement on Passenger Names Record (PNR) exchange will be explored in later chapters. The following section will analyse possibilities of and (potential) challenges for judicial scrutiny of EU CTP.

Judicial Scrutiny: Ensuring Compliance with (the Rule of) Law and Protecting Human Rights

While one cornerstone of democratic legitimacy is parliamentary scrutiny, modern democratic societies also understand their citizens as holders of rights which need to be protected by an effective judiciary. The powers of parliamentary bodies to impose a sanction on, or restrict certain actions of, policing bodies is insufficient to ensure individual rights and liberties of individuals. Academic scholars identified the protection of basic rights as well as the compliance with law, including respect for human rights, as the 'twin pillars of good police forces in liberal-democratic societies' (Goldsmith, 1999: 34; cf Mendes, 1999: 13). The second cornerstone of democratic legitimacy is therefore judicial scrutiny, which includes compliance with the rule of law and the protection of human rights. For the study of EU CTP, it is adequate to refer to human rights as the core reference point for judicial scrutiny.

In principle, the police exercise 'their lawful powers given to them by governments in the name of the people, to protect the people and their institutions' (Alderson, 1984: 19). The relationship between the law and policing is complex and somewhat contradictory but might be summarized as follows: '(a)s law enforcement officials, the police are obliged to uphold the law while enforcing it against others who may have broken it' (Goldsmith, 1999: 33–34). Policing bodies therefore act on the thin line between the protection of individual rights and their endangerment through arbitrary conduct, which is why judicial control over executive action in European policing is deemed as necessary (Goldsmith, 1999: 35; Guild and Carrera, 2005: 4; Edwards, 2005: 151).

While the relationship between policing and the law is already a complex one in the domestic framework, in the context of transnational policing and intelligence gathering this relationship is even more complicated. The activities then involve the domestic laws of at least two countries. The challenge for the EU is that law is 'part of a value system into which we are progressively socialized by all the institutions with which we have contact and of which we are a part' (Morgan and Newburn, 1997: 179). Guild and Carrera (2005: 8) have argued that, within the MS with a long tradition of the rule of law, citizens have developed trust in the judicial protection against executive incursion. Yet the Central and Eastern European countries that have joined the EU in recent years have, of course, a peculiar recent history of the relationship between citizens and security authorities. The post-communist states inherited security bodies, but also judicial systems, 'that were not trusted by their own people' (Henderson, 2005: 1). Reforms during the 1990s were speeded up to a considerable extent due to the EU's 'coercive power' (Henderson, 2005: 7) to grant EU membership only to those countries that had sufficiently reformed their sector of internal security. This was also of importance to the existing MS, as their data protection standards in the field of police and judicial cooperation would be affected by low standards in the new MS (eg, information shared via Europol could end up in those countries and could have been more likely subject to misuse). As a consequence, in those post-communist states

> sophisticated international police cooperation structures have...been developed, with the widespread use of police liaison officers, which required among many other preparations training in the necessary linguistic skills.... Further examples of the demanding legislative requirements for guaranteeing justice and home affairs cooperation was the passing of data protection acts... This was a precondition for establishing the trust necessary for data exchange internationally, while also representing an improvement in civic rights domestically (Henderson, 2005: 18).

A high level of trust certainly does not come naturally when one considers policing activities at the transnational level. The law in European countries has developed in various ways and the judicial systems and legal regulations differ to a considerable extent from country to country. As a consequence, European police cooperation is often based on bilateral police agreements. However, if the EU wants to implement EU-wide regulation, it needs to ensure, as a basic premise, that the legal definition or the legal terminology is consistent. As already mentioned in the previous chapter, the introduction of the EU-wide definition of terrorism must be understood as a step in this direction (Council, 2002a).

The legal framework for certain forms of EU-wide cooperation is complex and often involves a considerable amount of paperwork.[6] The more complex and time-consuming legal restrictions are, however, the greater the danger of delaying an operation—which could potentially harm the overall effectiveness of the police operation. Also, it appears that policing bodies prefer more informal forms of cooperation to avoid the legal restrictions of formal ones. One could therefore object that conformity with law, and in particular international human rights, might weaken CT efforts. However, the Council of Europe's Parliamentary Assembly (PACE) (2005: point 2) argued convincingly that, on the contrary, such conformity is 'not a weakness in the fight against terrorism but a weapon, ensuring the widest international support for actions and avoiding situations which could provoke misplaced sympathy for terrorists or their causes'.

The protection of individual rights is usually ensured by a system of judicial oversight. The term refers to 'a system of rules that is both enforceable by an independent judicial authority, and accessible by any citizen on a basis of equality' (Lord, 1998: 96). Thus, it includes oversight of institutions exercised by courts. As will be analysed in depth in Chapter 7, the challenge is which judicial bodies are responsible with respect to CT activities of the EU. While national bodies remain of primary importance for the time being, the chapter will show that European activities in the field of policing are also subject to the European Court of Human Rights (ECtHR). The ECtHR, which is not an EU body, but acts at the wider European level, focuses, among other issues, on the proportionality of remedies such as surveillance and screening. Moreover, the European Court of Justice (ECJ) and its Court of First Instance (CFI) have dealt with the protection of individual rights regarding CT policies (Guild, 2008).

Apart from a court system, a further mechanism to ensure the protection of individual rights is a quasi-judicial complaint body, such as an ombudsman, to which citizens have access and to which they can complain about the misuse of power or bad conduct through the policing actors (Lord, 1998: 80; Den Boer and Fernhout, 2008). However, as will be discussed in connection with Europol's complaint body, such bodies are softer in many senses than courts, also because they usually hold much weaker sanctioning powers.

[6] This is, for example, the case concerning Joint Investigation Teams (JITs) which can involve Europol staff. The case will be discussed in the following chapter; but see also Rijken, 2006; Rijken and Vermeulen, 2006.

Finally, the statutory footing of transnational police activities needs to be taken into account. The EU's third pillar was well known for the creation of bodies and administrative agreements decided on without any (considerable) involvement of parliaments (Chalk, 2000: 197). More generally, networks are often based on informal Memoranda of Understanding (MOUs) between the regulatory agencies and EU-wide policing is often based on a framework decision, whose precise legal effect remains unclear (Guild and Carrera, 2005: 3).

Having explored possible mechanisms of parliamentary and judicial scrutiny, the final section of this chapter will discuss some implications of the secret field of CTP for a scrutiny system as established previously in this chapter.

Challenges for Scrutiny in the Security Sector: Transparency v Secrecy

The security sector in which actors such as the police, intelligence, and the military work, is often described as being a distinct policy field with respect to public control, civil participation, transparency, and accessibility. Security matters are of a sensitive nature and considerations of national security are widely acknowledged to justify a certain degree of secrecy (Halperin and Hoffman, 1977: 1). Secrecy refers to the intentional blocking of information and 'the resulting concealment' (Bok, 1989: 6). Consequently security matters do not fit easily with demanding concepts of scrutiny, accountability, and transparency; a certain exception to the rule of openness remains acceptable to the public. However, the last couple of decades in Western democratic societies have slowly seen an emergence of understanding that the security sector ought to be 'one part among others' of democratic governance. Some go as far to suggest that secret activities are a fundamental paradox in a democracy. Here, the term democracy refers to the ideal notion of 'open society' which is responsive and works through transparent and flexible political mechanisms. Governmental or executive secrecy is not foreseen in such a system.

In such a society, any kind of secret activity by an executive agency must be understood as a challenge to the basis of that society in question. In a decision in March 1998 concerning the Treaty on European Union (Maastricht Treaty), the German Constitutional Court referred to transparency in the exercise of power as 'one of the essential conditions for the democratic legitimacy of the EU's institutional system' (Monar, 2005b: 209). Transparency refers to the notion that 'the process of making decisions should be understandable and open and the decisions themselves should be reasoned and based on information that is publicly available' (Harden, 1996: 134). In particular, a high level of transparency is a prerequisite for any effective scrutiny system (Harden, 1996; Harlow, 2002; Eijkman, 2006: 414). Without information, it is impossible to hold actors to account.

Yet, most observers would argue that a considerable restriction of openness is necessary in the field of security. For intelligence services, secrecy is thought of as 'a virtue as well as a necessity' (Hulnick, 1999: 463) and a pre-condition for an effective service (Glees and Davies, 2006: 849). While details about the work and mandate of intelligence services were kept in the dark by governments for a long time, more and more services were put on statutory footing, in particular from the mid-1970s onwards. This was for a variety of reasons, such as 'scandals' which were publicly revealed and caused great concerns in the public as well as court judgments at the European level. Since then, the necessity of a democratic basis for intelligence services has slowly spread. In addition, most European secret services went 'through a regulatory revolution in the 1990s in which the European Convention on Human Rights was written into their core guidance. Everywhere, secret services are being monitored and examined, if not always called to account' (Aldrich, 2009b: 892).[7] It seems fair to argue that 'it is now generally accepted that democratic control contributes to the acceptance and legitimacy of the work of intelligence services' (De Smet, 2008).

The increased use of intelligence concerning fighting organized crime and transnational issues are understood as a further reason to open the doors of the intelligence services for certain accountability procedures. Those activities are said to have created 'new audiences such as the courts and a greater interest in a much wider group of consuming departments' (Robertson, 1999: 123). Those audiences have a strong interest in understanding where certain information comes from in order to judge its reliability, the relevance and effectiveness of subsequent activities based on that information, and so on.

However, secretiveness is deeply ingrained in the daily work of intelligence services. For example, services work on a 'need-to-know' principle—ie the individual officer is informed about an investigation, or case, only insofar as absolutely necessary for their conduct of work. The same can be observed in the field of high policing. While this is partly introduced to protect the employee (against interrogations and espionage from outside, for instance), internalizing this principle leads to a general secrecy of the staff of intelligence services (Brodeur, Gill, and Töllberg, 2003: 4). An over-emphasis on secrecy has consequences for scrutiny efforts, for example insofar as staff might not talk openly to scrutiny bodies.

Clearly, the security sector—and the field of CT in particular—remains less transparent and accessible than other policy fields, but it has arguably experienced a considerable procedure of 'normalization' since the 1970s. Lustgarten (2003: 323) has identified two key elements of a democratic anchorage in the field of contemporary national security governance: 'a) effective public decision-making in the choice of the aims and operative framework of the agencies and b) creation of oversight machinery that is capable of ensuring that they respect

[7] France was an exception for a long time. A parliamentary intelligence oversight committee was finally created in 2007. While the committee's mandate and powers are severely limited, this move nevertheless indicates that France too 'has admitted that matters of intelligence concern the Parliament' (Lepri, 2011: 215).

democratic values.' Those criteria are very similar to the ones elaborated on previously referring to the importance of democratic procedures and institutions *as well as* democratic values and including features of public scrutiny and the protection of human rights. Since the investigations by the 9/11 Commission into the failures of intelligence that (possibly) led to the terrorist attacks, many scrutiny procedures—by parliamentary and expert committees as well as legal investigations—have been initiated in Western countries with respect to intelligence and police, often related to the fight against terrorism.[8] At the same time, more professionals from the field of CT, and intelligence more broadly, appear to write about their experience (Rimington, 2002; Hayman, 2009).

Another recent development is the increasing appearance of intelligence personnel in court trials, which provides some insight into their work. Finally, the recent media coverage of police and intelligence work is remarkable. Individual national police bodies and intelligence services in Europe usually communicate in various forms with the media. In recent years, more police and intelligence services, including Europol, have created press offices and employed official spokespersons, which indicates a growing need to manage the public's demand for information. Yet the high level of secrecy is pointed to as a key reason for a limited role of the media in the oversight of intelligence services. In the German context, for example, Geiger (2007: 35) argued that it is rare that the media discusses a particular operation, or investigation, or reveals a scandal.

Indeed, wide-ranging information about EU CTP is sparse. While it appears that EU-wide legislation in this field is widely available, many debates, recommendations, meetings of working groups, cooperation, and rivalry between institutions and information about the work of the Counter-terrorism Coordinator or CTNs are much less accessible. This fits with wider descriptions about the current era of 'excessive secrecy' (Aldrich, 2009a).[9] Only thanks to information freedom groups, in particular the London-based group Statewatch, are citizens provided with lots of information about EU policing, which was originally restricted to a small number of readers.

---

[8] Examples are, the Menezes inquiries; the reports by the PACE and the EP into the involvement of European countries in the CIA's extraordinary rendition programme; the court trial concerning the extraordinary rendition of Abu Omar in Milan and the legal investigations into the torture allegations by Binyam Mohamed in the UK; the parliamentary probe into the role of the *Bundesnachrichtendienst* (BND) and other security institutions in Iraq as well as cases of extraordinary rendition (in particular with respect to Khaled El-Masri) in Germany; and the judgments of, and ongoing trials before, the ECJ concerning the freezing of assets of terrorist suspects based on a UN Resolution and respective EU legislation (Independent Police Complaints Commission, 2006a, 2006b; Marty, 2006, 2007c; European Parliament, TDIP, 2007; Goetz and Sandberg, 2009; Mohamed, 2009; *Der Spiegel*, 2009; Guild, 2008).

[9] Authors referring to an increase in secrecy point to, for example, an 'increasing use of State secrecy provisions and public interest immunities for instance by Germany, Italy, Poland,... the United Kingdom or the United States to conceal illegal acts from oversight bodies or judicial authorities, or to protect itself from criticism, embarrassment and—most importantly—liability' (Scheinin, 2009: para 59; see also International Commission of Jurists, 2009).

Overall, transnational policing has only a 'low public visibility' (Loader, 2002) as it is thought of as being far removed from the individuals' everyday lives, usually responding to threats that are 'placeless' (eg illegal migration, cross-border drug trafficking) or very technical and secretive to deal with (eg money-laundering and the freezing of terrorist assets). The opaque nature of cross-border networks adds to this challenge. However, more formal networks, such as Europol, are increasingly providing information for the press and the wider public about their successes and other news. This might become an increasingly important role for Europol, as it could promote itself as the centre of European-wide policing. Unsurprisingly, such bodies tend to promote themselves exclusively in a good light and would avoid reporting about failures, shortcomings, or contested issues.

Surely, the secretiveness surrounding CT operations makes it very difficult to claim an overall effectiveness of CT actors, and the provision of security in general. For example, is CT work effective if there is no terrorist attack? What if nobody had planned an attack anyway? Clear indicators for an analysis of effectiveness in this field are lacking (Den Boer, 2002: 284). However, some authors have suggested more indirect measures. One yardstick would be to measure the *desired* outcome of a policy or operation against the actual results—which ought to be done by means of an independent evaluation (Müller-Wille, 2006; Finnemore, 2005: 201). If the CTNs were effective in providing security, they could be regarded as legitimate in this sense (a form of 'output legitimacy' in the words of Scharpf (1999)). Anderson (1995: 267), for example, assumes a certain degree of public support for international policing arrangements. Similarly, a 2009 opinion poll seems to suggest that citizens want the EU to be engaged in internal security, and CT in general, but this is not very reliable information given the general way the questions were asked (Commission, 2009a). To justify activities at EU level in this field, however, the EU's former Counter-terrorism Coordinator Gijs de Vries (2003: 13) stated in 2003 that

> (i)t is clear what European citizens want. They want the Union to address their concerns and help solve their problems. They want the European Union to...take on, effectively and democratically, those cross-border problems, which the nation-states of Europe are unable to deal with on their own. No more, no less.

Yet, after the rejection of the Constitutional Treaty through the French and Dutch citizenry, the subsequent long and hampered ratification procedure of the Lisbon Treaty, and the ongoing debates about adequate financial crisis management, such a statement needs to be read with great scepticism, as it appears less clear what European citizens want (or do not want) from the EU.

Given the lack of openness of the security sector and the difficult task of conducting the job effectively, authorities in the field of CTP tend to enjoy a considerable degree of professional autonomy. To some extent, the simple fact that mechanisms of parliamentary and judicial scrutiny exist helps to create and ensure a certain degree of public confidence. The mechanisms ensure the 'rightness'—both in a legal, but also a wider democratic, or normative sense—of the CT actors' actions. They potentially establish public trust in the correctness and adequateness of behaviour and sufficient jurisdictional and/or bureaucratic boundaries to avoid misconduct or wrongdoing. Nevertheless, it emerges from the debates about the legitimacy of policing that there appears to be an overall consensus that the more intrusive the work, the more important is the process for accountability and oversight (see also Treverton, 2009: 254). Instead of understanding scrutiny procedures as a hurdle for effective work, it must be understood as a procedure of quality control and therefore something good for the performance of the security sector.

Comparative scholarly work on police and intelligence suggests that policing activities are deeply embedded in different social and cultural histories—and so are the mechanisms to ensure their legitimacy. What then are the rules, guidelines, and traditions that frame the work of a network such as Europol, which comprises of representatives of all twenty-seven MS, plus a considerable amount of liaison partners from non-EU countries (cf Chapter 3)? Previous academic work has maintained that the linkage between the security providers acting under the EU's umbrella and the citizens appear to be weak. In particular owing to the intergovernmental nature of the former third pillar, individuals had few channels to ensure an impact on the field. While the decision-making procedures have changed under the Lisbon Treaty, as will be analysed in Chapter 6, it remains to be seen how far this really opens towards a greater involvement of the citizenry. Also, the fact remains that the AFSJ, due to its quick evolution, and EU security governance comprise of complex and opaque structures (Rees, 2003: 122). When the creation of the AFSJ was announced at the Tampere Council in October 1999, the idea was to base the AFSJ 'upon the principles of transparency and democratic control, as well as upon an open dialogue with civil society in order to strengthen the acceptance and support of citizens' (Eder and Trenz, 2003: 113; see also Council, 1999b). It is widely agreed, however, that the AFSJ is far from meeting those ideals at the moment. The lack of accountability is often pointed out as a crucial problem. Neil Walker (2004: 27) has stated that the intensified European policing activities pose new challenges of 'transnational executive accountability'. Traditional yardsticks of effective monitoring, for example, seem not to fit appropriately (Walker, 2004).

One particular problem lies in the fact that the key responsible body is the European Council which is 'not a body which by any means can be forced out of office or to resign' (Monar, 2005b: 218). It comprises representatives of the MS, usually from the executive part of government, and the individual members of the body could be held accountable by their own parliaments (Harden, 1996: 132). Harden (1996) has called this 'indirect democratic legitimation'. But Monar critically pointed to the problem of diffused political leadership at the EU level. He stated that

> the difficulties for national parliaments to effectively scrutinise collective decision-making by their representatives at the Union level are well known, and outside of the legislative domain national parliaments have most of the time to content themselves with general statements of government policy before political leadership decisions are taken at the EU level and general statements on outcomes after they have been taken, with parliamentary majorities expected to 'rubber-stamp' those in one way or another. Looking at it critically one could say that responsibility in the context of collective Council leadership is assumed rather than real and certainly not compatible with that which national constitutional frameworks normally provide for (Monar, 2005b: 218).

The Council, in other words, 'operates largely in secret' (Harden, 1996: 133).

The opaque nature of CTNs intensifies these problems. In general, networks are understood to be providers of 'a decentralized, flexible, individualized, and creative response to a public problem' (Goldsmith and Eggers, 2004: 123). Yet, exactly those characteristics make it inherently difficult to scrutinize networks and hold them to account (Goldsmith and Eggers, 2004: 41; Benner, Reinicke, and Witte, 2004: 198). Networks include members from various policy levels and a mixture of decentralized and centralized, vertical and horizontal, regional, national, and transnational organizational structures (Stegmaier and Feltes, 2007: 20). This is why the recent literature dealing with problems of accountability in network-like and transnational settings seems to agree that a broader and more flexible system of accountability is needed (eg Bovens, 2007a, 2007b; Goldsmith and Eggers, 2004). Actors in networks are assumed to have both national and transnational components of responsibilities (Slaughter, 2004b: 171). Consequently, a scrutiny system focusing only on the domestic home institutions is not seen as sufficient on the international level and has to be complemented by a form of *collective* accountability and oversight. Ideally, those forms of accountability would complement each other and not lead to a conflict of accountability.

The opaque distribution of power appears to be the crucial problem of networks with respect to scrutiny. As the literature on security networks suggests, more and more complex structures are created around the globe in order to produce or ensure 'security'. Those new structures are likely to lead to a new distribution of power (Gill and Phythian, 2006: 173). As stated in the previous chapter, networks can be a means of power diffusion. The crucial questions to ask about a network are then 1) who has access to the network in question (and who is excluded) and 2) what do actors really diffuse, share, or exchange?

Critical voices argue that the networks of bureaucratic and professional police elites act 'largely disconnected from the process of... democratic scrutiny, whether at national or European levels' (Loader, 2002). In addition, the question of who leads or controls a security network is not easily answered given that many security networks are 'composed of relatively autonomous security auspices and providers' (Lippert and O'Connor, 2006: 58). One key question with respect to European policing is at which policy level the networks and their participants ought to be held to account. Is democratic scrutiny within the MS sufficient or is an extra scrutiny body for European policing necessary (see also Bovens, 2007a: 467)? Loader (2002) distinguished the literature between the one fallen into the 'national sovereignty trap' which reduces the problem of legitimacy to the remoteness of European policing forms from national mechanisms of oversight, and the one reducing legitimacy to social legitimacy and, consequently, linking it only to effectiveness. To him, the proper political level to address the deficit, however, should be mainly 'in the place at which it arises—by strengthening *European* political institutions, or by establishing more robust connections between national *and* supranational modes of governance' (Loader, 2002; emphasis in original). By now, transnational 'police co-operation has long been characterized by light regulatory regimes at best, and by informality and "*ad hocery*" at worst. In such barren terrain, there is little opportunity for robust systems of accountability to take root' (Anderson, 1995: 263; emphasis in original).

Overall, the chapter's exploration of the literature on legitimacy and democratic governance in an international context showed that, in an international setting, legitimacy is widely referred to as a question of democratic quality. The chapter has identified parliamentary scrutiny and judicial scrutiny as two crucial features to ensure the democratic anchorage of policing bodies. Through parliamentary bodies as well as judicial authorities the work of CTP bodies can be democratically legitimized. Those two forms of external scrutiny become of particular importance to transnational, networked forms of policing, as internal and executive forms of accountability are insufficiently capable to ensure a thorough scrutiny of activities in this realm. Given the complexity of network structures and the fact that EU policing bodies include both national participants as well as EU bodies, it became clear that external scrutiny mechanisms are needed both at the national and the European level. A well-balanced mixture of *ex post facto* and proactive means is important to ensure that policing bodies can be appropriately and efficiently held to account. Such arrangements can only work properly, however, if an adequate level of transparency is fulfilled to ensure access to information. The struggle for transparency in this field is sharpened by a (well-justified) need for a high level of secrecy, an overall secrecy culture in the security sector, and a high degree of professional autonomy in the field. Network structures across borders contribute to the opaqueness to a considerable extent.

The careful and thorough examination through parliaments and the judiciary can proceed in various ways, as explained in this chapter. It remains to be seen in the following chapters, which of such mechanisms are available and in place with respect to the EU's CTNs. While those mechanisms are well established in European countries (though, of course, different in their history, form, and rigour), scrutiny bodies are normally restricted to their domestic framework and lack authority outside their own country (Scheinin, 2009: para 48; Aldrich, 2009b: 901). It is contested in the literature whether they, and democratic principles, structures, and values in general, can be easily transferred to the international level. The following chapters, in particular Chapters 6 and 7, will shed some light on this question in the context of CTNs and EU CTP.

Many aspects of the right 'balance' between security and liberty are well known in several European countries which have fought similar struggles in recent decades (eg, *Klass and Others v Federal Republic of Germany*[10]). In the heated atmosphere of post-9/11, international bodies such as the CoE and human rights organizations have (again) been promoting a *proportionate* answer to terrorism. This principle is not new, of course, and has long been established in various European and global codes.[11] These international norms are said to have a big impact on the reform of police practices, mainly because they 'require governments to establish systems of review and oversight for abuses of force and coerced confessions' (Chevigny, 1999: 79). The challenge is, however, that proportionality—which is sometimes expressed as the principle of the minimum use of force in national law—is a relational indicator and it is therefore impossible to generate precise yardsticks, which would be valid under any circumstances. The principle refers to the idea that 'an optimal system of security would be one in which security is neither quantitatively excessive (to the detriment of objectives other than security) nor qualitatively invasive (to the detriment of personal freedoms) and which satisfies conditions of collective accountability, effectiveness and justice' (Johnston, 2006: 34).

This chapter has identified external scrutiny as one key mechanism to ensure such a proportionate response. While parliamentary and judicial scrutiny as explored earlier might not be able to totally ensure that misuse is prevented in all places at all times, they nevertheless provide important tools to do so. Before an in-depth analysis of mechanisms of parliamentary and judicial scrutiny, it is necessary to gain a better understanding of how networked cooperation is taking place at the EU level. To do this, the next chapter will focus on Europol's network, which is (also) tasked with fighting terrorism.

---

[10] *Klass and others v Federal Republic of Germany* Series A No 28, (1978) 2 EHRR 214.

[11] Crucial reference texts are the CoE's Code of Police Ethics; the UN's Code of Conduct for Law Enforcement Officials as well as the UN's Basic Principles on the Use of Force or Firearms by Law Enforcement Officials. See also Goldsmith, 1999: 42–3; Chevigny, 1999: 78.

3

The European Police Office: a Network Perspective

Europol provides a particularly powerful example for how the EU's field of internal security is governed 'through the sharing and pooling of sovereignty' (Bignami, 2007: 680). As of 2010, Europol's logo includes lines 'derived from a spider's web which represents exchange of information, networking and the cooperative nature of work' (Europol website—'Visual Identity'). Analysing Europol using a network lens embraces its institutional, socio-political environment and takes its structural linkages seriously (see also Gerspacher and Dupont, 2007; Deflem, 2006a). This way, we can gain a deeper understanding of Europol's role, structure, and the (potential) powers and impact it can have. A network perspective illustrates better why it is increasingly difficult—both for citizens as well as for scrutiny bodies—to grasp the extensive connections that Europol has established with other bodies.

Striving for the role of the EU's 'criminal information hub' (Europol, 2011b: 59), Europol has been facing severe hurdles on the way. Despite its name, Europol is not a federal police office. There has been no clear transfer of national sovereignty from the participating states to Europol and, instead, it has developed in a network-like structure. In addition, its mandate and powers do not even come close to those of a federal police agency, such as the German *Bundeskriminalamt* (BKA). Secondly, Europol's activities have not much in common with the traditional work of the uniformed police in the streets, having the function of maintaining the social order and legitimately using force (Reiner, 2000). Thirdly, not only police officers work at Europol but also staff of other law enforcement authorities, such as customs, and, much less so, security services. One key objective of this chapter is therefore to provide an overview of what Europol actually *is* and *does*, what its mandate is and what kind of activities it covers, in particular with respect to combating terrorism.

Tackling Crime through Networking: From the European Drugs (Intelligence) Unit to the European Police Office

From its very beginning, Europol was set up as a network. The informal TREVI group, as briefly sketched in the first chapter, was the key coordinating body for European law enforcement bodies before the EU formally brought internal security to its political agenda with the TEU, which entered into force on 1 November 1993. In the mid-1980s, the TREVI group established a pan-European liaison system to fight, in particular, drug trafficking. A proposal of 1985 suggested the creation of a European central service for information exchange in the field of combating drug trafficking (Fijnaut, 1993: 14). For this purpose, a working group set up guidelines in order to establish 'a system of drug liaison offices posted in each member state, as well as in producer and transit countries' (Occhipinti, 2003: 32–33), which were approved through the TREVI ministers in December 1987. At the 1990 European Council in Dublin, an Action Programme was agreed with the aim of creating 'a network of national drugs intelligence units in each member state for the pooling of information' (Occhipinti, 2003: 34) and to establish a coordinating body—a European Drugs Intelligence Unit (EDIU; later referred to as EDU).

Helmut Kohl, then Chancellor of Germany, promoted the idea of a general Central European Criminal Investigation Office in 1991 (Rupprecht, 1993: 41). His initiative aimed at the creation of the body in two phases, 'with the first entailing information exchange and the second regarding independent investigative powers' (Occhipinti, 2003: 35). Yet, several governments objected to his idea. While some feared the loss of sovereignty by granting executive powers to a European police force, others argued that the lack of legal harmonization concerning policing and criminal procedures posed a serious hurdle. Both the British and French governments were rather sceptical about the idea; and the governments of countries such as Belgium, Spain, and Portugal considered it only as a long-term possibility (Ingleton, 1994: 35).

Yet, the intention to set up a European police body was written into the political agenda and, in the same year, concrete plans were discussed at the 1991 Intergovernmental Conference on Political Union (Occhipinti, 2003: 35). Ideas for a European police agency ranged from a 'Mini-Europol, a Europol with only coordinating competences or operating only as an information network... [to]... a Europol with a broad spectrum of non-executive central functions—for example criminal laboratories, common identification systems and so on' (Rupprecht, 1993: 42). The results of the negotiations, published as a Declaration on Police Cooperation in the Appendix to the 1993 TEU, maintained guidelines for a potential European police body, which was meant to assist national criminal investigations and should be able to analyse, pool, and assess information.

At the time of drafting the Declaration, it was widely acknowledged that the EDU would become the embryonic cell of a future Europol. While TREVI's Working Group on Europol prepared the framework and mandate for a future Europol, a 1993 Ministerial Agreement concerning EDU/Europol maintained that the body would be a *non-operational* organization and that it would be prohibited from the transmission of personal information to non-MS and international organizations (Santiago, 2000: 45–46). The EDU started its work on 3 January 1994 focusing on the fight against drugs.

Details about the liaison arrangements of EDU/Europol were agreed in a 1995 Joint Action Plan (Council, 1995b). Each EU country should send (police or customs) liaison officers to EDU's headquarters to serve as intermediates between the unit and the MS. Liaison officers from one country were grouped as a team and given a liaison office, which would legally remain 'the sovereign territory of the respective member states' (Occhipinti, 2003: 52). The liaison officers were required to cooperate but 'act as a non-operational team for the exchange and analysis of information and intelligence' (Council, 1995b: Article 2.2). Given that two or more MS were affected by the crime, liaison officers were mandated to work in the fields of illicit drug trafficking, illicit trafficking in radioactive and nuclear substances, crimes involving clandestine immigration groups, and illicit vehicle trafficking.

The exchange of information among states about such cases should 'take place solely on a bilateral basis via the liaison officers of these States' (Council, 1995b: Article 4.1). The EDU was not allowed to store personal information centrally and no personal information should be transmitted to non-MS or international organizations (Council, 1995b: Article 4.2). With respect to oversight, it was maintained that the Council 'shall exercise general oversight over the activities' of the EDU based on reports by the head of the body (Council, 1995b: Article 6). Given that the liaison offices were sovereign territory of the MS, the national ministers were ultimately in control of the liaison officers (Occhipinti, 2003: 52).

Europol's legal basis

While it was quickly agreed that Europol should be based on an international treaty, the agreement on such a text and the ratification process took time. On 1 October 1998, two years after its signature, the Council Act of 26 July 1995 drawing up the Convention on the establishment of a European Police Office (hereafter Europol Convention) entered into force and Europol started its full activities on 1 July 1999 (Council, 1995a). The Convention set up a European Police Office with legal personality and a headquarters in The Hague. It maintained that Europol's overall objective is to facilitate the exchange of information and intelligence, to analyse information, and to support investigations in the MS, for instance by notifying national authorities of relevant information and by maintaining computerized databases.

Europol National Units (ENUs) were created in each MS, which would function as the only liaison body between Europol and national law enforcement authorities. Europol would be administered by a Management Board (comprising one representative of each MS and of the Commission, the latter having observer status only), the Director (appointed by the Council of the EU), the Financial Controller (appointed by the Management Board), and the Financial Committee (including one representative from each MS). The Convention provided for the creation of a database, the Europol Information System (EIS), but restricted its use by maintaining that the EIS 'must under no circumstances be linked to other automated processing systems, except for the... systems of the national units' (Council, 1995a: Article 6.2).[1] The EIS includes personal data likely to assist in identification but also details such as: criminal offences; means which were or may have been used to commit the crimes; suspected membership of a criminal organization; and previous relevant convictions. Next to the EIS, Europol can create work files where data can be stored on the criminal offences for which it is competent, including data on related criminal offences.

The original Convention was amended and expanded through various protocols. For example, Europol's original mandate did not cover terrorism but it was quickly added to its remit. A Council Decision of 3 December 1998 instructed Europol to deal with crimes committed or likely to be committed in the course of terrorist activities against life, limb, personal freedom, or property provided for it, but the ratification procedures took until the year 2000 (Council, 1998).

To 'start a new operative period' (Bundesministerium des Innern, 2007b), three crucial amendments entered into force in 2007. The first amendment concerned the introduction of Joint Investigation Teams (JITs), a tool to cooperate in operations of national law enforcement authorities. The EU Convention on Mutual Assistance in Criminal Matters provides for the creation of JITs among law enforcement bodies in at least two EU MS (Council, 2005c). Such teams can be set up by at least two EU MS for the purpose of the execution of a criminal investigation (Rijken, 2006: 101). The JIT Protocol, which was signed in 2002 and entered into force on 3 April 2007, grants Europol the competence to participate in JITs as well as the right to ask national law enforcement authorities to initiate an investigation (Council, 2002f). An interviewee involved in the creation of the JIT framework described it as an important tool for Europol, but acknowledged that, in practice, JITs are a complicated feature, in particular owing to the various national legal restrictions (Interview A; see also Rijken and Vermeulen, 2006).

[1] The Convention comprised more data protection arrangements, which will be discussed in Chapter 5.

Secondly, the JIT Protocol led to changes concerning a 1997 Protocol which granted Europol officers full immunity 'from legal process of any kind' (Council, 1997: Article 8.1a) in respect to their official activities. Given Europol's widened mandate, the provision of full immunity was widely considered as inadequate by observers and the so-called Immunity Protocol was amended. The new Protocol on the privileges and immunities of Europol, the members of its organs, its Deputy Directors, and its members implies a waiver of immunity for Europol officials acting within the framework of JITs (Council, 2002g).

Finally, the Danish EU Presidency suggested further amendments in July 2002 to allow Europol more flexibility and to strengthen its operational support function (Council, 2002e). The Protocol, signed in 2003 and entered into force on 18 April 2007, provided for amendments to the Convention with the aim to widen Europol's mandate and powers. For example, the Protocol facilitated cooperation between Europol and third parties, widened Europol's mandate by allowing it to deal with a wider range of crimes, and enhanced the sharing of personal data with a wider range of institutions (Bruggeman, 2007: 2).

Yet, overall, the Europol Convention was criticized for many years as not providing an adequate legal basis. Owing to the increasing tasks Europol carries out on behalf of the Union and its right to transfer personal data to several non-EU parties, criticisms became even louder in recent years (Apap, 2006: 4). In addition, the three amendments of 2007 demonstrated that the Convention only provided for a very time-consuming process to change Europol's mandate and remit. Given these difficulties, the general aim was to agree on a new legal basis, partly 'so that Europol's legal framework can be adapted more rapidly in response to trends in crime' (Council, 2008b).

In particular, during the negotiations of the Hague Programme in 2004, the agenda of which was clearly affected by the terrorist attacks of 11 September 2001 and 11 March 2004, discussions about the broadening of Europol's mandate arose (Council, 2004c). The overall tendency among policy-makers was the will to shift Europol's mandate from focusing on specific crimes towards (organized) crime in general and from handling information towards gaining more operative powers (Apap, 2006: 1–2).

For completely different reasons, the EP had pushed for initiatives to change Europol's legal basis for some time. So far, the EP had had a very limited role in the intergovernmental decision-making processes within the third pillar, including Europol. As a consequence, the EP suggested in 2003 to replace the existing Europol Convention with a Council Decision (European Parliament, 2003). Such a move would imply that decisions relating to Europol would no longer be taken by the Council acting unanimously but would need to be adopted by qualified majority and by co-decision with the EP (Apap, 2006: 4). The EP also requested to be 'provided with the legal means and institutional framework to enable it in the future to exercise genuine democratic control' (Apap, 2006). Finally, it called for arrangements to amend the funding of Europol by replacing the contributions of MS with funding from the EU budget.

Indeed, the JHA Council on 4–5 December 2006 agreed to replace the Europol Convention by a Council Decision (Council, 2006d). The Commission was quick to present a draft Decision only two weeks later, but a consensus on the wording was only reached some 15 months later in April 2008 (Commission, 2006; Presidency of the Council of the EU, 2008). As of 1 January 2010, the Europol Council Decision (ECD) is Europol's new legal basis and provides for changes concerning Europol's mandate and its powers (Council, 2008b). The Council Decision is a secondary EU law instrument, ie, EU action rules now apply to Europol. Up to then, Europol formally operated outside the EU Treaty (Lavranos, 2003: 261). Europol's remit is no longer limited to organized crime but has been extended to thirty-two crimes in total (Council 2008a, Article 4.1). Crucially, amendments to the legal basis, formerly requiring unanimity, only require a qualified majority vote in the Council and changes to the ECD can be made without a ratification process (Article 34 TEU; Lavranos, 2003: 261). That governments actually agreed to drop national vetoes on decisions about policing was considered an extraordinary move (Brady, 2007b: 1). Moreover, the entry into force of the ECD also affected Europol's parliamentary scrutiny, as will be discussed in Chapter 6. Finally, Europol is now subsumed under the jurisdiction of the ECJ (cf Chapter 7). However, the immunity clause remains untouched apart from Europol staff involved in JITs.

The changes as of January 2010 are accompanied by further amendments on the basis of the Lisbon Treaty. In particular, the provisions outlined in Article 88 TFEU strengthen the position of Europol through the incorporation of legislative regulations that explicitly determine its status and the range of its operations.

Europol's remit

The network covers a wide range of types of crime. Article 2 of the ECD states that its overall objective 'shall be to support and strengthen action by the competent authorities of the Member States and their mutual cooperation in preventing and combating organised crime, terrorism and other forms of serious crime affecting two or more Member States'. According to this mandate, Europol's role is a supportive, informative, and coordinating one. Supporting between 10,000 and 15,000 cross-border investigations per year, Europol's focus is on investigative and analytical intelligence, the collection and analysis of data from network participants, such as law enforcement authorities, and the transfer of information and intelligence to those network participants or EU bodies, as necessary (Europol, 2011b, 2009b; Bignami, 2007: 666; Højbjerg, 2004: 51–52). All these tasks are obviously quite different from traditional tasks of law enforcement authorities.

The pre-condition for covering any crime is that 'two or more Member States [are affected] in such a way as to require a common approach by the Member States owing to the scale, significance and consequences of the offences' (ECD,

Article 4). If those requirements are met, Europol can become active with respect to terrorism, organized crime, and various types of serious crime, including unlawful drug trafficking, trade in human beings, and motor vehicle crime (Council, 2009a: Annex).

Most cases in which Europol gets involved take place within the territorial area of the EU, but this does not necessarily have to be the case. Some operations cover a much wider geographical space, such as Operation Koala concerning child pornography. Based on information from Australian authorities, which reached Europol via Interpol, the Operation involved security authorities from nineteen countries (Europol, 2008b: 19–20; Europol, 2009b: 19). Also, Europol supported a joint police action between the Bank of Spain Investigation Unit (BIBE) of the Spanish Judicial Police, the Colombian Secret Service Agency, and the US Secret Service against a Colombian criminal group, which produced and distributed counterfeit euro and US dollar banknotes. According to Europol (2008b: 25), the operational part of the case took place entirely in Colombia. Thus, it seems fair to argue that there are basically no geographical limits to Europol's activities. The examples also illustrate the increasing capacities of Europol to coordinate or support transnational operations (see also Santiago, 2000: 52; Occhipinti, 2003: 2). To do so, Europol's databases are a particularly important resource for this kind of activity.

Europol's databases

To fulfil its mandate and connect its participating parties, Europol comprises the Europol Computer System (TECS), an information system which consists of three elements: the Europol Information System (EIS), Analysis Work Files (AWFs), and the Index System, which is a kind of search engine to cross-check both the EIS and the AWFs for information.

The EIS stores data related to persons who are 'suspected of having committed or having taken part in a criminal offence in respect of which Europol is competent or who have been convicted of such an offence' as well as those 'regarding whom there are factual indications or reasonable grounds... that they will commit criminal offences in respect of which Europol is competent' (ECD, Article 12.1). The EIS is fed with data by the MS (through the ENUs) and can be accessed by Europol staff and liaison officers. To improve information sharing and a better and quicker flow of information, access for national authorities has been facilitated since 2007 (ECD, Article 13; Bundesministerium des Innern, 2007b).

The AWFs are topical files containing criminal intelligence, for example related to terrorism, cocaine trade, outlaw motorcycle gangs, child pornography, and Euro counterfeiting (for the AWFs related to terrorism see page 80). The raw information is either obtained from the EIS or from other sources (via liaison officers or JITs, for example) and are then analysed by Europol staff. AWFs might also include 'data on a wide range of persons who might be called to testify in investigations' (Occhipinti, 2003: 61), such as victims and associates of suspects. Information in AWFs can directly be used in a JIT (Bundesministerium des Innern, 2007b). Moreover, national experts from third countries can be directly involved in an analysis group. The explicit reason for this has been the cooperation with the US in the fight against terrorism (Bundesministerium des Innern, 2007b).

These databases are Europol's analytical 'treasure' and they are used as an investigative tool by national authorities. To understand Europol better as a network-as-actor, the analytical character of Europol's work is of relevance. This body has not only been established to share and exchange information, but also to analyse independently incoming information and provide other bodies with the intelligence product. In other words, next to the facilitation of information exchange among the network participants, the central office is a consumer of the information itself: it 'consults the system to conduct long-term strategic analyses on different types of crime, which are then circulated to national police forces' (Bignami, 2007: 666). This also includes the possibility to assist national criminal investigations by the means of information analysis. That Europol has its own analysis capabilities made it a very special transnational policing body before ICPO-Interpol slowly started to catch up in this field in recent years (House of Lords, EU Select Committee 2003: 7, fn 10; ICPO-Interpol website).

Understanding Europol as a Network

Europol's set-up and structural arrangement is unique. One important aspect has been pointed out by Hartmut Aden (2001) who draws a line between elitist and everyday forms of cooperation. Few experts are intensely involved in police cooperation across borders and most of them work in criminal investigation departments, thus highly specialized units. Such elite groups work far removed from the concerns of daily police work, and Aden (2001: 103) has described Europol as 'an even more elitist agency for criminal investigation'. Yet, there are interconnections between elitist and everyday policing:

> (e)litist cooperation projects such as Europol interfere with local or regional policing, when they coordinate decentralised police action or provide support for concrete cases of investigation. Generally, high level cooperation units provide intelligence (mainly data from their electronic data bases such as...the...Europol Information System), coordination and technical support (Aden, 2001: 104).

It seems therefore important to provide a more holistic approach to Europol and include such connections between Europol and other actors.

As a formal network, Europol comprises a headquarters and national participants. As Bignami (2007: 665) has suggested:

(a) national agency—one node in the network—gathers the information. Another national agency—a different node in the network—acts upon the information. Such government action can take a number of different forms: further information gathering through surveillance and other investigative techniques, asset seizure, arrest, deportation, and prosecution.

This description is a useful starting point to explore Europol's structural arrangements.

Europol's 'hub': the headquarters

More than 700 people work at Europol's premises (Europol, 2011e). There has been an annual increase of staff numbers since 1999. The majority of personnel are Dutch, which is hardly surprising given that Europol's headquarters is based in the Netherlands and the majority of support staff are likely to be based there. In terms of national representation across staff, the Dutch are followed by German, British, and Belgian personnel. Alongside Europol staff, Europol Liaison Officers (ELOs) are based in the Europol premises.

Europol Liaison Officers

In 2010, 129 ELOs were based at Europol (Europol, 2011b: 10). By creating specific national units in each Member State and using ELOs to coordinate with them from Europol's headquarters, the aim was to 'ensure that there was a single authority in each Member State responsible for passing information to Europol and receiving analyses from them' (House of Lords, EU Select Committee, 2003: 10). Each ENU can allocate one or more liaison officers to Europol, depending on the respective decision by Europol's Management Board (decisions about liaison officers have to be made unanimously). The ENU can also authorize other national bodies to send liaison officers. The ELOs seconded to Europol headquarters by one country are grouped together as Europol Liaison Bureaux (ELBs). Within the network, the liaison officers have the duties of providing Europol with information and intelligence from their seconding units and vice versa and to provide information and advice in the analysis of information concerning their seconding state (Santiago, 2000: 49). The individual ELOs are subject to the national law of their home state. Therefore the heads of the national units (HENUs), but ultimately the individual national ministers are in charge of the liaison officers' work (Occhipinti, 2003: 52).

Based on this information, one can argue that the central secretariat of Europol is organized as a star network: Europol's central secretariat is the centre of a network of national units. Those units provide information to Europol, and vice versa, via their Liaison Bureau at Europol's headquarters. A simplified virtualized model looks as follows (Figure 3.1):

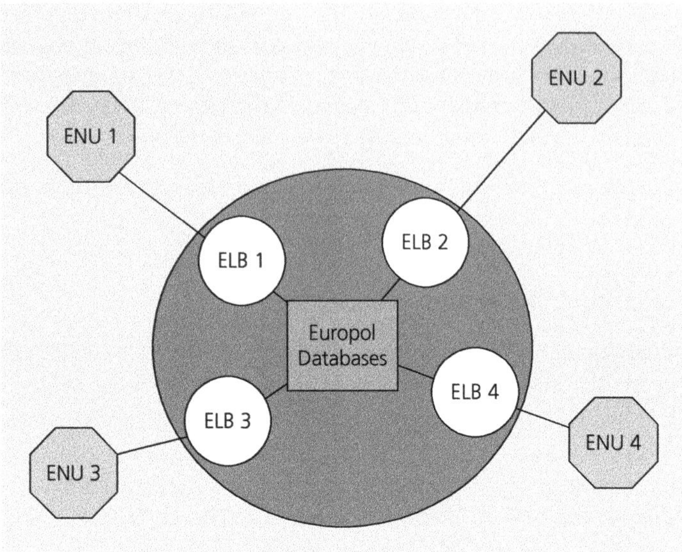

Figure 3.1 Europol's Liaison Network (EU Member States Only)

Key

ENU: Europol National Unit

ELB: Europol Liaison Bureau

In recent years, the number of ELOs has been continuously increasing; most of them are seconded from police forces (Europol, 2009b: 55–92, 2008b: 52–86). One liaison officer estimated that 85–90 per cent of ELOs are purely police-related (Interview E). There are, however, also officers from the Gendarmerie, customs, and intelligence services.

For analytical purposes, the formal information exchange procedure between the ENUs and the central secretariat needs to be distinguished from rather informal (bi- or multilateral) contacts among liaison officers. While I have so far described the relationship between the ENUs, via their liaison officers based at Europol, and Europol's secretariat, the liaison officers based at Europol also interact directly with each other (Interviews E, V, W; Brady, 2007b: 4).

Cooperation among liaison officers

According to the Council Decision establishing the European Police Office, ELOs 'assist in the exchange of information from their National Units with the Liaison Officers of other Member States under their responsibility in accordance with the national law; these bilateral exchanges may also cover crimes outside of the competence of Europol, as far as allowed under national law' (ECD, Article 9.3(d)).

Despite the lack of official information about this, it can be argued that information sharing among liaison officers bypassing the Europol databases has established the biggest share of information exchanged within the Europol network. Two interviewees suggested that around 70 per cent of all the information shared at Europol headquarters is shared among ELOs only and is not fed into Europol's central databases (Interviews P, W). Santiago (2000) documented in his research that, despite the adopted centralized mode of information exchange by the Europol liaison network, in practice national officials preferred to deal directly with the other national liaison officers. Yet, there is little information available on the kind of information that is shared among liaison officers and the ways this is done. According to the collected interview material, it seems that in particular timely and sensitive information is shared directly, avoiding the formalized and lengthy process via Europol's central secretariat.

When asked for an example of a situation in which liaison officers, or their ENUs, would prefer direct contact, one interviewee outlined a hypothetical, but close-to-reality scenario. He referred to the coordination of the surveillance of a drug delivery (Interview E). According to this example, police officers in one country realize that a lorry packed with drugs will soon cross the border, but they do not want to stop the lorry before its drivers will meet the next contact partner. In such a situation, the interviewee suggested, the national officials would contact their liaison bureau at Europol, which would subsequently approach the liaison bureau of the lorry's target country. Together, they would then arrange the takeover of the surveillance at the border. In such a situation, 'the simple fact of having officers from 27 European countries on the same corridor in The Hague is an unparalleled resource in day-to-day police co-operation' (Brady, 2007b: 5). However, the speedy and operational exchange of information is, of course, only possible when the seconded officers are granted 'the necessary authority at home to help other colleagues resolve cross-border issues' (Brady, 2007b: 5).

Of course, 'police officers never really disclose the informal contact network they have built over the years' (Alain, 2001: 124). But the importance of close and informal cross-border contacts among police officers is also reported in other studies. For example, Alain conducted interviews with French and Belgian police officers who used to meet regularly for exchanging inquiry techniques. Alain could show that those meetings were also *informally* used to exchange sensitive information regarding specific individuals' police files and criminal networks. Given the legal framework of cooperation, an exchange of sensitive data at such meetings was clearly illegal (Alain, 2001: 120).

Liaison arrangements with EU bodies and databases

Next to the EU MS, so-called third parties are allowed to base permanent liaison officers at Europol's premises. Third parties are non-EU states, international organizations, or regional bodies. Most of these liaison arrangements were only agreed on in the last decade. So far, Europol itself has only opened one liaison office abroad, in Washington DC, where two liaison posts were created in 2002. In addition, Europol has institutional contact with various EU bodies, too. There is also an ongoing discussion about connecting the various EU databases, including Europol's, with each other. It is therefore necessary to differentiate between institutional and virtual forms of cooperation at EU level.

Institutional cooperation

The Europol network includes various EU-bodies or institutions closely related with the EU and working at EU level. One example is Europol's cooperation with The European Agency for the Management of Operational Cooperation at the External Borders of the Member States of the European Union (Frontex), which started its work on 3 October 2005. Comprising the national border guard authorities of the MS, Frontex is to ensure a 'high and uniform level of control of persons at and surveillance of the external borders' (Europa, 2006). Its operations focus on tackling illegal migration flows from African countries heading to the southern EU MS (Frontex website; Monar, 2008: 116). For this purpose, Frontex liaises closely with other security authorities. While it signed an agreement with Europol on 27 March 2008, it also collaborates with non-EU authorities, including the US Department of Homeland Security (DHS), Interpol, Albania, Georgia, and the United Nations High Commissioner for Refugees (UNHCR) (Frontex website).

The first operational cooperation with Europol was project AGELAUS. This awareness programme 'focused upon standard procedures of dealing with minors...arriving from third countries by air at the external borders of the EU' (Frontex, 2007). Europol also provides Frontex 'with intelligence gathering during operations...and contributes to the Frontex Annual Risk Assessment' (Salgó, 2009: 7). Frontex also regularly contributes to several of Europol's crime assessment reports.

A second important EU partner for Europol is Eurojust, which was established in 2002 to strengthen the cooperation among judicial authorities within the EU MS with respect to cross-border investigations and prosecutions. Its caseload has been growing continuously, from 202 registered cases in 2002 to 1424 in 2010 (Eurojust, 2011: 76). Of those cases, Eurojust registered thirty-nine new operational terrorism cases in 2008, twenty-one cases in 2009, and twenty-eight in 2010 (Eurojust, 2011, 2009). To avoid duplication of analysis work, a new agreement between Europol and Eurojust aimed towards 'a structural relationship in their respective core business' (Council, 2008d) and enhanced cooperation (Council, 2007j). The Agreement, which entered into force on 1 October 2009, gives Eurojust the right to open an AWF and strengthens Eurojust's overall role in the context of the AWF (Europol, 2009b). Eurojust is currently associated with 15 AWFs (Eurojust, 2011: 53). The Agreement also provides for the exchange of general and, crucially, personal data. In early 2011, the cooperation was further intensified on the basis of a Memorandum of Understanding.

Apart from such formal cooperation, there are several other EU bodies, or bodies attached to the EU, which are important nodes in Europol's network. These bodies are officially categorized as External Associates by Europol. With respect to CT, it refers to the CTG, SitCen, the PWGT, the Terrorism Working Group, and the PCTF (Europol, 2006: 17).[2]

The cooperation with the PCTF provides an impressive example of the (informal) contacts Europol has with such institutions. Before its transfer into the COSI, the PCTF's key function was to 'exchange, *in cooperation with Europol*, experience, best practices and information on current trends in cross-border crime and contribute to the planning of operative actions' (Council, 1999b; emphasis added). The PCTF also started to plan 'joint European operations against organised crime networks with Europol and Interpol' (Brady, 2007b: 3). The first proper operation, which became publicly known, was Operation Callidus, an investigation related to child pornography directed by Swedish authorities in May 2005. The typical setting of such an operation was that it was guided by a *driver*, a team leader from a country 'directly affected by a particular criminal network and responsible for leading operations against it' (Brady, 2007b).

The key methodology of the PCTF was the COSPOL system which is still in place. The overarching objective of this multilateral law enforcement tool is 'to achieve tangible operational results in terms of arrests of top level criminals and the dismantling of criminal and terrorist organisations or networks, whilst ensuring that the Member States' competent authorities *make use of Europol's analytical support, in particular its Analysis Work Files (AWFs)*' (Council, 2007f; emphasis added).

Following a model of intelligence-led policing, the PCTF could set up COSPOL groups which can be 'used primarily as a means of targeting top organised crime enterprises ..., but also to address the Council priorities in the fight against terrorism' (Council, 2007f). To reach this objective, COSPOL groups work closely together with Europol. The groups can be 'closely linked to AWFs in order to exploit Europol's intelligence and analytical support and also to reinforce the intelligence cycle, so that the results of COSPOL activity can be fed back into Europol. If applicable, Joint Investigation Teams (JITs) may be set up' (Council, 2007f). Also, Europol's criminal threat assessments (OCTAs) should be distributed as soon as possible 'so that planning for future COSPOL activity can be undertaken at the earliest opportunity. Vice versa, Europol shall be consulted and provide advice for the selection of new COSPOL areas of activities, in order to ensure that Europol can plan and provide the necessary resources and expertise' (Council, 2007f).

Europol's instruments support the accountability procedure of COSPOL projects, a typical example of peer review in a network setting. When setting up the COSPOL decision in 2007, the Council (2007f) recognized a

[2] Non-EU related associates have been the UN Counter-Terrorism Committee (CTC) and the US.

> need for a mechanism by which the performance of each group can be measured and a system of accountability whereby the groups are answerable to the Police Chiefs Task Force. As such, COSPOL should be measured, using existing Europol tools, via the input, output, and outcomes of the related AWFs at Europol and also on its concrete law enforcement results in the MS.

However, the PCTF did not have to report to any political body.

While Europol was involved in projects of the PCTF, the PCTF could have an impact on strategic decisions with respect to Europol, as 'the PCTF should use its strategic meeting in Council structures to advise Europol if its future work programme should be broadened to incorporate new areas of business' (Council, 2007f). For this purpose, the PCTF agreed in 2007 to establish the European Network of Advisory Teams (EuNAT) as a cooperation mechanism with permanent linkage to Europol. The EuNAT Strategic Board comprises the EuNAT founders Belgium, Croatia, Germany, the Netherlands, Switzerland, and the UK as well as Europol and currently meets twice a year. The cooperation mechanism among law enforcement bodies has been set up 'to provide a mechanism for facilitating immediate international co-operation when responding to the threat of kidnap, hostage taking, and extortion, where human life is at risk. Moreover, EuNAT is a platform for sharing good practice and learning in this specific field' (Europol, 2008c). The cooperation includes mutual cooperation and assistance.

Interface with Common Security and Defence Policy

Europol's network is increasingly stretching into the field of the CSDP (see also Kaunert, 2010a). The enhancement of closer cooperation between the JHA sector, including Europol, and the CSDP is part of a wider EU agenda aiming to foster coordination between the military and civilian dimension of crisis management, also between the CSDP and JHA authorities (Presidency of the Council of the EU, 2009; De Vries, 2008: 366). Europol could potentially gain a key role in this context, in particular with respect to more efficient intelligence capabilities (De Vries, 2008: 366). On 6 June 2008, the JHA Council called for the establishment of a mechanism for the exchange of information between Europol and the EU's civilian CSDP missions in order 'to ensure continuity in the fight against organised crime, and to help to reinforce security and stability, both in the areas where ESDP missions are deployed and in the EU' (Council, 2008g). The information would be channelled via the Council General Secretariat and the exchange does not include personal data (Europol, 2009b: 52). Former EU Counter-terrorism Coordinator Gijs de Vries (2008: 366) has suggested that the systematic exchange of operators of CSDP missions with Europol would help the latter 'to provide a more comprehensive assessment of developments in terrorism and other forms of crime—including, crucially, the nexus between the two'. Moreover, the Stockholm Programme suggests that Europol should play a role in promoting standards and good practice for European law enforcement cooperation in non-EU countries (European Council, 2010: 4.3.1). First steps into this direction have been Europol's efforts to transfer EU practices concerning combating terrorism to the Western Balkans. While the overall agreement between Europol and Solana did not provide for the exchange of personal data, the exchange between the EULEX Kosovo Mission and Europol explicitly includes such data. However, cooperation between Europol and the EU Police Mission in Bosnia and Herzegovina does not include the exchange of personal data. Finally, in this context it is notable that Europol has been implementing 'a process to establish security equivalency between Europol and cooperation partners in accordance with EU and NATO standards, to allow the exchange of higher classified information' (Europol, 2009b: 37).

The cooperative mechanisms described in this sub-section are typical mechanisms within transnational networks. For example, Bignami (2007: 664) pointed out that within such networks, national officers use techniques such as 'information exchange on best practices, promulgation of standardized regulation, and mutual assistance in enforcing that regulation'. In addition to such institutional linkages, Europol has increasing access to virtual databases.

Virtual channels

The idea to connect Europol with other existing databases concerning law enforcement or intelligence was already discussed before Europol actually became operational (see, for example, Council, 1999c). While Article 6 of the Europol Convention maintained that '(t)he computerized system of collected information operated by Europol must under no circumstances be linked to other automated processing systems, except for the automated processing systems of the national units' (Council, 1995a: Article 6), there was always a fine distinction drawn between allowing *access* and *linking* those databases in order to allow access for Europol. The prioritization of the fight against terrorism at the EU level facilitated some of the contested proposals of interconnecting existing individual databases, including the Schengen Information System (SIS) and its anticipated successor SIS II, the Visa Information System (VIS), and the European Fingerprint Database (Eurodac).

Europol's EIS and the SIS are the two biggest information-sharing networks concerning EU policing. While the databases contain very different information, the systems of data sharing are similarly structured in the sense that they each have national offices (the Supplementary Information Request at National Entry (SIRENE) bureaux are responsible for SIS). In practice, these offices are often based in the same national departments (examples are the Criminal Intelligence Department of the Estonian Central Criminal Police; Britain's Serious Organised Crime Agency (SOCA); and even the EU candidate state Turkey has already established an Interpol-Europol-Sirene Department within the Turkish National Police). Only in the aftermath of the 9/11 attacks was Europol granted access to SIS, though excluding matters concerning asylum (Council, 2005d).

The decision to allow Europol access must also be understood as a step to increase Europol's operational powers further. Details are still under discussion due to ongoing technical problems in establishing SIS II and reasons related to data protection (Commission, 2011a; House of Lords, EU Select Committee, 2007c). There are also political concerns about the creation of SIS II and its connection with Europol (see Chapter 5). Given Europol's legal mandate, Europol has 'no power to take any action based on the alerts which it accesses' (House of Lords, 2007c: para 107). To circumvent this legal restriction, 'Europol will contact the Member State concerned and ask for permission to use the alert and, if necessary, ask for supplementary information' (House of Lords, 2007c: para 108). The information subsequently provided by the MS in question can then be used as a MS contribution—'(t)hus Schengen information becomes Europol information' (House of Lords, 2007c) and could be further distributed. A transfer to third countries is forbidden in the SIS II legislation, however. Dutch legal experts on the SIS pointed out that they were 'particularly concerned about the possibility of such information falling into the hands of the security services, because this meant losing control of how the information was used' (House of Lords, 2007c).

In addition to the SIRENE database, the Visa Information System (VIS) is being created as an instrument of the EU's common visa policy. Once fully implemented, it will collect and store personal data, including biometric information (eg, fingerprints and photographs) of up to 70 million third-country nationals applying for a visa in the Schengen zone (Commission, 2009c; Monar, 2008: 117). As VIS is based on the Schengen regulations, it comprises Norway, Iceland, Liechtenstein, and Switzerland, but not the UK and Ireland (see also Commission, 2009d). Europol has been granted access to the VIS on the basis of a Council Regulation and the related Council Decision (Commission, 2005d; Council, 2007b). Although the purpose of this database is not police-related, the Decision allows Europol access to the VIS database, though subject to certain conditions. For instance, the MS, which entered the data in question into the VIS, has to agree that this information can be accessed by Europol.

Finally, there is a pending proposal, which would grant law enforcement agencies as well as Europol access to Eurodac, the database containing fingerprints of applicants for asylum and illegal immigrants (Commission, 2010b). In April 2008, a senior official at the Commission explained in an interview that there were two diverging positions about the extension of the Eurodac database. Apart from this general statement, the interviewee refused to discuss the diverse opinions and concerns any further (Interview X). The debate was widely understood to be a 'hot potato', as the opening of Eurodac towards police authorities was yet another example of 1) function creep in the sense that databases established for one purpose (here, immigration control) are later used for a different one (law enforcement) and 2) the nexus between illegal immigration and terrorism. In particular, data protection bodies and civil rights activists have raised serious concerns, in particular with respect to data protection principles, about granting law enforcement authorities access to this database. In general, it is questionable 'whether it is acceptable to subject anyone on the Eurodac database to a greater level of surveillance than others in the population' (Mitsilegas and Baldaccini, 2007: 9). In terms of data protection principles, it is also a question of whether the original purpose of a database can be extended to a very different purpose.

Cooperation beyond the EU

That there is frequent European cooperation beyond 'EU territory' became already obvious in the portrait of the liaison arrangements (pages 67ff). Europol's cooperative network is stretching even further than that, though. Since 2002, the body has been legally allowed to establish and maintain relationships with bodies from third countries and other international organizations (Council, 1995a: Article 42(2)). The nature of the relationship is usually described in cooperation agreements between Europol and the third state or non-EU related body in question. Basically, there are two different types of such agreements, namely strategic and operational ones. Strategic agreements do not provide for the exchange of personal data, but are limited to technical and strategic information. In contrast to that, operational agreements explicitly allow the exchange of personal data, ie data relating to an identified or identifiable natural person (Apap, 2006: 1). The agreements were not publicly available before early 2005 when Europol placed them on its website (Peers, 2005: 204).[3] One of the most important relationships for the EU in the field of CT is the one with the United States (Rees, 2011) and Chapter 7 will explore in depth this relationship, including Europol's links to the US.

This overview of the most relevant links and connections that Europol set up with other institutions and the connections between Europol's databases and other information systems provides a broad picture of Europol's inter-agency relations. The overview also showed that it is useful to understand Europol as a network, ranging from the narrow circle of its central secretariat and its liaison arrangements with EU MS to the vast range of formal and informal contacts with other bodies. Despite the danger of over-simplifying the picture, Figure 3.2 seeks to give a visual illustration of what the overall Europol network looks like:

[3] The agreements are available at <https://www.europol.europa.eu/content/page/protecting-europe-21>.

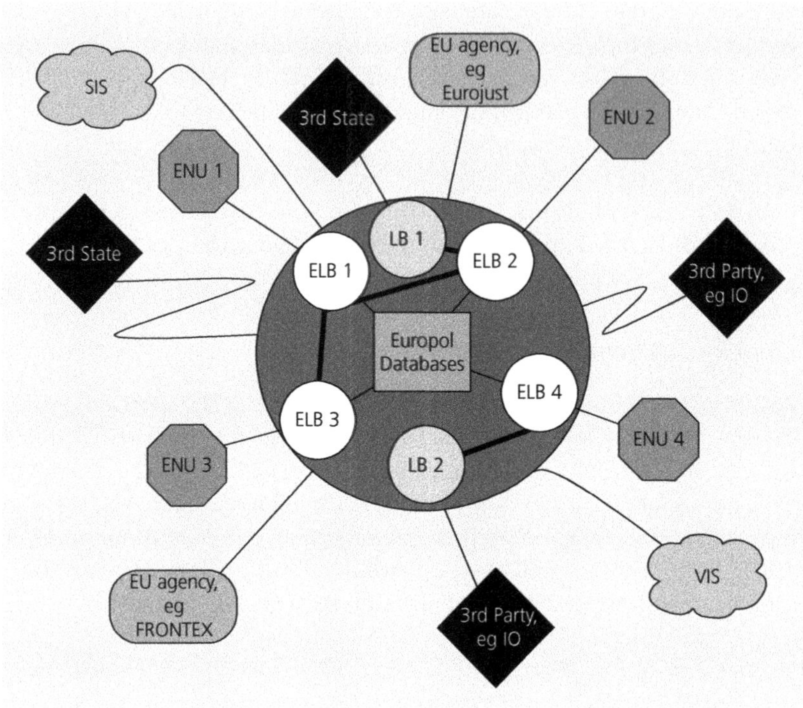

Figure 3.2 Europol's Extensive Network

Key

ENU: Europol National Unit

ELB: Europol Liaison Bureau

IO: International Organization

LB: Liaison Bureau of a Third Party based at Europol headquarters

SIS: Schengen Information System

VIS: Visa Information System

This figure does not show linkages among the various actors outside of the Europol framework (such as bilateral contacts between ELOs). That the whole area of EU internal security is rather well connected, has been shown early by Bigo (1994, 2000b). For the purpose of this research, however, it was important to identify key arrangements between Europol's hub, the central secretariat, and the participating nodes, the national units and third parties as well as the databases to which Europol is, or will be, connected. Finally, the liaison officers based at Europol headquarters have developed a separate network of personal and institutional contacts, both among the ENUs as well as with the Liaison Officers from third countries or other third parties. Those 'informal' contacts are not covered by any regulation concerning Europol, but by their national law only.

Europol is not only continuously expanding its liaison and informational network but, at the same time, its mandate and powers have also widened and expanded to a considerable extent. The following section will explore Europol's remit in the field of combating terrorism.

Europol as a Network-as-actor in the Field of Counter-terrorism

As explained on page 62, terrorism became part of Europol's mandate in 2000. Similar to other types of crime, the justification of Europol's engagement in the fight against terrorism has been that the 'transnational nature of this threat requires an EU-wide response' (Europol, 2008a: 5).

Shortly after the terrorist attacks of 9/11, the Council agreed to establish a team of national counter-terrorist specialists at Europol 'with the task to collect and analyse data concerning current threats and provide operational and strategic analysis' (Lavranos, 2003: 262). As a consequence, a temporary Counter-terrorism Task Force (CTTF I) was set up composed of liaison officers from police and intelligence services with an expertise in counter-terrorism (Council, 2001a; Lefebvre, 2003: 531; Bergenstrand, 2004: 88). The hastily arranged group became operational on 15 November 2001, yet it was dissolved at the end of 2002 (Europol, 2002). In the aftermath of the 2004 Madrid Bombings, the Task Force was reactivated, partly in order to support the investigations by Spanish authorities. The CTTF II also assisted MS with, for example, investigations into the financing of terrorism and terrorist recruitment (Europol, 2007c: 13). This Task Force was later transformed into a First Response Network (FRN; see page 79). Today, Europol's Serious Crime Department hosts a permanent Counter-terrorism Unit, comprising of fifty CT experts (Europol, 2011d). It spans a wide field of activities.

Check the Web

Europol supports national authorities in countering the use of the internet for terrorist purposes. In October 2004, the CTTF II initiated a project on web-based Islamist activities. European security authorities continue to be concerned that, for example, '(s)o-called terror manuals provide instructions on how to produce weapons, how to carry out attacks, how to take hostages and how to build bombs' (Council, 2007e). The original project was later transferred to Europol's Counter-terrorism Unit and, in accordance with the policy recommendations in the EU's Strategy for Combating Radicalization and Recruitment to Terrorism, Europol now pools information about terrorist-related activities on the internet (Europol, 2008a: 9; Council, 2005e). One year after the adoption of this Strategy, the information platform Check the Web was launched at a meeting of the Europol Management Board on 8–9 May 2007 and presented as a key instrument to fight terrorist radicalization, recruitment, and training on the internet (Council, 2007d).

The platform provides contact information, links to jihadist websites, messages, and propaganda of terrorist organizations as well as results of analysis

(Council, 2007d). It allows the storage of personal data. Given the nature of the project, the initiative targets open sources. In addition, language skills and expertise of national authorities are listed. Through their ENU, national authorities feed the platform with information, which can then be accessed by national experts as well as Europol staff. National contact partners can be contacted immediately. Apart from the information platform, the network offers expert meetings and the possibility of joint projects (Bundesministerium des Innern, 2007a; Council, 2007d). One publicly revealed example for a joint project was the analysis of al Qaeda's 'PR unit' named *As-Sahab* (Council, 2007d); another one concerned the support by the Check the Web team of an operation by Greater Manchester Police Counter-terrorism Unit (Europol, 2011b: 28).

Apart from the Check the Web initiative, Europol continues to analyse further features related to radicalization and recruitment, 'such as extremists returning from armed struggle in conflict zones, terrorist organisations, the role of religious converts and women with regard to radicalisation, training venues in the EU, and "home-grown terrorism"' (Council, 2007a).

Security of explosives

In the 2004 Declaration on Combating Terrorism, the European Council (2004b) emphasized the need 'to ensure terrorist organisations and groups are starved of the components of their trade' by ensuring 'greater security of firearms, explosives, bomb-making equipment and technologies'. One of the key measures undertaken to reach this objective was the setting up of a public-private Explosives Security Experts Task Force (ESETF) with a view to preparing recommendations for actions in this field. The ESETF's recommendations were transferred into the Action Plan on Enhancing the Security of Explosives (Council, 2008c). Among the tasks listed in the Action Plan, which the JHA ministers agreed in April 2008, are three with particular relevance to Europol: the European Bomb Data System (EBDS), the Early Warning System for arms, explosives and chemical, biological, radiological, and nuclear materials (EWS), and the European Explosive Ordnance Disposal Network (EEODN).

The EBDS constitutes 'a common EU system enabling authorised governmental bodies at EU and Member States level to have 24/7 access to relevant information on incidents involving explosive devices' (Council, 2008c). Co-funded by the Commission, Europol has developed the system, which has been operational since October 2010 (Europol, 2011b: 29).

The EWS links public security authorities of the MS and Europol. It extends the existing EWS of the G6 group comprising of France, Germany, Italy, Poland, Spain, and the UK (Council, 2009d: 3).[4] The aim is to provide for early warnings

[4] The G6 was established in 2003 as an informal group of the Ministers of Interior of the six countries mentioned. It is, in particular, working on matters of terrorism and immigration.

on issues, such as immediate threats, theft of explosives or detonators, suspicious transactions, and the exploration of new modi operandi (Council, 2008c). Europol was said to be 'the only European law enforcement organisation with the necessary network infrastructure and applicable confidentiality regulations' (Commission, 2007a: 9) for the creation of such a database. Already in 2007, Europol's Counter-proliferation Programme was extended to a new category that facilitates the information exchange among national experts on explosive devices and arson (Europol, 2008b: 24).

In addition to the EBDS and the EWS, the EEODN, created in May 2008, aims to foster knowledge about explosive materials, in particular concerning their disposal, among specialized national units from the police, military, and other authorities.

First Response Network

As a successor of the CCTF II, the FRN was launched in 2006 but became operational only on 2 July 2007 (Europol, 2008b: 24). In case of a major terrorist incident, a MS can activate the Network, which will then set up a team to support the immediate investigation for a maximum of eight weeks (Torda, 2007). For the first time, Europol activated the FRN in the wake of the incidents in Norway in July 2011.

ATLAS Platform

Europol provides a secure communication channel and platform, which is used by a group of special intervention and counter-terrorism teams, called ATLAS (Europol, 2009b: 32; Europol, 2008b: 31). Created under the umbrella of the PCTF at the extraordinary Council following the 9/11 attacks, the overall purpose of ATLAS was described in the Commission's 2008 Crime Prevention Work Programme as follows:

> With the objective of strengthening and developing cooperation, where necessary through organizational and operational arrangements, between Police, Customs, Security Services and Special Forces in the Crisis Management of terrorist incidents, ATLAS encompasses twenty-nine authorities of twenty-seven MS (Commission, 2007a: 9).

The EU has been promoting an intensified cooperation of special units in the fight against terrorism. Given the secrecy surrounding national law enforcement authorities 'specialised in the control of a crisis situation' (Council, 2006a), it is little surprise that the ATLAS group was never mentioned by interviewees when they were asked to outline the EU's CT efforts. One interviewee who works on terrorism-related issues, but is not directly based in Europol's Counter-terrorism Unit, claimed he had never heard of the cooperation and suggested he could not imagine cooperation between special forces being in any way related to Europol (Interview R).

Yet, the ATLAS cooperation was only formally institutionalized through a Council Decision in 2008 (Council, 2008e). Ludo Block (2007) claimed that the involved special intervention units themselves would prefer an informal framework 'that allows the network to draw up its internal rules, procedures and organizational arrangements'. For this cooperation, the Commission granted €900,000 and €1 million respectively in 2008 and 2009 to support activities, such as 'joint training activities, support for the acquisition of equipment at disposal of all authorities, exchange of best practices and other co-operation initiatives' (Commission, 2007a: 9). The ATLAS platform will shortly be transferred to Europol's new Platform for Experts (EPE) (Europol, 2011b: 20).

Further Activities

An overview of *operational* support provided by Europol (2011b: 25) to MS suggests that nearly 6 per cent of such support in the year 2010 concerned terrorism. In 2007, Europol was involved in around twenty terrorism-related investigations in Europe (Council, 2007c). It is extremely difficult to get information on record about the cases in which Europol is involved and in which way it participated in the investigations. From the information available it appears that, if applicable, national authorities make use of Europol's AFWs. With respect to terrorism, there are currently two AWFs: AWF 008 comprises information on Islamic extremist terrorism and AWF DOLPHIN contains data on other (non-Islamist) terrorist-related groups (Interviews N, W; Europol, 2007c: 17). Currently, Europol is working on a joint terrorism database (Europol, 2011b: 29).

Europol's 2007 Annual Report gave some rare insights into Europol's involvement in the CT operations of the MS. For example, the French National Police and Belgian authorities set up a JIT in 2007 to investigate a terrorist group. The team covered both the Belgian Operation Nougaro and the French Operation Artigat (Europol, 2008b: 55). According to Europol (Europol, 2008b: 61), its Counter-terrorism Unit 'provided analytical support and deployed analysts in the field during the arrest operations'. Another French operation, code-named Safari, was led by the Anti-Terrorist Division of the Central Directorate of Judicial Police (*Sous-Directorate Anti-Terroriste*) and, in close cooperation with Europol analysts, tackled members of the Liberation Tigers of Tamil Eelam (LTTE) in France (Europol, 2008b). Finally, the report mentions Operation Welfare, in which Europol's AWF on Islamist extremism and terrorism was used by Austria to locate and dismantle an Islamic fund-raising organization and individuals suspected of illegal financing of Islamic extremists (Europol, 2008b: 54). The 2008 Annual Report refers to Operations Cantata and Submarino concerning Islamic terrorism groups in Spain, for which the Spanish authorities called the Europol mobile office (Europol, 2009b: 81). Mobile offices allow direct access to Europol databases (De Buck, 2007: 263).

Europol has also created a unit of counter-terrorism financial specialists and analysts in order to support the US Terrorist Financing Tracking Programme, which entered into force on 1 August 2010 (Europol, 2011a: 15). This Programme, aimed at identifying and pursuing terrorists and their donors, and Europol's role in it, will be discussed in depth in Chapter 7.

To complete the picture, Europol's Counter-terrorism Unit was mandated to cover maritime piracy as well at the beginning of 2010. So far, it focuses 'on the identification of key perpetrators, logistical assets and financial flows linked to this criminal activity' (Europol, 2011b: 29).

EU Terrorism Situation and Trend Report (TE-SAT)

Apart from the direct support of an investigation of MS or the participation in a JIT, the delivery of threat assessments and reports is a relevant feature in order to explore the democratic legitimacy of Europol. This section will focus on Europol's key product in the field of terrorism, the annual TE-SAT.[5] Europol's former director Max-Peter Ratzel claimed that the TE-SAT has become one of the 'important awareness tools for decision makers at European level' (Europol, 2008a: 5). The TE-SAT has a wider audience than just the National Units of Europol. In particular, it is striking to find indications that Europol's products are used to steer and justify EU politics in the field of internal security.

TE-SATs are a mixture of descriptions of the status quo regarding terrorism in the EU and more analytical reports of future trends. A TE-SAT is 'a situation report which describes and analyses the outward manifestations of terrorism, ie terrorist attacks and activities' (Europol, 2008a: 6) focusing on an overview of the EU-wide situation. The data collection covers both 'terrorist attacks, activities and arrests in the EU... and terrorist attacks outside the EU in which EU interests were affected' (Europol, 2008a: 8). Based on this, the TE-SAT provides a trend assessment whereby a trend 'can be defined as a general tendency in the way a situation is changing or developing' (Europol, 2008a : 6).

The publication series was introduced after the 9/11 attacks to provide the Terrorism Working Party (TWP) of the Council of the EU and the EP with regular information about terrorism (Europol, 2011c: 8). At that time, Europol was not primarily responsible for the reports, but they were already based on Europol files and further analysis. The TE-SATs were presented by the respective Presidencies of the EU Council. Europol's suggestion in 2006 to widen the data collection for the TE-SAT in order to improve the quality of the report was agreed on during the JHA Council on 1 and 2 June 2006.

Information for the TE-SAT can be provided from the MS, EU bodies, or third parties, such as Interpol (Europol, 2011b: 8; Europol, 2008a: 5, 7). The provision

[5] TE-SAT's counterpart regarding organized crime is the Organised Crime Threat Assessment (OCTA).

of information by MS is based on the Council Decision of 20 September 2005 on the exchange of information and cooperation concerning terrorist offences which requires MS 'to collect all relevant information concerning and resulting from criminal investigations conducted by their law enforcement authorities with respect to terrorist offences' (Council, 2005h).

The TE-SAT is a publicly available document and contains no classified information or information that might jeopardize ongoing investigations. Information is 'cross-checked and, in case of gaps, complemented by open source data systematically collected and processed by Europol' (Europol, 2008a: 8–9) and finally validated again by the respective MS. There is an advisory board of TE-SAT comprised of the two Presidencies during that year as well as representatives of Eurojust and SitCen. Apart from TE-SAT, Europol provides a variety of smaller and more specific products to its MS (cf Council, 2008k: Appendix B).

From the Europol Convention to a Council Decision…and further towards a European FBI?

Overall, it appears that European political decision-makers have accepted a much more active and expanded role for Europol than the one it was granted in the beginning. Certainly, Europol's operational limits remain considerable. It still has no executive powers. However, it has been argued already in 2000 that 'Europol fairly quickly moved into the coordination of operations and investigations across Europe' (Santiago, 2000: 73). More sceptical authors such as Bruggeman (2007: 1), however, describe the coordinating role of Europol as having rather little real impact so far 'since a lot of police officers in the field still work bilaterally (the so-called "old boys network")'.

It has become clear in this chapter that Europol has nevertheless established 'a fluent, multinational network of law-enforcement professionals' (Stevenson J, 2005: 211). In the beginning, MS had to be convinced of the quality of Europol's work and its work is still not very well known by many national security authorities (eg, Interview D). In a talk in 2008 under Chatham House Rules, a Europol official explained this in terms of the 'distinct police smell' which Europol lacked in the beginning, but which it has gained over time. Even Bruggeman (2007: 1) maintained that national law enforcement authorities now seem to be 'willing to use Europol as a valuable instrument for international co-operation'. Certainly, the recent changes of Europol's legal and institutional footing have aimed at fostering Europol's position in the wider context of EU policing. For example, Europol's remit is no longer limited to organized crime but has been extended to thirty-two crimes in total (Council 2008a, Article 4.1). Its access to several databases and national systems has been facilitated and the EIS is no longer limited to national units, as they can authorize other national authorities to have direct access to

Europol (although on a hit/no-hit basis only).[6] Mitsilegas and Baldaccini (2007: 3) have called this 'the end to the basic principle underlying the work of Europol, namely that the main channel of co-operation is between Europol and central national police units'. The national units have to be kept informed, however. In addition, to strengthen its analysis capabilities, Europol has stretched its network to include actors, such as forensic institutes—a move which 'has contributed to the first steps in using DNA in analysis processes' (Europol, 2009b: 33).

That the development of Europol took some time does not come as a surprise if Europol is analysed from a network perspective. The establishment of trust into the central 'hub', ie Europol's central secretariat and its products, as well as trust among the participants (countries, organizations, as well as individuals such as ELOs) is an essential element of the evolutionary process of a network. In its 2008 Annual Report, Europol (2009b: 33–34) stated a continuous increase in information exchange via Europol, including the increase of law enforcement cases initiated in relation to the exchanged information. It also suggested an improvement in MS' reporting of criminal investigations with respect to terrorist offences. While Europol is allowed to request information from MS, it rarely does so (Europol, 2009b). In October 2009, Europol's current Director Rob Wainwright stated after a meeting of the JHA ministers at Europol's premises as follows:

> The decision by the Swedish Presidency to host a Justice and Home Affairs meeting within our premises is a clear signal about the trust in Europol and about confidence in its role within the EU internal security structure. These high expectations will be met in the future by Europol acting as a stronger operational support centre in the EU for the combating of terrorism and international serious crime and by it becoming the EU's central information hub in these areas (Europol, 2009c).

One provision to foster exchange between national authorities and Europol is the provision for Europol to contact sub-national bodies directly, thereby bypassing the ENUs. This is in particular the case with respect to JITs. While the ENUs should be kept informed about it by Europol, Europol staff can take part in measures on the ground (Bundesministerium des Innern, 2007b). By participating in JITs, Europol staff ought to support the MS 'even more effectively' (Bundesministerium des Innern, 2007b) in the fight against terrorism or serious crime.

Another instrument for Europol to circumvent the lack of executive powers is the right to ask MS to start an investigation in specific cases. The MS can only reject this 'by giving good reasons' (Lavranos, 2003: 263). This option implies that Europol can not only act in a 'support capacity' but also as an initiator and

[6] In a hit/no-hit system, the enquiring party will only see whether the requested information is available (but not the detailed information itself). If this is the case, the party needs to contact directly the national authority which holds the information in question and ask for access.

coordinator of investigations, which is clearly more of a 'central capacity' (Lavranos, 2003) nature.

Given those possibilities, is Europol on its way to become a European FBI? The expansion of Europol's mandate and powers raised questions about the future role of Europol and led some to wonder whether Europol is on its way towards a federal police agency. Occhipinti (2003: 2) has argued early that 'at least in some regards, the EU seems to be on a path toward establishing its own federal police agency, much like the Federal Bureau of Investigation (FBI)'. Authors drawing a comparison with a national federal agency, such as Occhipinti and Jeffreys-Jones, are quick in pointing out that Europol 'is not nearly as supranational vis-à-vis the member states of the EU as the FBI is relative to the law enforcement agencies of the fifty United States' (Occhipinti, 2003: 3) and that the comparison with the FBI is somewhat inadequate with respect to the powers and discretion the police officers at the two different police agencies have (Jeffreys-Jones, 2007). Yet, they nevertheless find evidence to claim that it is worth discussing whether Europol is slowly on the way towards becoming such a federal body. One piece of evidence brought into the discussion is that the FBI's first task was to fight counterfeiting the dollar. Europol, as mentioned earlier, got its first 'proper' operational mandate with regard to Euro counterfeiting (Council, 2005a). However, Europol's limits are still enormous and the network will remain focused on its analytical capabilities in the near future.[7]

Nevertheless, the recent and ongoing changes due to the adoption of the ECD and the Lisbon Treaty suggest a shift towards a more active and powerful role for Europol in the European-wide fight against crime. While the overview of activities in the field of CT indicated that Europol has been slow in finding its role within the wider EU landscape of policing in this field, the network lens used in this chapter shed new light on Europol's position and its (potential) power within the wider field of EU security. Europol's revamped remit and the huge expansion of its network in recent years, covering several nodes within the EU and beyond, raise questions about its overall legitimacy. Before Chapters 6 and 7 will explore the parliamentary and judicial scrutiny of Europol and other EU efforts at CTP in depth, the following two chapters will widen the analysis of network patterns of international CTP. They will therefore move beyond Europol and widen the perspective to related activities of the EU in the fight against terrorism.

---

[7] For a sceptical view on Europol's current CT efforts see Bures, 2011: ch 4.

4

European Counter-terrorism in Transition: International Information Sharing and Proactive Policing

So far, the research has outlined the emergence of CTNs within the EU. Yet the EU's activities have not developed in a vacuum but are deeply interwoven with the actions within its MS and beyond. It is therefore sensible to widen the perspective at this point, in order to examine how the EU's networking activities relate to its broader CT environment. As established in the second chapter, democratic legitimacy is a contextual concept in the sense that the degree of legitimacy depends upon particular political and social circumstances and attitudes at a specific point in time. Before the analysis of 'formal' cornerstones of democratic legitimacy of CTP—namely parliamentary and judicial scrutiny—in the final two chapters, this chapter and the following will complete the picture of the networking efforts. While the following chapter will focus on the transatlantic dimension of EU CTP, this chapter aims to provide an exploration of wider changes in contemporary European CT, which have, or are likely to have, an effect on those scrutiny mechanisms.

In order to do so, the chapter will draw on two developments which are interrelated and that, in sum, can be understood as 'symptoms of deeper shifts' (Lyon, 2003: 3): international information sharing—via networks, across Europe and beyond, and the proliferation of features of proactive policing. The latter notion corresponds to a move from purely reactive law enforcement towards approaches that focus on the period *before* a criminal offence occurs—thus a more proactive, or preventive, approach.[1] Proactive CTP focuses on preventing terrorist attacks, and terrorism-related crime, from occurring in the first place. For this purpose, information and intelligence—as a processed form of information—become policing tools of utmost importance.

As suggested earlier, it seems useful to distinguish between three layers of networking in the context of the EU's CTP: the national level, comprising domestic bodies and sub-national entities; the EU level; and the bi- and multilateral networks comprising European members, but stretching beyond European territory. As will be shown, the emphasis on information sharing has implications at all of these levels. Three crucial consequences are at the centre of the discussion.

Firstly, the research has so far established that in order to collect, analyse, and distribute terrorism-related information, network structures are a formidable tool, insofar as they are meant to ensure a sufficient flow and provision of information. Yet, information from actors outside the established networks is also understood to be essential and, thanks to their loose structure, networks such as Europol increasingly allow for the inclusion of these actors, depending on the information needed. Secondly, the emphasis on information for the purpose of terrorism policing has led to an increasing use of both criminal and national intelligence. As a consequence, intelligence services and their informational products have become crucial for policing, and particularly preventing, terrorism. Therefore, this chapter includes crucial insights from the intelligence realm and focuses on increased cooperation. Thirdly, to gather information before a criminal offence has taken place, the police are instructed to strengthen their intelligence-gathering efforts. Some of those tools—including surveillance, database tools, and biometric techniques—have been and are being promoted and facilitated by the EU. Examples of this include the collection and storage of data in EU databases, such as SIS (II), VIS, and the fingerprint database Eurodac, and the creation of terrorist watch-lists.

The chapter will argue that these current trends in CTP pose challenges to democratic legitimacy. As argued throughout the book, the network structure makes it difficult to hold individuals to account and to monitor and oversee the work and actions of the network. This is more the case at the European and wider international level than at the national one; nonetheless, network structures are blurry and opaque at all levels. In addition, the mix of issues of national security and law enforcement—for example through the increased involvement of intelligence services—leads to a high level of secrecy. This hampers the scrutiny of the security authorities involved and raises questions about the relationship between secrecy and democratic legitimacy. The increasing cooperation of European security authorities with 'dubious foreign bedfellows' (Herman, 2004: 188) like Syria and Uzbekistan provides an excellent frame for exploring such challenges. The

[1] Scholars of police studies use various labels for proactive policing approaches, such as 'preventive' and 'pre-emptive' approaches as well as 'pre-crime' policing. Despite somewhat differences in definition and analysis, they all refer to the notion explained in the text.

increased use of proactive strategies and techniques appears to create considerable 'costs of counter-terrorism' (Donohue, 2008), most notably the infringement of individual freedoms and human rights.

The chapter starts with a focus on increased informational cooperation. The analysis will include the efforts to strengthen, or improve, the relationships between police and intelligence authorities, both within and across European countries and with third parties. To study the effects of increasing international demands and a preventive CT framework, the slow 'softening' of Germany's *Trennungsgebot*, a legal institution which prohibits cooperation between police and intelligence services, will be examined. The second section is concerned with wider international cooperation in this field, followed by a discussion of challenges posed to scrutiny bodies by such secretive collaboration. The final section explores the trend towards proactive CTP, including tools of surveillance and preventive measures.

Information Sharing across the EU

Collecting and analysing information about suspicious individuals and behaviour is understood to be of the utmost relevance for detecting terrorist suspects and intervening before the actual criminal offence. At the domestic level, European countries have fostered developments towards this in various ways, notably through structural changes, funding, legal regulations, and political will (Van Leeuwen, 2003; Haubrich, 2003; Foley, 2009; Wilkinson, 2007). The EU has always understood the provision of frameworks to facilitate and foster EU-wide information sharing as one of the fields where it can add value to the individual policing efforts of MS, and the fight against terrorism is no exception. One official involved in the creation of Europol remarked in 1997 that the 'need to collect, develop and share information with others is of paramount importance' (Robertson, 1997: 23) to the EU. He maintained that 'the emphasis is now on the development and sharing of law enforcement information, a process that is often contrary to commonly held notions of policing' (Robertson, 1997). As outlined in the first chapter, the EU did so by establishing various bodies, which channel information at the European level in the field of policing, such as Europol, Frontex, and the anti-fraud agency OLAF. In addition, some MS have collaborated as separate groups with the objective of moving forward and enforcing information sharing (the original Prüm Convention is the most crucial example in the field of CT). Post-9/11, the institutional efforts are accompanied by a plethora of legislation concerning the fight against terrorism.

However, despite policy documents and official statements, the EU's information-sharing efforts are hampered by various factors. The field is not developing as fast as many EU practitioners would like to see (Interview A). One crucial problem is that policing structures and policies are traditionally organized in a domestic framework and are deeply interwoven with the historical, political, and social context of the country in question. Therefore, the parameters of policing vary, also with respect to actors, mandates, structures, and legal frameworks. Owing to their diverse social contexts, security bodies develop their own institutional cultures over time (Pitschas, 2005: 153). There is no convincing systematic approach to studying the culture of security authorities—a situation that is partly due to the diffuse nature of the concept itself. The term police culture refers, for example, to a 'layer of informal occupational norms and values operating under the apparently rigid hierarchical structure of police organisations' (Chan, 1997: 43). While it is beyond the scope of this book to analyse this aspect at length, it is clear that the culture of a policing body is 'an important implicit and informal dimension' (Miller and Blackler, 2005: 31) which penetrates all aspects of police work, without necessarily being disclosed to the outside world (Anderson, 1993b: 62; Chan, 1997: 170). The cultural differences partly derive from the distinct structures of police organizations and the various degrees of discretion in Europe. Structural and procedural parameters, such as differences in criminal law and criminal procedures, matter insofar as they 'have a profound effect on the attitudes and behaviour of the police' (Anderson, 1993a: 32). There is not even a 'common definition of police or police powers throughout the [European] Community because of the divergent legal codes and traditions' (Anderson, 1993a). Fighting terrorism is the responsibility of a variety of actors. Also, the degree of openness towards the public and towards researchers varies considerably. Finally, the division 'of authority between general and specialised police units, between police and military, between police units and secret services... differs in an important way' (Aden, 2001: 100)—a fact which will be discussed later in the chapter with respect to the German *Trennungsgebot*. In the field of information exchange, such cultural differences, as described earlier, can lead to the misinterpretation of received data (Bignami, 2007: 673).

Cooperation despite the odds

Despite such considerable differences, cooperation happens on a daily and often routine basis across Europe. To ensure that their law enforcement and intelligence structures would be capable of improved information sharing, European countries started to re-examine and re-organize their CT policies and structures in the aftermath of the 9/11 attacks (eg, House of Commons Home Affairs Committee website: 'Project CONTEST'). Consequently, deep structural changes have been emerging in the domestic security architectures of many European countries in recent years (Glaeßner and Lorenz, 2005b; Wilkinson, 2007; Foley, 2009). Most notably, special CT bodies, such as fusion centres, usually comprising intelligence, police, and other law enforcement CT experts, are meant to provide a frame for pooling information (see also Chapter 1). Similar to others, the purpose of the German Joint Counter-terrorism Centre (GTAZ) is to overcome the decentralized structure of Germany's police and intelligence system by improving the coordination among its services (Neve et al, 2006: 45–46).[2] For the intelligence side, 'Alliance base', a cooperation centre set up by American intelligence authorities in Paris, has become a prominent example of the extent of operational cooperation in the field of CT (Priest, 2005b, 2005c).

The pressure towards pooling information in order to ensure a better flow of information is high. Take the considerable changes in the UK's CTP structure in recent years. Although the police forces are decentralized, four regional counter-terrorism units (CTUs) and smaller supportive counter-terrorism intelligence units (CTIUs) have been established in the aftermath of the London bombings on 7 July 2005 (Brown, 2008). Their mandate is to gather and assess intelligence from local forces and analyse issues on a regional basis, in order to inform the national intelligence picture. The CTUs are 'responsible for overseeing investigations into those who recruit terrorists and promote hate' (Brown, 2007). The CTIUs have similar tasks but no investigative role (UK Home Office, 2009: 63). Such efforts include not only structural changes, but also technical arrangements aimed at facilitating the interoperability of databases.

Approximation

The previous chapters have already indicated certain EU-wide developments in the context of CTP, which might be described as processes of approximation. The notion refers to a development towards a situation in which, for instance, structures, legal regulations, or cultures become similar, but certain differences remain.[3] First steps towards increased convergence between European policing structures and actions have already been described in 1993 by Malcolm Anderson (1993b: 51), who pointed out the move towards more centralized systems, common methods of handling criminal intelligence, the streamlining of procedures for communicating evidence between jurisdictions, and a standardized police terminology. This can be partly explained by functional necessity, but it can also be understood as a permanent mutual learning process through cooperation, including internship programmes, and liaison exchange (Anderson, 1993b; Interview D). Networks are useful tools for distributing and diffusing experiences and knowledge. On the one hand, they allow for cooperation of policing actors with varying structures and cultures. In the EU context, they allow the MS and their agencies ample room for interpretation and concrete implementation of instruments. Yet on the other hand, international cooperation of police forces can enforce the convergence of policing. Referring to

[2] To fight Islamist terrorism, the GTAZ comprises representatives of the Federal Police Office (BKA), the Federal Intelligence Service (BND) and thirty-nine other agencies. These include the Military Counterintelligence Agency (MAD), the Federal Office for the Protection of the Constitution (BfV), and representatives of the Public Prosecution Office (Bundeskriminalamt, 2008: 16–17).

[3] Harmonization would refer to a situation in which those issues would be 'the same', at least in a formal sense.

undercover policing, Aden (2001: 101) argued that '(p)olice cooperation circles not only diffuse the knowledge about undercover policing, but they also play a coordinating role'. One such example is Europol, which sometimes coordinates international 'controlled deliveries' concerning illicit substances.[4]

International cooperation can also set standards for the interoperability of different police technologies (Aden, 2001: 101). Centralized databases, such as the ones maintained by Europol and Schengen, require national units to adopt the technology to ensure they can participate in the network. In a similar vein, it could be argued that the strengthening of Europol leads to further approximation of national systems (eg, common definitions on certain types of crime and terrorism; national contact points; and so on).

In recent years, the EU has been pushing forward regulations and other instruments in the field of criminal law designed to provide a common ground concerning criminal law and respective procedures. Examples of this are the Framework Decisions which 'define certain criminal offences and determine the minimum penalties applicable in all Member States' (Lavranos, 2003: 273; see also Council, 2002a, 2002c). Lavranos (2003: 273) has described the creation of the European Arrest Warrant (EAW) as a first step towards a single European criminal code (offences covered by a future Europol with extended powers) and criminal procedural code (rules applicable to the activities of such an empowered Europol). The introduction of a European Evidence Warrant (EEW), aimed at accelerating and simplifying the gathering and transfer of evidence in international criminal proceedings, was a more contested move, but was formally agreed on 18 December 2008 (Council, 2008h).

To overcome the various ways in which countries perceive and assess threats, the EU increasingly provides European-wide threat assessments, both by Europol and SitCen. The latter provides threat assessments based on the sources provided to it by intelligence agencies and, to a lesser extent, by the military, the diplomatic services, and the police. SitCen aims to make useful contributions to operational issues, such as investigating terrorists' destinations, motives, and movements. Moreover, the EU Council is currently establishing common criteria for risk assessments concerning 'the potential threats related to terrorist offences and serious crime' (Council, 2009c).

The EU also tackles cultural differences by establishing and promoting best practices. The 1999 Tampere Council already called for the creation of a European Police Chiefs Operational Task Force (PCTF) designed to 'exchange, in co-operation with Europol, experience, best practices and information' (Council, 2004d) concerning policing. In addition, the Council of the EU establishes such guidelines in cooperation with national officials, so that national experiences of bureaucracy and administration seep into the European administration

[4] Within the EU, Art 73 of the Schengen Convention provides for controlled deliveries of drugs and psychotropic substances.

(Pitschas, 2005: 156). One example includes a handbook for police officers in the event of a terrorist attack (Interview T). Svendsen (2008: 661) suggested that establishing best practices and standards leads to a 'flattening' of hierarchies. Also, the European Police College (CEPOL) offers EU-wide courses on key police matters.

Hobbing takes a very critical stance on the question of European standards of policing. He points to a huge difference between political rhetoric and its actual transfer into police reality. According to him, the MS 'are far from applying common EU standards; neither do they even aspire to reach such concordance in the future' (Hobbing, 2008: 243). For this author, the overall problem is that state governments seem to resist any legally binding instrument in this respect. Even more informal instruments such as best practices include technical details, but no serious commitments to certain (normative) standards of policing (Hobbing, 2008: 246). Exploring the example of training for police forces of the MS which joined the EU more recently, Hobbing observed that the content of the seminars depended very much on the country, or group of countries, which were responsible for the individual training arrangement. Instead of teaching European-wide standards, these MS would rather get a patchwork overview of how things are done in various countries (Hobbing, 2008: 248).

The EU acknowledges the considerable differences between the MS, also because policing is still understood to be one of the crucial elements of *national* sovereignty. A network approach is a very useful structure in such a context as it grants the participants autonomy and yet they are able to cooperate. As a consequence, EU Framework Decisions and Recommendations concerning PJCC leave ample room for national governments to implement and interpret the texts.[5] Even with respect to Europol—the most integrated police network at EU level—its National Units as well as the liaison system at its headquarters in The Hague are handled differently in the participating countries (cf Santiago, 2000). Moreover, the language barriers remain substantial. Concerning Europol's AWFs, one interviewee expressed concern about the fact that several countries still provide information in their national language (Interview E). Such information has to be translated by Europol staff, which makes timely information exchange an impossible task and can lead to a misinterpretation of the information in question.

Having described some of the struggles that police cooperation at the EU level includes, the following section will explore two cases in which the EU appears to have had a catalyzing effect on the approximation of national standards, structures, and instruments. These are the cases of information sharing efforts, which are on the rise, and of instruments of proactive policing, which are increasingly being used.

[5] One example is the instrument of 'hot pursuit' which allows police forces of the Schengen group to pursue crime across national borders. The instrument is implemented and interpreted very differently in the various countries (Brady, 2007b: 3).

International Information Gathering and Exchange in the Fight against Terrorism: Cooperation with 'Friendly' and 'Not-so-friendly' Countries

The complex and opaque nature of international CT cooperation becomes obvious in the field of information and intelligence exchange. This section is meant to shed some light on recent developments in this field.

From the principle of 'need to know' to the principle of 'responsibility to share'?

In the intelligence literature, the emphasis on information sharing has been described as a move away from the principle of 'need to know' towards the principle of 'need to share' (Zegart, 2007: 67). The principle of 'need to know', deeply embedded in the realms of intelligence as well as high policing, refers to the fact that security officials ought to know only as much about a case, or investigation, as is necessary for their individual work. The more they know, the more vulnerable they are. The principle also allows for the managing of operations in such a way that they cannot be easily compromised. Similarly, 'need to know' is the overriding principle for sensitive information concerning police work (House of Commons, Home Affairs Committee, 2007: 46). Guidelines of Kent Police (2009), which due to the policing of the Channel have longstanding experience with international policing, maintain that 'only enough information needed to complete the task allocated should be given' to individual officers.

The 'need to know' principle certainly applies to CT activities given their sensitivity. A senior CIA official has argued, for example, that despite the CIA's Counter-terrorism Center's connections with various European security bodies, the Center worked on a strictly 'need to know' basis with its European allies in the context of High Value Detainees (HVDs) (Marty, 2007c: point 161).[6] Europol's AWFs are bound to the same principle—only a restricted number of people are allowed access to a certain file. Also, a British intelligence report has shown that the cooperation of MI5 with police forces continues to be conducted on a 'need to know' basis (Intelligence and Security Committee, 2009).

Many CT-related inquiries since 9/11 have required improved information sharing among security bodies. The 9/11 Commission criticized, for example,

[6] According to the definition provided by an unnamed Assistant General Counsel of the CIA, an HVD is 'a detainee who, until time of capture, we have reason to believe: (1) is a senior member of al-Qai'da or an al-Qai'da associated terrorist group...; (2) has knowledge of imminent terrorist threats against the USA...or its allies; or that has/had direct involvement in planning and preparing terrorist actions against the USA or its allies, or assisting the al-Qai'da leadership in planning and preparing such terrorist actions; and (3) if released, constitutes a clear and continuing threat to the USA or its allies' (quoted in US Department of Justice, 2005).

that '(t)here are no punishments for not sharing information. Agencies uphold a "need-to-know" culture of information protection rather than promoting a "need-to-share" culture of integration' (National Commission on Terrorist Attacks upon the United States, 2004: 417). The Commission recommended the sharing of information 'horizontally, across new networks that transcend individual agencies' (National Commission on Terrorist Attacks upon the United States, 2004: 418). Yet, to implement such a new approach appears to be cumbersome. Some observers suggested that security bodies lack the feeling of being 'a unified team' (Zegart, 2007: 104). Moreover, as David Omand (2009: 5) suggested, it would require the authorities 'to feel a "responsibility to provide"'. Although there are indications that, overall, there is more and improved information sharing, including the EU efforts described earlier in the chapter, neither for Europe nor for the US is there evidence that this move from a principle of 'need to know' to a 'responsibility to share' has yet become an intrinsic part of security bodies.

Concerning information sharing between police and intelligence authorities, the basic challenge lies in the different functions, competences, and mandates of the bodies. While intelligence services 'have the task of recognising ... future or current threats to the democratic legal order and to alert the competent authorities thereof ... [, the] police, in the framework of its judicial function, have the task of gathering information concerning offences with a view to their eventual settlement by a criminal court' (Vervaele, 2005: 3–4).

Also, the products differ. Information collected by intelligence services is, in principle, secret, but police information 'is subject to judicial testing as criminal evidence in the publicly accessible information' (Vervaele, 2005: 4). A third challenge is that the police can investigate intelligence agencies, a fact which presumably does not make the relationship easier (for the investigation of the London Metropolitan Police into intelligence activities concerning torture allegations see page 99).

One way of persuading security authorities to share more information is to establish structures that are 'more adaptive and flexible' (Neumann, 2009: 154). Since the 9/11 attacks, several Western European intelligence services are said to have 'opened up, doing away with much of the unnecessary secrecy that had hindered effective communication with other agencies and the outside world' (Neumann, 2009: 154–55). Notably, Svendsen (2008: 671) suggested that fusion centres

> have greatly improved the rate of exchange simply by providing a focus of existing threat assessments, and by housing representatives under one roof. The result is not only faster and better coordinated sharing of information among local agencies, but also an entity that is in constant touch with its overseas counterparts ...

Such fusion centres have to face enormous cultural, legal, and structural hurdles that are, in part, deeply rooted in the history of the societies in question. The following sub-section will analyse one such case in more depth, namely the German

GTAZ and the *Trennungsgebot*. From this case, important insights can be learnt for intensified information sharing beyond institutional affiliations.

The German '*Trennungsgebot*'

The EU-wide agenda of improved information exchange concerning police and intelligence is not necessarily consistent with all national frameworks. In particular, the cooperation between police and intelligence clashes with the *Trennungsgebot* ('law of separation'), a legal institution unique to Germany. Due to the extensive powers and role of the Secret State Police (GESTAPO) during the Nazi regime and the increased activities of the foreign intelligence service at that time, the German legal code includes an obligation to separate the work and functions of the police and intelligence services (both at the federal level and at the *Länder* level).[7] This obligation is detailed at various points in the legal acts concerning the police and intelligence services.

The *Trennungsgebot* has crucial consequences for various dimensions of the work of German police and intelligence authorities. Firstly, it implies the obligation of an *organizational* separation. Police and intelligence services are denied any direct organizational relationship; they are not allowed any direct connections; the intelligence services do not have any powers to control or instruct a police force; and there is no personnel overlap. Yet at the top of the bureaucratic hierarchy, the same office is responsible—for the federal level, the Ministry of Interior (König, 2005: 33–34). This organizational separation has been challenged considerably since the introduction of new anti-terrorism legislation in Germany in 2001 (see page 95). Secondly, the *Trennungsgebot* contains the obligation of strict separation of *competences*. At the core of this obligation is the prohibition of executive powers, such as arrest, for intelligence services. Thirdly, there is an *informational* component of the *Trennungsgebot*. This aspect lacks a clear definition, only vaguely referring to information sharing, but includes the prohibition of joint databases of police and intelligence actors. However, it seems nowadays widely accepted among German legal scholars that the *Trennungsgebot* does not totally prohibit all kinds of informational cooperation (König, 2005: 36).

This legal institution has been challenged, contested, and stretched since 11 September 2001. The process of centralization of CT efforts in Germany also brought police and intelligence services closer together, most notably through the creation of the GTAZ. In contrast to other joint CT centres in Europe, the GTAZ had to be structured in such a way as to fulfil the requirements of the *Trennungsgebot*. As a result, it comprises a police analysis and information point (PIAS) and an intelligence analysis and information point (NIAS). Police and intelligence officials occupy separate parts of the buildings and use different entrances. However, the spatial separation is widely understood to be artificial as members

[7] The legal-constitutional dimension of the *Trennungsgebot* remains contested.

of the two groups are allowed to come together for daily briefings in order to exchange topical findings, to establish assessments, to agree on individual measures, as well as in the framework of several working groups. Moreover, both parts of the GTAZ have access to the anti-terrorism database, containing basic information, such as names and addresses, of individuals linked to terrorist activities. Unless there is an emergency, further information is only accessible on request to the organization which fed the information into the database. The extended dataset includes categories, such as phone connections, bank account details, religious affiliation, participation in a terrorist training camp, contact persons, and so on.

The *Trennungsgebot* was challenged again in January 2009 by the introduction of the Law for the prevention of dangers of international terrorism through the Federal Criminal Police Office, aimed at increasing the preventive CT powers of the Federal Criminal Police Office (BKA).[8] This so-called BKA law expands the investigative powers of the BKA to a considerable extent. For instance, it provides for vastly expanded powers to gather information from phones, computers, and homes of suspected terrorists. Unless there is an emergency, those measures require court approval. Critics argue that the law provides for a new 'power complex... half CIA, half FBI' (Naumann, 2009). This caused particular concern, as the revamped institution will not be accompanied by a supervisory body. At the time of writing, there is yet another pending court trial before the Federal Constitutional Court about the legality of the new law.

To summarize, it seems that whilst German politicians keep paying lip service to the *Trennungsgebot*, its practical relevance is diminishing. The analysis suggests that the pressure on security bodies to jointly fight terrorism can be so high as to initiate a cultural change within the institutions. The approximation of tasks and functions of the police and the intelligence services has been implemented in recent anti-terror legislation. In particular, the 2001 anti-terror law provides the intelligence services with certain competences which traditionally belonged to the police, and vice versa (König, 2005: 302). While the organizational separation *de jure* and *de facto* is more or less still existent, the separation of competences is slowly becoming obsolete (König, 2005: 255).

König (2005: 302), who has provided an extensive legal study on the *Trennungsgebot*, argues that the process of European integration in the fields of police and intelligence will require a thorough revisiting of the *Trennungsgebot*. According to him, this will become a matter of urgency once the EU would further integrate intelligence services (König, 2005: 303). In the context of international cooperation, the *Trennungsgebot* has already caused certain problems. The German legal regulations are conceived of as complex and opaque by foreign security authorities. Also, practical challenges have appeared with respect to protecting sources and other interests, which have led to high levels of secrecy on the German side.

[8] For the law see <http://bundesrecht.juris.de/bkag_1997/index.html>.

The *Trennungsgebot* illustrates some important aspects for the overall research. On the one hand, it is an example of legal and cultural specificities of national security frameworks, and of the fact that they are rooted in history and legal traditions. It also shows that during times of emergency, or of an event with a deep impact on people's mindset, longstanding institutions can be surprisingly flexible and can adapt to a new situation (the repeated references to the dangers of *transnational* terrorism provided sufficient justification for the joint anti-terror database and the GTAZ). The example also illustrates that the European policing environment can create external pressure on national security arrangements. When I asked a German federal police official involved in police cooperation what they would make of the *Trennungsgebot* in the European context, they gave a vague answer acknowledging the existence of the legal institution, but arguing that it did not play an important role in the day-to-day work (Interview G).

This section described some of the information-sharing efforts within the EU and the challenges it faces. The following sub-section will broaden the focus by turning towards information sharing with non-EU countries and their respective security authorities. Countries involved in al Qaeda-related cases are sometimes quite distant 'and in many cases there are no pre-existing relationships between the relevant security agencies' (Neumann, 2009: 156).

Opening up networks for new actors: intensified international cooperation in the fight against terrorism

In the aftermath of 9/11, European security bodies started to open up their cooperative networks to new actors. Security authorities of countries related to al Qaeda cases, or those which are understood to provide the ground for jihadist radicalism, were approached and became involved. Some of those countries might be described as not-so-friendly ones, hence countries that have a bad human rights record, no substantive framework of the rule of law, and are well known for their mistreatment of detainees, the use of harsh interrogation techniques, and so on.[9] Several of those countries are understood to have a considerable knowledge about jihadist organizations that are active in Europe, which is why European security experts understand cooperation with them as absolutely necessary (Steinberg, 2009: 17). As stated in a British newspaper article: 'MI5 and MI6 officers argue that in the fight against global terrorism, they have no choice but to deal with foreign security and intelligence agencies *that have different standards*' (Norton-Taylor, 2009; emphasis added). Michael Herman (2004: 188) put it as follows: 'More international co-operation on terrorism means consorting with politically dubious foreign bedfellows.' Craig Murray (2007: 138), former British Ambassador to Uzbekistan, argued that the British government was

[9] Reports by the UN and organizations, such as Human Rights Watch and Amnesty International, list the human rights records of countries worldwide and provide studies on their CT efforts. For difficulties of investigating allegations of torture and ill-treatment see Nowak, 2009.

'accepting material from the torture chambers of Egypt, Pakistan, Jordan, Saudi Arabia and...other countries including even Sudan and Syria' as well as Uzbekistan in the aftermath of 9/11.

One exemplary case is Syria, which is listed as a state sponsoring terrorism by various Western countries and uses torture on a regular basis. The German government cooperated with Syria in 2002 concerning an interrogation, in a Syrian prison, of the German-Syrian Haydar Zammar, who allegedly supported terrorists. The then terrorism advisor for the German Chancellery, Guido Steinberg, gave a testimony to the Parliamentary Control Panel—which is responsible for the scrutiny of intelligence activities in Germany and which looked into the case of Zammar—arguing that all participating decision-makers were very aware of the possibility that Zammar would be subjected to torture in the Syrian prison, but they nevertheless decided to cooperate in his interrogation (Blechschmidt, 2007). The aim of the German security authorities was to gather information about jihadist networks from Syrian authorities, while the Syrian government was allegedly more interested in the surveillance of oppositional Syrians in Germany (Steinberg, 2009: 18). The German government apparently stopped the cooperation at some point, as it was 'unsatisfying' (Steinberg, 2009). Allegedly, the UK has also agreed on some form of CT cooperation with Syria during the visit of Foreign Secretary David Miliband to Damascus in 2008. There have also been claims

> that the British security agencies tipped off their Syrian counterparts to the alleged terrorist activities of...two British citizens [Maryam Kallis and Yasser Zahur Ahmed, who were arrested in Damascus on 17 March 2009] as part of a British-Syrian antiterrorism cooperation agreement concluded last November [2008] (Batal al-Shishani, 2009: 5).

Finally, Pakistan has become a very important partner (Ross, 2009; Hanning, 2008; Miller, 2009). Both the Federally Administered Tribal Areas and the North-West Frontier Province are said to be 'a centre of gravity for regional and international terrorism' (Hanning, 2008) and are supply and training bases, as well as refuge territory, for the Taliban and several terrorist groups. British police worked with Pakistani authorities to uncover plans to bomb Heathrow Airport in August 2006. The German BKA provided training and funding for Pakistani security authorities (Hanning, 2008).

One of the key motivations for European governments to cooperate with such countries is that, since the 9/11 attacks, the global intelligence community has identified human intelligence (HUMINT) as its 'best source' (Maddrell, 2009: 211) of information on terrorist suspects. HUMINT is supposed to provide timely and accurate information necessary to fight loose terrorist networks, such as al Qaeda. Much of such information currently comes from arrested terror suspects rather than spies in the field (Maddrell, 2009: 212). Former CIA director George Tenet (2007: 256) claimed, for example, that the information provided by arrested members of al Qaeda gave 'insight into people, strategy, thinking, individuals'.

Countries such as Syria, Egypt, and Pakistan, to name just a few, have arrested terrorist suspects who are then, in some situations, also interrogated by European officials. In other cases, information provided by such detainees is somehow shared with Western security authorities. The reports on individual cases of the CIA's extraordinary rendition programme illustrate the abuse of some of the imprisoned individuals. For example, the Italian citizen Abou Elkassim Britel was held in a Moroccan prison. In 2002, Britel was detained in Pakistan. After he was handed over to US authorities, they transferred him to Morocco where he was handed over to local intelligence officials (ACLU, 2009). The American Civil Liberties Union (ACLU) claims that he falsely confessed to terror allegations under torture and, as a consequence, is serving a nine-year sentence (ACLU, 2009). After a six-year long investigation into Britel's alleged involvement with terrorism, an Italian investigating judge 'found a complete lack of evidence linking him with any terrorist-related or criminal activity' (ACLU, 2009), and went on to dismiss the case in 2006. Britel now lives again in Italy.

Finally, Europol's intensive networking is another example of increasing cooperation between security authorities that do not share the same standards and values concerning human rights. A Council Decision of 30 November 2009 asks Europol to 'strive for the conclusion of a cooperation agreement...which allows for the exchange of personal data, unless decided otherwise by the Management Board [of Europol]' (Council, 2009g) with countries such as the Ukraine, Colombia, Israel, India, Morocco, and the Russian Federation. Such cooperation must be seen in a wider context, as it is usually part of a wider partnership programme—for example, Israel is one of the EU's 'neighbours' (cf European Union, Delegation of the Commission to Israel, 2007). The Council first decided in 2005 that Europol should aim for cooperation with Israel (Cronin, 2009). Europol's data protection authority, the Joint Supervisory Body (JSB), was asked to give its opinion with regard to the data protection regulation in Israel.[10] The opinion is not publicly available. In its Fourth Activity Report, the JSB (2008: 28) declared that

> from a data protection perspective no obstacles exist for Europol to start negotiations with Israel to prepare an agreement on the transmission of personal data by Europol to Israel. However, this conclusion was made conditional, meaning that certain issues are to be properly dealt with in the negotiations. The JSB particularly focused on the implementation of the agreement and direct applicability of the data subjects' rights; independent supervision with necessary competence and powers to investigate the law enforcement agencies; data quality issues; clear rules on the transmission of the sensitive data; time limits of the storage of the data; liability and legal remedies for individuals for the breaches of the agreement as well as for unauthorised or incorrect data processing; and data security issues.

Thus, while the JSB saw the need for substantial negotiations—including basic aspects of data protection regulation—it still suggested that there were no serious

---

[10] The role and function of the JSB will be explored in detail in Chapter 7.

hurdles for an agreement. Somewhat different from the JSB's summary of its opinion, David Cronin (2009), a journalist who has seen the internal report of the JSB to Europol, suggested that the report stated that Israel's data protection framework is flawed and therefore Europol should not make an agreement including the exchange of personal data and other police intelligence in the field against terrorism and organized crime before Israel adopts stricter regulation in this field. Human rights observers have also pointed towards Israel's well-known use of torture and ill treatment of detainees and warned that Europol would have no control over the use of its information by Israeli authorities (Cronin, 2009).[11] Yet it appears that the JSB focuses on technical issues, but does not provide a broader political discussion. Despite those negative reports, the Council pushed the agenda forwards (Council, 2009h). Asked about the plans to connect Europol closer with Israel's security authorities, a senior Europol official expressed serious concerns and great scepticism about those efforts (Interview H).

Through a data protection lens, the exchange of information with countries lacking a sufficient data protection regime increases the danger of 'los[ing] control over the information flow' (De Hert, 2004: 54)—a situation that weakens any data protection instrument. When a senior official at Europol was asked during an interview whether information concerning (former) Guantánamo Bay detainees, or gathered from Guantánamo detainees, could have been transferred via Europol's channels and whether Europol would be aware of it, they simply said that they would not get to know about it (Interview H).

In some cases of cooperation with 'dubious foreign bedfellows', allegations of torture involving European officials have been made. While this has become well known in the context of the CIA's extraordinary rendition programme (which will be discussed in the following chapters), there have been various other allegations, particularly in Britain. Several European governments have clearly denied any involvement in torture or harsh interrogation techniques, similarly to Britain's former Prime Minister Gordon Brown (2009), who has argued: 'Torture has no place in a modern democratic society. We will not condone it. Nor will we ever ask others to do it on our behalf.' However, some of the allegations against British intelligence officials were so serious that the Metropolitan Police started an investigation. Both MI5 and MI6 were facing charges concerning allegations of mistreatment of terrorist suspects held overseas (Barrowclough, 2009; Cobain, 2009b). Both agencies' directors insisted publicly that their services had, and would not, collude in torture. Yet MI5's Director also emphasized the need to use certain overseas intelligence in the post-9/11 period. Similarly, the head of the Secret Intelligence Service (SIS) argued in August 2009

[11] For instance, in May 2009, the UN's Committee against Torture (2009: point 19) expressed concerns 'that there are numerous, ongoing and consistent allegations of the use of methods by Israeli security officials that were prohibited by the September 1999 ruling [on the prohibition of torture] of the Israeli Supreme Court, and that are alleged to take place before, during and after interrogations'.

that his service's officials were not involved in any torture act, claiming that they were 'as committed to the values and the human rights values of liberal democracy as anybody else' (BBC News, 2009). Only one month later, however, SIS referred a case to the Attorney-General, asking for an investigation into the detainment of a non-British citizen and the potential involvement of British personnel (Evans M, 2009). The CPS decided not to charge individuals in this context but SIS is currently facing another police investigation concerning allegations of criminal wrongdoing in relation to alleged ill treatment and rendition of two Libyan dissidents (Crown Prosecution Service, 2012).

Concerning such sensitive forms of cooperation, European security officials tend to strive to avoid the public release of any related information. It seems that only under intense public or legal pressure do government officials justify such forms of cooperation. For instance, former Foreign Minister David Miliband insisted that the British interrogation policy in the aftermath of the 9/11 attacks should not be revealed to the public, although the topic is highly contested in the country. One of the facts that have been revealed so far is that, in 2002, an SIS officer who was interrogating a detainee held by the US military abroad asked London for advice because he had noticed a mistreatment of the interviewee. The officer received written instructions the following day and they were distributed among all intelligence officers of MI5 and SIS in the field (Cobain, 2009a). In this reply, the officers are clearly instructed not to condone torture and not to 'engage in any activity... that involves inhumane or degrading treatment of prisoners' (Cobain, 2009a). However, they were also advised that they are under no obligation to prevent detainees from being mistreated: '(g)iven that they are not within our custody or control, the law does not require you to intervene to prevent this' (Cobain, 2009a). Arguably, such an approach would be in contradiction to Article 4 of the 1984 UN Convention against Torture (CAT)—of which the UK is a signatory—which includes the obligation to avoid *complicity* in torture. As the UN's special rapporteur on human rights, Martin Scheinin (2009: 19), pointed out, 'active participation through the sending of interrogators or questions, or even the mere presence of intelligence personnel at an interview with a person who is being held in places where his rights are violated, can be reasonably understood as implicitly condoning such practices'.

Given the emphasis on information gathering by European security institutions, the question is whether and, if so, how far, to make use of information that might have been gathered by harsh interrogation techniques and possibly torture. In what concerns the UK, Sir David Omand (2009: 16; emphasis added), has described the current approach as follows: 'The present British policy is to accept information from *any source* that bears on [the UK's] major interests, at the same time as taking all reasonable steps to promote UK views over acceptable interrogation methods overseas.' According to this statement, any information appears to be acceptable if it is in the interest of the country, and a moral dilemma only arises with respect to the question of whether to share such information with 'dubious' countries. MI5 Director Jonathan Evans (2009) has confirmed this approach emphasizing that, after the 9/11 attacks, the MI5 had to rely on cooperation with countries with standards and practices 'very far from our own'. Given the way intelligence liaison works, he emphasized that MI5 does 'not control what other countries do, that operational decisions have to be taken with the knowledge available, even if it is incomplete' (Evans, 2009). Yet there are two dangers of such an approach. On the one hand, there is the 'slippery path' argument, which suggests that once cooperation with such agencies will be allowed, this will slowly become routine and the moral hurdles will appear less high. On the other hand, there is a danger that this attitude might slowly trickle down through the whole security apparatus.

Indeed, Omand (2009: 16) put the question of whether it 'will... continue to be sustainable in terms of Parliamentary acceptability that in return [for information] British intelligence information should be passed to other countries if that information might lead to action by others that would not be considered acceptable by the UK?' He seems to refer here to a wider—that is, international—responsibility of Western security authorities in the cooperation with certain partners, related to the notion of international fairness. Related to this, Pablo De Greiff (1999: 160) maintains that the current 'concepts of sovereignty and of democratic legitimacy lead to the idea that as long as a country respects democratic procedures, it can pass whatever laws its people consider appropriate for the regulation of social interactions within its own borders'. He wonders whether there is actually a moral responsibility for legislators to consider the consequences that their policies might have beyond their own borders (De Greiff, 1999: 161). This question ought to be extended to the executive on the ground, including policing and intelligence actors, and would be a formidable question to be discussed in scrutiny forums.

While the chapter has so far discussed information sharing as one form of preventive action to fight terrorism, the following section will discuss other developments, which can be categorized as instruments of proactive/preventive policing. Again, the distinction between police and intelligence measures becomes blurred in this field.

Towards Proactive Policing

This section deals with shifts towards proactive policing, focusing on police work and functions in the run-up to a crime, such as a terrorist attack. Preventive measures have been transferred into several European police laws since the 1990s. For instance, the German Federal police law was changed in 1997 to acknowledge that prevention was as important as post-crime investigations (BKAG §§ 2 I, IV, VI, 3 II of 1 August 1997). Yet, such a 'preventive' framework only refers to a move towards law enforcement actions *before* any actual offence or evidence of harm. It also refers to different methods of policing. To 'confront, disrupt and target threats before they emerge' (McCulloch and Pickering, 2009: 631) includes the criminalization of conduct by calling it terrorist-related, 'such as giving money to a charity or associating with what are deemed to be terrorist organizations' (McCulloch and Pickering, 2009:631). Moreover, the approach favours a networked model of police work by identifying information and intelligence sharing at the core of law enforcement work (Ratcliffe, 2008).

One of the consequences of this approach is that intelligence is more often used in criminal justice processes. McCulloch and Pickering (2009: 634) have argued that '(t)he blurring of evidence and intelligence is demonstrated in the expanded intelligence-gathering roles of police agencies and the granting of coercive police powers to security intelligence agencies as well as the quality of information used to support terrorism charges'. A further consequence is that intelligence gains an important role in the process of policing. The approach of 'intelligence-led policing' has become widespread, referring to a proactive approach in which intelligence and analysis are at the heart of decision-making (Ratcliffe, 2008). Though there is no agreed definition, 'intelligence-led policing involves the collection and analysis of information to produce an intelligence end product designed to inform police decision-making at both the tactical and strategic levels. It is a model of policing in which intelligence serves as a guide to operations' (Smith, 1997: 1).

Police agencies are increasingly taking over intelligence-gathering roles (McCulloch and Pickering, 2009: 634). Therefore, one consequence of the move towards preventive policing is that the police resort (more) frequently to what used to be means of intelligence services, such as undercover agents and surveillance (König, 2005: 35). The emphasis is now on 'routine ways in which focused attention is paid to personal details by organizations that want to influence, manage, or control certain persons or population groups' (Lyon, 2003: 5). Other instruments of proactive policing include data-gathering, -mining, and the use of joint databases. Such measures are potentially harmful methods, as they have implications for the individual's right to privacy (see Chapter 7; cf Miller and Blackler, 2005). In addition, the use of proactive means of policing is difficult to trace in networks, as information sharing via networks leads to 'a set of rules on the exchange of information that is intended to ensure that work within the networks cannot be easily observed by people or organizations outside' (Roberts, 2006: 139). In the following step of the argument, four examples of such measures, which are also increasingly used in the fight against terrorism, will be discussed.

Firstly, the police powers of stop and search under section 44 of the Terrorism Act 2000 in the UK allowed the British police to stop and search civilians ('terrorist suspects') without a warrant and without providing a good reason. France's post-9/11 anti-terrorism legislation grants the French police a similar right and 'this measure can also be employed by private security firms not directly accountable to the public' (Haubrich, 2003: 21). In the UK, the instrument was increasingly used by the police, but was criticized by human rights advocates. In January 2010, the ECtHR ruled the British stop and search powers illegal, maintaining that they were 'not sufficiently circumscribed' and lacked 'adequate legal safeguards against abuse'. Crucially, stop and search powers run contrary to the idea of a free society, one of whose cornerstones 'is the ability of its citizens to go about their business without the need to explain to anyone in authority what they are doing, and without the fear that they may be subject to arbitrary challenge or arrest' (Haubrich, 2003: 13). The regulation also raised concerns because of the potentially racial pattern of such searches (Travis, 2009). Allegations of racism concerning the British practices of stop and search had the twisted effect that the police subsequently tended to carry out searches of individuals who do *not* fit such a pattern, in order to 'racially balance' (Carlile, 2009) the statistics. Yet by 2009, none of all the searches provided for under Section 44 had led to a conviction for a terrorist offence (Carlile, 2009).

Moreover, the powers of stop and search are one example of a CT law which has been misused for other purposes after its implementation. The powers under section 44 were used in approaches to policing protests, for example (House of Lords/House of Commons, Joint Committee on Human Rights, 2009a; Liberty et al, 2003). This might simply be described as 'mission creep', but it was only possible because the law was not specific enough about the purpose and limit of the regulation. Eventually, the respective sections of the Terrorism Act 2000 were replaced by more limited powers in March 2011 under the Terrorism Act 2000 (Remedial) Order 2011.

Secondly, as will be explored in more detail in Chapter 7, the EU and the US use so-called terrorist lists. Some of those lists have been established for a particular purpose, such as the freezing of assets of terrorist suspects, while others are more general watch-lists of terrorist suspects. The most recent publicly available EU list concerning financial sanctions of terrorist suspects includes the names of twenty-six individuals (plus their ID card numbers, if applicable, and dates of birth) and twenty-five groups or other entities (Council, 2011c). National terrorist watch-lists have also been established.

The effectiveness of such lists is contested. The biggest national terrorist watch-list is the US government one, which is maintained by the FBI's Terrorist Screening Center. It is based on a 2003 presidential directive and includes information about individuals 'known or appropriately suspected to be or have been engaged in conduct constituting, in preparation for, in aid of, or related to terrorism' (US General Accounting Office, 2009: 2, fn 3). The watch-list records are included in the National Crime Information Center's Violent Gang and Terrorist Organization File, in order to allow law enforcement officials to exchange information related to terrorism (US Department of Justice, Office of the Inspector General, 2009). According to data the FBI provided to the Senate Judiciary Committee, 1600 names—including aliases—were, on average, added *daily* to the FBI's list between March 2008 and March 2009 (Pincus, 2009). According to the FBI, those individuals raised a 'reasonable suspicion'. Yet, a recent report provided by the Department of Justice Office of the Inspector General (2009) found that the part of the watch-list maintained by the FBI may contain a 35 per cent error rate. It also suggested that many entries on the list were out of date.[12]

It also seems that, at times, there are no consequences of being in such a list. A 2009 Report by the US General Accounting Office (2009) shows that, in 865 occasions out of 963, individuals registered on the watch-list were able to buy guns as well as explosives during a five-year period. While the names appeared on the list, there was no law prohibiting the purchase of weapons for registered individuals. Although the purpose of the list is not specifically to prevent the acquisition of weapons, the results of the report challenge the effectiveness of these lists as measures to prevent terrorist attacks. Rather, such lists carry a danger of easy misuse, as Chapter 7 will show in the case of the EU and UN lists (eg, bank accounts are frozen, cross-border travelling is denied, the right to a fair trial is not guaranteed, presumption of innocence is not given, and delisting is very complicated). To stay with the example of the FBI's efforts to establish a terrorist watch-list: the Bureau circulated a so-called 'no fly' list among private companies after the 9/11 attacks. This list, currently run by the US government and including roughly 9 per cent of the general FBI terrorist watch-list, featured hundreds of names of persons the agency wanted to talk to (Pincus, 2009). Despite indications of error entries, once established for a specific purpose—combating terrorism—this list was later used to deny jobs to, or arbitrarily discriminate against, innocent people (De Hert, 2005: 87). A prominent example for a false positive on the 'no fly' list was the late Senator Edward Kennedy (D-MA) (Kehaulani Goo, 2004) who happened to share his name with an entry on the list.

Thirdly, the increasing number of databases set up in the field of police and intelligence and their various interconnections are indicators of the increased use of instruments of data collection (for the UK see Omand, 2009; for a discussion about the EU's efforts concerning the 'interoperability' of European databases see the following chapters). In particular, the sharing of different data sets available to different governmental authorities is problematic from an ethical and data protection perspective: 'information gathered for one purpose should not be made available for another purpose, unless a specific case can be made out for doing so' (Miller and Blackler, 2005: 91). Moreover, Miller and Blackler (2005) argue that data sharing is not only an individual, but also a societal issue, as an image of a 'big brother' system of invasive inquiry and social control ought to be avoided. While the analysis of these authors focused on the domestic framework, it is similarly applicable to the European level.

The European Commission's efforts concerning the interoperability of the various EU databases (most notably SIS (II), VIS, and Eurodac) have led to a 2009

[12] For example, two of the people listed were dead. Also, more than 50,000 records did not contain a reason why the individual in question was on the list, which makes it impossible to remove them. At the same time, putting somebody on the list appeared to be a very time-consuming process.

proposal aimed at establishing one umbrella agency for all AFSJ databases (Commission, 2009b). The information stored in such databases might be gathered through well-established technologies, such as the use of fingerprints and vehicle registrations. Additionally, advanced biometric technologies have become available for the police, such as deoxyribonucleic acid (DNA) databases and face- as well as iris-recognition technologies. The Prüm arrangement, adopted at the EU level on 12 June 2007, includes the exchange of such data as DNA, fingerprint, and car registration data.

Fourthly, the retention of phone and internet traffic data is understood to play a key role in CT. A paper by the French government points out that this 'is often what makes it possible, notably in the case of the March 2004 Madrid attacks, to track down the terrorist network' (De Villepin, 2006). Electronic communications operators have been required by European countries to keep such data for different periods of time. In early 2006, an EU-wide directive on the retention of communications traffic data was adopted which requires the data to be kept for at least six months. The French paper maintains that this EU regulation 'will allow better cooperation among Member States in identifying terrorists' (De Villepin, 2006). As with other surveillance instruments, the surveillance of telecommunication links is slowly being transformed into an automatic process. For example, if based on a court order, the surveillance of telecommunications links has been legal in Germany since long before 2001, but the post-9/11 legislation seeks to automate this process (Haubrich, 2003: 12).

Overall, the policing of protests surrounding the World Trade Organization meeting in Seattle in November 1999 was a global phenomenon where preventive policing became most obvious for the broader public. Holding of people in temporary detention centres during the events, video surveillance, and repeated searches of protesters without charge are some of the most contested instruments of proactive policing. It seems, therefore, that there is a much broader trend in policing, although it is correct to assume that the pressure for CTP actors to be successful/effective in using such preventive measures is higher than in many other crime areas, given the potentially high number of casualties of a terrorist attack. The police method of crowd control called 'kettling', whereby police officers contain a crowd for a long time period within a limited area to prevent disruption by protesters, is one example. While it was always a contested method, the police had to face a public outcry after events during the G20 protests. The Independent Police Complaints Commission (2009) called for changes after the inquiry into the case of a woman who had been subject to kettling during the protests. Similarly, a report into the events by the UK Chief Inspector of Constabulary (2009), Denis O'Connor, marked the kettling practice as 'inadequate' and said it belonged to a 'different era' of policing. He warned that the police might lose public consent if they would continue using such methods.

Yet, in contrast to kettling, many preventive measures are often understood to be of a 'soft nature' and not particularly intrusive as they do not cause direct physical harm (De Hert, 2005: 86). Examples of this are video surveillance and the provision of fingerprints and DNA, but the terror lists are an even more indirect way of providing such information, as the individual is not directly involved in the process. While at the policy-making level there is a tendency to discuss such technologies and their effectiveness in isolation from ethical and social questions, critics highlight the dangers of such technology to both the individual and the whole of society. They emphasize that '(t)echnologies such as DNA profiling, databases and even [closed-circuit television] CCTV cannot be dissociated from ethical and social questions' (Anderson et al, 2009: 9) and are intimately linked to public perceptions of legitimacy and fairness of the police. New biometric technologies, for example, are qualitatively different from personal data traditionally collected by the state, as they can reveal more sensitive details about a person, including one's race, sex, ethnicity, and propensity for diseases (Neyroud and Disley, 2008: 3). Clearly, the sensitivity of such data 'engages the right to private life in a more profound way' (Neyroud and Disley, 2008: 3) than previous technologies did. On the quantitative scale, it is now much easier and cheaper to retain and store such data and to exchange information stored at various databases.

Given such differences both in terms of quality and quantity, critics refer to preventive measures as indicators for the existence of a 'maximum security society' (Marx, 1988), or 'controlling societies' (Gutwirth, 2002: 71), in which individuals are permanently under surveillance, information about them is stored in massive databases, and privacy is not respected. The UK's Information Commissioner pointed to a lack of public debate about this development, famously arguing that the British are 'sleepwalking into a surveillance society' (as quoted in Neyroud and Disley, 2008: 6). Neyroud and Disley (2008) use the example of the UK's increasing joined databases of various police forces to show that there is a high support among the public for data sharing and linking. Yet, they also warn that there is a great tension in the public in this respect, as others fear a surveillance system and the loss of individual rights and liberties (Neyroud and Disley, 2008: 3).

One crucial criticism is that such surveillance and database instruments often comprise sensitive material of 'innocent' individuals. For example, the UK's National DNA database, set up in 1995 and now one of the world's biggest DNA collections, contains profiles that can be retained 'even if a person is not charged or is acquitted' (Neyroud and Disley, 2008: 2). Critics point to the fact that DNA profiles of 'innocents' were not deleted and that young, black men were over-represented on the database. Moreover, the ECtHR found in December 2008 that keeping the DNA of innocent people for an unlimited time period contravened the ECHR (*S and Marper v UK*[13]). The judgment has led to a broader public debate and finally to the government proposing changes to the existing legislation.

---

[13] *S and Marper v The United Kingdom* (Applications no. 30562/04 and 30566/04) (2008) 48 EHRR 50.

One of the dangers posed by the use of such instruments refers to 'over-policing' (Chan, 1997: 21ff)—certain people or groups are more likely to be stopped, investigated, and suspected than others, which might be perceived as harassment of certain minority groups. This can easily lead to a damaged relationship and distrust between the police and those communities. From an operational point of view, this might cause members of those communities not to inform the police or collaborate with them and, thus, damage the success of an investigation (Chan, 1997: 2).

No European country has had a more intense debate about some of its recent legislative CT initiatives than the UK. Rare voices from the intelligence community could be heard in this context. For example, former MI5's Director General (DG) Stella Rimington has described the response to the 9/11 attacks as a 'huge overreaction' (quoted in Norton-Taylor, 2009). She accused the government of passing excessive anti-terrorist laws wanting their citizens to 'live in fear under a police state' (Norton-Taylor, 2009). Similarly, Baroness Eliza Manningham-Buller, also a previous DG of MI5, publicly criticized the government's idea of holding terrorist suspects without charge for forty-two days. In her 2008 maiden speech to the Lords, she said: 'I have weighed up the balance between the right to life—the most important civil liberty—the fact that *there is no such thing as complete security*, and the importance of our hard-won civil liberties. Therefore, *on a matter of principle*, I cannot support the proposal' (Norton-Taylor, 2009; emphasis added).

Manningham-Buller argued 'on a matter of principle' against this particular CT measure. As can be seen from this section, the instruments of proactive policing tend to touch on core values, or ethical principles, of individuals and societies. Yet the problem arising from policing networks, which distribute information gathered through such proactive means, refers to the notion of 'many hands'. The cooperative nature of activity in institutions, such as police and intelligence agencies, refers to an institutional context comprising 'many actions, outcomes and spheres of activity to which many different persons in fact contribute' (Miller and Blackler, 2005: 39). This dimension is very difficult to study, as the cloak of secrecy in the field of CT prevents the study of the moral attitudes of individual officers in greater depth. But it has been argued that modern intelligence as well as proactive police work includes the regular use of intrusive methods, which always implies 'breaking everyday moral rules' (Omand, 2009: 9). Given this (potentially) severe impact on individuals' freedoms and rights, efficient external scrutiny through parliaments and courts appears even more important (Gill and Phythian, 2006: 148). It is therefore to be welcomed that, while the intelligence services gained more powers through the anti-terrorism legislation after 9/11, services like MI5 are at the same time more 'under the spotlight, both politically and operationally, as never before' (Norton-Taylor, 2009).

In August 2005, British Prime Minister Tony Blair, referring to measures and efforts in fighting terrorism, argued that 'the rules of the game are changing' (UK Prime Minister's Office, 2005). This chapter has illustrated recent shifts in the field of CT within the EU and its MS, including two major features: a trend towards increased information sharing among European CT actors, but also with non-European authorities, as well as the increased use of instruments of proactive policing. Such a preventive CT approach is reflected, encouraged, and fostered by EU legislation and bodies, such as Europol.

Yet, the shift in CT touches on deep cultural and historically grown roots of national policing bodies and structures. Far from being a homogenous move in the Union, the emphasis on proactive CT efforts has highlighted some of the differences between national CT actors, partly referring to cultural aspects. Yet pressure for increasing information sharing, internationalization, and other forms of proactive policing helped to overcome some of those differences, as the example of fusion centres has shown.

Moreover, the logic of proactive CTP, with its insatiable hunger for information, makes European CT actors also very dependent on foreign partners. It is fair to describe the current political climate as promoting an 'imperative' for cooperation with foreign agencies (Svendsen, 2008: 672). While this chapter focused on 'not-so-friendly' partners and the ethical and legal dilemma such collaboration poses, the following chapter will analyse the closest cooperation between the EU and a non-EU partner, namely the US.

5

Stretching across the Atlantic: Transatlantic Counter-terrorism Initiatives

So far, the book has explored the increased density of police cooperation among European countries and at the EU level. The EU's post-9/11 CT agenda has clearly stipulated several of these efforts. Moreover, the previous chapter touched on the increased inclusion of non-EU partners in some of the CTNs. This aspect will be analysed in more depth in this chapter. It will focus on one particularly important and—as will be demonstrated—often dominant partner of the EU in fighting terrorism: the US. The American 'nodes' have a unique position in several CTNs comprising European participants, such as Europol or national law enforcement authorities, and this chapter will analyse this relationship in more detail.

While there had been some transatlantic cooperation on JHA matters before the 9/11 attacks, both the scope and the depth of the collaborative efforts were intensified to a remarkable extent in the first decade of the twenty-first century. The EU-US cooperation in the field of CT in this era embraces a wide range of areas, including border control, airline security, intelligence sharing, legal assistance, and the tackling of illicit money flows. In addition, the US continues to cooperate closely with national authorities of most MS. This chapter will provide an in-depth picture of the transatlantic collaboration in the context of CTP. Despite some challenges concerning the gathering of reliable information about the extent of cooperation on both sides of the Atlantic, the chapter will explore what is meant by policing terrorism through transatlantic channels since 9/11 through an examination of empirical findings.

For the exploration of the democratic legitimacy of CTNs with European 'nodes', it is important to analyse the involvement of non-EU partners within them. As emphasized in the first chapter, despite the ideal of networks as a web of homogenous nodes, power dynamics within the collaborative relationships are defining features of networks and affect their overall performance. If it appears that the US is a particularly dominant actor within the networks, this has an impact on the question of democratic legitimacy. Crucially, the policy priorities of the US government and its executive bodies are not legitimized, or necessarily shared, by EU citizens, and they have no direct ways of informing the American CT agenda. This aspect is often neglected in debates on the EU's CTP efforts. In addition, as the final section of this chapter will outline with respect to extraordinary renditions, the involvement of US authorities can raise severe problems of accountability and oversight which also concern and affect European partners.

The first section will briefly explore the intensified transatlantic collaboration on matters of policing, criminal justice, and in particular CT in the post-9/11 era. This will be followed by an examination of some of the major transatlantic efforts at policing terrorism, focusing on the creation of—institutional and personal—networks. This section will outline the wide range of networks which focus on the fight against terrorism, ranging from collaboration between customs officials to the sharing of sensitive data of air passengers to the CIA-led extraordinary rendition programme. The chapter then moves on to analyse the power dynamics within some of the established CTNs and critically examines the role of the US in EU-wide CTP. The final section will briefly explore some of the major challenges that the increased cooperation with non-EU parties present to scrutiny procedures.

Intensified Cooperation in the Post-9/11 Era

European governments and their security authorities have been cooperating with their American counterparts for a long time. Some authors have argued that they formed a 'security community' (Adler and Barnett, 1998), emphasizing shared identities, values, long-term interests, as well as frequent interactions. While NATO has been the main institutional basis for this cooperation, the emergence of the EU as a security actor stimulated new institutional dynamics. In the post-Cold War period, 'the security and prosperity of the United States and the EU remain inextricably linked', also because both parties have been facing 'a common set of challenges—from countering terrorism and weapons proliferation to slowing environmental degradation to ensuring the stability of international financial markets' (Archick and Morelli, 2011: 1). As these challenges cannot be satisfactorily addressed in a unilateral manner, US security authorities cooperate with their national counterparts in Europe, often on a bilateral and sometimes on a multilateral basis. Crucially for this research, they also increasingly (have to) take the EU into account.

In the immediate aftermath of the attacks of 11 September 2001, the EU and its MS stood close by the US. *Le Monde* dramatically editorialized 'We are all

Americans', and the German government ensured the state's unlimited solidarity with the US (Colombani, 2001; Schröder, 2001). NATO allies invoked the mutual defence clause, maintained in Article Five of the North Atlantic Treaty. At that point in time, the enormity of the terrorist attacks on the US would have prompted many heads of European governments to agree with the statement of the British Prime Minister Tony Blair (2001) that this was 'not a battle between the United States of America and terrorism, but between the free and democratic world and terrorism'. What followed was an unprecedented, wide-reaching effort to tackle terrorism across the globe with the US as the primary driver.

Andreas and Nadelmann (2006: vii) argue that '(t)oday's global counterterrorism campaign... very much builds on and extends policing capacities and initiatives originally developed to suppress drug trafficking and related money laundering'. This is certainly the case concerning the transatlantic cooperation on internal security, and CT in particular, which has been based on existing structures to combat transnational organized crime, developed during the 1990s (Den Boer, 2003; Rees, 2011: 154).[1] Some initiatives reach back even further, such as the deployment of US law enforcement officials at American embassies and consulates in Europe in earlier decades (Nadelmann, 1993b).

The initially sporadic cooperative efforts concerning JHA matters became more explicit and formalized in the 1995 New Transatlantic Agenda (NTA). The NTA maintained the aim of closer and systematic cooperation in four priority areas: the worldwide promotion of peace and stability, democracy, and development; responses to global challenges, such as transnational crime and terrorism; efforts towards expanding world trade and closer economic relations; and building transatlantic 'bridges' of people and communities. By now, cooperation takes place at the level of heads of state governments as well as senior and lower-ranked officials, via a range of channels, such as summits, dialogues, working committees, networks, regulatory cooperation agreements, task forces, road maps, and informal collaboration. In addition, the US House of Representatives and the EP established the Transatlantic Legislators' Dialogue in 1999 and, more recently and focused, the Transatlantic Parliamentary Group on Counter Jihadi Terrorism, also called the Transatlantic Group on Counterterrorism (cf Archick and Morelli, 2011). There is also active collaboration among civil society actors (cf Pollack, 2005). Cooperation concerning, among other issues, the fight against terrorism was further fostered through the Joint EU-US Action Plan, signed in 1995, in which the two parties stated their joint commitment to fight international crime, drug trafficking, and terrorism.[2]

Yet only in recent years have CT and related aspects of information sharing concerning law enforcement, border management, and other areas become a

---

1 For an overview of the origins of crime control in Europe and the US respectively see chapters two and three in Andreas and Nadelmann (2006).

2 A copy of the Treaty is available at <http://eeas.europa.eu/us/docs/joint_eu_us_action_plan_95_en.pdf>.

major focus of transatlantic cooperation. In this relatively short period of time, the previously existing—often informal and rudimentary—structures of cooperation in these areas were considerably expanded and deepened. Transatlantic cooperation in this field could easily develop from 'an international crime control infrastructure already in place' (Andreas and Nadelmann, 2006: 5), often simply adding a CT notion to the agenda (see also Rees, 2011: 162). This also applies to cooperation in longstanding multilateral forums, such as NATO, ICPO-Interpol, the Financial Action Task Force, and the UN.

In matters of CT, the US administration under President Bill Clinton (1993–2001) initiated several high-level summits, comprising representatives of the US, Germany, the UK, France, and Italy. The gatherings led to improved arrangements concerning, for example, 'the extradition of terrorists, the international criminalization of terrorist activities..., and a broadening of the scope of forensic investigation related to terrorist incidents' (Andreas and Nadelmann, 2006: 217). However, most efforts took place on a bi- or multilateral basis between the US and individual European countries, not between the EU and the US.

While the US continues to work with European partners on a bi- and multilateral basis when tackling terrorism, it strongly expressed an interest to cooperate to a greater extent with partners *at the EU level* in the aftermath of the 9/11 attacks. This move was facilitated by the fact that, after 9/11, 'for the first time, the European Union officially expressed its view as a Union on transatlantic cooperation in the fight against terrorism' (Fijnaut, 2004: 22). Both political and operational transatlantic collaboration were strengthened after 9/11. Notably, President Bush presented the European Commission's President on 16 October 2001 with a wide-ranging list of measures which he considered to be crucial for future US-EU CT cooperation, covering the areas of law enforcement and border control, terrorist financing, transport security, non-proliferation, and diplomatic actions.[3]

Overall, a continuous mutual interest in cooperation can be stated. By now, collaborative efforts at the institutional level include cooperation between EU institutions, such as Europol and Eurojust, and American law enforcement, intelligence, and judicial authorities. Beyond that, the European Commission cooperates with American governmental bodies, most notably the US Department of Homeland Security (DHS), in areas such as border control and information collection and exchange. In addition, the US has been involved in multilateral forms of cooperation with European partners (but outside the EU umbrella)—for example, in the form of the CT intelligence unit Alliance Base, set up in Paris by American intelligence authorities. The unit does 'not only pool[ ] intelligence but also plans and coordinates operations to monitor or disrupt terror cells' (Walsh, 2010: 107; Priest, 2005b).

The extent of the EU-US cooperation is not easily visible and obvious to the wider public, partly because some negotiations took place in secret. For instance,

[3] Statewatch made a copy of this letter available at <http://www.statewatch.org/news/2001/nov/06Ausalet.htm>.

The Guardian reported in September 2005 that 'documents show that secret talks between senior American and European officials cover a wide range of sensitive issues, including extradition, the exchange of personal data, the funding of terrorist suspects, intelligence-gathering, and organised crime' (Norton-Taylor, 2005). According to the journalist, 'EU governments have persistently tried to play down the extent of their cooperation with US agencies' (Norton-Taylor, 2005).

While a mutual interest of cooperation can be stated, the CT priorities pursued by the US clearly set the agenda for many transatlantic law enforcement initiatives. Though the 9/11 attacks were not the first terrorist attacks on US soil, they caused a unique response by the US government and led to wide-ranging changes of the American security apparatus.[4] Overall, the US developed a very broad CT strategy, understanding terrorism as a matter of national security rather than law enforcement. The 2002 US Counter-terrorism Strategy outlined a whole range of instruments, including diplomatic means, intelligence and law enforcement tools, financial instruments, and military force. CT law 'progressed in a piecemeal fashion, evolving from legislation on activities associated with terrorism to a more comprehensive approach' (Deflem, 2010: 29–30). The main legislative response was rushed through only five weeks after the 9/11 attacks: The Uniting and Strengthening America by Providing Appropriate Tools Required to Intercept and Obstruct Terrorism Act of 2001 (USA Patriot Act) expanded and revamped some existing legislation. It provided federal security authorities with a remarkable range of executive powers, in particular in areas such as surveillance and information gathering and sharing—'in some cases by creating novel mechanisms, but in others by simply extending capabilities already permitted in the fight against organized crime to CT' (Occhipinti, 2010: 169). Federal agencies, such as the FBI, were now allowed to 'search telephone, e-mail, and financial records without a court order through the use of National Security Letters..., a form of administrative subpoena issued without judicial oversight' (Chesterman, 2011: 97).

The wide range of internal security mechanisms to prevent and tackle terrorist attacks were bundled into the new policy area of homeland security, described as 'a concerted national effort to prevent terrorist attacks within the US, reduce America's vulnerability to terrorism, and minimize the damage and recover from attacks that do occur' (DHS, 2002). At the centre of this approach is the DHS, created by the Homeland Security Act of 25 November 2002. The creation of the DHS, comprising now more than 200,000 employees, represented 'the largest reorganization of the federal government since the early years of the cold war' (Andreas and Nadelmann, 2006: 200). For the US, protective efforts concerning terrorism

[4] Previous attacks include the 1972 Pentagon bomb attack by the Weather Underground, the World Trade Center bombing by Ramzi Yousef in 1993, and the 1995 bombing of the Murrah Federal Building, Oklahoma City, by Timothy McVeigh and Terry Nichols.

> include capabilities related to border protection and security; aviation security and screening; aerospace control; maritime/port security; cargo security; cyber security; nuclear, radiological, biological, and chemical materials and the ability to detect their illicit use; biometrics; critical infrastructure protection; force protection; all hazards preparedness; community engagement; and information sharing among law enforcement organizations at all levels (White House, 2011: 11; see also Dalgaard-Nielsen, 2006: 1).

Many of these policy concerns have been transferred into transatlantic initiatives, as will be demonstrated later in the chapter.

In addition, a range of new or revamped government institutions working on CT-related issues were created, and financial and staff resources of existing law enforcement and intelligence agencies were increased.[5] In 2004, for example, the FBI's personnel numbers had more than doubled since 2001. A Terrorist Threat Integration Center was created which was later amalgamated into the National Counterterrorism Center (NCTC), established by the Intelligence Reform and Terrorism Prevention Act of 2004 and overseen by the Office of the Director of National Intelligence. The NCTC's main purpose is the integration and analysis of all intelligence on terrorism and CT. It maintains the Terrorist Screening Database (TSDB) which is primarily fed by two sources: information regarding transnational terrorism flow from the NCTC and concerning domestic information from the FBI (Priest and Arkin, 2011: 84).

Like their European counterparts, as described in the first chapter, many of the US policing actors also increased their *international* efforts since autumn 2001. The FBI simply puts it as follows: 'Crime and terror have gone global. And so have we' (FBI website—'International Operations'). As part of its legal attaché programme, the organization has increased the number of employees stationed in its overseas offices by 'nearly 55 per cent' up to 289 employees between the years 2001 and 2011 (FBI website—'Ten Years After'). The FBI's office in Madrid provided investigative assistance following the string of train bombings in 2004, for example. Similarly, the efforts of the DHS increasingly stretch beyond American borders. For example, it increasingly ensures agreements with foreign partners concerning information exchange, such as the agreements with—so far—fourteen nations with reference to the exchange of biometric and biographic data on terrorists and criminals (DHS website—'About'). Another example concerns the United States Secret Service (2010) which, so far, has established two European Electronic Crime Task Forces, based in Rome and London. In cooperation with public and private European partners, the units are meant to tackle computer-related crimes, including terrorist-related features.

---

[5] For an official overview of the complex CT structures of the US government see <http://www.state.gov/j/ct/team/>. Priest and Arkin (2011) outline the mushrooming of government organizations working on CT and intelligence, in particular at the top secret level, and the overall growth of the sector in the last decade.

Clearly, the impact of the 9/11 attacks on the transatlantic cooperation on internal security matters has been significant. As Rees (2011: 154) pointed out, in particular the 'external dimensions of internal security have become some of the most important areas of development and the US has fashioned its closest cooperation with its European allies'. Transatlantic initiatives in this area are often agreed at EU-US summits. High-level meetings between ministers or senior officials contribute to further collaboration in areas, such as 'border protection issues, visa-free travel across the Atlantic, information sharing for law enforcement purposes to address international terrorism…, international organized crime…and drugs'[6] (European External Action Service—EU-US Cooperation website). International agreements with Europol were signed as well as agreements on information transfer concerning PNR and other data (see pages 119ff).

In its 2005 Strategy for the external dimension of JHA, the Council of the European Union (2005f) outlined that the EU would need to work closer with non-EU partners in order to effectively fight terrorism and crime. It maintained that the AFSJ's development 'can only be successful if it is underpinned by a partnership with third countries' (Council of the European Union, 2005l). More recently, the EU-US Joint Statement on Enhancing Transatlantic Cooperation in the Area of Justice, Freedom and Security (Washington Statement) of 28 October 2009 emphasized both parties' commitment to a deepening of their cooperation 'in the pursuit of greater justice, freedom and security' (Council, 2009e). The statement promises a 'close operational partnership leading to international agreements and working arrangements between the US and Europol, Eurojust and Frontex, respectively, and the posting of liaison officers at each other's diplomatic representations and at Europol and Eurojust'. Yet despite this assuring rhetoric, several authors have pointed out severe differences between the US and the EU on CT-related matters.

Cooperation despite Diverging Threat Assessments

Cooperation on CT has not always been a smooth transatlantic endeavour. In 1999, Bruce Hoffman (1999: 73) summarized the two different conceptualizations of terrorism:

> America's problem with terrorism has historically been international in nature, while the opposite has mostly been the case in Europe. Hence, two inevitably very different perceptions of and, indeed, responses to the problem. Moreover, whereas the United States tends to regard counterterrorism as something akin to a moral crusade, Europeans are far more sceptical of blanket approaches and rigid policies and instead adopt what they see as more practical and…more productive approaches.

[6] Examples are the High Level Contact Group, the High Level Policy Dialogue on Borders and Transport Security, and the High Level Group on Data Protection.

As a consequence, Hoffman (1999: 64) argued that '(t)errorism has long been a source of friction between the United States and Europe'. These existing frictions were intensified in the aftermath of the 9/11 attacks. Observers pointed out, for example, that the 'the United States and Europe disagree on . . . the precise nature of the terrorist threat, the best methods for managing this threat, and the root causes of terrorism' (Shapiro and Byman, 2006: 34). To put it in a nutshell, while the US understands terrorism to be a threat of national security, the EU has a 'lower threat perception' (Rees, 2011: 160).

Some authors distinguished between a 'war' and a 'crime/law enforcement' approach. The US government understood al Qaeda's attack as a declaration of war against its state, and the Department of Defense coined its subsequent efforts at combating terrorism the 'Global War on Terrorism' (GWOT) (Bellinger, 2007).[7] The Former US Vice President Dick Cheney described the wide-ranging war approach well:

> Once you go into a wartime situation and it's a strategic threat, then you use all of your assets to go after the enemy. . . . You use your intelligence resources, your military resources, your financial resources, everything you can in order to shut down that terrorist threat against you. . . . When you go back to the law enforcement mode . . . [you] are very much giving up that center of attention and focus that's required, and that concept of military threat that is essential if you're going to successfully defend the nation against further attacks (CNN, 2009c).

While the rhetoric and tone has changed, to some extent, since President Obama came to office, the US government continued to perceive of its struggle with al Qaeda and related terrorist actors as a war-like situation which justified, for example, the assassination of Osama Bin Laden on 1 May 2011.

Yet especially Bush's aggressive war approach raised concerns by Europeans, in particular after the invasion of Iraq as of March 2003. The EU's High Representative Javier Solana contrasted Europe's position to that of America by stating that 'Europe is not at war' (as quoted in Tremlett and Black, 2004). Similarly emphasizing the European understanding of terrorism as a matter of criminal justice, the UK Director of Public Prosecutions, Sir Ken Macdonald, explained in the aftermath of the 2005 London bombings that 'London is not a battlefield. Those innocents who were murdered on 7 July 2005 were not victims of war. . . . On the streets of London, there is no such thing as a war on terror' (Bannerman, 2007). Once publicly revealed (though still fragmentarily), the US's most controversial CT policies, such as the CIA's extraordinary rendition campaign and the secret detention policy, were criticized sharply by some European politicians and media outlets. As MEP Sophie In't Veld (2010) emphasized, such topics 'have seriously undermined trust in transatlantic relations'. In a similar vein, then EU Counter-

[7] In March 2009, the Department of Defense replaced the term GWOT by the phrase 'Overseas Contingency Operations' (Wilson and Kamen, 2009).

terrorism Coordinator Gijs de Vries (2006) argued that 'Abu Ghraib, Guantanamo and CIA renditions have damaged America's standing in the world and have compromised our common struggle against terrorism'.

An emphasis on either a warfare or a crime-fighting approach has consequences for the types of political response. The American post-9/11 CT approach was driven by the assumption that terrorism can be *stopped*. Bush (2001) maintained that 'the only way to defeat terrorism as a threat to our way of life is to stop it, eliminate it, and destroy it where it grows'. Given their historical experience with political violence, Europeans see CT rather as a long-term campaign, emphasizing preventive measures to stop radicalization in the first place. A second difference was that the 'US has mainly chosen to fight its war on terror abroad, whereas the Europeans have focused primarily on the threat at home' (Keohane, 2008: 137). The EU has focused on home-grown terrorism earlier than the US which marginalized the topic in the immediate post-9/11 era. Overall, the American assumption was that American Muslims were better integrated or less vulnerable to radicalization than their European counterparts, given the small number of domestic terrorist incidences in the US.

To be sure, the US did not entirely neglect the topic. A July 2007 National Intelligence Estimate, titled 'The Terrorist Threat to the US Homeland', pointed out the risks of an increasing number of violent Islamic extremists on American soil, for instance. In a similar vein, DNI Mike McConnell testified before the Senate Select Committee on Intelligence on 5 February 2008 that, '(o)ver the next year, attacks by "homegrown" extremists inspired by militant Islamic ideology but without operational direction from al-Qa'ida will remain a threat to the United States or against U.S. interests overseas' (as quoted in United States Senate Committee on Homeland Security and Governmental Affairs, 2008: 3).

Yet a widespread realization that home-grown terrorism was an important issue for the US too only came with incidences in 2009 in which several American citizens used terrorist methods. Schmitt and Shanker (2011: 212) suggest that, in total, 'there have been more than forty plots involving American citizens or permanent residents in the ten years since the 9/11 attacks, and roughly half of these were launched in 2009 or 2010'. In autumn 2009, for example, the American citizen David Headley was charged with involvement in planning a terrorist attack against employees of *Jyllands Posten*, the Danish newspaper that published the Prophet Mohammed cartoons in 2005. A few months later, on 5 November 2009, US military psychiatrist Major Nidal Hasan killed thirteen people and wounded more than thirty at Fort Hood, Texas. And in December 2010, Antonio Martínez, a Baltimore construction worker, was charged with attempting to kill American military personnel by the bombing of a military recruiting station in Maryland.[8] Events such as these

[8] For studies on home-grown terrorism in the US since 9/11, see Jenkins, 2010; Bergen and Hoffman, 2010; Schmitt and Shanker, 2011; and Bjelopera, 2011.

> threw a spotlight on the reality of a two-way threat posed by violent radicals in both the US and Europe.... These events forced a rethinking of the prevailing wisdom that characterized earlier transatlantic counter-terrorism cooperation where US-EU cooperation was organized principally against an inbound threat from Europe to the United States (Laurence, 2010: 1).

In particular, the US has become concerned about 'lone wolf actors': terrorists operating alone and without a wider support group (Bjelopera, 2011).

Despite this slow approximation in the threat assessments concerning home-grown terrorism, the US government continues to prioritize the efforts 'to engage the potential terrorist threat as far from its shores as possible and rely upon a series of layered defences' (Rees, 2011: 159). As Rees (2011: 160–61) described:

> Law enforcement, intelligence, immigration and customs officers based overseas were its first line of defence, preventing dangerous individuals and goods embarking for America. Coastal protection, airline and border security were the next line of defence, preventing entry onto US soil.

In contrast, EU governments 'were much more focused on the threat within Europe and on preventing bombings like those carried out in Madrid in 2004 and in London in 2005.... The Europeans are much less willing to conduct major military operations around the globe to hunt down terrorists' (Keohane, 2008: 137).

Given the diverging threat perceptions, it is little surprise that the US and the EU differ in their chosen CT priorities and means. Comparing the US and EU Counter-terrorism Strategies, one could suggest that the EU puts more emphasis on preventive measure than the US which (also) aims at the defeat of terrorist organizations. Yet others have pointed out that, despite such diverging conceptualizations, 'basic American and European values and interests have not diverged' (Gordon, 2003: 74). In a recent statement, the Council (2011b) re-emphasized that '(t)he terrorist attacks of 11 September 2001 shook all of us profoundly and changed not only our perception of terrorism but also our comprehension of the world as we knew it'. Laura Donohue (2008: 10) rightly pointed out that neither the 'war' nor the 'crime' approach is exclusive, and that it should be rather understood as a 'broad framing' which 'may influence the source of authority claimed and the extremity of measures sought'. Hence, while the US approach puts more emphasis on military tools, the '"war on terror", like the "war on drugs," primarily involves policing, not conventional soldiering' (Andreas and Nadelmann, 2006: 4). On the other hand, the 2003 ESS maintains that 'dealing with terrorism may require a mixture of intelligence, police, judicial, military and other means'.

Crucially, both sides have continuously emphasized their commitment to CT cooperation in the twenty-first century. The US Counter-terrorism Strategy of June 2011 maintains that the US will support European governments in their CT efforts, where needed (White House, 2011). Moreover, what the discourse about the allegedly diverging CT approaches tends to conceal is that, despite the '(a)pparent conflict on long-term strategy for countering international terrorism', there has been 'a significant increase in actual transatlantic policy co-operation... in the aftermath of 9/11' (Peterson, 2004). The following section will illuminate some aspects of this cooperation.

Transatlantic Networks on Counter-terrorism

Operational cooperation concerning the fight against terrorism continues to be mainly conducted bilaterally. For example, the US has longstanding cooperative mechanisms with countries, such as the UK, Germany, and France. Still, transatlantic cooperation in this field remains difficult due to the fact that it comprises a range of policy areas, the sensitivity of the topic, and the overall secretiveness of the field. Given this complexity, one could suggest that the US ought to find it convenient to use the EU as 'a single point of contact, rather than interacting with twenty-seven different European legal systems and legislative frameworks' (Rees, 2011: 162). This also means, however, that the EU-US agreements in the field of CT, for example, concerning judicial cooperation, 'rather supplemented, but did not totally replace, existing bilateral arrangements' (Occhipinti, 2010: 175).

The post-9/11 era with its emphasis on information sharing has stimulated the creation of a range of transatlantic networks to facilitate the exchange of raw data as well as intelligence at all policy-levels. The effects of the 2001 attacks in the US have been profound on internal security actors on both sides of the Atlantic. Basically, it forced them 'to learn the habits of external cooperation and information sharing' (Rees, 2011: 162). Multilateral pooling and sharing of CT-related information, and homeland security more broadly, has become a priority. This section will briefly explore how the main transatlantic networks concerning information sharing to fight terrorism have evolved in the post-9/11 era.

Cooperation between Europol and US authorities

As outlined on page 111, the 1995 Joint EU-US Action Plan aimed at strengthening practical cooperation between the two parties in general, and US authorities and Europol in particular. Still, cooperation between Europol and American institutions remained sporadic until 11 September 2001. This changed immediately afterwards, when Europol's then Director Max-Peter Ratzel allowed the exchange of data—including personal data—with US authorities, despite the lack of any formal exchange agreement. According to Europol's then legal basis, the transmission of personal data to a third party was only permitted if based on a legal agreement. With other parties, with whom Europol did not have a formal information sharing agreement, it was only allowed under exceptional circumstances. This refers to situations in which Europol's Director deems the transmission of data as 'absolutely necessary to safeguard the essential interests of the MS concerned within the scope of Europol's objectives or in the interests of preventing imminent danger associated with crime' (Council, 1999a, Article 2(2); amended in 2002 (Council, 2002d)). Ratzel made the case that the 9/11 attacks would justify such a transmission of data 'due to the life threatening situation at that time' (Council, 2005g; see also Chapter 6). He announced that Europol 'would share any information related to the attacks with the United States', and Europol officials, 'for example, helped U.S. authorities check European phone numbers called by the alleged hijackers'. (Occhipinti, 2003: 166).

This informal arrangement between Europol and the US created the basis for further negotiations between the two parties. The negotiations were the most extensive between Europol and a third country so far. They concluded in a first agreement of 6 December 2001 on the exchange of both strategic and technical information in the fight against a broad range of forms of international crime. It also provided for the creation of liaison offices both in the US and EU, and Europol opened a liaison office in Washington in 2002. A supplementary agreement of 20 December 2002 concerned the exchange of personal data, including the sharing of specific information about individuals. The agreements between Europol and the USA became directly binding law.[9] Notably, while the Europol-US agreements were negotiated in the framework of fighting terrorism, their scope went beyond this purpose (Occhipinti, 2010: 176).

However, the US authorities quickly appeared to be disappointed about the depth of cooperation. The anticipation 'that Europol would provide EU wide analytical assessments about crime as well as information on particular transnational cases impacting on the USA' remained somewhat unfulfilled (Council, 2005g: 15). The FBI had posted a liaison officer at Europol's headquarters when the temporary Counter Terrorism Task Force was established, but the US officials were disappointed about the lack of information sharing via Europol and withdrew the liaison post after only three months (Council, 2005g). As a consequence, the US considered 'the actual added value gained by US law enforcement authorities through the application of the cooperation agreements between Europol and the USA is deemed to be limited' and continued to use direct channels with EU MS rather than through Europol (Council, 2005g). The overall complaint in 2005 was that '(a)ny added value that Europol can provide is either not perceived or is deemed out-weighed by the benefits to be derived from dealing with Member States directly' (Council, 2005g).

Yet, Europol's 2007 Annual Report listed four US liaison officers—apart from the FBI, the United States Secret Service, the Drug Enforcement Administration, and the US Postal Inspection Service are listed (Europol, 2008b: 84–85). While there are no US statistics available on the scope of transatlantic cooperation with Europol, the Europol US Liaison Office provided figures in a secret report, suggesting that 18.6 per cent of correspondence with US authorities concerned terrorism (Council, 2005g: Annex 3).

[9] The agreements are accessible via Europol's website.

Since then, Europol has been interlinked with US authorities in several ways. For example, features of the US-EU data sharing initiatives include 'a regular interchange between the US Department of Justice and Europol' (Rees, 2011: 166–67). Moreover, Europol became the EU oversight body for transatlantic data transfer under the umbrella of the Terrorist Finance Tracking Programme (TFTP). There are also more far-reaching plans under discussion. For example, the EU Coordinator has suggested that '(t)he US should be fully associated with relevant Europol projects and Analytical Work Files' (Council, 2010c).

Another field of mutual concern and intensified cooperation, in which Europol is increasingly involved, is the tackling of cyber crime. As Europol's Director, Rob Wainwright, explained:

> Cybercrime is borderless by nature—this also makes criminal investigations more complicated for law enforcement authorities. To effectively tackle cybercrime, adequate cross-border provisions are needed, and international cooperation and mutual assistance within EU law enforcement, and between the EU and third countries, needs to be enhanced (Europol, 2011f).

The internet is used as a strategic tool for terrorists and their supporters, for example with reference to the incitement of terrorism, recruitment, fund-raising, and potential attacks on critical infrastructures, such as energy production plants.

At the EU-US Summit of 20 November 2010, a Working Group on Cyber-Security and Cyber-Crime was established with the overall aim of tackling threats to the internet and digital networks (Council, 2010b). The priorities of the Working Group were agreed upon in April 2011. These include efforts to remove child pornography from the internet, a field which has previously been subject to considerable transatlantic cooperation. On 3 November 2011, the EU and US carried out their first joint cyber security exercise (Cyber Atlantic 2011).

Various actors are involved in fighting cyber crime on both sides of the Atlantic. The responsibilities within the US are split, in particular between the DHS and the Departments of Justice, State, and Commerce. Similarly, several EU institutions are involved in this area. Within the European Commission, for example, the Commissioner for Home Affairs is responsible for the policies on cyber crime and the Commission's Vice-President leads on cyber security. Yet on the operational side, Europol has become the leading institution.

The Stockholm Programme provided the basis for Europol's increasing engagement in the strategic analysis on cyber crime. Europol is involved in the European Cybercrime Task Force, for example. The task force's overall purpose is the facilitation of fighting cyber crime and it also comprises representatives of Eurojust and the European Commission (Europol, 2011a). Europol has released a first Threat Assessment on Internet Facilitated Organised Crime (iOCTA), an abridged version of which is publicly available. The iOCTA 'assesses current and future trends in cybercrime, and informs both operational activity and EU policy' (Europol, 2011a). Its cyber crime database can be used to provide MS 'with investigative and analytical support' (Europol, 2011a). The 2011 iOCTA outlines further plans to coordinate cyber crime—related reports by MS in this context, such as an Internet Crime Reporting Online System and an Internet & Forensic Expert Forum, are currently in development. Moreover, Europol has expressed an interest of being the host for the planned EU Cyber Crime Centre. This will be decided some time in 2012.

Apart from the cooperation between US authorities and Europol, a second major field of cooperation concerned airline security and the exchange of travel documents. The key features of this field will be explored in the following.

Airline security and travel documents

Aviation security, as Mark Salter (2008: 245) observed, comprises a 'complex web of state and non-state security actors that…provide security'. Prior to 9/11, the EU did not comprise of common aviation security regulations, but it set up a first regulatory framework for managing aviation security in the immediate aftermath. Commission officials, national institutions, and the European Aviation Safety Agency are involved. In addition, 'the European Civil Aviation Conference…engages in regular audits and provides assistance' for national authorities (Heng and McDonagh, 2011: 322).

The 2007 US National Strategy for Aviation Security proposes a 'risk-based, cross-discipline, and global approach to aviation security' (US DHS, 2007: 11). Already since the 1990s, the US government had used passenger lists to screen travellers and persons on watch-lists, or in whom they had some other interest, before they depart on a journey. In the aftermath of 9/11, the focus shifted to thwarting potential terrorists who are so far unidentified by using more of the detailed information collected by airlines and travel agencies when an individual books a flight (Chertoff, 2006). For this purpose, the US government introduced the US Aviation and Transportation Security Act on 19 November 2001 to collect data about passengers entering, transiting, or leaving the US by air. Air carriers, including European ones, were requested to provide the DHS and the Bureau of Customs and Border Protection with certain so-called Passenger Name Record (PNR) data. PNR data refer to the 'files created by the airlines for each journey any passenger books. They are stored in the airlines' reservation and departure control databases' (Europa, 2007). Among other things, the information refers to details about departure and return flights and special services required on board. The European Commission and the DHS finally signed an agreement on 28 May 2004, allowing for the transfer of thirty-four pieces of information about airline passengers of flights originating in the EU to US authorities, such as contact numbers, bank and credit card numbers, and home and e-mail addresses (Council, 2004g). Such information would be analysed in conjunction with current intelligence to identify high-risk travellers before they board their planes (House of Lords, EU Select Committee, 2007a: para 2). The information could be stored for up to three and a half years. As Chapter 7 will analyse in depth, the initial agreement was annulled on the basis of a judgment of the ECJ of 30 May 2006. A new EU-US agreement was finally signed on 29 June 2007 (Council, 2007g). In December 2010, the Council outlined for the Commission the negotiating guidelines for a further revision of the agreement. This process is still ongoing at the time of writing.[10]

The PNR agreements are a crucial part of a wider emerging transatlantic aviation security framework. One further feature was the controversial introduction of the US Visa Waiver Program (VWP) which requires individuals travelling to the US to have a biometric identifier in their (newly issued) passport. This requirement posed serious challenges for the EU's new MS. The VWP was finally expanded on 17 November 2008 to include the Czech Republic, Estonia, Hungary, Latvia, Lithuania, and the Slovak Republic; Malta was invited on 30 December 2008 (cf Occhipinti, 2010: 180–81). Yet in order to meet the requirements of the VWP, the European states

> had to complete bilateral deals with US on the exchange of DNA, fingerprints and other personal information for use in criminal or terrorist investigations.... (T)he new participants were also required to utilize the new pre-clearance programme, which became known as the Electronic System for Travel Authorization (ESTA) (Occhipinti, 2010: 181–82).

The recognition that there was an increasing threat of home-grown terrorism in Europe raised even further concerns about European travellers to the US. At a meeting in Toledo on 21 January 2010, the US and EU signed a Joint Declaration on Aviation Security. During the meeting, representatives of the Commission, the DHS, and European national ministries discussed 'current terrorists threats, in particular the attempted attack on an aircraft approaching Detroit on 25th December 2009, ways to strengthen international security measures and standards for aviation security, and an upcoming global dialogue on securing international travel' (US DHS, 2010).

As was the case with a few of the other initiatives described earlier in the chapter, the collaboration with American partners, originally based on a US security strategy, also led in this case to calls for an EU-wide system. An EU-wide PNR system was described by the EU Coordinator as

> an excellent example of the kind of information gathering which is needed to tackle the increasingly diversified nature of the terrorist threat. Patterns of travel, for example, which can be derived from visa and PNR information, offer a means of detecting and following people who travel to conflict zones for terrorist training and then return to Europe (Council, 2011a: 4).

In addition to strengthened security efforts concerning air travel, the US also stimulated efforts to secure cargo shipping, as will be briefly outlined in the next section.

---

[10] For a proposed Council Decision on the PNR agreement see Commission (2011b).

Container Security Initiative

In January 2002, the US Customs Service—which became the Bureau of Customs and Border Protection (CBP) in March 2003—launched the Container Security Initiative (CSI), aimed at addressing 'the threat to border security and global trade posed by the potential for terrorist use of a maritime container to deliver a weapon' (CBP website). The CSI is basically a pre-screening, or pre-clearance system. To avoid severe constraints at US ports by lengthy checks, the US officials decided to 'push out the border' (Koslowksi, 2006: 95). As part of the system, US customs officials are deployed at foreign ports. Together with local customs officials, they aim at detecting and inspecting high-risk cargo bound for the US. The cargo containers can then reach the US with all paperwork submitted prior to arrival (Andreas and Nadelmann, 2006: 208).

The US originally collaborated with eight European countries on a bilateral basis on this matter, based on CSI Statements of Principle. However, the European Commission eventually stepped in as the initiative concerned the single market. The negotiations between the Commission and the respective US authorities led to an EU-US agreement in November 2003. Currently, the CSI operates in fifty-eight ports worldwide, including ports in ten European countries, such as the UK, the Netherlands, Germany, and Italy. While the 2003 agreement is, in principle, reciprocal—European officials could be based at US ports, this has not happened in practice (Koslowksi, 2006: 96). The cooperation was intensified on the basis of a second agreement in 2004.

Further discussions took place in April 2004, when the US and the EU initiated the High Level Policy Dialogue on Borders and Transport Security. The US specified further rules in 2007, demanding a full pre-screening (the '100 per cent requirement'). However, in summer 2011 Homeland Security Director Janet Napolitano explained that the US would not insist on this at the moment (DW World, 2011). Pushed by the US government, customs cooperation remains high on the political agenda, however. For example, at the time of writing the two parties had roughly agreed on a Mutual Recognition of a Customs-Trade Partnership against Terrorism (C-TPAT), to be signed in spring 2012. The C-TPAT was developed by the US as a public-private cooperation, aiming at the approximation of standards concerning security requirements in cargo trade, in particular with respect to the private industry.

Yet another area of concern is the fight against terrorist financing. Again, this is an example of a network effort which also includes private actors to a considerable extent.

Terrorist Finance Tracking Programme

To detect and track terrorist suspects, or their financial donors, the US Treasury implanted the TFTP, a programme that concerns the collection of financial transaction data. The arrangement concerned the Society for Worldwide Interbank Financial Telecommunication (SWIFT), a company which 'handles about 80 per cent of all global wire transfer traffic' (De Goede, 2011: 3). Though SWIFT is based in Belgium, it owns a data processing centre in the US. The TFTP allows its staff—by means of administrative data—to request data concerning financial transactions from this SWIFT centre (Monar, 2010: 143). While the majority of SWIFT's data concerns European customers, Americans and others are also affected.

An evaluation pointed out that the results of inquiries under the umbrella of the TFTP, shared with European authorities, have supported several terrorist investigations. According to an EU-restricted report, TFTP information 'provided new leads, corroborated identities, and revealed relationships among individuals responsible for this terrorist plot' in the aftermath of the London bombings (Bruguiére, 2010). Another example concerns the attempt to bring down transatlantic flights using liquid explosives in 2006, in the aftermath of which 'TFTP information provided information which assisted in the investigation and conviction of individuals responsible for this attempted attack' (Bruguiére, 2010).

The ways in which the data was checked and transferred suggests a close collaboration between American officials and SWIFT personnel. De Goede (2011: 7) describes the process of networking well:

> American Treasury officials are not given complete access to SWIFT database, but sets of data are selected by SWIFT, 'black-boxed' and made accessible to the officials. Treasury searches continue to be supervised by security-cleared, SWIFT employees, called 'scrutineers', who have 'round-the-clock' and 'real-time' access to the justification for individual searches, and the power to query or block Treasury's searches.

When the *New York Times* brought this data transfer initiative to the attention of the wider public, the EP and civil rights organizations criticized the arrangement sharply, emphasizing that American officials had easy access to Europeans' financial transfers (De Goede, 2011: 2). The Working Party 29 reported in November 2006 'that the data transfer procedure from SWIFT to the United States Treasury entailed a "lack of transparency and adequate and effective control mechanisms", representing "a serious breach" of the EU Data Protection Directive' (De Goede, 2011: 4). After lengthy discussions, in particular focusing on data protection issues, a revised agreement between the EU and the US on the exchange of such financial information was achieved in 2010. Despite ongoing concerns about transparency and judicial supervision of the transatlantic programme, the European Commission (2011c) proposed in July 2011 the creation of an EU-wide Terrorist Finance Tracking System.

To demonstrate the wide range of network-like structures and initiatives which have evolved in the post-9/11 era, the following sub-section will briefly outline a network in the field of intelligence.

Extraordinary rendition campaigns

The final CTN which will be explored in this chapter concerns the CIA-led extraordinary rendition and secret detention programme. On 26 September

2002, Cofer Black (2002), Director of the CIA's Counter-terrorist Center from 1999 until May 2002, explained to the Congressional Joint Inquiry Into 9/11 that he would only say so much about the operational side of the agency's CT programmes: 'This is a highly classified area. All I want to say is that there was "before" 9/11 and "after" 9/11. After 9/11 the gloves come off.' While the CIA had been conducting renditions before the terrorist attacks, a classified Presidential Decision Directive of 17 September 2001 reportedly widened the rendition activities by providing for the creation of overseas detention facilities for interrogations (see also CIA Inspector General, 2004). The rendered individuals are either handed over to national authorities of third countries or transferred to a secret overseas prison run by the CIA (a so-called black site). While the CIA is the leading party, it cooperates with foreign state authorities (eg, intelligence, police, and border personnel) as well as private companies which are, for example, providing and staffing planes or consulting the CIA on interrogation techniques. At the CIA-run black sites, interrogators question the detainee, often using harsh methods, and several former detainees have alleged that they were mistreated and/or tortured while interrogated by CIA officials (eg, International Committee of the Red Cross, 2007). As the case of Abu Omar, which was briefly sketched in the Introduction to this book, indicated, several individuals who have been subject to the extraordinary rendition and secret detention programme of the CIA were residents or citizens of a European state.

An inquiry by the CoE described the US efforts as a global 'spider's web' of rendition flights and alleged that fourteen European governments allowed the web to spread over Europe, participating in the CIA's programme (namely Sweden, Bosnia-Herzegovina, the UK, Italy, the former Yugoslav Republic of Macedonia, Germany, Turkey, Poland, Romania, Spain, Cyprus, Ireland, Portugal, and Greece) (Marty, 2006: para 284ff). The form of involvement varied: some European officials were either involved in the preparation of the abduction, the rendition process itself, or the preparation and conduct of interrogations at a secret detention (Hillebrand, 2009). Others simply tolerated secretive actions by the CIA on their territory. The follow-up report concluded that there is factual evidence that the CIA operated secret detention centres for some years in Poland and Romania (Marty, 2007c).

The examples of transatlantic CTNs provided in this section illustrate the complex pattern of transatlantic initiatives in this field which have emerged since late 2001, in particular. At several points, the discussion has already hinted at the question of whether the US-EU cooperation is always one between two equal partners or, rather, whether it is driven and dominated by the American CT agenda. This question will be addressed in the following section.

Equal Partners?

Some of the high-ranking EU officials who have been interviewed for this research described the US as the 'foremost partner of the EU in the fight against terrorism' and described the overall EU-US CT cooperation as 'excellent' (Interviews X, M). Moreover, the brief evaluation of the major US-EU initiatives in this field confirms a mutual interest on CT cooperation in the US and EU. As described in Chapter 1, a mutual interest is crucial for the creation and continuous work of CTNs. Nevertheless, the analysis in this chapter suggests that some of these networks appear to be dominated by the US, suggesting rather unequal network-like relationships.

To some extent, this appears to be a matter of resources, structures, and size. The American CT apparatus is enormous in comparison to that of the EU, but also that of European governments. There is no convincing comparative study on CT spending, partly because it is so difficult to estimate the budgets in this secretive field but also because of the overlap between CT measures and other security efforts. Still, the dimensions of the American and the EU budgets are simply worlds apart. It has been suggested that the US spent over one trillion US dollars on CT since 2001, excluding the costs of the wars in Iraq and Afghanistan (Mueller and Stewart, 2011: 2). The total EU spending on CT measures has been estimated to have grown from around €5.7 million in 2002 to around €93.5 million in 2009—this excludes any spending by the MS (Wensink et al, 2011). Such differences obviously result in greatly varying capabilities and they also lead to structural imbalances between the two actors (Argomaniz, 2009: 120).

Moreover, the US has been more determined and proactive in its emphasis on international data sharing and other CT efforts. This was embedded in a CT strategy which quickly developed in the aftermath of the 9/11 attacks. The EU, although demonstrating activism right after the attacks, has been slower in developing a wider strategy, as outlined in Chapter 1. Concerning most transatlantic CTP initiatives, 'the EU has found itself reacting to a US agenda that it has been unable to influence' (Rees, 2011: 162). In the case of airline security and the CSI, for example, the US 'initially bypassed the EU level' when negotiating arrangements with European partners on a bilateral basis (Occhipinti, 2010: 178). Moreover, with regard to airline security, the TFTP, and the CSI, the US imposed new, or revised guidelines unilaterally (see also Occhipinti, 2010: 177–178).

Several European interviewees have critically maintained that information sharing between US and EU authorities in the field of CT has been rather a one-way street. Concerning the exchange with Europol, it was said that the '(t)he US wants to get everything', but that the information flow *from* the US was very limited (Interview V). Similarly, interviewees pointed out that there was a wider 'imbalance' concerning transatlantic information sharing, one of them stating that '(w)ith the US, it is never an equal cooperation' for the EU in the field of CT (Interviews V, L). In this context, another interviewee emphasized the differences in how information is classified and evaluated in the US and the EU (Interview X): US authorities tend to share information with very low security classification only, while the EU is much less restricted. According to the interviewee, US agencies tend to classify much more information than their European counterparts, which causes problems concerning the fulfilment of existing agreements regarding information exchange (see also Ratcliffe, 2008: 229; Roberts, 2006: 141ff; Zegart, 2007: 90). Referring to the fact that a certain piece of information is classified, the US partners would often refuse to share it with their European counterparts. With respect to agreements on information exchange, this can easily lead to an imbalanced handling of the agreement, which one party might understand to be unfair.

Yet the imbalance of EU-US networks goes even further. What has become apparent in the analysis of transatlantic CTNs in the field of data sharing is that, in various cases, the continuous efforts of US authorities at ensuring law enforcement cooperation with the European partners must be described as a strategy of 'coercive co-optation involving a mix of sticks and carrots' (Andreas and Nadelmann, 2006: 220). The 'carrots' are usually offers 'of preferential access and other privileges to those who did comply' (Andreas and Nadelmann, 2006: 220). The stick can be the denial of entries into the US. This has been the case with respect to air security, for example. At times, the US appeared to have put pressure on individual EU countries to push EU-wide initiatives, for example in the context of the VWP and the PNR agreements (Interview Z). The stick can also stand for the threat that the EU would pose European lives at risk if it would not agree to a certain CT initiative. Concerning the rejection of the SWIFT Interim Agreement, US Treasury Undersecretary Stuart Levey warned that the loss of the TFTP 'would be a deeply regrettable and potentially tragic mistake' allowing 'undetected and undeterred' terrorists 'to abuse the integrity and openness of the world's financial system' (as quoted in Monar, 2010: 148). In May 2010, US Vice-President Joe Biden argued before the EP: 'The longer we are without an agreement on the Terrorist Finance Tracking Programme, the greater the risk of a terrorist attack that could have been prevented' (White House, 2010).

From the analysis in this chapter of the transatlantic CTNs, it appears that the EU tends to be very—and some observers would say, too—attentive and acceptant when it comes to US-led initiatives concerning the policing of terrorism. This observation is in accordance with Anne-Marie Slaughter's (2009: 113) suggestion that the US will be the 'central player in an integrated world' that creates and leads transnational networks, decides on who is included and who is not, and determines the agenda.

Concerning EU-US CT cooperation, the EU had to adopt responses to terrorism in the post-9/11 era that 'did not fit easily with the European threat perceptions and strategy of response' (Argomaniz, 2009: 120). Examples of this include the CIA extraordinary rendition programme, the PNR agreements, and the CSI. In this regard, there can be little doubt that the EU had to adopt security practices and CT measures that have been literally 'made in the USA' (Pawlak, 2009). Argomaniz (2009) therefore suggested to understand the EU as a 'norm-taker' in the context of the PNR agreements: the EU adopted the norms established by US border security and did little to oppose the dominant US position in these negotiations. The debate is an illuminating example of the impact that negotiations with non-EU countries potentially have on the EU's internal security framework and practices. An MEP described the influence of the US government on the decision-making at EU level with regard to security measures in the fight against terrorism, including PNR exchange, as 'massive' (Interview J). As Argomaniz (2009: 126ff) has argued, the PNR agreements do not refer to a partnership, but an asymmetric relationship. He points out that

> the transmission of air passenger data to the US had never been part of the EU antiterrorist agenda until the unilateral US authorities' decision to oblige European carriers to provide this data. PNR exchange had been neither part of the EU antiterrorist action plan nor previously discussed in JHA meetings (Argomaniz, 2009: 125).

Moreover, Bush's list containing areas suitable for fostering transatlantic CT, produced on invitation by the President of the European Council, was criticized by some observers. Statewatch (2001) described it as 'a sweeping agenda covering unregulated and unaccountable powers affecting criminal investigations, suspects' rights, the retention of telecommunications data, border controls and asylum policies'. Pawlak (2009: 10) suggested that the incident clearly 'demonstrated that American involvement in EU security policies remains a sensitive topic'. Asked about the influence the US has on EU CT-related decision-making, one interviewee stated that originally 'European governments nearly blindly follow[ed] the Bush administration with regard to counter-terrorism' (Interview J). Similarly, giving the examples of the VWP, PNR, and data protection, other interviewees said that 'there is a lot of pressure by the US' concerning EU decision-making on CT (Interview L). Yet the US itself appears to grant not much room for external influence on its policy processes (Pawlak, 2009; Rees, 2011: 161).

The US government had an indirect impact on some European CT initiatives by presiding over the G8 in 2004, as G8

> recommendations were typically introduced at the EU-wide level through the group's EU members. Critics saw this as a prime example of 'policy laundering': the utilization of U.S.-dominated international forums that lacked transparency and democratic oversight as a vehicle to promote more invasive policy measures that would otherwise fail to be approved via traditional domestic political procedures (Andreas and Nadelmannn, 2006: 220).

The influence that the US can play out through transatlantic CTNs is more direct and profound. The negotiations about certain CT tools and demands concerning information sharing had an impact on the EU's agenda and the ways in which CTP has been approached in the aftermath of 9/11. Such powerful influence is not an entirely new phenomenon in the field of transatlantic cooperation on JHA matters. Nadelmann (1993b) referred to an early example where Europeans rejected US drug enforcement undercover methods, but incorporated them eventually into European policing practices. Some CT tools, originally developed in the EU-US context, have been, or are likely to become models for cooperation with other partners—one example is the EU-Canada PNR agreement of 2005 (Interview M). Finally, several of the US-led initiatives have stimulated similar arrangements within the EU, as has been the case concerning the TFTP. As a consequence, one observer described the US as an 'agenda-setter' (Pawlak, 2009: 1).

Given the powerful position of the US concerning the EU's field of CTP and the fact that the EU appears to have comparatively little influence on the American CT agenda, the question of how to scrutinize the collaborative activities becomes even more urgent. Drawing on scrutiny procedures concerning the extraordinary programme, the remainder of the chapter will emphasize some of the major general challenges in this respect. The following two chapters will then explore more specific aspects of both parliamentary and judicial scrutiny concerning CTNs.

Challenges for scrutiny

Opening up information sharing networks to new partners raises serious questions about the democratic scrutiny of the arrangements. Given the understanding of the US that terrorism is rather a matter of national security than criminal justice, one of the effects is that more and more 'aspects of criminal justice associated with counter-terrorism take on the level of secrecy associated with national security' (McCulloch and Pickering, 2009: 638). For scrutiny bodies, information sharing in such a secretive field poses challenges to their own 'information gathering', ie, for the collection of evidence, both with respect to factual information and to witnesses. While those institutions have been sporadically exposed to those challenges before, nowadays there seems to be an increase of terrorism-related court trials with an international dimension, and an increasing international dimension of parliamentary inquiries (or inquiries by independent commissions initiated) can be observed (Neumann, 2009; Eurojust, 2008). One illuminating example is the court trial in Milan, Italy, concerning the 'extraordinary rendition' of Abu Omar.[11]

After five years of investigation, a ruling of the Milan court on 4 November 2009 turned the case into 'the first in the world in which CIA operatives have been tried for their role in capturing prisoners abroad and illegally transferring them to other countries after the 11 September terrorist attacks' (Goetz and Sandberg, 2009). Observers of the closing remarks by state prosecutor Armando Spataro argued that it 'has rarely been possible to reconstruct an undercover CIA operation in such minute detail' (Goetz and Sandberg, 2009). Twenty-two Americans, all on trial *in absentia*, were found guilty, twenty-one of them sentenced to five years and one to eight years. Three Americans were granted diplomatic immunity from prosecution and the cases against them were dismissed. While two Italians were sentenced to three years for aiding the plot, the cases against the former head of Italy's military intelligence service SISMI and his deputy were dismissed because of state security provisions (CNN, 2009a). As the Italian government declined to seek the extradition of the Americans from the US, it is

[11] So far, this has been the only extensive trial of a European court which explored a rendition case in full and clearly identified the parties involved in the rendition.

unlikely they will ever have to serve their sentence. Early on in the investigation, Spataro argued that the

> kidnapping of Abu Omar was not only a serious crime against Italian sovereignty and human rights, but it also seriously damaged counterterrorism efforts in Italy and Europe... In fact, if Abu Omar had not been kidnapped, he would now be in prison, subject to a regular trial, and we would have probably identified his other accomplices (as quoted in Whitlock, 2005).

Yet the prosecutor had to face serious hurdles during the investigation. Crucially, Italy's Constitutional Court ruled in March 2009 that several pieces of evidence were classified as state secrets and that their disclosure could harm national security. The state secrets privilege works similarly in other Western countries, basically allowing the respective governments 'to resist court-ordered disclosure of information during litigation if there is a reasonable danger that such disclosure would harm the national security' (Liu, 2009: 1). As a consequence, all documents referring to connections between SISMI and the CIA in the context of this investigation were classified, and Spataro could not make use of a considerable amount of his evidence (Goetz and Sandberg, 2009). He argued in his closing remarks that '(c)lassifying documents as state secrets cannot, in a democracy, be accepted as a pretext for covering up a kidnapping' (Goetz and Sandberg, 2009). In addition to those restrictions, Spataro had to face personal challenges:

> his phone has been tapped, SISMI has placed him under surveillance and the agency has planted moles in his immediate surroundings. The Italian intelligence agency has even asked journalists to sound out the details of his inquiries... He has even been investigated on suspicion of betraying state secrets (Goetz and Sandberg, 2009).

A crucial challenge the court had to face concerned aspects of state secrecy. On the one hand, as described earlier in this chapter, the US understands terrorism to be a matter of national security. On the other hand, the rendition campaigns are activities by intelligence services—the CIA, in the case of the US. As a consequence, the sensitivity of the material and the overall secrecy of the field put considerable hurdles on any investigations. For example, on 23 September 2009, the US granted court trial immunity to one of the American then suspects, Air Force Colonel Joseph Romano, in the Milan case. The government invoked jurisdiction under NATO's Status of Forces Agreement which 'applies to suspected crimes overseas by military personnel performed "in the course of official duty"' (Stewart, 2009). Those immunity clauses had been criticized by the CoE's rapporteur Dick Marty (2006, 2007c) in his reports on European involvement in the CIA's extraordinary rendition campaign. The Milan case is remarkable—and unique—in this context. The Italian Minister of Justice supported the decision of court trial immunity by the US. However, the Court decided to ignore this: Romano did not escape a conviction and is one of the Americans convicted (CNN, 2009a). Due to the European Arrest Warrant, the convicted Americans cannot travel to an EU country without risking their surrender to Italy.

Similar to some other inquiries into cases of extraordinary rendition, the Milan case referred to a

> general principle or convention that intelligence information received by one State from another will not be released into the public domain or otherwise used without the consent of the state supplying it. This principle is often referred to as the 'principle of control over intelligence'... (*Mohamed v Secretary of State* (2009): point 15i[12]).

A separate court case in London, related to an alleged case of extraordinary rendition concerning Binyam Mohamed, led judges to reject the notion that this is an absolute principle, however, as 'it is a convention as opposed to a matter of legal obligation. It clearly does not have the status of a rule of customary international law' (*Mohamed v Secretary of State* (2009): point 71).

While the peculiar nature of the extraordinary rendition cases might challenge scrutiny procedures to an unusual extent, it has become clear nevertheless that cooperation with foreign partners poses particular challenges. Crucially, the excessive degree of secrecy causes serious problems for scrutiny bodies. The investigations into such actions are hampered by a mixture of legal barriers (invoking the state secrecy privilege), claims that the release of information would harm national security and, potentially, personal threats against the inquiring personnel (as it was the case during the investigations in Milan). The fact that these activities often involve national security intelligence—in contrast to purely criminal intelligence—makes such cases extremely lengthy and complicated. The final statement of the prosecutor in Milan involved in the case of Abu Omar took fifteen hours to read out—an indication of the meticulous work that is necessary to present sufficient and coherent evidence in such cases.

Building on these findings, the following two chapters will analyse parliamentary and judicial scrutiny procedures in length, taking into account several of the empirical cases outlined in this chapter. As the chapter has outlined, CT cooperation across the Atlantic has become a crucial component of the complex US-EU security relationship. The CT cooperation between the EU and the US appears to be similarly governed to the EU-wide cooperation in this field, with an emphasis on flexibility, informality, and speed (see also Pawlak, 2010). Working in network-like structures allows for a pragmatic approach: information sharing and other types of cooperation can take place without the 'nodes' necessarily agreeing about all details. Yet the EU and US appear not be equal partners in this endeavour. The evidence used in this chapter strongly indicates that the respective US authorities are the much more powerful network members, compared to their EU counterparts. A major concern arises from the fact that the transatlantic cooperation might be even less subject to scrutiny than EU-wide efforts. The following chapters will also shed some light on this matter.

[12] *Mohamed, R (on the application of) v Secretary of State for Foreign and Commonwealth Affairs* [2009] EWCH 2549 (Admin).

6

The Parliamentary Scrutiny of European Counter-terrorism Cooperation

The previous chapters have drawn the picture of a changing pattern of European CTP. As Neyroud and Beckley (2007: 3) have pointed out: if the *context* of policing is changing, so are the *challenges*. In a time when '(n)ational boundaries are more and more irrelevant' (Neyroud and Beckley, 2007: 13) in the prevention and detection of crime, one such key challenge for the democratic legitimacy of CTP concerns the question of parliamentary scrutiny of the related policies and activities.

In Europe, executive bodies, such as police and intelligence authorities, and their activities are overseen and controlled within the domestic framework. A very important dimension of this refers to the scrutiny of the executive by parliamentary bodies. This also applies to the realm of CT and the related actors, structures, policies, and overall performance, as outlined in Chapter 2. Parliamentary scrutiny ought to ensure the accountability to a democratically representative elected body 'capable of determining the broad direction of policy' (Morgan and Newburn, 1997: 196). The actors are to give an account of their actions or policies and to outline and, if necessary, justify certain strategies, practices, or institutions (Simmons, 1999: 740). Although the individual scrutiny powers and mechanisms of parliaments vary, accountability to parliaments is often understood as the most important form of accountability in democratic regimes (eg Bovens, 2007b).

However, the increasing processes of Europeanization/internationalization of policing challenge such national scrutiny arrangements or, at least, suggest their reach to be insufficient. Increased information sharing and joint analysis efforts as well as the proliferation of liaison networks and international teams, whether they are based on bi- or multilateral agreements, present challenges to domestically oriented scrutiny frameworks. In addition, the pattern of European policing incorporates several different levels: the cooperation takes place partly within the EU, partly among the Schengen states only, partly bilaterally between individual countries, and partly beyond the EU (Schulte, 2001: 146). This mixture of activities and levels is accompanied by an increasing involvement of intelligence services in policing, in particular with respect to combating terrorism (Neyroud and Beckley, 2007: 14).

The aim of this chapter is to explore the powers, functions, and degree of involvement of parliaments in scrutinizing such complex collaborative patterns, with a particular focus on EU CT cooperation. To analyse parliamentary involvement in such a policy field includes two key dimensions, namely the extent of participation of parliamentarians and the degree of parliamentary control and oversight (Borrás and Conzelmann, 2007). From a perspective of democratic governance, the involvement of parliamentarians refers to the idea of a parliament as a forum where questions of values and principles involved in policy choices can be debated, dilemmas are resolved, and questions at stake are brought closer to citizens (Tsakatika, 2007: 554–55). Parliamentary accountability, on the other hand, can be understood as an authoritative democratic check on rule-making (Tsakatika, 2007: 554). This includes supervisory functions such as the monitoring and reviewing of the actions of executive bodies (Griffith, 2005). Concerning police and intelligence cooperation, the power to oversee the budget, and thus public funds, is a crucial feature of oversight.

With respect to the EU's decision-making process, parliamentary scrutiny refers to the impact and the powers of parliamentary bodies at the EU as well as at the national level. Consequently, the roles of the EP as well as the NPs will be analysed by means of illustrative examples. In the first section, the originally 'consultative' role of the EP and NPs concerning PJCC is briefly discussed, with a particular focus on European CT cooperation. This is followed by an exploration of several empirical examples to illustrate in greater detail current specific challenges for parliamentary scrutiny with respect to EU-wide CT cooperation and between the EU and non-EU partners. To complete the picture, the third section will briefly discuss (potential) forms of cooperation between parliamentary actors.

The Role of Parliaments in the Scrutiny of the Field of PJCC

The provisions of the 1993 TEU, as described in Chapter 1, provided for formal and systematic cooperation of the EU MS in the area of JHA. Since internal security issues are deeply interwoven with the concept of national sovereignty, the TEU introduced an intergovernmental 'European Union method', which required unanimous agreement of all MS in the Council of Ministers (House of Commons, Home Affairs Committee, 2007: para 40). While some AFSJ policies experienced a change of decision-making process through the Amsterdam Treaty, the area of PJCC remained intergovernmentally organized.

The Lisbon Treaty provided for substantial changes. By 'merging' the first and third pillar, matters of PJCC 'move[d] into the generally applicable mechanisms of the Union' (House of Lords, EU Select Committee, 2008: point 2.4). This has a considerable impact on the institutional balance of the decision-making process in this field, strengthening, in particular, the role of the EP in it. Yet PJCC remains to a considerable extent in the hands of the MS, through their Ministries of Justice and of the Interior, given the remaining dominant role of the Council in this area. The Council still holds most of the power in this field, although other Community institutions are increasingly involved as well, in particular the Commission (Spence, 2007b: 9; Kaunert, 2006). In the following, the EP's role concerning PJCC will be discussed.

From the marginalization of the European Parliament toward the Lisbon Treaty

The fact that, prior to the Lisbon Treaty, the policy field of PJCC was intergovernmentally organized, prevented serious involvement from the EP whose powers and capabilities to scrutinize this policy field were strictly limited. Yet, in comparison to the time before, the Amsterdam Treaty of 1999 provided the EP with a few more competencies in the then third pillar. Crucially, Article 39 TEU required the Council to consult the EP before it adopts any legally binding measures under the third pillar. This had to happen at least three months in advance, so that the EP had time to deliver its opinion. However, the EP's opinions were non-binding documents: the Council had to hear the EP's opinion about any legally binding measures, but it was not obliged to take any suggested amendments into account. Given the sometimes short time for the EP to provide an opinion and the freedom of the Council to ignore this, the EP's role concerning agreements under this pillar was very limited. Moreover, the procedures described earlier 'reduce(d) the opportunities for public debate' (Balzacq, 2008: 93–94). Similarly, the EP's powers concerning the control and oversight of Europol were strictly limited under the Europol Convention (Anderson, 1995: 254). There was no formal mechanism for direct parliamentary scrutiny by the EP. As Europol's budget was based on intergovernmental financing, the EP also had no 'power of the purse' in this context.

The implementation process of the EU CT policy presents a striking example of the fact that the EP remained largely excluded from policies under the then third pillar. In that process, the EP had merely consultative powers (Monar, 2005a: 450). In its first two sittings following the 9/11 attacks, the EP agreed 'on the need to strengthen the repression of terrorist acts through the reinforcement of the international cooperation in the field of gathering and processing information, and the harmonisation of judicial and legal systems' (Tsoukala, 2004). An MEP pointed out that there was an overall agreement in the EP that the EU should become a more active player concerning CT (Interview F). However, no particular measures of legal acts were discussed during those two sessions after 9/11, and the EP had little impact on the following decision-making process.

The Lisbon Treaty brought substantial changes to the EP's role concerning matters of the former third pillar. The handling of this area is now more in line with normal EU procedures, where the Commission makes proposals and the EP and the Council co-legislate on equal footing (including qualified majority voting in the Council). Concerning matters of PJCC, legislative proposals can be made by MS numbering at least one-quarter of the total—currently seven MS. This means certain MS could proceed with measures of PJCC while others would not participate.

While parliaments have gained an explicit mandate in overseeing Europol through the Lisbon Treaty, Article 88 of the TFEU maintains that the EP and the Council have to 'lay down the procedures for scrutiny of Europol's activities by the European Parliament, together with national Parliaments'. This is an ongoing process, with a new Europol Regulation to be expected in the next few years. A crucial change in the EP's role concerning the oversight of Europol already came with the institutional transfer of Europol to an EU agency. This move implied that the EP has now budgetary appropriation and discharge functions, as Europol's revenues are now entered in the EU's general budget (cf Wills et al., 2011: 177–178).

Moreover, the Lisbon Treaty provides for a potentially considerable extension of the EP's powers concerning the external sphere of PJCC. According to Article 218(6) of the TFEU, the Council has to obtain the consent of the EP with respect to agreements between the Union and third countries or international organizations (unless the agreement concerns exclusively the common foreign and security policy). In practice, this means that the EP has now the right to veto the conclusion of such agreements.

While it remains to be seen how the EP will use this new power in the long term, it gave a flavour of it when it rejected the EU-US SWIFT agreement on the sharing of financial data in February 2010, despite the strong support by the Council and the Commission. The vote was described as 'one of the so far not so many historic votes of the Parliament on an EU external relations issue' (Monar, 2010: 143). Following the EP's rejection of the original agreement, a new EU-US agreement was concluded in June 2010, 'including enhanced stipulations concerning the protection of data and the right of redress for citizens' (De Goede, 2011: 2). In this case, the EP has demonstrated that, although it is not formally involved in the negotiation process and therefore has a limited role in the context of international agreements, nevertheless 'some democratic oversight has finally been introduced over what was hitherto a matter purely of closed diplomatic negotiations at the European level' (Curtin, 2011: 23). Monar (2010: 149) optimistically argues that 'the Council and Commission will from now on have to give more consideration to the principles of necessity and proportionality as regards the use of personal data for international law enforcement cooperation purposes'.

The role of the National Parliaments

All NPs—forty parliamentary chambers in twenty-seven countries—maintain individual procedures by which to scrutinize EU affairs. While the processes vary, the overall purpose for all of them is 'to reinforce democratic control over EU matters and to ensure democratic accountability in EU decision making' (Conference of Parliamentary Committees for Union Affairs of Parliaments of the European Union (COSAC) website—'scrutiny'). Most of the parliaments have established a committee on European affairs, which is sometimes supported and/or advised by sectoral (sub-)committees. Scrutiny is either exercised through a 'document based' system focusing on the examination of EU documents, such as legislative proposals, or it is based on a 'mandating model', which allows the respective Committee to 'give a direct mandate to their governments before ministers can endorse legislation in Council meetings' (COSAC, 2005; for an overview on the different systems see COSAC, 2007: 14–19). Some parliaments have developed a hybrid model and a few have chosen 'more informal channels of influence' (COSAC, 2007: 7).

With respect to matters concerning PJCC before the Lisbon Treaty, the role of the NPs has been described as a 'non-role' (Lodge, 2007) given the severe limitations and restrictions parliaments experienced concerning matters of policing, also with respect to the scrutiny of CTP. In addition, there is a trade-off between the powers of the EP and the NPs. While the TEU had granted the EP the right to be consulted in this field, '(i)n practice the European Parliament received laws only after they have been enacted by the Council. Normally, its national counterparts had better opportunities to influence the legislation processes in the third pillar, due to the unanimity requirement' (Lummer, 2008a).[1] Over time, however, the NPs lost powers to the EP in some areas of the AFSJ, as the decision-making mode concerning several aspects—most notably issues of immigration and asylum—was changed from unanimity to qualified majority voting in the Council as of 1993. This meant that NPs 'could now no longer influence decisions at EU level by pressuring their governments to veto a certain law' (Lummer, 2008a). Overall, it is fair to argue that, over time, the 'EP was more successful than the NPs in gaining powers of scrutiny, co-decision and access to the levers of power' (Lummer, 2008a) concerning the AFSJ. Notably, the Lisbon Treaty introduced the co-decision procedure to measures concerning PJCC.

However, the national constitutions, or quasi-constitutional frameworks, provide for different rights of parliaments. Parliamentary powers vary with respect

[1] Each MS has a right of veto under the unanimity rule and the rule can therefore be used to block the decision-making process.

to the access to AFSJ-relevant information, the involvement in discussions of draft EU decisions, and the overall influence they have over their governments concerning decision-making in this field. While 'some NPs are confronted with a lack of formal participation rights,... others enjoy extensive information and participatory rights' (Lummer, 2008b). Generally speaking, NPs did not have 'prior power to become involved in the *negotiation* of Conventions, Protocols or implementing measures' (Peers, 2005: 203; emphasis in original) concerning PJCC, whereas the EP had at least the right to give an opinion on legislative proposals.

As a consequence of those different procedures, the level of information of NPs concerning matters related to the AFSJ varied immensely. Overall, NPs tended to receive the relevant EU documents at a pretty late stage of the negotiations. This was further complicated by the overall lack of information they received about the complicated and technical policy process on the EU level (see also Lummer, 2008a). To improve this, the 1999 Treaty of Amsterdam had already attached a legally binding protocol on the role of parliaments in the EU which required a better flow of information to the NPs and that EU documents should be forwarded to parliaments immediately, for example. The lack of information and the unwillingness of authorities to provide evidence in parliament or in public were even more severe concerning the sensitive area of CT.

Detailed comparative information about the ways in which NPs scrutinize matters of police cooperation is hard to find. A rare exception is the 2008 questionnaire that the Secretariat of the Conference of Community and European Affairs Committees of Parliaments of the European Union (COSAC) circulated among NPs to inquire into their scrutiny procedures of the Schengen process (COSAC, 2008: Annex). The questionnaire was driven by the question as to whether the particular sensitivity of the issues, which were touching on questions of asylum, security, and individual freedoms, had pushed the NPs to reinforce their general scrutiny procedures of EU policies in this particular area (COSAC, 2008: ch 4 and Annex). The result was that most NPs, including the German and the Belgian ones, continued to use their normal scrutiny procedures which are usually not binding for the government in question. The report distinguished between *direct* and *indirect* involvement of parliaments. Direct involvement refers to NPs which express their views to their respective government about an issue *prior* to the meetings of the JHA Council, as is the case in Finland, Sweden, and the Polish *Sjem*. Other NPs control their government in a more indirect manner, for example by providing an opinion on the basis of an EU text submitted by their government or by simply exchanging information with their government (eg, both French chambers and the National Assembly of the Republic of Slovenia). Such an exchange can happen in a very informal manner. Even certain parliaments of countries that do not participate in the Schengen agreement scrutinize the views of their government (concerning the UK, this happens mainly through the House of Lords' European Scrutiny Committee and the House of Commons' Home Affairs Committee). Several parliaments are not formally involved at all, such as those of Spain and Romania. Few countries have substituted their normal scrutiny procedures by special arrangements for Schengen or JHA issues (eg, Italy and the Netherlands). The German *Bundestag* and the Austrian *Nationalrat* reinforced their monitoring towards their government concerning JHA issues:

> In the German *Bundestag*, the scrutiny of EU-documents relating to the Schengen area is firstly scrutinized by the Internal Affairs Committee, then the European Affairs Committee and finally in the plenary. The Federal government has to report before and after the meetings of the Justice and Home Affairs Council to the Internal Affairs Committee on the different aspects of the Schengen *acquis* and on the enlargement of the Schengen area (COSAC, 2008: 39).

Despite such provisions, the role of the NPs in the field of European police cooperation has been criticized from various sides. For instance, Jörg Monar (2008: 120) has argued that there is a 'problem of ineffective national parliamentary scrutiny procedures' simply due to the increasing volume of JHA legislation. That leads to delays in ratifying regulations, which have been agreed on at EU level (one example for this was the delayed ratification of various amendments to the old Europol Convention). Asked about parliaments' involvement concerning AFSJ matters, an MEP pointed out during an interview that they were critical of the fact that the NPs were very much focused on national matters and would not feel responsible for the scrutiny of the EU's then third pillar. The EP would liaise with NPs but this 'prove(d) to be difficult' (Interview F). One expert in the field of data protection in the third pillar also expressed the impression that NPs either had no time, did not take the time, simply had no interest, or did not prioritize the area of police cooperation (Interview G). In addition, MS have their own cultures of accountability, as Monica den Boer (2002: 278) has illustrated.

Yet the various ways of scrutiny could ensure a wide legitimacy of the EU (see, for example, Presidency of the Council of the EU, 2001b). Notably, the Lisbon Treaty draws a new picture of the NPs' role in future EU activities. Article 12 TEU simply states: 'National Parliaments contribute actively to the good functioning of the Union.' Title V of the TFEU describes such contributions with respect to the AFSJ, referring to the participation in the evaluation of EU policies in the AFSJ, the scrutiny of Europol (Article 88 TFEU), and a strengthened involvement in the activities of Eurojust. A key function for the NPs is to ensure the compliance with the subsidiarity principle of the proposals submitted in this area.[2]

The Lisbon Treaty's Annex includes two Protocols, which are highly relevant for the role of NPs: the Protocol on the role of national parliaments in the European Union and the Protocol on the application of the principles of subsidiarity

[2] De Hert (2004: 63) has pointed out that the principle of subsidiarity was rarely taken into account regarding the former third pillar. The Lisbon Treaty introduced an Early Warning Mechanism which enables NPs to monitor compliance with the subsidiarity principle across the EU. For an overview on the differences of and the discussion about subsidiarity control in NPs see <http://www.cosac.eu/en/info/earlywarning/>.

and proportionality. The former obliges the EU institutions to provide NPs 'with all the necessary and relevant information to carry out their work' (COSAC, 2008: 21). The procedures by which the NPs ensure compliance with the principle of subsidiarity are described in the latter Protocol. The Danish Parliament has pointed out that this provision 'has a strong potential to engage national parliaments since it encourages them to get involved in the early stages of the decision making process' (COSAC, 2008: 28). Yet while the scope of activities for NPs has—potentially—been significantly broadened concerning PJCC, it is too early to examine the NPs' adaptation of their newly gained powers.

Currently, there is no literature which describes the role of parliaments concerning CT cooperation in a coherent or extensive manner.[3] In the following, several examples of CT cooperation within the EU as well as between the EU and a third country will therefore be explored to gain a deeper understanding of the restricted role of parliaments in this field.

Parliamentary Scrutiny in Practice

As explained in Chapters 1 and 3, the EU's CT efforts include forms of cooperation among its MS as well as between the EU and non-EU countries. Among other practices, the EU is involved—though often in an indirect manner—in activities such as 'tracking, detaining and prosecuting terrorists; denying terrorists financial and material resources; encouraging, supporting and technically assisting third countries in tackling terrorism; and addressing the social and political resources drawn on by terrorist and criminal networks' (Spence, 2007b: 12). To prepare and empower the EU's legal framework as well as the relevant institutions for an active role in CT after the 9/11 attacks, the Council of Ministers and the EU Commission tabled a plethora of draft legal agreements and adjustments. At the same time, the EU and Europol negotiated with key partners, such as the US, about ways to strengthen cooperation in this area (cf Chapter 5). The following sub-sections will analyse the involvement of the parliaments in some of the key debates and negotiations.

Scrutinizing Europol

The role of parliaments concerning issues related to Europol was previously regulated in the Europol Convention.[4] Article 34 required that the EP shall be 'consulted' with respect to any amendments of the Convention. Otherwise, the

[3] Individual cases have been referred to in various publications, though, and will be used in the following section.

[4] This section is based on an earlier article by the author titled 'Guarding EU-wide Counter-terrorism Policing: The Struggle for Sound Parliamentary Scrutiny of Europol', *Journal of Contemporary European Research* 7/4 (2011), 500–19.

Council Presidency was only required to send a special report to the EP on Europol's work once a year. The substance of the reports was limited by 'the obligations of discretion and confidentiality' (Article 34(2)), which were not further described. As a consequence, the EP was not much involved in the legislative decision-making concerning Europol's remit or powers. Moreover, it could not 'reject legislation or propose measures on its own initiatives' (Apap, 2006: 3) and was therefore not involved in the prioritizing of Europol's activities. Neither did the EP comprise any powers of 'real parliamentary supervision' (Fijnaut, 2002: 16).

With respect to Europol, there was a lack of regulations concerning NPs. The MS were meant to individually deal with the parliamentary role (Article 34(3) of the Europol Convention). The ratification process of the Europol Convention provided the NPs with no power to amend the text. The choice for them, if national procedures required involvement by parliament at all, was simply between ratifying the Convention or not (Peers, 2005: 203).

For example, when the Europol Convention was originally established, neither the EP nor the NPs were consulted in the negotiations or the process of the drafting. When questioned about the involvement of parliament in drafting and approving the Convention in the British House of Commons (1996) on 11 January 1996, the then British Home Secretary, Michael Howard, replied in writing as follows: 'The final text of the Europol convention was published, and laid before Parliament, on 8 December last year. Drafts of the convention were not public documents and therefore were not published nor made generally available.' Tellingly, he added that '(t)he police service were closely consulted throughout the negotiation of the convention through police representative organizations' (House of Commons, 1996). Thus, while parliaments and the wider public were not involved in the negotiations at all, executive authorities were much more so.

The parliamentary role was similarly restricted concerning proposals for amending the Europol Convention and the Protocols thereto. In this process, again, they did not have an impact on the text, but only decided whether or not they wanted to ratify the amendment. This is a significant problem with respect to Europol since, as Aden (2001: 112) stated, '(o)nce established, international bureaucratic institutions such as Europol will leave little scope to be reshaped by democratic institutions'.

In 2002, the Dutch Parliament circulated a questionnaire among the parliaments of the then MS to understand how other NPs dealt with the subject of Europol (Fijnaut, 2002). Though few countries replied, it became clear that parliaments found it difficult to assess Europol's work. Information of 2005 nevertheless maintains that several parliaments had mechanisms in place to examine Europol's budget and the protocols, which amended the Convention (see COSAC, 2005: 89–94).

In some respects, there was an indirect way for NPs to influence decision-making about Europol: they could do it via the minister who represents the state in question in the Council. The Council had 'to approve the draft agreement negotiated by the Director of Europol' (Lavranos, 2003: 272) with its partners, for example. Helpful in this respect was the Protocol on the role of NPs in the EU in the Annex of the TEC and TEU, which maintained that NPs had the right to be fully informed by their governments and EU institutions. As the discussion that follows about agreements between Europol and the USA will show, this indirect way of influencing the minister might not always work well, however. Obviously, it would be important that the parliaments would have sufficient time and be provided with sufficient information so that there is a fair chance to influence the outcome (eg by scrutinizing documents, such as data exchange agreements). The lack of both pre-conditions—sufficient time and sufficient information—to ensure an effective procedure of parliamentary scrutiny was criticized, for example, by the House of Lords' Select Committee on European Union (2003) in 2003 with respect to the Europol-US Agreement on the transmission of personal data.

In the context of Europol, parliaments struggled to find ways of scrutinizing its performance, at least prior to the changes under the Lisbon Treaty. This was due, for example, to a lack of regular reports on police cooperation between national authorities; insufficient information to assess effectiveness and appropriateness of its activities; and the lack of an independent assessment of Europol's operation (Peers, 2005: 202).

Given those limitations, observers had called for a long time to improve the democratic control of Europol in general, and its parliamentary oversight in particular. Indeed, crucial changes concerning Europol's scrutiny were put in place on the basis of Europol's new legal framework, the ECD, and the Lisbon Treaty. The changes appear to be partly contradictory, in particular with respect to the role of the NPs, and it remains to be seen how the NPs will get involved in Europol. The major (potential) changes will be discussed in the following.

The transfer of Europol's former legal base, a 'patchwork system of conventions' (House of Commons, Home Affairs Committee, 2007: para 96), into the ECD provides for a more integrated and solid legal basis (see also Chapter 3). Crucially with respect to parliamentary scrutiny, this move includes that Europol's funding is now provided for by the European Community budget and no longer relies on national contributions. Consequently, the EP is granted substantial budgetary oversight rights.

In addition, the ECD facilitates future amendments of Europol's legal base, which previously had to be ratified by national procedures. This takes away the only slightly powerful mechanism by which NPs used to have an impact on Europol's work. Some NPs expressed concern that their role in scrutinizing Europol was being further limited and that they would not be involved in future changes of Europol's legal basis (see, for example, House of Commons, Home Affairs Committee, 2007: para 101). A few NPs have desired for years a stronger role for the NPs in the accountability procedure of Europol (for example, see House of Lords, EU Committee, 2003).

Paradoxically, the Lisbon Treaty is likely to strengthen the parliamentary scrutiny of Europol and, most notably, provides the possibility for some form of joint scrutiny of Europol by the EP and NPs (House of Commons, Home Affairs Committee, 2007: para 98). So far, the European governments have been keen on keeping the EP excluded from decision-making with respect to Europol ever since its establishment. Even the decision to turn Europol into an EU agency was provided for in a manner which ensured a marginal role for the EP in the negotiation process only. The Lisbon Treaty provides for co-decisive powers for the EP. Therefore, at a time when the Treaty was agreed, MS finally ratified and implemented some important protocols which were necessary in order to agree on the ECD replacing the Convention (as described in Chapter 3). If they had not found an agreement and the Lisbon Treaty had entered into force—as foreseen—at the end of 2008, such a regulation would have had to be negotiated with the EP (Monar, 2008: 121).

Europol has become an active international actor in recent years, which includes its networking efforts to ensure information exchange with security authorities in third countries and organizations. If its activities refer to sensitive information, as is the case, for example, with respect to the exchange of personal data, they might infringe interests of civil liberties. It is therefore important to see how, if at all, parliaments are involved in this external dimension of Europol's activities. Therefore, the involvement of parliaments in the negotiations about two such agreements between Europol and US authorities will be explored in the next sub-section.

The debate about the Europol-USA agreements

As described in the previous chapter, Europol signed two information sharing agreements with the US in the aftermath of the 9/11 attacks, one of which allows for the exchange of personal data. In general, Europol is only allowed to share information with third parties based on a legal agreement. However, Europol's then-Director Max-Peter Ratzel used an emergency clause in the Europol Convention, which allowed him to waive this requirement 'due to the life threatening situation at that time' (Europol, 2005). Consequently, information exchange concerning CT could take place between Europol and US authorities. The use of the emergency clause was criticized widely and the lack of a proper legal basis for the information exchange led, according to voices in the USA, to a situation in which the European authorities 'were unwilling to share the information with the USA via the Europol channel' (Europol, 2005). To overcome those concerns, Europol and the US negotiated the two agreements mentioned earlier. These agreements are far-reaching agreements in comparison to other agreements between Europol and third parties. In particular, the extensive supplementary agreement was understood as a way to provide a wide legal basis for a strengthened operational cooperation between the EU and the USA.

The EP and the NPs were excluded from the negotiations about the agreements. After the first agreement had been made public, the EP quickly requested to be 'fully informed and consulted *before* the adoption of *any* EU-USA cooperation agreement in the field of JHA' (European Parliament, 2001; emphasis added). However, this (non-binding) request had no serious consequences.[5] The second Europol-US Agreement was made available to parliaments before the final meeting took place, but only briefly before the adoption of the text. In theory, the NPs' opinion could have had an impact on their government's position. Yet in practice the draft Agreement was made available to NPs only at a time 'when it appeared that the text had already been agreed with the United States' (House of Lords, EU Committee, 2003: para 49). In the case of the British House of Lords' Select Committee on European Union, the Committee's members pointed out that 'none of the Committee's main concerns were satisfactorily met by the Government, and the Agreement was finally approved by the Council in December [2002], when the Government overrode scrutiny reserves from both Houses of Parliament' (House of Lords, EU Committee 2003: para 50).

The concerns raised by various parliaments and other observers about the second agreement were substantial and far-reaching and referred, among other issues, to the following:

- The sensitivity and scope of the information, which can be shared according to the agreement. The term personal data in the agreement refers to 'any information relating to an identified or identifiable natural person' (Article 2 Supplementary Agreement). If deemed necessary, information referring to political opinions, race, religious or other beliefs, health, and sexual life may be exchanged (Article 6 Supplementary Agreement). As Europol was not allowed to store such information in its own information system, the House of Lords' EU Select Committee (2003) concluded that the Europol-US Agreement 'provided for the exchange of data for purposes much wider than Europol's remit'.
- The wide scope of the agreement regarding the multitude of US authorities, which are granted access to the information provided by Europol (Article 7 Supplementary Agreement; Balzacq, 2008: 91). This point of concern was strengthened by the fact that the US was unwilling to provide a list of agencies which would be allowed to access or to request data provided by Europol (House of Lords, EU Committee, 2003).
- The lack of an adequate data protection law in the US. That the US did not provide a list of agencies with access to the shared data makes it very difficult to ensure that Europol data would be 'subject to broadly equivalent data protection standards' (House of Lords, EU Committee, 2003: 51).

---

[5] For example, the EP remained completely excluded from further such agreements, such as the two agreements between the EU and the US on extradition and mutual legal assistance in criminal matters on 25 June 2003 (Monar, 2004: 406).

Clearly, the negotiating parties of the Europol-US agreements did not provide for any active involvement of the parliaments. Moreover, Article 14 of the agreement required a first evaluation only within two years after the agreement entered into force. Such a report was provided by Europol's Management Board in 2005, but it was directed to the Council and public access to it is restricted (Europol, 2005). It seems that this report was never discussed at a parliamentary level (and there is no formal requirement to do so). Finally, it has been criticized that no non-governmental organizations had been involved in the consultation process prior to the agreements, as was the case with other Europol-related agreements (House of Lords, EU Committee, 2003: para 49). Once the British House of Lord's Select Committee on European Union stated this fact, it started to involve non-governmental organizations, such as the civil rights group Statewatch, into their own consultations (House of Lords, EU Committee, 2003).

The only way parliaments got slightly more involved in the second Agreement is because of a change of Europol's Convention which itself became necessary due to a clause in that Agreement. The Agreement allows the US, under certain circumstances, to participate in Europol's Analysis Groups which includes access to the respective AWFs. This article required a change of the Europol Convention, as the old version denied third parties direct access to the AWFs (Council, 2004a; Europol, 2005). The involvement of NPs depended, again, on the national ratification procedures.

The transatlantic CT collaboration has not only a law enforcement dimension, but also an intelligence one. This happens primarily outside the formal EU realm, but the multinational dimension of such cooperation has been considerably strengthened since September 2001. One peculiar case is the CIA's extraordinary rendition campaign. The following sub-section will briefly explore how such an informal CT collaboration is scrutinized by European parliaments.

Investigations into the CIA's extraordinary rendition programme

The CIA's extraordinary rendition programme is a particular form of intelligence cooperation in the fight against terrorism. Alarmed by reports by investigative journalists and serious concerns about human rights abuse in the context of the rendition campaign, the PACE, comprising MPs of the forty-seven MS, mandated an inquiry committee to investigate into the CIA's detention programme in 2005. Its rapporteur Dick Marty (2006, 2007c) published his first findings in June 2006, followed by a final report in 2007 (hereafter referred to as First and Second Marty Reports). The EP quickly decided to follow this path and set up a Temporary Commission on the alleged use of European countries by the CIA for the transportation and illegal detention of prisoners (TDIP). The TDIP Commission published its final report in January 2007 which basically confirmed and repeated most of Marty's findings (European Parliament, TDIP Committee, 2007).

In its report, the EP's Committee bluntly criticized the lack of cooperation of individual EU officials and institutions in the investigation. The collection of information appeared to be a challenging task or, in other words, some EU bodies were apparently very reluctant to assist the Committee's work. The Report criticized the refusal of the then Europol Director to appear before the Committee and the unsatisfactory answers of the then EU Counter-terrorism Coordinator (European Parliament, TDIP Committee, 2007: para 28–29; Interview I). To mention explicitly the name of certain individuals who where unwilling to cooperate with the Committee can be understood as a procedure of 'naming and shaming', one more example of the various social mechanisms in which forms of accountability can take place.

Otherwise, the impact of the Report has been limited. For example, in July 2007 the EU Commissioner for JHA urged the governments of Poland and Romania to conduct an in-depth investigation into the allegations against them concerning their complicity in rendition flights and the tolerating of detention facilities. However, as of spring 2008 neither government had replied (Tran, 2008). The EP itself discussed for some time internally whether and, if so, how to follow up the TDIP report (Interview I). According to an MEP, a further engagement in this sensitive issue was partly prevented amid party struggles due to the fact that EP elections were taking place in June 2009 (Interview I). In December 2008, the Conservative and Socialist groups in the EP rejected a request by the Liberals, the Greens, and the Communist groups to debate the CIA's extraordinary rendition programme and Guantánamo in a plenary session of the EP that month (Ludford, 2008). An extensive follow-up on the report appears unlikely at the time of writing.

The Swedish Parliament was the only parliament which investigated allegations of the involvement of state authorities in relation to the CIA's clandestine activities *prior* to the reports of Dick Marty and the TDIP Committee. A probe took place in Sweden between August 2004 and May 2005 concerning the cases of Mohammed al-Zery and Ahmed Agiza, who were expelled by the Swedish government in December 2001. The government had asked the CIA for assistance by means of an aircraft and the two men were transferred to Egypt, their country of origin, by a CIA team (Grey, 2006: 25). They were handed over to Egypt's General Intelligence and Security Service and were subsequently imprisoned. The Parliamentary Ombudsman and the Swedish Parliament consequently published reports focusing on the involvement of their government in these issues (Riksdagens Ombudsmän, 2005; Swedish Parliament, 2005). While the probe did not have serious political consequences, the Swedish government granted the two men financial compensation in 2008.

The reports at the European/EU level pushed formal parliamentary investigations into various aspects of the rendition campaign in several countries. This has been the case in the UK, Romania, and Germany, for example. The investigations differ both in terms of their mandate and rigour. Concerning the UK, increasing public pressure and serious allegations expressed in, for example, the Second Marty Report concerning the potential use of the island of Diego Garcia—British overseas territory—by US authorities to secretly detain terrorist suspects, led the British Parliament to start an investigation in October 2007 (Marty, 2007c: point 70). As part of its inquiry into overseas territories, the Foreign Affairs Committee, an all-party parliamentary body, pursued the allegations. While it did not provide any evidence of the use of Diego Garcia facilities as a 'black site' prison, the UK government had to admit in early 2008 that the island had indeed been used for refuelling stops during two US rendition flights in 2002 (House of Commons, Foreign Affairs Committee, 2009). In reply to a request under the Freedom of Information Act by MP Andrew Tyrie, the Foreign and Commonwealth Office maintained that the US government denied that there had been any further use of UK territory, the Overseas Territories or the Crown Dependencies for rendition flights (Foreign & Commonwealth Office, Counter Terrorism Department, 2008).

In July 2008, the House of Commons Foreign Affairs Select Committee (2008) urged the government to investigate American claims that Great Britain's territory had not been used for renditions. Emphasizing a 'legal and moral obligation', it also requested that the government should explore the US government's use of interrogation techniques, such as waterboarding. In clear terms, the Committee (para 9) argued that '(g)iven the clear differences in definition, the UK can no longer rely on US assurances that it does not use torture, and we recommend that the government does not rely on such assurances in the future'. Finally, it asked the government to investigate allegations that the UK had 'outsourced' the interrogation of six terror suspects to Pakistan's Directorate for Inter-Services Intelligence, where they were interrogated and possibly tortured by British intelligence officers (BBC News, 2008).

The case of the British resident and former Guántanamo detainee Binyam Mohamed opened up a discussion about another aspect of the rendition campaign. Mohamed's release from Guantánamo Bay in February 2009 and his allegations of complicity of his ill-treatment and torture against unknown UK officials during his stay in secret prisons in Pakistan and Morocco raised calls for a full inquiry by the Government.[6] The parliamentary Joint Committee on Human Rights (JCHR) investigated 'possible criminal wrongdoing by the intelligence and security service personnel' in Pakistan, with a particular focus on the activities of MI5 and SIS within that region in recent years (Goldenberg, 2009a). The Committee also looked at the legal provision which allegedly offers British intelligence officers immunity in the UK for any crimes committed overseas (the Committee's Chairman has called it the 'James Bond-style get-out clause'). Both the Foreign Secretary and the Home Secretary refused to give oral evidence to the JCHR. The Report of the JCHR (2009: 38) sharply criticized the status quo of accountability mechanisms concerning international intelligence cooperation:

---

[6] An MI5 officer interrogated Mohamed when he was held incommunicado in Pakistan. Also, Mohamed claims that the people who tortured him in Morocco were receiving questions from British intelligence (Goldenberg, 2009b).

> We fully accept that intelligence co-operation is both necessary and legitimate in countering terrorism, and that a degree of state secrecy is justifiable in this area. However, there must be mechanisms for ensuring accountability for such co-operation.... Our experience over the last year is that Ministers are determined to avoid parliamentary scrutiny and accountability on these matters, refusing requests to give oral evidence; providing a standard answer to some of our written questions, which fails to address the issues; and ignoring other questions entirely. Ministers should not be able to act in this way. The fact that they can do so confirms that the system for ministerial accountability for security and intelligence matters is woefully deficient.

Given such serious shortcomings and the remaining unanswered questions, the Committee concluded 'that there is now no other way to restore public confidence in the intelligence services than by setting up an independent inquiry into the numerous allegations about the UK's complicity in torture' (Report of the JCHR, 2009: 40). This is now unlikely to happen. While the Prime Minister announced before Parliament on 6 July 2010 the creation of the Detainee Inquiry with the aim of looking 'at whether Britain was implicated in the improper treatment of detainees, held by other countries, that may have occurred in the aftermath of 9/11', the secretive working procedures of the Inquiry were sharply criticized by some observers (Detainee Inquiry website). The Inquiry was prematurely concluded in January 2012 due to investigations by the Metropolitan Police with respect to alleged renditions of two men to Libya.

Other parliaments conducted investigations with little success. Only three brief examples shall be given in the following (cf Statewatch website—'Observatory on "'rendition"'; Borelli, 2011; Hillebrand, 2009). The Romanian Senate investigated the claim that a secret prison existed on Romanian territory. The head of the investigation committee, Norica Nicolai, emphasized the lack of any evidence that the CIA operated a prison in Romania or used facilities to interrogate people on Romanian territory (International Herald Tribune, 2008). Yet the investigations by Romania were criticized by the EU for a lack of rigour (Tran, 2008).

In Germany, a parliamentary investigation touched partly on a case of alleged rendition and it presented its final report of 1430 pages after three years of work in summer 2009 (Deutscher Bundestag, 2009). The probe was widely thought of as unsatisfactory, in part because the mandate was too broad covering various allegations against the Federal Intelligence Agency (BND). Given the complexity of its mandate, the investigative committee appointed an expert investigator in July 2007. In his report of 2008, the investigator warned that an investigation could only be completely successful if the US authorities would cooperate and provide sufficient information (Blechschmidt, 2008). He admitted that, given the reluctance of US authorities to cooperate, he had to rely on random information about potential rendition flights and he could not come to a reliable conclusion (Deutscher Bundestag, 2009: 59–60). The Committee also pointed to the lack of cooperation of both the German government and the BND with respect to its investigation into individual cases of extraordinary rendition (Deutscher Bundestag, 2009: 433). The inquiry emphasized the need for reforms for the Standing Parliamentary Control Panel (PKGr) to control the German intelligence services which had been already discussed for some time (Deutscher Bundestag, 2009: 352ff; Biermann, 2008).

After allegations by an American television programme in August 2009 that the Lithuanian government had provided American authorities with secret detention facilities, the National Security Committee of the Lithuanian Parliament conducted a probe into these allegations. In December 2009, the Parliament announced that the Lithuanian security services had provided the CIA with two secret facilities (BBC News, 2009). However, the Report claimed that there was no evidence to confirm an involvement of the then President or Prime Minister. Then President Rolandas Paksas testified before the Committee that the security service asked for his permission to accept foreign terrorist suspects in Lithuanian facilities in 2003. He claimed to have denied the request, though. The head of the State Security Department—Lithuania's secret service, Povilas Malakauska, resigned during the parliamentary investigation (Whitlock, 2009). The Committee called for prosecutors to launch an investigation into the actions of the State Security Department. The government rejected the findings of the Report (CNN, 2009b).

Though this section could only give a short overview, the parliamentary investigations into allegations of extraordinary rendition illustrate a lack of parliamentary scrutiny of transnational activities of intelligence services. The reports by Dick Marty and the TDIP Committee, accompanied by further inquiries by human rights organizations, pointed to a serious lack of accountability with respect to the involvement of European security authorities in some of the illegal renditions. Yet most NPs have been slow to pick up the allegations in these reports concerning their respective countries and to conduct more detailed investigations at the national level. Once they do start an investigation, however, they have to face serious hurdles given a lack of transparency and willingness to cooperate by governmental authorities, both from their own country and the US. Yet, according to some, including the British JCHR, only a complete picture would restore public confidence in the actions of security authorities.

So far, aspects of law enforcement and intelligence cooperation in the fight against terrorism have been analysed. The following sub-section will focus on yet another transatlantic form of cooperation, but this time in an area which might be described as an administrative form of CTP, namely data sharing. Data sharing both among MS and between the EU and other partners became a key aspect of the EU's efforts in the fight against terrorism. Some light will be shed on parliamentary involvement concerning, exemplarily, the PNR-Agreements between the EU and the US.

Data sharing between the EU and third countries: The debate about the Passenger Name Record Agreements between the EU and the US

As described in the previous chapter, PNR data refers to files created by airlines, comprising personal information, and which are shared between European governments and foreign authorities, such as American ones. However, according to Article 25 of the EU's Data Protection Directive 95/46/EC, EU companies—including air carriers—are not allowed to transfer EU citizens' data to another country when an adequate level of data protection cannot be ensured (Argomaniz, 2009: 123). It is widely acknowledged that the EU's data protection regime is more rigorous than the American one (eg, see Bignami, 2007; Whitman, 2004; Donohue, 2008: 206–209). Since the European air companies would face high penalties in case of acting against the EU law, there was an urgent need to find a common basis for the transmission of personal data by EU transport companies to the US authorities (Guild, 2007: 1). Thus, the PNR agreement, which was the result of the negotiations starting at this point in time, has never been a *joint* initiative of both the US and the EU, as Thierry Balzacq (2008: 92) has rightly pointed out. This endorses the argument developed in the previous chapter concerning the imbalance of the EU-US CT collaboration.

The first agreement between the European Commission and the American DHS with respect to PNR of 28 May 2004 allowed for the transfer of thirty-four pieces of information about airline passengers of flights originating in the EU to US authorities, such as full names, contact numbers, bank and credit card numbers, and home and e-mail addresses (Council, 2004g). Such information would be analysed in conjunction with current intelligence to identify high-risk travellers before they board their planes (House of Lords, EU Select Committee, 2007a: para 2). The information could be stored for up to three and a half years.

Since this agreement was negotiated under the EU's first pillar (as a measure of common market policies), the Agreement could only enter into force after the EP would have agreed on the text according to the 'Community method'. In this case, the EP rejected the Agreement in March 2004. Its key concern in terms of substance was related to data protection issues and it complained that it was not involved in the negotiations (Spence, 2007b: 21). The EP decided to take the agreement to court. It challenged the legal basis on which this agreement was grounded and requested an opinion from the ECJ on the legality of the proposed adequacy decision.[7]

[7] An adequacy decision is a decision 'adopted by the European Commission on the basis of Article 25(6) of Directive 95/46/EC, which establishes that a third country ensures an adequate level of protection of personal data by reason of its domestic law or the international commitments it has entered into' (European Data Protection Supervisor's website—'Glossary'). Adequacy depends on features such as the nature of information as well as the law and security measures in force in the country receiving the data (Donohue, 2008: 208).

The ECJ indeed found that the agreement required a different legal basis describing PNR as an issue of criminal law legislation (third pillar) and not a social and economic matter (first pillar). On this basis, the Court nullified the agreement on 30 May 2006. Paradoxically, this ruling must be considered as an 'own goal' for the EP, since transferring the PNR issue from the first to the third pillar meant that the Parliament lost its right of consultation on the negotiations and the ECJ's jurisdiction would not cover the new agreement anymore (see also Argomaniz, 2009: 124). Therefore, from this point in time the EP was formally excluded from any further negotiations. As the ECJ had required, the parties of the agreement quickly adopted a new agreement on the correct basis on 19 October 2006, but it was only agreed on as an interim solution which would expire on 31 July 2007. The Agreement comprised the Council Decision, the Agreement itself, and a letter of interpretation dated 11 October 2006 from the DHS. A crucial change from the original agreement was the introduction of 'letters of understanding', which allow a party to make (unilateral) changes on the database management system 'without any public debate or parliamentary control' (Balzacq, 2008: 92).

The EP tried to regain an influential role in the debate about a new long-term agreement which would enter into force on 31 July 2007. For example, MEP Sophia in't Veld drafted a report on the issue (European Parliament, 2006a). Based on this report, the EP adopted a non-legislative resolution, requesting that, concerning the EU-USA PNR agreement, the Council should provide the EP with full co-decision rights, in particular so that the EP could ensure the safeguarding of European data protection standards in future agreements (European Parliament, 2006b).[8] It also suggested being involved in forthcoming negotiations between the EU, the US, Canada, and Australia 'with a view to... establishing a global standard for the transmission of PNR, if that is deemed necessary' (European Parliament, 2006b).

A permanent agreement was finally signed between the Presidency, on behalf of the EU, and US authorities on 29 June 2007 (Council, 2007g). It includes several changes from the original agreement: there are nineteen categories of information; passenger data can be stored for fifteen years; some data implied stricter access rules; there was a change from the 'pull' system to a 'push system' (ie, the US cannot access airline databases immediately, but has to require information on a case-by-case basis); the DHS was allowed to pass the data to other US security agencies; and the agreement would be valid for seven years (cf Guild, 2007). The DHS is supposed to 'filter out and not use sensitive information contained in PNR data, save exceptional cases where life is at risk' (Europa, 2007). For the purpose of preventing and fighting terrorism and other serious crime, US authorities have direct access to the DHS database.

---

[8] This could be done by invoking the so-called passerelle clause, allowing the Council to move policy areas from decision-making by unanimity in Council and consultation of Parliament to qualified majority voting in Council and co-decision with the EP.

The EP criticized the new Agreement in a Resolution of 12 July 2007. It objected to not being consulted on the agreement and raised concerns about the 'open and vague definitions and multiple possibilities for exception' (European Parliament, 2007a). Overall, the EP understood 'the substance of the data protection undertakings' to be inadequate (House of Lords, EU Select Committee, 2007a: para 51–52). In addition, a few NPs tried to stand up to the Council and make their voices heard during the negotiation period (see, for example, the detailed report by the House of Lords' EU Select Committee, 2007a). The PNR Agreements fell under standard scrutiny procedure of most of the NPs. A new agreement is currently under discussion (Commission, 2011b). This time, it requires the approval by the EP.

In the meantime, the focus of the debate moved away from sharing data between the US and the EU towards a European-wide sharing of PNR. The Commission (2007b) announced a proposal on a European PNR Agreement in summer 2007, which would be very similar to the American PNR System. A first attempt into this direction had already been made in a 2003 Commission Communication on the 'Transfer of air passenger name record (PNR) data: A global EU approach' (Commission, 2003). One of the justifications given by a Commission official was, according to Argomaniz (2009: 130), that 'it would have been difficult to explain to European passengers that US authorities would receive more information than their own national services'.

Finally, the discussion of the introduction of an EU-wide PNR scheme is accompanied by a debate about the use of PNR data for law enforcement purposes. On 6 November 2007, the Commission (2007b) tabled a draft Council Framework Decision on the use of PNR data for law enforcement purposes. It maintained that the air carriers, which collect PNR data for in- and outbound EU flights, should make this data available 'to specialized national units carrying out risk assessments and law enforcement and counter terrorism missions' (Commission, 2007b). The UK government pushed for an extension of the original proposal including data from internal EU flights, sea, and rail travel.[9] The EP's LIBE Committee raised concerns about the plan on the basis that: 1) it is not justified legally; 2) the compatibility with fundamental rights is doubtful; and 3) the effectiveness of this measure with respect to the fight against terrorism remains unclear. It also criticized the lack of a sunset clause in the text. Therefore, instead of formulating a formal opinion on the framework decision, the EP adopted a resolution drafted by MEP Sophie in't Veld which included the concerns about the Commission's proposal and suggested amendments for a framework resolution on the use of PNR data for law enforcement purposes. Moreover, the proposal's suggestion of profiling—whereby the PNR data on passengers will be run 'against a combination of characteristics and behavioural pattern' (Commission, 2007b)—caused

[9] For a critical stance on this within the UK see the Second Report on PNR by the House of Lords EU Select Committee (2008: x).

concerns about racial profiling with individual MEPs (EP, LIBE Committee, 2008).

One of the ongoing criticisms about the PNR-related debates is the lack of an evaluation of their effectiveness. For example, the EP questioned whether the collection of PNR data is useful for massive profiling or data mining in order to seek potential terrorists. Apparently, a joint EU-US evaluation took place in 2005, but the report has not been published. Moreover, 'EU officials were forced to sign confidentiality agreements exposing them to criminal sanctions for any breach and their access to some records was limited by US authorities' (Argomaniz, 2009: 134, note 8). Concerning the use of PNR data for law enforcement purposes, the Council (2007i) has released an opinion by its legal service about the Draft Decision, but the crucial parts of the opinion were blacked out.

There is another dimension of data sharing in the context of CTP which refers to the interoperability of databases in order to allow a quick and possibly automatic exchange of data. Concerning European-wide databases, this has not only been discussed since 9/11, but was already tabled as an issue in 1999. A serious debate only broke out in the context of CT cooperation post-9/11, however.

The interoperability of European databases: the political/normative dimension

One of the key aspects of the 2004 Hague Programme was maximization of interoperability between EU databases, in particular concerning the reciprocal access to national databases and access to existing central EU information systems (Commission, 2005b). Databases were meant to be established or updated in a way that would make them 'interoperable' and easily accessible for various authorities despite the different categories of data which have been established for different purposes (Mitsilegas and Baldaccini, 2007). Key AFSJ databases are the VIS, SIS (II), and Eurodac, as earlier chapters have outlined.

In 2005, the Commission (2005e: 3) published a Communication on improved effectiveness, enhanced interoperability, and synergies among European databases in the area of Justice and Home Affairs which claimed that interoperability was a technical, rather than a legal or political concept, and the 'question of whether the data exchange is legally or politically possible or required' was not addressed. The Commission's efforts to reduce the issue of interoperability to a technical matter led to severe criticism. Scholars have argued that 'the selection, work and evaluation of a particular model of interoperability are not immune from legal requirements and political debates' (Balzacq, 2008: 93). Beyond this, interoperability 'has technical, semantic, social, cultural, economic, organisational *and* legal dimensions' (De Hert/Gutwirth, 2006: 23; emphasis in original). An involvement of parliaments would therefore be appropriate.

The fact that interoperability is also a political issue can be seen in the fact that the 2005 Communication strives to create a new field of security wherein proactive policing and intelligence-led policing are merged: 'whereas the former uses...soft security (nonverified information, often based on interpretations, informers, open sources), the latter uses *all* available information techniques of crime analysis [such as the use of profiling]' (De Hert/Gutwirth, 2006: 30; emphasis in original). A direct implication of the interoperability of such an approach would be that not only information based on facts would be used for policing matters, but also data that resulted from opinions and personal assessments of the situation. In addition, police and intelligence services would be required to handle data in order to draft policies on increasingly similar target populations (migration, asylum, drug trafficking, visa sponsors, and terrorists).

Another political aspect of interoperability is the question of who is granted access to which databases. This will be briefly discussed using the example of Europol. As Chapter 3 has established, Europol has been granted access to the VIS and the SIS (II), and future access to Eurodac is likely (Commission, 2009f). The access to VIS is regulated via central access points, which makes monitoring easy. The MS in question needs to express its consent before Europol can retrieve information. While this is understood by some as an important safeguard for individuals, Europol allegedly understood it to be 'detrimental to the fight against terrorism' (Balzacq, 2008: 89) and would have preferred automatic access.

Finally, the discussion of interoperability includes a move away from the original purpose of the databases to a new way of using and interpreting the data for unforeseen purposes. In this vein, the Commission's Communication freely declared that the aim of the paper is 'to highlight how, beyond their present purposes [the databases SIS, Eurodac, and VIS] can more effectively support the policies linked to the free movement of persons and serve the objective of combating terrorism and serious crime' (Commission, 2005g: 2). In the case of SIS (II), Balzacq (2008: 84) argued convincingly that the justification that it needs to be used for the fight against terrorism has transformed the database 'from a "support tool" for the free movement of persons and police co-operation to an investigative tool'. The use of SIS for 'police information purposes in a broad sense' (Council, 2002h) was initially not foreseen. In the meantime, however, additional agencies such as Europol, Eurojust, national judicial authorities, and vehicle registration authorities have been granted access to SIS. Overall, the Commission argued after 9/11 that 'Europol needs to have the greatest possible access to European databases' in order to be able 'to carry out a complete strategic analysis including risk assessments in the field of crime' (Council, 2002h: 3). The overall idea was that the 'SIS can substantially assist in the identification of terrorist suspects' (Aus, 2003: 32). The Council followed the Commission's opinion and agreed on a Decision of February 2005 which 'introduced both new functions for the SIS, including the fight against terrorism, while allowing Europol to access data' (Balzacq, 2008: 86; cf Council, 2005d).

With respect to the Eurodac database, a Commission Communication of 24 November 2005 described the lack of access for law enforcement authorities as a shortcoming in the fight against terrorism (Commission, 2005e). A first draft Council Decision to grant that access was tabled in December 2006 (Council,

2006b). On 10 September 2009, the Commission (2009e) has indeed proposed a Framework Decision which would grant the national law enforcement authorities as well as Europol access to Eurodac. A scrutiny mechanism by parliaments is not foreseen.

The integration of the provisions of the Prüm Treaty into the EU framework

The final discussion will focus on the so-called Prüm Treaty and its integration into the EU framework. This agreement comprises several issues which previous examples touched on, such as a strengthened law enforcement cooperation, data sharing, and the access to databases in the context of CT. At the same time, this is one example of an international agreement which was set up completely outside the EU framework, but quickly became (nearly) fully integrated into EU law.

Signed on 27 May 2005 by the heads of government of Austria, Belgium, France, Germany, Luxembourg, the Netherlands, and Spain, the Prüm Convention aimed at, in particular, improved exchange of information for law enforcement purposes among the participating countries by granting reciprocal access to national databases on DNA profiles, fingerprints, and vehicle registration data (cf Chapter 1; Council, 2005j: ch 2). The Convention was entirely 'negotiated between the interior ministries of the founding countries without any information or oversight by national parliaments or the European institutions' (Lummer, 2008a). Moreover, the Convention established a framework 'whose rules are not subject to Parliamentary oversight [and therefore] impacts on the EU principle of transparency' (Balzacq et al, 2006: 17).

The text was subject to national ratification procedures in several countries but the example of Germany shows serious problems with the system. The draft Prüm Treaty needed to be ratified by the *Bundestag*, which only received the document in April 2006, thus about eleven months after it was signed in Prüm. The draft was then declared 'urgent' and left the Parliament with only a few weeks for scrutiny 'and merely thirty minutes for discussion and vote in the plenary' (Guild and Geyer, 2007). In the plenary debate of 19 May 2006, 'coalition MPs did not even bother to speak but instead submitted their statements in writing. Consequently only three MPs from the opposition gave a short speech, concentrating less on the content of the Prüm Treaty but criticising...the entire procedure' (Guild and Geyer, 2007).

Before the Convention was ratified by all parties, the Commission (2005f) already tabled a Proposal for a Council Decision in order to make the Prüm provisions a legal requirement for all MS. It became quickly obvious that 'Prüm was never more than a stepping stone to an EU-wide instrument' (House of Lords, EU Select Committee 2007b: para 29). This first step towards the integration of the Prüm Treaty in EU law has been decided without any consultation of parliaments or prior impact assessment.

The EP organized a Joint Parliamentary Meeting with the NPs on 2–3 October 2006 during which several MPs raised serious concerns about the way the Prüm Group sought 'to pre-empt EU decision-making processes, by making arrangements of their own, and offering them to other Member States on a take-it-or-leave-it basis' (quoted in Guild and Geyer, 2007). The Council nevertheless tabled a draft Council decision to incorporate the Prüm Treaty into law on 19 January 2007. A revised version of this draft was published for consideration at the JHA Council in February 2007, without an explanatory memorandum, an impact assessment, or an estimate of the cost to the MS (House of Lords, EU Select Committee, 2007b: para 46). At the meeting, the Council agreed on the integration into the EU framework of all parts of the Prüm Treaty relating to PJCC. Only Article 18, which provides for cross-border police intervention in the event of imminent danger, was eliminated from the subsequent draft.

Based on Article 39 of the Treaty, the Council is obliged to consult the EP. It did this with respect to the Prüm Convention on 28 February 2007 and asked the Parliament to deliver its opinion by 7 June 2007. The EP's LIBE Committee issued its report on 24 April 2007. While it supported the idea of applying the Prüm Convention to all MS, it suggested the need for a different legal base, namely a Framework Decision under Article 34(2) (b) of the EU Treaty instead of a decision pursuant to Article 34(2) (c). Article 34(2) (c) would allow the Council later to adopt implementing measures by a qualified majority without consulting the EP. The EP issued its final opinion on 7 June 2007 regretting the urgency of the decision, the lack of impact assessment or evaluations, and the lack of an adequate framework decision for the protection of personal data in PJCC (European Parliament, 2007b).

The timing is crucial in order to understand the way the Council was planning to deal with the EP's opinion. Prüm was the 'baby' of the German Council Presidency and the last JHA Council of this Presidency was scheduled for 12–13 June 2007. The Presidency clearly hoped to agree on the implementation of the Prüm Treaty into the EU framework at this Council. However, the timing allowed the Council only a couple of working days to consider the opinion to be delivered by the EP and it appears that the Presidency had 'little intention of being influenced by the views of the Parliament' (House of Lords, EU Select Committee, 2007b: para 55). The decision was indeed agreed at the June JHA Council (Council, 2007b).

The implementation of the Prüm Treaty has been debated in various NPs (eg, House of Lords, EU Select Committee, 2007b). Often, the discussions in the relevant (sub-)committees seem to be reduced to practical questions of implementation, technical issues such as the compatibility of technical systems and standards, access to databases, and perhaps effectiveness (see, for example, Parliament of Ireland, Joint EU Scrutiny Committee, 2007).

Given the difficulties for parliaments to scrutinize policing matters both at the EU and at the national level, it has been suggested that increased cooperation between the parliamentary bodies might facilitate the work (Wagner, 2004). The final section will therefore briefly discuss forms of cooperation between parliaments in this field.

Cooperation between European Parliaments

In institutional terms, the need for, and the current lack of, effective cooperation between the EP and NPs concerning JHA matters has been mentioned several times in this chapter. It is therefore necessary to explore this issue briefly. Inter-parliamentary cooperation is aimed at improving the overall quality and efficiency of parliamentary involvement in EU decision-making and could therefore contribute to its democratic legitimacy.

Communication and inter-parliamentary cooperation among the various European parliaments has already been taking place in various ways. The primary and most institutionalized coordinating body is the COSAC, which provides a forum for members of the EU-affairs committees of the NPs as well as EP delegates. The overall aim is to share best practices and policy developments. Another mechanism of exchange between the EP and NPs is the annual conferences of the Speakers of European Parliaments, which promotes information exchange and general cooperation (Lummer, 2008a).

In addition, there are more informal forms of cooperation. For example, rather sporadic meetings of standing committees take place. Also, EP committees sporadically invite their national counterparts to their meetings to discuss new Commission legislative proposals. The EP's LIBE Committee has been particularly active in setting up meetings which are organized on specific topics and bring together MEPs and their national colleagues concerning matters of JHA and CT cooperation. Several such meetings have taken place with respect to Europol in 2006, for example. The LIBE Committee has also established several public hearings on particular problems to start an issue-specific debate, such as the one on Prüm in May 2007. There is also the informal network of the representatives of NPs in Brussels, which is understood by some as a 'crucial channel of communication and information' (COSAC, 2008: 29). Moreover, some NPs, such as the Slovakian and the Polish ones, consider regional cooperation between smaller groups of states as important (COSAC, 2008: 30). Finally, since 2002 the EP also has observer status in NATO's Parliamentary Assembly and may take the floor in debates. It also used to sit in meetings of the former Assembly of the Western European Union (WEU) Assembly, has contact with the PACE and, as described in the previous chapter, with the US Congress.

Concerning Europol, one idea to increase the powers of the NPs and the EP resulted in setting up a joint parliamentary committee comprising representatives of all parliaments and which would be responsible for scrutinizing Europol's work. In a Communication Paper in February 2002, the Commission suggested the creation of such a committee, which would meet twice a year. A sub-group of the Committee should ensure closer contact with Europol but a legal-technocratic problem became quickly obvious: only primary European legislation (ie, European treaties themselves) has the power to establish formal parliamentary committees of any kind. Consequently, a rather informal group was created, called 'Parlopol'. Together with the EP and the Commission this group suggested to the Council various measures to strengthen the EP's democratic power of oversight. For example, it recommended a formal exchange of information between Europol, the EP, and NPs as well as the creation of a joint committee comprising members of the EP and NPs with respect to police cooperation, the right to invite Europol's Director and to make them accountable to the Parliamentary Committee in question, the extension of Europol's Management Board to include two representatives of the Commission and two of the EP, and an equal involvement (ie like the Council) of the EP in the procedure for the appointment and dismissal of Europol's Director (Bruggeman, 2006: 8). While some of those recommendations have had an impact on the legal changes with respect to Europol, others—for example the introduction of seats for Members of the EP in Europol's Management Board—have not been accepted.

Bringing the empirical strands of this chapter together, it is clear that the parliamentary scrutiny of European CT cooperation has been weak so far. Obviously, forms of cooperation differ in the legitimacy problems they pose. But all examples suggest that, in one way or another, parliaments were either excluded from, not capable of, or not overly enthusiastic about getting involved in such sensitive matters at EU level. This is in particular notable as the marginalization of the EP and its national counterparts concerned, in particular, the years following the 9/11 attacks—thus the period during which most of the EU's CT efforts were planned, shaped, adopted, and institutionalized.

The changes under the Lisbon Treaty concerning the EP's involvement in the AFSJ must be understood as 'a way of strengthening the EU's democratic accountability' (European Parliament, 2007c: para 1c). While it is too early to judge how well the EP is going to use its new powers in this field, first indications are that it is attempting to become an important player in the EU's CT policy-making. This will be a learning process, of course. The fact that the EP—through its move to bring the first PNR Agreement before the ECJ—basically excluded itself from the further negotiation process, raises questions about the EP's capabilities to scrutinize such wide-reaching decisions. To be fair, the EP usually works under time pressure when it is asked to give an opinion or agree on a Council Decision. Also, the fact that the ECJ indeed nullified the agreement shows that the EP rightly understood the Agreement as illegal. However, it has been suggested that the result—that the EP would be excluded—came as a surprise for the EP (Interview J).

The picture is less clear with respect to the NPs. It remains to be seen how the partly contradictory regulations of the two legal texts concerning parliaments will be interpreted and how actively, if at all, the individual NPs will try to gain a more powerful and influential role in the decision-making process. What seems to become a more unlikely option now is that national governments will continue to 'actually use the European level for reducing... parliamentary scrutiny' (Monar, 2005a: 450) by bypassing levels of competences. The way the Prüm

Treaty was introduced to the European framework is a crucial example for playing the institutional levels within the EU in such a way: certain political issues are moved to a different institutional level (for example, from the national to the European level) where the political goals are most likely to be achieved. Such a transfer often meant that '(d)emocratic procedures [were] replaced by undemocratic and unaccountable networks serving highly particularistic or dominant interests' (De Hert, 2004: 59) in order to achieve a very contested political issue.

As the examples analysed in the chapter have clearly confirmed, 'in the transnational state system where governance transcends national jurisdictions and simultaneously valorizes the national security function, there are no confident and clear lines of political accountability' (Sheptycki, 2007: 71). While certain traditional mechanisms of accountability apply to European CT cooperation (eg the possibility for parliaments to have meetings, hearings, and start an investigation or publish a report), such instruments are often undermined by a lack of information and an unwillingness of both EU and national officials to support such efforts. The investigations into the extraordinary rendition campaign confirm the problem of finding information and evidence concerning CTNs. Chalk (2000) seems to be right in suggesting that such traditional mechanisms of democratic control 'are not always adequate to monitor informal informational contacts between executives and opaque communities'.

Indeed, one major point of current debates concerns the access that parliamentary bodies have to sensitive information concerning policies and practices under the AFSJ. While operational, strategic, and data protection concerns jeopardize full transparency concerning CT efforts, an *excessive* level of secrecy might undermine legitimacy by 'depriving the public of information as a premise for partaking in public discussion' (Tanchev, 2005: 113–114; see also Aldrich, 2009a). EU institutions, for example, often refuse to release documents concerning AFSJ matters. With respect to the EP, the current system of receiving classified information in the AFSJ field has been described as 'inadequate' (Wills et al, 2011: 30). Such a 'Top Secret Europe', as Deidre Curtin (2011) has recently dubbed it, diminishes the effectiveness and quality of parliamentary involvement. Parliamentary bodies rely on information for their scrutiny efforts. It remains to be seen how the EU will tackle this matter in the long term. The lack, so far, of public information about the COSI, the new—and potentially very powerful—body in the EU's policy area of internal security suggests that the EU is still far away from meeting its ideals of transparency in this area (Hillebrand, 2010).

The analysis of current processes, challenges, and shortcomings of parliamentary scrutiny of EU CTP will be followed by an exploration of the challenges to judicial scrutiny in the following chapter. As Chapter 2 outlined, tools of judicial scrutiny accompany parliamentary mechanisms to ensure—ideally—a high level of democratic legitimacy.

7

The Protection of Fundamental Rights in the Context of European Counter-terrorism Policing

In July 2001, the EP's LIBE Committee (2001: para X) regretted in a report 'the European Union's slowness in responding to the terrorist threat and the fact that there is as yet no coherent and legally binding set of coordinated measures'. This arguably changed a couple of months later when the EU started to rapidly develop legislation on CT. Particular attention has been paid to strengthening and expanding data-sharing efforts concerning PJCC, both within the EU and beyond, and this is an ongoing development. One result of the EU's CT legislation and the increased powers of some institutions, such as Europol, is that it allows for 'a space in which abuses of police powers may occur' (Anderson, 2008: 106).

Following on from the exploration of the parliamentary scrutiny of the EU's efforts at CTP, this chapter seeks to explore the judicial scrutiny in this field. The safeguarding of fundamental rights, freedoms, and the rule of law are crucial elements of democratic, liberal political systems. Those features, it has been argued, are also of particular relevance concerning policies of the AFSJ, 'as these entail many implications on the status of the individual that go beyond traditional "person-state" relations within a nationally confined legal system' (Carrera and Geyer, 2007: 3).

While operational powers such as arrest, detention, trial, and sentence are usually regulated at the national level, it is the EU's emphasis on information sharing and exchange, more recently confirmed in the Internal Security Strategy (ISS), which is a particular concern. This has become the area in which 'the possibilities of direct abuse of fundamental rights through police malpractice' (Anderson, 2008: 120) in the EU context are most likely to be found, and it is this field only which will be in the spotlight in this chapter.

In democratic systems, the judiciary is the institution to uphold the law, enforce democratic rights and procedures, and thereby prevent the abuse of power by the government (Caparini, 2007: 15). The judiciary is also conceived as 'the guarantor of human rights in the fight against terrorism' (International Commission of Jurists, 2004). Judicial oversight and legal accountability is therefore important for the democratic legitimacy of European CTP, as outlined in Chapter 2.

The upholding of human rights and sound legal accountability are of particular significance in times when over-reactions to the terrorist violence by governmental bodies might lead to the employment of oppressive CT measures. The erosion of individual rights and freedoms by security authorities might lead to a decrease of democratic legitimacy in the long-term (Gill and Phythian, 2006: 155). Policing work potentially challenges several fundamental rights, as maintained in the ECHR and, more recently, in the Charter of Fundamental Rights of the European Union (hereafter EU Charter), such as the rights to privacy, freedom of expression, personal liberty, and a fair trial.[1] This chapter is therefore concerned with the question of how, and to what extent, networked information sharing structures aimed at tackling terrorism are judicially scrutinized at the European level.

Judicial scrutiny can be ensured in a variety of ways. The first section of the chapter analyses the problems surrounding judicial scrutiny of EU-wide CT actions through the courts at European/EU level, focusing on the case law concerning the 'terrorist lists'. As will be explored, a particular problem arises from the fact that the overall framework of the EU measures in this context is set by UN resolutions.

The second section will focus on the right to privacy and, in particular, related features of the protection of personal information. Given the increased use of data-transferring processes concerning police cooperation, especially concerning CT, proper standards for the collection, storage, and transmission of personal data are of great significance in the EU context. This is reflected in the fact that the protection of personal data is now recognized as a specific fundamental right in Article 8 of the EU Charter (see also Bigo et al, 2011: 24). Data protection regulations are very specific, however, and the EU's framework remains incoherent.

[1] The EU Charter, containing a list of rights and freedoms under the titles Dignity, Freedoms, Equality, Solidarity, Citizens' Rights, and Justice, gained full legal effect with the entry into force of the Lisbon Treaty.

The section is therefore limited to the exploration of one framework, namely the one related to Europol.

Human Rights Protection in the Context of the EU's Counter-Terrorism Activities

In its CT Strategy, the EU commits itself 'to combat terrorism globally while respecting human rights..., allowing its citizens to live in an area of freedom, security and justice' (Council, 2005b). Human rights law refers to 'agreed values, standards or rules regulating the conduct of states' (Baehr, 1999: 1) towards all individuals, which can take the form of treaties, customary law, but also soft law, such as UN General Assembly Resolutions (Wiegand, 2008: 51). Drawing on the UN Charter, which comprises the key fundamental rights and freedoms, the most important, and legally binding, global treaties concerning human rights are the International Covenant on Civil and Political Rights and the International Covenant on Economic Social and Cultural Rights. Also important concerning current CT efforts is the Convention against Torture and other Cruel, Inhuman or Degrading Treatment or Punishment.

For the European context, the most important reference is the ECHR which 'contains affirmative statements of political and civil rights... [and] expressly permits limitations of most of the enumerated rights' (Sottiaux, 2008: 19; cf Council of Europe, 1950). All members of the CoE, including all EU MS, are party to the Convention and its Protocols which aim to secure democracy and to guarantee human rights and fundamental freedoms. As an enforcement mechanism, and to safeguard the application of the ECHR, the ECtHR was set up. Any person can take a case against a state to this fully judicial organ, and its judgments enjoy legally binding force.

This human rights framework puts limits on the possibilities of states as well as the EU to act, in particular in the field of security. At the same time, states are under the positive obligation to protect their population. Under particular circumstances, this obligation might require the states 'to take preventive operational measures to protect an individual whose life is at risk from the criminal acts of another individual' (Lemmens, 2004: 226).

Consequently, the ECHR makes a distinction between absolute, limited, and qualified human rights. The latter two can be restricted by authorities if there are good reasons for doing so. For these categories of rights, the UN High Commissioner for Human Rights (United Nations Economic and Social Council, Commission on Human Rights, 2002: para 14; emphasis added) established the following guidelines:

> principles of *necessity* and *proportionality* must be applied. The measures taken must be *appropriate* and the *least intrusive* to achieve the objective. The discretion granted to certain authorities to act must not be unfettered. The principle

of non-discrimination must always be respected and special effort made to safeguard the rights of vulnerable groups.

As 'a constitutional instrument of European public order' (*Loizidou v Turkey* (1995), § 75[2]), the ECHR is an important point of reference for police conduct and cooperation treaties. It outlines 'the minimum standard which police officers from all European countries have to respect when they cooperate' (Aden, 2001: 106). In addition, the ECtHR's case law continuously 'develops pan-European legal principles' (Cameron, 2005: 35).

The Convention and the case law of the ECtHR have also been applied many times by national courts concerning cases which involved conflicting claims of security and liberty related to terrorism. According to Sottiaux (2008: 18), the 'international character of a supervising body... allows it to take a more independent and detached stance from domestic legislative and executive attempts to curb fundamental rights'. In the heated atmosphere of the post-9/11 era, this observation seems to be of particular importance. While at the domestic level the fight against terrorism might lead to an over-reaction, a more distant and internationally oriented authority seems more likely to keep 'a clear head' and be less vulnerable to political pressure. One example for this is the 1979 ECtHR decision in the case *Ireland v United Kingdom*[3] concerning the use of means of Highly Coercive Interrogation, referring to the 'five techniques'. The Republic of Ireland had complained to the ECtHR that the British government—more specifically, interrogators of the Royal Ulster Constabulary, supervised by the British Army—had applied emergency procedures against suspected terrorists in Northern Ireland as of 1971. In its judgment, the Court considered the techniques of hooding, wall-standing, subjection to noise, relative deprivation of food and water, and sleep deprivation to be cruel, inhuman, and degrading and therefore to be breaching the ECHR. This was the first inter-state case ever brought before the ECtHR and British policy was shaped by the fact that there were binding international standards which applied to the CT response in Northern Ireland and that they might be held accountable internationally for failure to comply with them.

Surely, with respect to reviewing intelligence and police work, an international court such as the ECtHR is primarily a 'fire brigade system... [which]... starts working only when a problem seems to have emerged' (Cameron, 2005: 37). Yet over the years, both the CoE and the ECtHR also 'played an important role in shaping the criminal policy of Member States and in strengthening international cooperation against crime' (Verbruggen, 2004: 311). Concerning intelligence, the ECtHR has so far mainly addressed cases in which the (in)adequacy of the legal framework regulating the action, such as surveillance, collection, and the use of intelligence, had to be scrutinized (Cameron, 2005: 38).

---

[2] *Loizidou v Turkey* Series A No 310, (1995) 23 EHRR 513.
[3] *Ireland v The United Kingdom* Series A No 25, (1979-80) 2 EHRR 25.

In principle, EU legal acts concerning policing, including CT instruments, can also be subject of applications to the ECtHR (Callewaert, 2007). Moreover, the ECtHR's case law suggests that states have to ensure that their activities within the framework of international organizations 'are being exercised in conformity with the Convention' (Callewaert, 2007: 514; see also *Matthews v United Kingdom* (1999)[4] and *Bosphorus Airlines v Ireland* (2006)[5]). Yet in contrast to its MS, the EU itself is not (yet) a contracting party to the ECHR. The Lisbon Treaty has opened the door for the EU's accession to the ECHR—a move which would clarify the ECtHR's judicial competence. So far, the degree of legal uncertainty has been considerable in the context of the EU's CT activities, as recent high-profile cases concerning the so-called 'terrorist lists' will outline in the following.

The European Court of Human Rights and the 'terrorist lists'

There are currently three major 'terrorist lists', established by the UN and the EU for the purpose of tackling the financing of terrorism. The lists comprise individuals or entities suspected of having links with terrorism and who ought to be subject to measures, such as the freezing of financial assets and the severe restriction of travel and freedom of movement (European Parliament, 2009b: 30). These targeted sanctions can seriously harm individuals.

The first lists were established on the basis of the 1999 UN Resolution 1267 on sanctions against the Taliban regime in Afghanistan and successive Resolutions 1333 and 1390. The lists, regularly updated by the UN's Al-Qaida and Taliban Sanctions Committee, provide names of individuals and entities associated with the Taliban and/or Bin Laden or al Qaida, broadly defined (United Nations Security Council, 1999). The updated, consolidated list of 30 July 2010 comprised 443 names (European Center for Constitutional and Human Rights (ECCHR), 2010: 12–13). The members of the UN were obliged to implement the list. As those sanctions touch on the EU's common market, however, the EU had to adopt the list as well (Common Position 2002/402/CFSP and EC Regulation 881/2002).

In addition, the 2001 UN Resolution 1373 demands from the UN MS to sanction terrorists, terrorist suspects, or associates to allow for the freezing of their assets. It encourages MS to create their own lists rather than providing a list of names.[6] The EU implemented the Resolution by Common Position 931/2001/CFSP and Regulation EC 2580(2001) (Council, 2001e, 2001d). The EU's list is occasionally updated in total secrecy, based on information provided by national judicial and security authorities (Guild, 2008: 174). The list of December 2011 contains twenty-six individuals and twenty-five organizations, maintaining the

---

[4] *Denise Matthews v The United Kingdom* (application no. 24833/94), (1999) 28 EHRR 361.

[5] *Bosphorus Hava Yollari Turizm ve Ticaret Anonim Şirketi v Ireland* (application no. 45036/98), (2006) 42 EHRR 1.

[6] For a discussion of the implementation of this Resolution in the British context see Anderson (2011).

name, date, passport number, and city of birth of the affected individual as well as the related terrorist group (Council, 2011c).

The lists have been severely criticized by various bodies, such as PACE and human rights organizations (eg ECCHR, 2010; PACE, 2008a, 2008b; Marty, 2007a, 2007b; Statewatch website—'Terrorist' lists). Various concerns have been stated: the secretiveness of creating the lists; the affected individuals or groups are not informed about the listing; the procedure for de-listing is unclear; and the question of compensation remains open. Overall, the PACE rapporteur Dick Marty (2007a: point 6) was sharply critical of the lists for 'doing flagrant injustice to many persons against whom there is no proof of any wrong doing'.

Among others, two affected Spanish parties, Mr Segi and the group Gestoras Pro Amnistía, complained to the ECtHR against their listing on the basis of the EU Common Position 931/2001. They argued that their listing was in breach of their rights to freedom of expression and association as well as their property rights, as maintained in Articles 10 and 11 ECHR (Callewaert, 2007: 516). Concerns were also raised that the right to presumption of innocence was flouted and the rights to fair hearing and fair trial were violated, that the right to judicial remedy was not ensured, and that the circumstances under which the applicants' names were added to the list were troublesome (Wiegand, 2008: 77). However, the ECtHR decided the application to be inadmissible. As an EU Common Position is not directly applicable in a MS, the applicants could not claim to be *direct* victims of the Common Position.[7] Only if the state in question would have implemented concrete measures, could the applications be subject to formal judicial review, according to the Court's judgment (*Segi and Gestoras Pro Amnistía v 15 EU Member States* (2002)[8]). The Court therefore denied in this case judicial accountability at the European/CoE level. The judgment also pointed out that the international character of the lists made *any* judicial redress against the instruments impossible. Yet the affected individuals of this case as well as several other affected parties turned to the ECJ.

The European Court of Justice and the 'terrorist lists'

Overall, the ECJ's scrutiny over measures concerning PJCC or the EU's external affairs has been very limited. Given the EU's pillar system, the ECJ was not per se competent as these issues were not part of the 'communitarized' area (Carrera/Geyer, 2007: 3; Kahlke, 2004: 52). Individual MS could make a declaration accepting the jurisdiction of the Court but this was a voluntary choice, according to Article 35 of the Amsterdam Treaty. Furthermore, the 'public order exception' in this Article specifically stated that the ECJ shall have

[7] The victim status is of great relevance, as one of the admissibility conditions of the ECtHR is that the applicant must be victim of an alleged human rights violation (ECHR, Art 34).

[8] *Segi (and others) and Gestoras Pro Amnistía (and others) v Austria, Belgium, Denmark, Finland, France, Germany, Greece, Ireland Italy, Luxembourg, Portugal, Spain, Sweden, The Netherlands, United Kingdom* (applications no. 6422/02 and 9916/02) (2002) ECHR 2002-V.

> no jurisdiction to review the validity or proportionality of operations carried out by the police or other law enforcement services of a Member State or the exercise of the responsibilities incumbent upon Member States with regard to the maintenance of law and order and the safeguarding of internal security (Douglas-Scott, 2008: 23).

This loophole will be overcome by provisions of the Lisbon Treaty. After a transition period, the full powers of the ECJ will become applicable to the acquis of the former third pillar as of 1 December 2014, according to Article 10 of Protocol 36 on transitional provisions. Yet so far, there is 'no possibility for individuals and companies to bring direct actions for the annulment of third pillar measures' (Douglas-Scott, 2008: 23). Citizens also remain excluded from gaining redress against Europol at the ECJ (for more details see the section on Europol later in the chapter).

The fact that, hitherto, the ECJ has been only marginally competent in third pillar matters has raised concerns, as it led to an inadequate control of the institutional balance given the EU's competencies in this area (EU Network of Independent Experts on Fundamental Rights, 2003: 9). The ECJ is 'no longer an absent player' in matters concerning the AFSJ, however, and has incrementally started to contribute to the configuration of the AFSJ by giving preliminary rulings on the validity and interpretation of EU legislation (Sanfrutos Cano, 2008: 52). In 2003, the Court made its first judgment concerning matters under the third pillar, with reference to a provision of the Schengen Convention (joined cases *Gözütok and Brügge* (2003);[9] Thwaites, 2003). That the ECJ—and the attached Court of First Instance (CFI)—might become powerful players in the scrutiny of the AFSJ can also be seen from two other cases concerning the 'terrorist lists', namely the prominent ones of *Kadi* and *Al Barakaat*, which were dealt with jointly by the Court.[10]

According to the UN's Sanctions Committee, Yassin Abdullah Kadi, a resident of Saudi Arabia, and the Al Barakaat International Foundation, established in Sweden, were associated with Bin Laden and, consequently, were included in the terrorist list for their funds to be frozen. Their names were reproduced in the Annex of Council Regulation 881/2002 (Council, 2002c). Mr Kadi and Al Barakaat brought their case before the CFI claiming that the Council was not competent to adopt the regulation at issue and that it infringed several of their fundamental rights, in particular, the right to property and the rights of the defence. Similar to the judgment of the ECtHR in *Segi and Gestoras Amnestía*, the CFI dismissed the appeal and decided that the EU courts had, in principle, no jurisdiction to review the validity of the regulation (joined cases *Kadi and Yusuf and Al Barakaat v Council and Commission* (2005)). The Court argued that because the lists were based on an obligation circumscribed by the relevant UN resolutions,

---

[9] Joined Cases C-187/01 and C/385/01 *Gözütok and Brügge* [2003] ECR I-1345.

[10] The CFI is an independent court attached to the ECJ, composed of twenty-seven judges, one from each MS. Appeals are sent to the ECJ.

the EU authorities 'had no autonomous discretion' (*Kadi* (2005)[11] § 214; *Yusuf and Al Barakaat* (2005)[12] § 265). The responsibilities arising under the UN Charter would prevail 'over any other obligations, including the obligation under Community law to respect fundamental rights' (*Kadi* (2005) §§ 181–84; *Yusuf and Al Barakaat* (2005) §§ 231–34).

Mr Kadi and the Al Barakaat group filed appeals against those rulings before the ECJ. In its judgment on 3 September 2008, the ECJ set aside the decision by the CFI and came to a very different decision (joined cases *Kadi and Al Barakaat* (2008)[13]). It argued that the Regulation 2580/2001 falls into the context of the internal and autonomous legal order of the Community within which the ECJ has jurisdiction to review the validity of measures in the light of fundamental rights (European Parliament, 2009b: 48–49). In other words, an international agreement ought not to undermine the Union's commitment to fundamental rights. It pointed out that there might have been a way of implementing the UN Resolution without excluding judicial scrutiny of its lawfulness. The Court annulled the relevant implementing measures and declared that they violated fundamental rights protected by the EC legal order (De Búrca, 2009: 2). It decided that crucial aspects of judicial review were dismissed in the listing procedures: 'the rights of the defence, in particular the right to be heard, and the right to effective judicial review of those rights, were patently not respected' (ECJ joint cases, *Kadi and Al Barakaat* (2008)). The Council ought to inform the person or entity concerned about the grounds of their listing, at the latest promptly after the decision was made, 'in order to enable those persons or entities to exercise . . . their right to bring an action' (*Kadi and Al Barakaat* (2008) § 336). As this did not happen in the case of Mr Kadi and Al Barakaat, their listings infringed their right to legal remedy (*Kadi and Al Barakaat* (2008)).

Notably, the Court explicitly discussed a scenario in which 'safety or the conduct of the international relations of the Community and of its Member States may militate against the communication of certain matters to the persons concerned and, therefore, against their being heard on those matters' (*Kadi and Al Barakaat* (2008) § 342). This would not mean, however,

> that restrictive measures such as those imposed by the contested regulation escape all review by the Community judiciary once it has been claimed that the act laying them down concerns national security and terrorism. . . . In such a case, it is none the less the task of the Community judicature to apply, in the course of the judicial review it carries out, techniques which accommodate . . . legitimate security concerns about the nature and sources of information

[11] Case T-315/01 *Yassin Abdullah Kadi v Council of the European Union and Commission of the European Communities* [2005] ECR II-3649.

[12] Case T-306/01 *Ahmed Ali Yusuf and Al Barakaat International Foundation v Council of the European Union and Commission of the European Communities* [2005] ECR II-3533.

[13] Joined Cases C-402/05 P and C-415/05 P *Yassin Abdullah Kadi and Al Barakaat International Foundation v Council of the European Union and Commission of the European Communities* [2008] ECR-I 6351.

> taken into account in the adoption of the act concerned and...the need to accord the individual a sufficient measure of procedural justice (*Kadi and Al Barakaat* (2008) § 343).

The judicial struggle with respect to the terrorist sanctioning regime is worth exploring in such length not only because the rulings illustrate the different positions of the judicial bodies and the current 'jungle' of judicial oversight at the European level, but also because they are examples of CT measures introduced by an international body—the UN. Bodies such as the UN and EU, as Gráinne de Búrca (2009: 9) has explained, 'tend to concentrate and to enhance executive and bureaucratic power... [but tend] not to provide for the accountability and oversight mechanisms which are characteristic of the state context'. Agreements reached at the EU level, for example, often exclude, or are accompanied by, less effective national mechanisms of judicial and democratic control (Bigo, 2006b: 24–40). Victims of such measures often have difficulties in finding ways of judicial redress against such policies and acts of international bodies. This was demonstrated by the cases concerning terrorist lists.

De Búrca (2009) argued that the lack of judicial oversight is due to the idea that such bodies do not possess legal or operational powers, which would allow them to affect individuals directly, but that this perspective does not account for how international organizations have evolved over time. Concerning the Kadi and Al Barakaat cases, she pointed out that the primary responsibility lies with the international bodies which establish such blacklists, not the states implementing such mandatory decisions (de Búrca, 2009: 11). For the future, de Búrca (2009: 13–14; emphasis added) warns that

> the problem may... be that the proliferation of international organizations and institutions, rather than multiplying the potential sites and mechanisms of accountability and jurisdictional oversight, in fact leave *a vacuum of legal responsibility* where the international organization itself envisages no legal mechanism for review, and the national or intermediate levels of authority consider that they are not themselves responsible for the act in question and that they lack jurisdiction to question the accountability of the other or 'higher' level of authority.

Against this background, the judgment of the ECJ concerning the second Kadi/Al Barakaat decision must be understood as a remarkable move. As Elspeth Guild (2008: 181) has pointed out, this judgment implied that the EU 'as security actor is changed from one unaccountable to the individual to one which must justify its actions where those actions harm the individual'. She interprets this as a move towards the recognition of a more direct relationship between the EU and the individual (Guild, 2008: 182).

The severe criticisms and judicial judgments of the 'terrorist lists' have led to some procedural changes at the EU level. These include the creation of a formal sanctions committee, stricter review procedures, a notification system for listed individuals, clarifications concerning de-listing applications, and the move from an automatic implementation of the UN 1267 lists at the EU level to one of 'controlled compliance' which allows for the consultancy of advisory committees and the listed individuals and groups (cf ECCHR, 2010: 18–20). In addition, Article 275(2) of the TFEU provides for the right to judicial review, one of the deficiencies pointed out in the 2008 *Kadi* judgment. Some shortcomings remain at the EU level, in particular with respect to the overall secrecy of the listing process. However, more recently it is in particular the foundation of the EU lists—the UN Resolutions and listing procedures, which continue to be sharply criticized due to the lack of transparency, involvement of a more democratically accountable body, such as the General Assembly, and judicial review of the listing procedures.

Apart from the challenges posed to the EU by international CT obligations, the following sub-section will demonstrate that the EU's arrangements with third parties, such as the US, also challenge sound judicial scrutiny.

Information exchange between the EU and a third party: the example of the EU-US Passenger Name Record Agreements

As outlined previously, information sharing is at the hub of the EU's cooperative CT efforts with third parties, such as the US. The arrangements usually include regulations of data processing and protection. In the following, I will briefly explore the challenges discussed in the case of the EU-US PNR Agreements (see also Chapters 5 and 6). The US is the example of a third party with, as it is widely acknowledged, 'different' data protection standards than the EU (Council, 2008h).

The first PNR agreement was based on European Community law (first pillar) and therefore the EU Data Protection Directive (DPD) was relevant which maintains the EU's data protection framework (Council, 1995c). Most important in the context of this book is that Article 25 of the DPD does not allow for transfer of data unless an appropriate protection of personal data can be granted (Argomaniz, 2009: 123). Yet, the ECJ annulled the PNR agreement on 30 May 2006, maintaining that it was founded on an incorrect legal basis (as explained in the previous chapter). A new Agreement was put on a different legal basis. Consequently, it fell outside the scope of Community law and, therefore, the DPD (*Parliament v Council and Commission* (2006)[14]). There was no overarching data protection framework for the second and third pillars at that time.[15] Consequently, the PNR data exchange would not be subject to any European rule on data protection, if the new agreement would not specify respective regulations (Sanfrutos Cano, 2008: 57). The PNR Agreement of 29 June 2007 therefore included several changes. From the data protection perspective, a crucial concern is that US law requires the DHS to share PNR data

[14] C-317/04 *European Parliament v Council* and C-318/04 *European Parliament v Commission* [2006] ECR I-4721.

[15] A first general data protection framework for the third pillar—the Data Protection Framework Directive (DPFD)—was adopted on 30 December 2008 (Council, 2008f; cf page 171).

with other US agencies (House of Lords, EU Select Committee, 2007a: para 62). As a consequence, once the data arrives in the US, it cannot be controlled anymore and the data might even become accessible to third countries through further information sharing (Wiegand, 2008: 91). Neither is there an independent authority which could supervise the application of the rules set by the PNR agreement. Given these shortcomings, the EP criticized the data protection framework in this context as inadequate (House of Lords, EU Select Committee, 2007a: para 51–52).

Similar to the challenges identified in previous chapters concerning CTNs, it is again the *international* collaborative dimension which causes great concerns about accountability and oversight in the context of the PNR Agreements. Yet the following section will rather focus on the EU context. Even there, collaborative network structures appear to be insufficiently covered by data protection regulations.

The Lack of a Rigorous Data Protection Framework

Francesca Bignami's work (2007: 674) shows the advantage of understanding law enforcement collaboration as a networked form of cooperation with respect to the field of data protection:

> Personal information can be collected by one national agency, used by a second for conducting surveillance, and transferred to yet a third for purposes of freezing financial assets or bringing a criminal prosecution. If only one of these many actors violates the right to privacy, individuals are at risk. All the other participating agencies, though entirely rights-abiding at home, become complicit in this privacy violation: they either supplied the personal information that produced the rights breach or they acted upon bad information, thus compounding the rights breach.

In its current form, the EU's data protection regime is fragmented. The DPD does not apply to the processing of personal data in the course of an activity which falls outside the scope of Community law (European Parliament and Council, 1995). Article 3(2) explicitly mentions the exceptions of public security, defence, state security, and the activities of the State in areas of criminal law. The DPD is therefore not applicable to data processing concerning PJCC.

The lack of a common legal data protection framework concerning EU-wide policing efforts meant that MS had to apply their individual frameworks to a certain situation. As a consequence, different rules could be relevant for a particular situation' (Mitsilegas and Baldaccini, 2007: 10) and these unilateral frameworks could hamper information sharing among MS. In addition, some PJCC-related bodies, such as Europol and Eurojust, have their own data protection authorities (for Europol see page 172).

To overcome complete fragmentation in this field, the EU started to develop pan-European data protection standards which all members have to adopt

(Bignami, 2007: 664). A General Framework Decision on data protection in the third pillar was discussed for years (European Parliament, 2009a: 22). On 4 October 2005, the Commission proposed a draft Council Framework Decision on the protection of personal data processed in the framework of PJCC (Commission, 2005c), including, among other features, 'general rules on the lawfulness of processing personal data, rights of the person whose data are processed, confidentiality and security in processing, judicial remedies, . . . [and] supervisory authorities' (Douglas-Scott, 2008: 20).

However, 'essential national security interests and specific intelligence activities in the field of national security' (Commission, 2005c) remain excluded. After a long struggle between the Commission, the EP, and the Council and periods of redrafting, including some scrutiny reservations by the parliaments of Denmark, Italy, Netherlands, Sweden, and the UK, the DPFD was adopted under the German EU Presidency on 30 December 2008 (Council, 2008f). The DPFD became the main reference point regarding data protection concerning matters of PJCC. Yet it only applies to the *cross-border* exchange of personal data *within* the EU. The DPFD does not apply to domestic data within individual MS. Neither is it applicable to data exchange beyond the EU (the transatlantic efforts at information sharing are excluded, for example). Moreover, the specific regulatory instruments applicable to, for example, Europol, Schengen, and Eurojust with their individual supervisory bodies remain in place (cf Bigo et al, 2011: 97–98). These limitations have led to suggestions that the DPFD 'reads like the turning away from the concept that personal data is in principle protected against complete state access' (European Parliament, 2009a: 22). The European Data Protection Supervisor (2008), Peter Hustinx, maintained that, despite being 'a first step', the Framework Decision is 'not fully satisfactory'. Moreover, one interviewee pointed out that there is no 'naming and shaming policy' in the Council. That is to say that the Council's members would not blame an individual country for wrongdoing. They further raised the concern that there is no assessment of measures taken by countries (Interview B).

A more general problem with data protection legislation in this context is that it is rather reactive than proactive, in particular when it comes to the rapid development of new surveillance and information technologies and procedures. Indeed, the emergence of new technologies, including the facilitation of automatic interoperability, was a key push factor for a debate about the establishment of a general data protection framework for JHA-related matters (Alvaro, 2006).

This section has identified some severe shortcomings and an overall lack of coherence of the EU's data protection framework, in particular with respect to international information exchange. While a new data protection regulation is currently under discussion, this has been an intractable development so far.[16] To

[16] For an overview of reform suggestions concerning the EU data protection framework, see <http://ec.europa.eu/justice/data-protection/index_en.htm>. For an in-depth discussion see Bigo et al, 2011.

provide a fuller picture of the data protection mosaic at EU level, the following section will focus on one specific data protection regulation of great importance concerning CTNs: Europol's data protection framework.

Europol and Data Protection

The EU strives for strengthened police cooperation in preventing and combating terrorism and serious crime. In this context, key operations of Europol relate to the storing, processing, and analysing of personal data in cases where two or more MS are affected.

Overall, the legal base of Europol is fairly detailed. Aden (2001: 106; emphasis in original) argues that Europol's 'concept of legitimacy follows the classical German idea of a *Rechtsstaat* in which executive intrusions on individual rights are only legitimised if they are allowed by a legal base, normally by a parliamentary law'. However, as has been described in Chapter 3, the role of parliaments concerning the development and establishment of Europol's legal framework—the Europol Convention, its amendments, and the ECD—has, so far, been fairly limited. According to the idea of the separation of powers and the concept of checks-and-balances, the executive should be scrutinized by both the judiciary and legislative in order to ensure rightful conduct. In the following, aspects of the judicial scrutiny of Europol's data processing and sharing will be explored.

The JHA Council and Europol's Management Board

Before the entry into force of the Lisbon Treaty, Europol was solely accountable to the JHA Council, through the Europol Management Board. While the Council continues to 'provide the general framework for European police cooperation and decide how far practice can go in the concrete situation' (Aden, 2001: 111), a crucial change of the Lisbon Treaty has been that Europol is now governed by the Council as well as the EP (Article 88 of the TFEU). Together, they now guide and monitor Europol's work through mechanisms such as the appointment of the Director, priority-setting, and budget provisions, according to the ordinary legislative procedure. Administrative oversight and guidance continues to be provided by the Europol Management Board, comprising one representative from each MS and one from the Commission (ECD, Article 37). The Board is obliged to meet at least twice a year, and the chair rotates with the EU presidencies. Decisions in the Board were previously taken by unanimity but are now taken by two-thirds majority.

It has been explained previously that there is no judicial control at the EU level which would be comparable to the control of the executive at the national level (Kahlke, 2004: 45). In accordance with this observation, the scrutiny procedures by judicial institutions concerning Europol have been described as being 'fragmented' (Puntscher Riekmann, 2008: 26). Declaration 7 of Article 30 of the TEU, annexed to the Final Act of the Intergovernmental Conference of Amsterdam, stated that 'action in the field of police cooperation..., including activities of Europol, shall be subject to appropriate judicial review by the competent national authorities in accordance with rules applicable in each Member State' (as quoted in Puntscher Riekmann, 2008: 26–27). The protection of fundamental rights also lies in the hands of the national courts. For example, information provided to Europol via the ENUs are controlled by the national judicial instances and 'a second legality check was not found necessary' (Bruggeman, 2006: 5). The national courts share the judicial oversight of Europol with the ECJ (Puntscher Riekmann, 2008: 26). Yet, as explained earlier, up to December 2014 the ECJ has only limited responsibilities concerning issues related to police work.

The actual abilities of the national courts to offer legal protection with respect to Europol are fairly limited. This is also due to the immunity of Europol officers, the inviolability of Europol archives, and the overall obligation of discretion and confidentiality (ECD, Article 41; Council, 1997: Articles 3 and 8; see also Chapter 3). In practice, this means that neither Europol officials nor the national liaison officers based at Europol's headquarters can be put to trial in case of a violation of Europol's legal framework (Kahlke, 2004: 45). However, Europol's Director is obliged to lift the immunity 'in cases where the immunity would impede the course of justice and can be waived without prejudice to the interests of Europol' (Council, 1997: Article 12). This power of the Director has been criticized as being insufficient to provide for adequate legal redress in case of wrongdoings, however. As David Heath already stated in 1997 before the House of Commons (1997),

> (t)hat is equivalent to leaving it to a chief constable to decide whether it is in the interests of his constabulary that an officer in this country [i.e. the UK] should be immune from prosecution.... We are being asked to give officers of Europol a degree of immunity that is not, and would not, be afforded to members of our own constabulary.

Moreover, it is an executive body—Europol's director, controlled by the Council, who decides on the waiving of immunity (Kaiafa-Gbandi, 2001: 254).

Based on Article 17(2) of the Immunity Protocol, the Protocol must be reviewed in case the functions of Europol would go beyond those set out in Article 3 of the original Europol Convention (Council, 1997). This took place for the first time with respect to the creation of JITs, the teams that can be requested to be set up by any MS concerned with the investigation of an offence with a cross-border dimension (see Chapter 3). According to the JIT Framework Decision, 'Europol officials may assist in all activities and exchange information with all members of the team' (Rijken and Vermeulen, 2006: 170; Council, 2002g). Thus, the Decision provides for 'direct liaison' between Europol and a JIT (as opposed to an indirect one via ENUs only). In this case, it has been argued, the functions and role of Europol officers are executive investigative ones. Consequently, Europol officials participating in a JIT do not have immunity from prosecution for any criminal act they might commit in this context and they are subject to the law of the MS in which the JIT operates (Rijken and Vermeulen, 2006: 170).

Apart from the immunity regulation, the legal protection by courts is also fairly limited owing to the specific institutional arrangement of Europol in the context of data protection, namely the JSB.

Data protection regulations

Given Europol's focus on information sharing and analysis, a key aspect of its work is related to the handling of personal data. Information privacy, or data protection, is considered a fundamental entitlement in Europe (ECHR, Article 8). As a qualified right, it can be restricted, for example for reasons of public safety or in order to protect the rights of others, and it therefore needs to be balanced against collective interests, such as national security. This is particularly the case if the police work crosses jurisdictional spheres and relies heavily on the exchange of data. This describes Europol's institutional position and functions well. According to a CoE Recommendation, the collection of personal data for police purposes should be limited 'to such as is necessary for the prevention of a real danger or the suppression of a specific criminal offence' (Council of Europe, 1987: Principle 2.1).

Since inaccurate or misinterpreted information can harm citizens, governments are constitutionally restricted in their use of personal information within the national framework. In Europe, 'the government's access to and use of personal information is regulated as a personal data processing continuum in which no stage is considered more or less harmful than the next. Privacy rights apply throughout. Moreover, privacy principles cover *all* personal information' (Bignami, 2007: 672; emphasis in original).

While already at the national level shared data could be misinterpreted, this risk becomes even greater in the context of CTNs. Different judicial spheres are now increasingly overlapping despite the existence of 'cultural, social, organisational and legal differences between the data exchanging law enforcement authorities' (European Parliament, 2009a; see also Anderson, 1993a: 29).

Europol's network has its own data protection authority, the JSB (ECD, Article 34). The JSB has been established as a joint control body, composed of representatives of national data protection supervisory bodies (NSBs). Its primary tasks are to supervise the use of personal data by Europol and the compatibility with the right of informational self-determination as well as to give advice on data protection aspects of Europol's work (JSB website). Part of this task is to check whether a newly created AWF (cf Chapter 3) and the collection and analysis of personal data accord with privacy principles (Bignami, 2007: 682).

The responsibility to ensure rightful data handling and data protection lies with the JSB and the NSBs respectively. The NSBs are to scrutinize the activities of the ENUs in question as well as those of Europol 'in order to ensure that individual rights of citizens are secured when processing personal data' (Puntscher

Riekmann, 2008: 27; cf. ECD, Article 33). In addition to the NSBs and the JSB, the European Data Protection Supervisor is entitled to monitor the activities of Europol, but its opinions are not legally binding.

The JSB's mandate also refers to the JSB as the contact point for individuals who requested access to information about them at Europol but who feel they did not receive a satisfactory reply. It therefore has to find a 'balance between desirable public access and the need to protect sensitive intelligence' (House of Lords, EU Select Committee, 2003: 18). One means of JSB's work are inspections at Europol headquarters. Every two years, results of its work are published in activity reports, which are sent to the EP and the Council and which are publicly available on the JSB's website (ECD, Article 34(6)).

The JSB has the power to cut off national monitoring in the sense that if it has come to a final decision on the legality of an act of data processing, this decision cannot be questioned in a court (ECD, Article 34 (8); Kahlke 2004: 46). Yet the JSB is not a full judicial body, but rather an administrative, quasi-judicial body without sufficient competencies to constitute an adequate instance of judicial control or provide for full legal protection (Puntscher Riekmann, 2008; Kahlke, 2004: 46). Moreover, Article 34(2) of the ECD only maintains that 'Europol shall assist the Joint Supervisory Body in the performance of the latter's tasks' without further clarification of procedures in case of Europol's refusal to do so. If the JSB identifies wrongdoing by Europol it will inform its Director and, if any difficulty arises, it can alert the Management Board (ECD, Article 34(4)). Overall, the JSB lacks powers which would ensure a strong oversight. Despite being described as an independent body, the JSB can also advise Europol on matters of the use and processing of data—it is therefore not entirely independent, but rather an integral part of Europol (ECD, Article 34(3); Kahlke, 2004: 46). The principle of the separation of powers does not seem to apply here: a case might occur in which the JSB first advises Europol on a particular legal issue only to examine it later itself (Kaiafa-Gbandi, 2001: 254). Consequently, the JSB has been criticized for lacking objectivity, in particular with respect to the first agreement between Europol and the USA on the transmission of personal data. For example, the 2003 Report on Europol by the HL's EU Select Committee (2003: 17) stated that the JSB was closely involved in the negotiation but that it might not have maintained the usual independent position. The Committee felt 'that on some issues it [ie the JSB] had let its acknowledgement of the political imperative to secure an agreement override its responsibility for ensuring essential data protection safeguards'.

Owing to the restricted competences of the ECJ, an affected individual cannot appeal to the Court in the case of potentially erroneous data processing at Europol. Instead, each MS in accordance with its national law is liable for any damage caused to an individual as a result of erroneous data processing (ECD, Article 52). Here again, the restrictions of the national courts mentioned earlier have to be considered. The ECJ has only an interpretative role for Europol's legal base. With respect to 'the right of access, correction or deletion of personal data'

(ECD, Article 52) the competent authorities are the JSB and the national courts (ECD, Articles 30–32). The national level will be described further in the next subsection.

More recently, Article 28 of the ECD required the creation of the post of a Data Protection Officer (DPO) in addition to the JSB and the NSBs. The DPO's main tasks are to assure the compliance of data processing at Europol with the ECD and its general lawfulness. Yet, although formally independent, both the DPO and the JSB bodies appear to be fairly close to the executive. The JSB secretary is based in the Council premises in Brussels, providing an annual report to the EP and some other actors (Interview B). The DPO is proposed by Europol's Director and confirmed by the Management Board.

Data protection at the national level with respect to Europol

For the national level, the MS are requested to 'guarantee a level of data protection which corresponds at least to that which results from the application of the principles of' the 1981 Council of Europe's Convention on Personal Data Processing into national law (ECD, point 11; Council of Europe, 1981). Only then are the national authorities allowed to enter information into or extract information from the Europol system. In principle, an affected person can appeal to a national court concerning data collection (Kahlke, 2004: 57). However, an individual is usually not aware that his or her data is fed into Europol's EIS or an AWF. Neither would he or she be informed if the data was transferred either from a national authority to Europol or from the EIS to an AWF. Thus, at least the transfer from the EIS to an AWF lacks a clear legal basis (Kahlke, 2004: 57). Europol's annual reports to the EP do not contain any information about individual processes of data collection. The Management Board and the Council only exercise personal control. The question is therefore that of who could potentially identify a breach of law in this context.

Provisions for data protection at both the centre and at the level of the national nodes

One general requirement for data protection rules is *specificity*. That includes the precise definition of the type of data, its purpose, the amount of time it is allowed to be stored, and the provision of measures to ensure that no unauthorized parties can access the information. Those specifications provide for both Europol's central secretariat and the national nodes. The information which can be stored in Europol's databases and the AWFs have to refer to one of the types of crime listed in the Annex of the ECD. The nodes as well as the centre, or hub, also have to ensure that unauthorized staff or bodies do not gain access to the databases and information systems (Bignami, 2007: 683).

A second general principle is that of *proportionality*, which 'implies, among other things, that data are not excessive in relation to the purposes for which they are stored, and that they are deleted if they are no longer necessary for these purposes' (Lemmens, 2004: 229; see also Council of Europe, 1981, Article 5c). In general, the storage of personal data is to be reviewed after three years (ECD, Article 20). With respect to the EIS, it is the responsibility of each national authority to review the information it fed into the system and to ensure that it is still stored for the original investigative purpose (ECD, Article 20). The information can otherwise be automatically deleted from the EIS.

These restrictions for data collection and storage are accompanied by handling codes that are attached to Europol data files. This is a technical instrument, which allows Europol to restrict the transmission of personal data contained in the files (House of Lords, EU Select Committee, 2003: 17). Finally, individuals can check whether information about them is stored in one of Europol's databases and that this information can be corrected if proven to be wrong or be deleted in case its storing breaches the data protection rules. National data protection bodies are the contact point for citizens in this respect, which will forward the request to Europol. If not satisfied with the answer provided by Europol, the individual can approach the Appeal Committee of the JSB.

While the level of control of the data exchange via Europol was understood by some as adequate for Europol's original purposes (Anderson, 2008: 116), two crucial developments in the context of the fight against terrorism seem to challenge this understanding: the increasing interoperability of EU databases as well as the tendency towards increasing executive investigative powers of Europol (for example, through the creation of JITs). While JITs have been briefly explored (page 173), the following sub-section will focus on aspects of interoperability.

Interoperability of databases and EU-wide data exchange

As explained in the previous chapter, Europol's access to the VIS, SIS (II), and possibly Eurodac opens up a new dimension of EU-wide data exchange. On 24 November 2005, the Commission (2005g) called for the expansion and interoperability of the existing European databases, 'motivated by a perceived need for the improvement of internal security due to terrorist attacks'. The term 'interoperability' is defined as the 'ability of IT systems and of the business processes they support to exchange data and to enable the sharing of information and knowledge' (Commission, 2005g; for a critical stance on the emphasis on technology—and not the political and legal dimensions—see European Data Protection Supervisor, 2007b). The need to strengthen the links between databases in the AFSJ is one of the key elements of the EU Counter-terrorism Strategy (Council, 2005b; cf Chapter 1).

A crucial concern refers to one of the key principles of data protection, namely the specificity of the *purpose*. Each of the EU databases referred to with respect to the interoperability has been established for a limited purpose (Mitsilegas and Baldaccini, 2007: 4; Interview B). VIS and Eurodac have been set up with respect to the assessment of visa and asylum applications respectively, while Europol's database, as well as some features of SIS (II), refer to police cooperation and CT. Those databases also underlie different data protection regulations (Mitsilegas and Baldaccini, 2007: 5). While Article 6(2) of the Europol Convention prohibited connecting the EIS to any other automated processing system apart from the ENU systems, this is not a concern of the ECD.

Closely related to the idea of interoperability is the effort to improve and extend the EU-wide data exchange concerning police and judicial cooperation to fight terrorism (Council, 2003b). The 2004 Declaration on combating terrorism called for legislation 'simplifying the exchange of information and intelligence between law enforcement authorities of the Member States' (Council, 2004b). Based on this, the European Commission (2004) suggested several instruments to ensure a 'free circulation of information between the law enforcement authorities', the first of which was 'the principle of equivalent access to data between law enforcement authorities'. This 'principle of availability' arose from the assumption that the 'mere fact that information crosses borders should no longer be relevant' (European Parliament, 2009a; cf Commission, 2005b). The 2005 Proposal for a Framework Decision on the exchange of information under the principle of availability strived for the availability of law enforcement relevant information to competent authorities and Europol, including DNA-profiles, fingerprints, vehicle registration information, and communications data (Commission, 2005a: Articles 3(a), 6).

Yet this proposal never reached the final stage, as, in the same month, the Swedish government suggested the adoption of a Framework Decision on simplifying the exchange of information and intelligence between national law enforcement, in particular as regards serious offences including terrorist acts (Council, 2004f; hereafter called the Swedish Initiative). In contrast to the principle of availability, the Swedish Initiative aimed for much more direct access to information upon request. However, the Initiative states: 'The absence of a common legal framework for the effective and expeditious exchange of information and intelligence between law enforcement authorities of the Member States is a deficiency that will have to be remedied' (Council, 2004f: preamble). The Initiative was turned into a Framework Decision in 2006 which refers to 'any type of information or data' held by law enforcement authorities, public authorities, or private entities and which is available to law enforcement authorities 'without the taking of coercive measures' (Council, 2006c: Article 2(d)). Yet MS 'shall, where permitted by and in accordance with their law, provide information or intelligence previously obtained by means of coercive measures' (Article 1(6)). The Framework Decision excludes explicitly secret services or units dealing with, in particular, national security from the information and data exchange procedure (Article 2(a)). However, it also grants MS the right to define the competent law enforcement authorities. Therefore, if 'in an individual Member State the separation between police forces and secret services blurs or does not exist, the possibility that those services nevertheless become engaged in the transnational information exchange is actually given' (European Parliament, 2009a: 16).

With respect to data protection, Article 8 of the Swedish Initiative maintains that requests for information and intelligence are subject to the national data protection laws of the receiving state, whereas personal data must be protected in accordance with the CoE's 1981 Convention for the Protection of Individuals with regard to Automatic Processing of Personal Data and the Additional Protocol of 8 November 2001 with respect to Supervisory Authorities and Transborder Data Flows (Council of Europe, 1981, 2001). More generally, the Framework Decision allows that a MS can refuse the provision of certain information, if its provision would harm its 'essential national security interests' (Article 10(a)). A questionnaire concerning the Swedish Framework Decision revealed that there remain crucial 'difficulties for the exchange of data which lie in the different legal provisions authorizing police agencies to exchange personal data across national borders. The replies clearly show that there is no common regulation of data access among law enforcement authorities' (European Parliament, 2009a: 2; for the replies to the questionnaire see Council, 2005i).

The 2005 London bombings led to a Decision on the exchange of information and cooperation concerning terrorist offences, which calls for the expansion of the scope of information shared 'to all stages of criminal proceedings, including convictions, and to all persons, groups or entities investigated, prosecuted or convicted for terrorist offences' (Council, 2005h: preamble, para 4). The MS are required to transmit information concerning criminal investigations, prosecutions, and convictions for terrorist offences to Europol and Eurojust (Article 2(3)). Moreover, Article 2(6) of the Decision calls for each MS to make all data related to terrorist crime accessible as soon as possible. This is the core of the 'principle of availability'—the central pooling of information at the national level and widest possible distribution among MS.

Even at the national level, however, serious problems of information sharing in the field of CT remain (Council, 2008a). Unsurprisingly, the legal and technological challenges led to an 'unsatisfactory' implementation of the 2005 Decision on the exchange of information and cooperation concerning terrorist offences, according to the Counter-terrorism Coordinator who himself refers to a report by Europol (Council, 2008a, 2005h). According to that report, the key 'obstacles to a systematic transmission of information relating to investigations' appear to be:

- the refusal by certain national judicial authorities to transmit information relating to investigations in progress;
- agencies with dual competencies in law enforcement and security are experiencing legal difficulties in identifying what can be shared with Europol;
- the requirement laid down in Article 2(3) of the Decision maintaining that the information affects, or is likely to affect at least two MS (Council, 2008a).

In order to improve the exchange of CT information, the Counter-terrorism Coordinator suggested several instruments, which overall refer to technological and legal harmonization, cultural approximation of police work, and organizational centralization of national CT efforts (Council, 2008a).

Finally, the Prüm Treaty, which has been explored in the previous chapter, needs mentioning. One of the key issues of the Prüm arrangements is the exchange of data, including sensitive information, such as DNA samples. It is fair to say that the seven original contracting states of Prüm 'have acted as a "laboratory", working out the complicated technical arrangements for querying each others' police databases quickly and effectively in a small group' (Brady, 2007a: 21–22). It has been suggested that the Prüm Treaty breached Community law, to be more precise the 'principle of loyalty' under Article 10 TEC stating that the MS 'shall abstain from any measure which could jeopardise the attainment of the objectives of this Treaty' (Balzacq, 2006: 2–3; see also House of Lords, EU Select Committee, 2007b: 11–12). The European Data Protection Supervisor suggested that the Treaty breached Community law, because the participating MS have avoided the requirements of enhanced cooperation. Crucially, he pointed out that this is a theoretical argument only, as neither the ECJ nor any other court has jurisdiction to decide on this question (House of Lords, EU Select Committee, 2007b: 12).

Similarly, the transfer of the Prüm Treaty into EU law has been criticized, as the transfer of a 'privately negotiated' treaty into the EU acquis—ie, not all MS were involved in the negotiations about the original Prüm Convention—'does not fulfil the requirements of legitimacy. It appears underhanded and dishonest' (Guild as quoted in House of Lords, EU Select Committee, 2007b: 11). The Prüm Decision clearly 'pushed the legislative process as far as it is possible at the time being' (European Parliament, 2009a: 20). In the process of adopting the framework decision on Prüm, national data protection authorities could 'play a role of consultation in the national implementation, and at the European level, via the "Article 29 Working Party", but without the possibility to stop the procedure' (Bellanova, 2008: 207); and the European Data Protection Supervisor's opinion on the matter was not legally binding. Overall, the involvement of national data protection authorities and the EDPS was quite marginal (cf Bellanova, 2008: 205).

Analysing all these instruments which aim to facilitate EU-wide mechanisms of data exchange—such as the stalled Principle of Availability, the Swedish Initiative, and the Treaty of Prüm, it appears that it becomes increasingly 'difficult for individuals to track and trace information held about them and passed from one member state to another (and even to third countries) or even to determine if the information held about them is accurate' (Douglas-Scott, 2008: 18).

The Commission is not satisfied with the current extent and reach of information exchange at EU level, however. For example, it criticized the Swedish Initiative for not obliging Member States to provide information (Commission, 2005a). Both the Prüm Treaty and the Swedish Initiative do not favour *direct* information exchange between authorities (European Parliament, 2009a: 18–19). However, for the time being several serious (and also practical) problems are apparent even in the restricted systems when it comes to enhanced data sharing. Apart from the different technological data systems, one crucial challenge is that MS collect, categorize, handle, and interpret data related to crime differently. This became very apparent in the discussion about the establishment of the European Criminal Records Information System (ECRIS) which was not set up as a central database, but as a decentralized system (the MS host their own databases). This is due to the fact that crime data remains very diverse within Europe and a common nomenclature of criminal offences would be needed to avoid misinterpretation and failures.

Such restrictions have to be welcomed from the perspective of data protection, as they seem to be necessary given that the 'dangers of inaccurate information are multiplied when information is exchanged between states' (Cameron, 2005: 43). As mentioned earlier, there are significant differences between the data-exchanging law enforcement authorities. Moreover, some countries seem to lack a clear approach on how to share information on criminality at the international level.[17] The complexity of data-sharing mechanisms (partly EU-wide regulated, partly by individual agreements) has also been identified as a challenge for national authorities (Magee, 2008: 60, § 129). While this might create problems concerning data protection, it might also lead to less efficiency. The UK, for example, 'does not have a very good reputation in the EU in terms of responding to requests for information from other countries' (Magee, 2008: 61, § 135). The country has also been criticized by Interpol's Secretary General for not making use of Interpol's list of 11,000 terror suspects, for example (Magee, 2008: 61, § 133). This can be understood as one of the downsides of networking, as the voluntary nature and the granting of autonomy of the individuals nodes can lead to non-commitment, which in the long run might harm the overall purpose or reputation of the network. The establishment of trust and a certain routine appears to be of great importance. This can be seen from the example of the Scottish Crime and Drug Enforcement Agency (SCDEA). Apparently, the SCDEA staff members 'were initially nervous about using Europol for data security reasons, but as they used it more and more they have gained such confidence that they have seconded a member of staff there' (Magee, 2008: 63, § 141).

Finally, while the roles of national authorities and EU bodies, such as Europol and Eurojust, are fairly well defined, 'it is above all the operational nature of cooperation within intelligence agencies and investigations which requires constant improvement' (European Economic and Social Committee, 2008: § 3.13). Currently, there seems to be no assessment of the degree of access that secret services have to the systems of transnational information exchange (see also European Parliament, 2009a: 23). Neither is the role of the private sector transparent. To give just one example concerning the fight against terrorist financing: the sharing of intelligence 'between the private sector and financial intelligence units (FIUs), between FIUs and other component national authorities, between all these authorities and Europol and Eurojust constitutes one of the main priority

[17] 'There is no clear UK strategy for sharing international information on criminality which sets out what we want to achieve, or our preferred routes for doing so' (Magee, 2008: § 127).

areas of current European legal instruments' (European Parliament, 2009b: 3). FIUs can be of administrative or judicial nature and they have 'different levels of cooperation amongst themselves and with Europol' (European Parliament, 2009b: 4; 20).[18]

The final sub-section of this chapter will explore the dimension of information exchange beyond the EU, hence the information exchange with non-EU countries or other public or private entities, thus, with third parties. I will draw on the example of Europol's agreements with the US.

Data protection rules for the exchange of information with third parties

As described earlier, Europol's network includes third parties. On 27 March 2000, the Council authorized Europol's Director to open negotiations on agreements with third parties, 'subject to compliance with a strict procedure, where this cooperation could result in the transmission of personal data' (EU Network of Independent Experts on Fundamental Rights, 2003: 23). With some of them, it also exchanges personal data. The pre-condition for such an exchange is, however, that those third parties provide an *adequate* level of data protection within their State/entity (ECD, Article 23(6) (b)). Adequacy in this context refers to the guarantees of the CoE's Convention on Personal Data Processing and the supervision of data protection rules by an independent government body (Bignami, 2007: 683). One exception to this rule refers to cases where Europol's Director 'considers the transmission of the data to be absolutely necessary to safeguard the essential interests of the Member States' or 'in the interests of preventing imminent danger associated with crime or terrorist offences' (ECD, Article 23(8); former Article 18 of the Europol Convention). One example for such an extraordinary situation was the exchange of information between Europol and US authorities after the 9/11 attacks.

Similar to the agreements on information exchange between the EU and third parties, such as the PNR agreements discussed previously, the agreements between Europol and third parties and the data protection procedures accompanying such an exchange remain challenging from a data protection perspective. There remains a need for adequate data protection safeguards. One concern is the lack of transparency: where does the information go that Europol provides and for what purpose is it used. The other concern is how trustworthy the information is that Europol receives from third parties and how much information is available about the process of gathering that information. Again, the Europol-USA Agreements give illuminating insights to this complex problem. This appears to be a rather one-way provision of data so far, as has been described in the previous two

[18] Many FIUs participate in the Egmont Group, created in 1995, which allows the exchange of intelligence via a secure website (cf website Egmont Group). The FIUs can share financial intelligence through a secure system (European Parliament, 2009b: 21–2).

chapters. Nevertheless, the paper version of the Agreement understands it as a two-way-system.

In particular, the (second) Agreement on the exchange of personal data has been criticized for the lack of serious data protection regulations and an insufficient level of protection of fundamental rights (eg Lavranos, 2003: 270). To begin with, the definition of the term personal data in the Agreement as referring to 'any information relating to an identified or identifiable natural person' is very vague. It is also widely agreed that the data protection standards in the US are far looser and less strict than the ones on the European continent. Therefore, it cannot count as an 'adequate' level of data protection. This overall deficit is also not covered by particularly specific regulations and therefore the use of the information is not clearly limited. The Agreement remains very unspecific in this context. It provides for the exchange of information for purposes such as 'the prevention, detection, suppression, investigation and prosecution of any specific criminal offences, and for any specific analytical purposes, to which such information relates' (Article 5(1)). Moreover, the information can be accessed by 'competent U.S. federal authorities' (Article 7(1))—a term which is not further specified—and by 'competent U.S. state or local authorities provided that they agree to observe the provisions of this Agreement' (Article 7(1) (b)). Given those wide provisions, it is no exaggeration to state that 'neither Europol nor the EU Member States will have any control over which American authority is using the data and for what purposes' (Lavranos, 2003: 269).

It remains somewhat unclear how Europol checks incoming information for reliability and lawfulness. Europol staff have a system to judge the validity of a piece of information which rates both the validity of the source (weak or strong) and the validity of the information as such (Interview C). What this control system does not cover is information about *how* the information in question was gathered. It is, however, essential in democratic societies 'that not only the results of each crime investigation but more specifically the way in which evidence has been obtained can be judicially supervised' (De Witte, 1993: 97).

Surely, this is not a problem of information exchange with third parties only. This is also an inherent risk within Europol's network of national units. How information is gathered is something that is very difficult to control from a distance. However, it is assumed that European states share certain principles of the protection of fundamental rights and, consequently, would roughly have a similar level of protective regulations. On 6 April 2009, however, the Council (2009h) authorized Europol's Director to enter into negotiations with Israel with a view to concluding an operational cooperation agreement, thus an agreement including personal data. Europol is also in negotiations with Russia with a view to concluding a strategic and operational cooperation agreement.[19] Given reports by human rights organizations about the conditions of imprisonment in such

[19] The current 2003 Europol-Russia agreement does not include the exchange of personal data.

countries, one may wonder how far the protection of fundamental rights can be granted in cooperation with them.

Taken together, the findings of this chapter point out some severe weaknesses concerning the judicial scrutiny of EU-wide CTP. While compliance with the rule of law as such is not a democratic value, a smooth, effective, and powerful system of judicial scrutiny is an important cornerstone of democratic legitimacy. It is meant to protect individuals from wrongdoing through executive bodies. Yet the increased Europeanization, and also internationalization, of CT efforts, and the inherent crossing of jurisdictions has led to a situation in which the protection of individuals' rights and freedoms is less stringent in comparison to a purely domestic framework. Overall, the judicial accountability system for European CT activities has proved to be rather weak so far.

To some extent, the Lisbon Treaty has brought, and is to bring, significant improvements and will increase legal certainty in the longer term. A crucial step in this respect will be the extension of the ECJ's jurisdiction to review and interpret AFSJ-related matters as of December 2014.

Yet the Lisbon Treaty, and in the specific case of Europol the ECD, also opens the door for further intensification of networking across the EU and beyond. Due to the move from unanimity to qualified majority voting in the Council concerning the field of PJCC, the Lisbon Treaty now allows MS to create cooperative links 'as they deem appropriate between the competent departments of their administrations responsible for safeguarding national security' (Carrera and Geyer, 2007: 5).

Some problems identified in this chapter lie at the national level, rather than at that of the EU. Many European governments have introduced CT measures in recent years which have undermined 'cherished values and resulted in serious violations of human rights' (International Commission of Jurists of the Eminent Jurists Panel, 2009). National CT legislation has not always been subject to careful scrutiny concerning the risk of abuse of fundamental rights (Anderson, 2008: 116). Unsurprisingly, this development had an effect on the EU as a whole. For example, its CT and policing activities are mainly steered by the MS through the Council. As shown earlier, problems at the national level concerning the handling of data exchange as well as the increased integration of secret and intelligence services in CT activities might raise challenges which are virtually transferred to the European level through the process of data transfer. The cases of individuals whose rights were harmed due to their listing by the UN and EU as 'terrorist suspects' show that the legal remedies at the European level are not strong. One author suggested a virtual lack of respect for the rule of law and freedom and justice in the EU's former third pillar (Douglas-Scott, 2008: 28).

Of course, there have always been tensions between the duty of political entities to protect their citizens against terrorism and their obligation to respect human rights. The fundamental right to life is understood to imply a 'right to protection from terrorism' (PACE, 2004). Acknowledging the need for certain measures to tackle terrorism does not mean, however, to justify the impingement of human rights and civil liberties. From a human rights perspective, 'there are values higher than the security of the State' (Cameron, 2004: 346). As the UN's former Secretary General Kofi Annan and many others have emphasized in recent years, the respect for human rights, fundamental freedoms, and the rule of law are essential values and should be prioritized in the fight against terrorism (United Nations Security Council, 2003; Council of Europe, 2002; International Commission of Jurists, 2009). This might occasionally be seen as an 'obstacle to a short-term "effective" measure' (Cameron, 2004: 346), but

> it is possible to fight terror effectively while still respecting human rights.... Many rights can be limited explicitly by reference to national security and public order, and...the case law of the [ECtHR] allows States to take into account the terrorist context in relation to other rights, and subject them to implicit, more far-reaching limitations (Cameron, 2004: 346).

Conclusion

Policing terrorism through networks has become a ubiquitous, though seldom visible phenomenon in the transatlantic realm. The aim of this book was to advance the understanding of the implications of such policing structures for the relationship between the citizenry and the policing actors. It analysed the challenges that collaboration through networks in this field pose to democratic legitimacy. Democratic legitimacy was described as the glue which bonds the citizenry and governmental authorities, including the executive. This book shed light on this relationship in the context of EU-wide CT cooperation.

The proliferation of network-like structures is intimately related to the strong emphasis on the sharing of information and intelligence in the fight against terrorism. Taken together, both phenomena are one of the most striking features of government reactions to the dramatic terrorist attacks on 11 September 2001. To some extent, their incremental evolution was overshadowed by governmental efforts on both sides of the Atlantic to revamp their CT efforts, by creating new bodies, initiating structural and institutional changes, and expanding the mandates, powers, and budgets of the respective institutions. One aim of this book was therefore to make the two phenomena more visible, outlining their character in the context of European-wide CTP.

This book demonstrated that the EU is a significant actor facilitating and fostering collaboration in the field of European-wide CTP. The EU was previously active concerning PJCC. Yet the events of 9/11 and the 2004 Madrid Bombings were catalysts for an emerging EU CT policy. While fighting terrorism had been on the European agenda since the 1970s, it was only at the beginning of this century that there emerged an EU CT policy worthy of the name. The book therefore focused on the Union's role in CT activities, the emerging liaison structures within the EU and beyond, and the challenges its practices raise with respect to policing.

Democratic thought rests on the idea that governments require public consent for their actions. In this book, democratic legitimacy was approached from a liberal perspective given that the EU's MS define themselves as liberal, representative democratic entities. At the minimum then, the efforts in the field of CTP should fulfil criteria of democratic legitimacy based on this liberal self-perception. This refers, in particular, to mechanisms to ensure democratic procedures, compliance with the rule of law, and the protection of human rights.

The overall argument of the book was that the collaborative forms and practices of CTP emerging under the EU's umbrella are, so far, insufficiently accompanied by forms of parliamentary and legal scrutiny. In other words, the parliamentary and judicial mechanisms meant to ensure democratic procedures, human rights, and compliance with the rule of law are weak in this field. This is in particular problematic given the fact that instruments of CTP easily touch on, and sometimes severely infringe, individuals' freedoms and fundamental rights. While it seems that police as well as, to some extent, intelligence cooperation is a day-to-day phenomenon and fostered by European policy-makers, such cooperation includes the risk of harm to individuals. Properly functioning monitoring and accountability mechanisms would therefore be of great importance to ensure that security concerns do not overshadow human rights and individual freedoms unduly.

The advantage of networks' loose forms of cooperation for the participating authorities is that they can keep their autonomy as well as authority, at least to some extent, over their actions. For example, Storbeck (2009: 163) pointed out that information sharing in models such as Europol works well, as national authorities retain the right to withdraw data, or decide not to feed data into a file for specifically explained reasons, or they can restrict the use of data for particular purposes. Crucially, networks can be tailor-made and are flexible. They can accommodate a range of actors, or nodes, and allow for a variety of structural forms of collaboration depending on the particular need. This is crucial for the field of CTP. The first chapter portrayed the EU's policing efforts as a complex web of cooperation among a variety of actors. It appeared that the EU's (former) third pillar provides a fruitful ground for CTNs. Yet these networks add another layer of complexity to the EU's field of PJCC with its overall plethora of actors and high degree of opaqueness.

The network approach provides a fresh perspective on questions of democratic legitimacy. Emphasizing parliamentary and judicial scrutiny as key mechanisms to ensure democratic legitimacy, the approach put forward in this book stresses the rights and liberty of the individual and approaches governmental use of power from a critical perspective. Drawing on the work of David Beetham and others, the protection of fundamental rights is understood as an intrinsic part of democratic systems, as it ensures that people can live freely in a democratic system.

At the core of this research project was Europol and its role in the 'polycentric world of nodal governance' (Wood and Shearing, 2007: 114). In recent years, it has increasingly taken on operational functions which has led to calls for improved external scrutiny. Chapter 3 explored Europol's wide-reaching network. This liaison system is, especially concerning non-European parties, still under construction, but it raises major questions about Europol's scrutiny.

In order to grasp the deep impact of recent CT efforts on national policing structures and to comprehend the EU's actions concerning CTP more fully, the book analysed the wider implications of current actions. It suggested that the standard reactive model of policing—sometimes referred to as the 'fire brigade' model, as a case is dealt with only once the fire is underway—is giving way to a more proactive policing model in the fight against terrorism. Information sharing and other proactive measures, such as the freezing of financial assets, the creation of huge databases and procedures of data-mining, the exchange of PNR records, and the listing of terrorist 'suspects' on watch-lists are all means aiming to prevent a terrorist attack and disrupt a (potential) criminal offence—to intervene before a crime has actually happened. The justification for such means lies in the fact that

> (i)ndividuals involved in clandestine violence make a concerted effort to remain hidden. To try to ferret out those guilty of complicity in acts of violence, the state must use patterns and individual characteristics, which involve, at the crudest level, ethnicity, religion, gender, and age. For this reason, measures frequently infringe on the rights of individuals who have nothing to do with terrorism (Donohue, 2008: 26–27).

The excessive use of such instruments and methods, however, raised concerns about 'surveillance creep' (Marx, 1988) being inherent in such policing structures. To what extent this preventive framework is taking over the criminal justice framework remains contested and varies among the peculiar national settings. Some authors see a striking development towards such a proactive approach (see, for example, Amoore and De Goede, 2008; McCulloch and Pickering, 2009).

Why then is parliamentary scrutiny so weak given the significance of CTP-related actions? Chapter 6 demonstrated that the way the field of PJCC has been structured in the EU led to a marginalized role for the EP with respect to accountability and oversight of Europol, and the policies concerning PJCC more broadly. Neither are the NPs much involved. Most notably, there appears to be a lack of adequate mechanisms of parliamentary scrutiny when it comes to cooperation beyond the EU. Previous chapters gave examples with respect to the collaboration with the US—through the exchange of PNR data, for example, as well as the CIA's extraordinary rendition programme. Finally, the cooperation under the Prüm framework suggested that national governments seek to avoid public debates and lengthy ratification procedures in the field of CT.

While Chapter 6 illustrated the weaknesses of parliamentary scrutiny concerning CTNs in the EU realm in the first decade of the twenty-first century, it acknowledged that the Lisbon Treaty brought considerable changes. Crucially, by 'merging' the first and third pillar, it provides for co-legislation of the EP with respect to all policy fields of the AFSJ. Being co-legislator, the EP is to become increasingly involved in matters of PJCC. With new rights comes greater responsibility, and the EP will be partly in charge of shaping the future field of EU-wide policing. The implications of the Lisbon Treaty for the role of the NPs are less clear and only time will show whether the parliaments will use the opportunity to gain a more powerful role in this field.

With respect to judicial scrutiny, the mechanisms vary, but key actors are the national courts, the ECtHR, and—increasingly—the ECJ. The analysis found that, although there are some mechanisms of judicial scrutiny in place concerning EU-wide efforts, a 'vacuum of legal responsibility' (de Búrca, 2009: 13–14) has emerged with respect to some of the CTP efforts which have been initiated or facilitated at the EU level. This became particularly obvious in the context of the so-called 'terrorist lists', established both by the EU and the UN. Similarly, while the analysis has shown that the EU has some data protection rules in place concerning policing, and Europol in particular, it appeared that significant gaps in the data protection framework remain, especially with respect to data exchange with third parties. A coherent data protection framework which will also apply to PJCC is an urgent concern in this respect (see also Bigo et al, 2011). Overall, the chapter pictured the judicial scrutiny in the field of EU CTP as patchy. Yet, as the UN special rapporteur on the right to health, Paul Hunt, pointedly illustrated: 'The rule of law cannot be applied selectively.... [It] is not to be turned on and off like a tap' (as quoted in Strange, 2005).

Taken together, the insights from this book refer to a substantial legitimacy gap between the EU and its citizens in the field of CTP. Increased connections and interdependencies in the field of policing result in a greater vulnerability of the—already fragile—relationship between individual citizens and security providers. As Dahl (2000: 183) stated it remains to be seen how, if at all, democracies will find a way to strengthen democratic accountability in the international arena. The pattern that emerged from this book is that democratic procedures have difficulties in keeping pace with the increasing international networking of European CT actors. Democratic scrutiny mechanisms might, for example, find it difficult to 'keep pace with changes in intelligence-gathering, storing and sharing' (International Commission of Jurists, 2009). Networks cannot be held accountable only by hierarchical, national structures. Earlier chapters illustrated that current scrutiny procedures appear to stand somewhat in contrast to the overall agreement that effective, or successful CT relies on cooperation between agencies, in particular international liaison. The systems of parliamentary and judicial scrutiny, as established in the MS and, much less so, at the EU level, continue to struggle with the increasing internationalization of their respective executive organs.

For example, the EP continues to be marginalized with respect to international agreements, such as the ones between Europol and US authorities. It is Europol's JSB which provides an opinion on a draft agreement if it concerns the exchange of personal information and also reviews the overall compliance with the agreement afterwards. As explored in the sixth Chapter, the EP has gained some important powers in this respect under the Lisbon Treaty, by having to give their consent to such an agreement (Article 218 of the TFEU). However, the EP 'is not informed and does not play any formal role in the drafting of such agreements or, indeed, their review once they have been signed' (Wills et al, 2011: 27). The analysis in Chapter 7 provided a sceptical perspective on the JSB's performance so far. To strengthen the democratic accountability of such agreements, the discussion about the new Europol Regulation should consider giving the EP a more active role in negotiations with third parties over PJCC policies.

Democracy requires, as a pre-condition, an informed electorate. Only a well-informed citizenry can participate in a meaningful way in democratic procedures. However, the pattern emerging from this research suggests that the current field of European CT policing does not meet such requirements. In particular, the network-like structures, the EU's complicated decision-making system, the overall secrecy surrounding CT policing, including secret and informal agreements and meetings behind closed doors, and the great distance between the individual citizen and the policing actors at the centre of this research prevent a sufficient degree of information flow and transparency. European parliaments can play an important role here, for example with respect to initiating public discussions about the aims and means of CTP. For operational reasons, secrecy is essential in this 'least conspicuous' (Brodeur and Dupont, 2006: 11) part of policing. Yet the lack of transparency generates ethical dilemmas and fundamental normative concerns. Significantly, it prevents individuals from being properly informed about the policy field, and the work of the executive bodies it entails.

So far, the extent, form, and content of many collaborative efforts explored in this book are not known to the wider public and even interested observers find it difficult to gain access to relevant information. The educational role of scrutiny bodies has been emphasized several times in this book. In relation to the public, parliamentary bodies are vital to ensuring that the public understands the purpose and necessity of police and intelligence activities.

Yet parliaments themselves struggle with gathering information about the EU's AFSJ. While the Lisbon Treaty has improved the general flow of information from the executive organs of the EU to the EP as well as the NPs to a considerable extent, a contested issue remains the EP's access to classified information about CTP, and information on AFSJ policies more broadly. Due to a lack of clear procedures and legal regulations, the information flows between the Council and agencies such as Europol and Frontex on the one hand and the EP on the other hand in this context are ad hoc and often cumbersome (see also Wills et al, 2011: 30). The EP should push towards concluding formal agreements in this context. The Framework Agreement on relations between the European Parliament and the Commission, signed on 20 October 2010, might be a starting point to explore the options.[1] However, the Council (2010d) has sharply criticized the Agreement with respect to the transmission of classified information from the Commission to the EP.

One of the features of an 'emerging EU executive order' (Busuioc et al, 2011: 849) is that strategies for tackling terrorism and other types of crime and risks to the EU are developed by the new COSI and the Commission (Europol, 2011e). These strategies obviously affect further priority-setting, budget and other resource allocations, tools, and structures concerning AFSJ policies. It is too early to make any claims about the COSI. One area of concern is, however, the active role that agencies, such as Europol, appear to have in the agenda setting and policy-making of the Committee. As such, they can (potentially) have a direct affect on EU policy-making in this area. The JHA agencies also delivered preparatory work for the ISS, for example. There is a danger that 'the dividing lines between policy advice and actual policy-making can become blurred in practice ...; this creates possibilities for agencies to influence and shape future policy' (Curtin, 2011: 10). Parliaments are simply to be informed about the proceedings of the COSI. It remains to be seen what the quality of the information is that parliaments receive from the COSI, or about its work.

As mentioned earlier in this book, a forthcoming Europol Regulation is currently in preparation. Again, this is, so far, not subject to a public discussion. The EP had called for a first proposal to be drafted six months after the Lisbon Treaty entered into force. However, the Commission (2010c: 32) indicates in the Action Plan Implementing the Stockholm Programme that it will only present a first draft in 2013. Europol's legal basis, the ECD, is currently evaluated by the Commission and the Europol Management Board (Europol, 2011e). Before European parliamentarians, Europol's Director argued that 'Europol is funded by EU tax payer money so we have a duty, as servants of the public, to be transparent and we welcome any changes which will improve this transparency' (Europol, 2011e). The EP needs to seize the opportunity to clarify some of the outstanding issues concerning its role in Europol's scrutiny in the new Regulation.

The thorough investigations into the extraordinary rendition campaign by Dick Marty for PACE and the EP's ad hoc Committee are worth considering in this context. Only amid such European-wide investigations has a considerable extent of the 'global spider's web' (Marty, 2006: 9) of rendition flights and secret detention become clear. National scrutiny bodies remain hesitant to investigate the potential involvement of their respective governments. I have therefore suggested elsewhere that one could understand transnational bodies, such as the EP and PACE as 'gap-fillers'—they might take charge of an issue in cases where NPs fail to engage with an issue or when the issue affects more than two European countries (Hillebrand, 2009).

[1] The Agreement is available at <http://ec.europa.eu/dgs/secretariat_general/relations/relations_other/docs/framework_agreement_ep-ec_en.pdf>.

Despite the focus on EU-wide CTP, the network lens required the inclusion of international actors into the analysis, one of which is the US. The empirical findings suggest that the relationship between the EU and the US in this field is close, but complicated. The US government under President Bush understood itself as fighting a war on terror: 'Make no mistake about it, we are at war' (as quoted in Stevenson R., 2005). The US approach to CT has not changed in a substantial manner under Barack Obama. The administration avoids using war terminology but it has not initiated major changes, partly blocked by Congressional opposition. Overall, it took a very pragmatic stance on existing CT efforts. For example, the closure of the Guantánamo detention facility did not meet the deadline of January 2010 and is unlikely to happen in the near future. Several detainees will remain imprisoned under US custody without ever being tried or prosecuted. Under Obama's administration, other controversial measures, such as the targeted killing of individual terrorists, or terrorist suspects, have sharply increased. It appears that the policies, which emerged in the post-9/11 period, are a long-term trend rather than a short phase.

Despite differences between the US and European governments in conceiving the dangers of contemporary jihadist terrorism and the proper means to fight it, transatlantic cooperation in this field has been continuous. One of the findings of this research is that the US was very keen on a strong involvement in Europol's network, yet at the same time seemed to lack a reciprocal understanding of networks. Instead, US authorities appear to request information from their European partners yet do not share their own information. Several interviewees pointed to this lack of reciprocity by American security authorities. It appeared that American officials tend to ask for all sorts of information and assistance from their European partners, but tend not to provide reciprocal services or goods. A similar result emerged from the analysis of the PNR data exchange. The US remains the 'elephant in the room' in the area of PJCC, pushing and affecting the EU agenda in this field.

Apart from the US, the increased cooperation of the EU with countries using draconian measures in their criminal justice system, having a record of ill treatment of suspects, or using the military for policing purposes raises fundamental questions. This is the case both at the EU level and the bilateral level. The need for closer collaboration with such countries to gather information that would make European countries safer allowed for partnerships which had been previously avoided for ethical and political reasons. The long-term implications of cooperation with such partners are not assessable yet, but the increased public concerns in countries such as the UK about this topic illustrate the uneasiness of many citizens about these practices.

Besides cooperation with individual countries, the EU's relationship with other international CT actors requires more systematic analysis. Several chapters have touched on the relationship with the UN, but an in-depth study of the power relationship(s) between those two bodies in the field of CT was beyond the scope of this book. While the UN is not a traditional policing actor and, being an international organization, is not thought of as having a *direct* impact on an individual's life, one finding of this research is that this is the case with some of its CT activities. As the discussion about the creation of the 'terror lists' and the financial sanctioning of terrorist suspects in Chapter 7 has shown, the tools of global regulations, as agreed in the UN Security Council, can require a regional actor to apply regulations which can have a devastating effect on the individual. One crucial question is how far UN policies and regulations actually 'steer' EU policies. In the field of JHA, the answer to the question who guides EU policy would usually be the MS, or sometimes the European Commission. But this book has suggested that there is also a 'top-down' impact. Results of such a study would also be of interest to the broader (international) governance literature. The network lens does not only allow studying relations between actors and structures in depth, but it is also useful to study 'the changing nature of political authority' (Eilstrup-Sangiovanni, 2009: 194).

While this research analysed an emerging authority in the field of CT, namely the EU, the analysis posed some questions long familiar to anyone concerned with the nexus between security and liberty. Crucially, what are the relative values of security on the one hand and individual liberties and human rights on the other hand? Every (attempted) terrorist attack raises new claims for increased executive powers and infringements on individual liberties and human rights. One example has been the debate in countries, such as the US, Germany, and the UK, about the increased use of 'naked scanners' to increase airport security after the failed bomb attack on 25 December 2009 on Northwest Airlines flight 253 from Amsterdam to Detroit. Executive authorities usually justify the need for restrictive measures by referring to the increased safety of the public that would be gained by using those methods and instruments. Yet it is a false conclusion to think that security measures, and the loss of liberties through them, could be easily 'balanced' by a higher level of safety. The discussion about measures of proactive policing showed that more intrusive measures do not necessarily lead to more security. Security authorities have so far not shown that such measures are particularly effective. Assurances of more safety and security cannot easily make up for the loss of liberties or the infringement of human rights. Indeed, less freedom and fewer rights can make individuals and communities feel less secure.

Debates about the legitimacy of CTP in networked structures tend to draw on longstanding dichotomies, such as liberty versus security and repression versus protection. How much security (provision) does a democracy need, and how much can it take? While such issues are already contested in the domestic framework, they are likely to become even more complex and contested at the international level. The concern is the erosion of individual rights and freedom through policing policies which allow an excessive infringement of human rights (Anderson, 2002: 238). Many measures and structures of CTP, also in the European context, were introduced in the name of security under the lasting impression of the 9/11 attacks, making (too) many compromises at the expense of individual freedoms. More than a decade after the attacks, the democratic legitimacy of European CTP needs to be carefully reconsidered.

References

Aden, Hartmut (2001), 'Convergence of Policing Policies and Transnational Policing in Europe', *European Journal of Crime, Criminal Law and Criminal Justice* 9/2, 99–112.

Adler, Emanuel and Barnett, Michael (1998), *Security Communities* (Cambridge: Cambridge University Press).

AFP (2009), 'France and Spain set up joint body to fight terrorism', 29 April, Madrid.

——(2008), 'France, Spain close ranks on ETA, Mediterranean Union, migration', 10 January, Madrid.

Alain, Marc (2001), 'Transnational Police Cooperation in Europe and in North America: Revisiting the Traditional Border Between Internal and External Security Matters, or How Policing is Being Globalized', *European Journal of Crime, Criminal Law and Criminal Justice* 9/2, 113–29.

Alderson, John (1984), *Human Rights and the Police* (Strasbourg: Council of Europe).

Aldrich, Richard (2009a), 'US-European Intelligence Co-operation on Counter-Terrorism: Low Politics and Compulsion', *British Journal of Politics and International Relations* 11/1, 122–39.

——(2009b), 'Beyond the vigilant state: globalisation and intelligence', *Review of International Studies* 35/4, 889–902.

Allum, Felia and Siebert, Renate (eds) (2003), *Organised Crime and the Challenge to Democracy* (London: Routledge).

Alvaro, Alexander (2006), 'Proposal for a recommendation to the Council on interoperability and synergies among European databases in the area of justice and home affairs', European Parliament, Session Document B6-0336/2006, 8 June.

American Civil Liberties Union (ACLU) (2009), 'Italian "Extraordinary Rendition" Victim Still Held In Morocco Based On Tortured Confession', Press Release, 25 June.

Amoore, Louise and De Goede, Marieke (eds) (2008), *Risk and the War on Terror* (London: Routledge).

Anderson, David (2011), 'First Report on the operation of the Terrorist Asset-Freezing Etc. Act 2010 (Review Period: December 2010 to September 2011)', Presented to Parliament pursuant to Section 31 of the Terrorist Asset Freezing etc. Act 2010, December 2011 (London: The Stationary Office).

Anderson, Malcolm (2008), 'Law enforcement cooperation in the EU and fundamental rights protection', in Martin Maik (ed), *Crime, rights and the EU: the future of police and judicial cooperation* (London: Justice), 105–20.

——(2002), 'What future for counter-terrorism as an objective of European police co-operation?', in Malcolm Anderson and Joanna Apap (eds), *Police and justice co-operation and the new European borders* (The Hague/London/New York: Kluwer Law International), 227–40.

——(1995), 'Controlling European Police Institutions', in Malcolm Anderson, Monica den Boer, Peter Cullen, William Gilmore, Charles Raab, and Neil Walker (eds), *Policing the European Union* (Oxford: Clarendon Press), 250–78.

Anderson, Malcolm (1993a), 'The British Perspective on Internationalization of Police Cooperation in Western Europe', in Cyrille Fijnaut (ed), *The Internationalization of Police Cooperation in Western Europe* (Deventer: Kluwer), 19–39.

——(1993b), 'The French Police and Cooperation in Western Europe', in Cyrille Fijnaut (ed), *The Internationalization of Police Cooperation in Western Europe* (Deventer: Kluwer), 49–83.

—— Den Boer, Monica, Cullen, Peter, Gillmore, William, Raab, Charles, and Walker Neil (eds) (1995), *Policing the European Union* (Oxford: Clarendon Press).

Anderson, Ross et al (2009), 'Database State', Report commissioned by the Joseph Rowntree Reform Trust Ltd. Online access at <http://www.jrrt.org.uk/publications/database-state-full-report>.

Andreas, Peter (2003), 'Redrawing the Line: Borders and Security in the 21st Century', *International Security* 28/2, 78–112.

Andreas, Peter and Nadelmann, Ethan (2006), *Policing the Globe* (Oxford: Oxford University Press).

Andrew, Christopher (2009), *The Defence of the Realm: The Authorized History of MI5* (London: Allen Lane).

Ansell, Christopher (2000), 'The Networked Polity: Regional Development in Western Europe', *Governance* 13/3, 303–33.

Apap, Joanna (2006), 'Session 2: What Future for Europol?: Increasing Europol's Accountability and Improving Europol's Operational Capacity', DG Internal Policies of the Union, Policy Department C, European Parliament, 7 September 2006, Brussels.

——and Carrera, Sergio (2004), 'Progress and Obstacles in the Area of Justice and Home Affairs in an Enlarging Europe: An Overview', in Joanna Apap (ed), *Justice and Home Affairs in the EU: Liberty and Security Issues after Enlargment* (Cheltenham: Edward Elgar Publishing), 1–24.

Archibugi, Daniele and Held, David (1995), *Cosmopolitan Democracy: An Agenda for a New World Order* (Cambridge: Polity Press).

Archick, Kristin and Morelli, Vincent (2011), 'The U.S. Congress and the European Parliament: Evolving Transatlantic Legislative Cooperation', Congressional Research Service Report R41522, 7 June 2011.

Argomaniz, Javier (2011), *The EU and Counter-Terrorism: Politics, Polity and Policies after 9/11* (Abingdon: Routledge).

——(2009), 'When the EU is the "Norm-taker": The Passenger Name Records Agreement and the EU's Internalization of US Border Security Norms', *Journal of European Integration* 31/1, 119–36.

Arquilla, John and Ronfeldt, David (eds) (2001), *Networks and Netwars* (Santa Monica, CA: RAND).

Aus, J.P. (2003), 'Supranational Governance in an "Area of Freedom, Security and Justice": Eurodac and the Politics of Biometric Control', Working Paper No 72, University of Sussex: Sussex European Institute.

Baehr, Peter (1999), *Human Rights Universality in Practice* (Basingstoke: Palgrave Macmillan).

Balzacq, Thierry (2008), 'The Policy Tools of Securitization: Information Exchange, EU Foreign and Interior Policies', *Journal of Common Market Studies* 46/1, 75–100.

——(2006), 'The Treaty of Prüm and the Principle of Loyalty (art. 10 TEC)', DG Internal Policies of the Union, Policy Department C, European Parliament, Brussels.

—— Bigo, Didier, Carrera, Sergio and Guild, Elspeth (2006), 'Security and the Two-Level Game: The Treaty of Prüm, the EU and the Management of Threats', Working Document No 234, January 2006 (Brussels: Centre for European Policy Studies).

Bannerman, Lucy, 'There Is No War on Terror in Britain, says DPP', *The Times*, 24 January 2007.

Barrowclough, Anne (2009), 'MI5 chief Jonathan Evans defends use of "torture intelligence"', *The Times Online*, 16 October.

Batal al-Shishani, Murad (2009), 'Al-Qaeda Investigation Raises Questions on British Counterterrorism Cooperation with Damascus', *Terrorism Monitor* 7/15, 5–6.

BBC News (2009), 'Binyam blames UK for mistreatment', 13 March.

——(2008), 'UK "must check" US torture denial', 19 July.

Beetham, David (2008a), 'Defining and Justifying Democracy', in David Beetham, *Democracy and Human Rights* (Cambridge: Polity Press), 1–29.

——(2008b), 'Liberal Democracy and the Limits of Democratization', in David Beetham, *Democracy and Human Rights* (Cambridge: Polity Press), 33–49. First published in *Democratization* 4/1, 76–93.

——(2008c), 'Human Rights and Democracy: a Multi-faceted Relationship', in David Beetham, *Democracy and Human Rights* (Cambridge: Polity Press), 89–114.

——and Lord, Christopher (1998), *Legitimacy and the European Union* (New York: Addison Wesley Longman).

Bellanova, Rocco (2008), 'The "Prüm Process:" The Way Forward for EU Police Cooperation and Data Exchange?', in Elspeth Guild and Florian Geyer (eds), *Security versus Justice?: Police and Judicial Cooperation in the European Union* (Aldershot: Ashgate), 203–23.

Bellinger, John (2007), 'Armed Conflict with al Qaeda?', available at <http://opiniojuris.org/2007/01/15/armed-conflict-with-al-qaida/>.

Benner, Thorsten, Reinicke, Wolfgang H, and Witte, Jan Martin (2004), 'Multisectoral Networks in Global Governance: Towards a Pluralistic System of Accountability', *Government and Opposition* 39/2, 191–210.

Bennhold, Katrin (2006), 'Europe, Too, Takes Harder Line on Terror Suspects', *New York Times*, 17 April.

Bergen, Peter and Hoffman, Bruce (2010), 'Assessing the terrorist threat', A Report of the Bipartisan Policy Center's National Security Preparedness Group, 10 September 2010.

Bergenstrand, Klas (2004), 'The European Intelligence and Security Community and the Fight against Terrorism', in EULEC (ed), *European Cooperation against Terrorism: Conference* (Nijmegen: Wolf Legal Publishers), 83–9.

Biermann, Kai (2008), 'Geheimdienste: Parlamentarier wollen Kontrolle verbessern', *Die Zeit*, 7 March 2008.

Bignami, Francesca (2007), 'Towards a right to privacy in transnational intelligence networks', *Michigan Journal of International Law* 28/3, 663–86.

Bigo, Didier (2006a), 'Internal and External Aspects of Security', *European Security* 15/4, 385–404.

——(2006b), 'Globalized (In)Security: the Field and the Ban-opticon', in Didier Bigo and Anastasia Tsoukala (eds), *Illiberal Practices of Liberal Regimes: The (In)Security Game*' (Paris: L'Harmattan), 5–49.

Bigo, Didier (2000a), 'When Two Become One: Internal and External Securitisations in Europe', in Mike Williams (ed), *International Relations Theory and the Politics of European Integration, Power, Security and Community* (London: Routledge), 171–205.

——(2000b), 'Liaison officers in Europe', in James Sheptycki (ed), *Issues in Transnational Policing* (London: Routledge), 67–99.

——(1994), 'The European internal security field: Stakes and rivalries in a newly developing area of police intervention', in Malcolm Anderson and Monica den Boer (eds), *Policing across national boundaries* (London: Pinter), 162–73.

——et al (2011), 'Towards a New EU Legal Framework for Data Protection and Privacy: Challenges, Principles and the Role of the European Parliament', Study for the European Parliament, Policy Department C, Doc. PE 453.216.

Bjelopera, Jerome (2011), 'American Jihadist Terrorism: Combating a Complex Threat', Congressional Research Service Report R41416, 15 November 2011.

Black, Cofer (2002), 'Unclassified testimony of Cofer Black at the Joint Inquiry into the terrorist attacks of September 11, 2001 by the House Permanent Select Committee of Intelligence and the Senate Select Committee on Intelligence' (Washington, DC, 26 September 2002).

Blair, Tony (2001), 'Statement in Response to Terrorist Attacks in the United States', London, 11 September 2001.

Blechschmidt, Peter (2008), 'Sonderermittler stößt an Grenzen', *Süddeutsche Zeitung*, 14 April.

——(2007), 'Syrische Folterpraxis war in Berlin bekannt', *Süddeutsche Zeitung*, 14 December.

Block, Ludo (2007), 'Europe's Emerging Counter-Terrorism Elite: The ATLAS Network', *Terrorism Monitor* 5/5, 10–12.

Boehm, Franziska (2009), 'Confusing fundamental rights protection in Europe: Loopholes in Europe's fundamental rights protection exemplified on European data protection rules', Law Working Paper No 2009–01, Faculty of Law, Economics and Finance, University of Luxembourg.

Bok, Sissela (1989), *Secrets: On the Ethics of Concealment and Revelation* (New York: Vintage Books).

Borelli, Silvia (2011), 'Rendition, torture and intelligence cooperation', in Hans Born, Ian Leigh, and Aidan Wills (eds), *International Intelligence Cooperation and Accountability* (Abingdon: Routledge), 98–123.

Born, Hans (2004), 'Towards Effective Democratic Oversight of Intelligence Services: Lessons Learned from Comparing National Practices', *Connections* 3/4, 1–12.

——and Johnson, Loch (2005), 'Balancing Operational Efficiency and Democratic Legitimacy', in Hans Born, Loch Johnson, and Ian Leigh (eds), *Who's watching the Spies?: Establishing intelligence service accountability* (Dulles: Potomac Books), 225–39.

Borrás, Susana (2007), 'Governance Networks in the EU: The case of GMO policy', in Martin Marcussen and Jacob Torfing (ed), *Democratic Network Governance in Europe* (Basingstoke: Palgrave-Macmillan), 232–50.

——and Conzelmann, Thomas (2007), 'Democracy, Legitimacy and Soft Modes of Governance in the EU: The Empirical Turn', *European Integration* 29/5, 531–48.

Bossong, Raphael (2008), 'The EU'S Mature Counterterrorism Policy—A Critical Historical and Functional Assessment', LSE Challenge Working Paper, June 2008.

Bovens, Mark (2007a), 'Analysing and Assessing Accountability: A Conceptual Framework', *European Law Journal* 13/4, 447–68.

——(2007b), 'New Forms of Accountability and EU Governance', *Comparative European Politics* 5/1, 104–20.

Bowling, Ben (2009), 'Transnational Policing: The Globalization Thesis, a Typology and a Research Agenda', *Policing* 3/2, 149–60.

——(2006), 'Sovereignty vs. Security? Transnational Policing in the contemporary Caribbean', *Caribbean Journal of Criminology & Social Psychology* 10/1–2, 1–21.

Brady, Hugo (2009), 'Intelligence, emergencies and foreign policy: The EU's role in counter-terrorism' (London: Centre for European Reform).

——(2007a), 'The EU and the fight against organized crime' (London: Centre for European Reform).

——(2007b), 'Europol and the European Criminal Intelligence Model: A Non-state Response to Organised Crime', Doc. ARI 126/2007, 1 December (Madrid: Real Instituto Elcano).

Bretherton, Charlotte and Vogler, John (2006), *The European Union as a global actor*, 2nd edn (Abingdon: Routledge).

British Embassy, Warsaw (2007), 'Working together to tackle organised crime: UK-Poland security agreement enters into force', Embassy News, 1 August.

Brodeur, Jean-Paul (2007), 'High and Low Policing in Post-9/11 Times', *Policing* 1/1, 25–37.

——(1983), 'High policing and low policing: remarks about the policing of political activities', *Social Problems* 30/5, 507–20.

——and Dupont, Benoît (2006), 'Knowledge Workers or "Knowledge" Workers?', *Policing and Society* 16/1, 7–26.

—— Gill, Peter, and Töllberg, Dennis (2003), 'Introduction', in Jean-Paul Brodeur, Peter Gill, and Dennis Töllberg, *Democracy, Law and Security: Internal security services in contemporary Europe* (Aldershot: Ashgate), 1–8.

Brown, Gordon (2009), 'Written Statement to the House of Commons on Detainees', House of Commons Hansard Ministerial Statements for 18 March, Column 55WS.

——(2008), 'National Security Strategy statement', 19 March.

——(2007), 'Statement to the House of Commons on National Security', House of Commons Hansard Debates for 14 November 2007, Column 667.

Bruggeman, Willy (2007), 'The future of Europol and its limits', 10 April. Online access: <http://www.europarl.europa.eu/hearings/20070410/libe/bruggeman_en.pdf>.

——(2006), 'What are the options for improving democratic control of Europol and for providing it with adequate operational capabilities?', DG Internal Policies of the Union, Policy Department C, European Parliament, Doc. IP/C/LIBE/FWC/2005–24, 16 February, Brussels.

——(2004), 'Policing in a European Context', in Joanna Apap (ed), *Justice and Home Affairs in the EU: Liberty and Security Issues after Enlargement* (Cheltenham: Edward Elgar Publishing), 175–89.

Bruguiére, Jean-Louis (2010), 'Second Report on the Processing of EU-Originating Personal Data by the United States Treasury Department for Counter Terrorism Purposes: Terrorist Finance Tracking Programme', EU Restricted, January 2010. Available via Statewatch at <http://www.statewatch.org/news/2010/aug/eu-usa-swift-2nd-bruguiere-report.pdf>.

Bukow, Sebastian (2005), 'Deutschland: Mit Sicherheit weniger Freiheit über den Umweg Europa', in Glaeßner, Gert-Joachim and Lorenz, Astrid (eds), *Europäisierung der inneren Sicherheit: Eine vergleichende Untersuchung am Beispiel von organisierter Kriminalität und Terrorismus* (Wiesbaden: VS Verlag für Sozialwissenschaften), 43–62.

Bundeskriminalamt (2008), 'Das Bundeskriminalamt: Das Profil' (Wiesbaden: Bundeskriminalamt).

Bundesministerium des Innern (2007a), 'Start des europäischen Informationsportals "check the web" bei Europol', Press Release, 9 May.

——(2007b), 'Deutsche Ratspräsidentschaft begrüßt Inkrafttreten der Erweiterung der operativen Befugnisse für Europol', Press Release, 20 April.

Bures, Oldrich (2011), *EU Counterterrorism Policy: A Paper Tiger?* (Farnham: Ashgate).

——and Ahern, Stephanie (2007), 'The European Model of Building Regional Cooperation Against Terrorism', in David Cortright and George Lopez (eds), *Uniting Against Terror: Cooperative Nonmilitary Responses to the Global Terrorist Threat* (Cambridge: MIT Press), 187–236.

Bush, George (2001), 'Address to a Joint Session of Congress and the American People', Washington DC, 20 September 2001.

Busuioc, Madalina, Curtin, Deirdre, and Groenleer, Martijn (2011), 'Agency growth between autonomy and accountability: the European Police Office as a "living institution"', *Journal of European Public Policy* 18/6, 848–67.

Callewaert, Johan (2007), 'The European Court of Human Rights and the Area of Freedom, Security and Justice', *ERA Forum* 8/4, 511–18.

Cameron, Iain (2005), 'Beyond the Nation State: The Influence of the European Court of Human Rights on Intelligence Accountability', in Hans Born, Loch Johnson, and Ian Leigh (eds), *Who's watching the spies?: Establishing Intelligence Service Accountability* (Dulles: Potomac Books), 34–55.

——(2004), 'General Human Rights Principles Relevant to US-EU Counterterrorism Cooperation', in Cyrille Fijnaut, Jan Wouters, and Frederik Naert (eds), *Legal instruments in the fight against terrorism: a transatlantic dialogue* (Leiden: Martinus Nijhoff Publishers), 343–59.

Caparini, Marina (2007), 'Controlling and Overseeing Intelligence Services in Democratic States', in Hans Born and Marina Caparini (eds), *Democratic Control of Intelligence Services: Containing Rogue Elephants* (Aldershot: Ashgate), 3–24.

Carlile, Alexander (2009), 'Report on the operation in 2008 of the Terrorism Act 2000 and of part 1 of the Terrorism Act 2006', June 2009 (London: Her Majesty's Stationery Office).

Carrera, Sergio and Geyer, Florian (2007), 'The Reform Treaty & Justice and Home Affairs: Implications for the common Area of Freedom, Security & Justice', Centre for European Policy Studies, Policy Brief No 141, July, Brussels.

Castells, Manuel (1996), *The Rise of the Network Society*, First Volume of the Trilogy 'The Information Age: Economy, Society and Culture' (Oxford: Blackwell Publishing).

Chalk, Peter (2000),'The Third Pillar on Judicial and Home Affairs Cooperation, Anti-Terrorist Collaboration and Liberal Democratic Acceptability', in Fernando Reinares (ed), *European Democracies Against Terrorism: Governmental policies and intergovernmental cooperation* (Aldershot: Ashgate), 175–210.

——(1996), *West European Terrorism and Counter-Terrorism: The Evolving Dynamic* (Houndmills: Macmillan).

Chan, Janet (1997), *Changing Police Culture: Policing in a Multicultural Society* (Cambridge: Cambridge University Press).

Chertoff, Michael (2006), 'A Tool We Need to Stop the Next Airliner Plot', *Washington Post*, 29 August.
Chesterman, Simon (2011), *One Nation Under Surveillance: A New Social Contract to Defend Freedom Without Sacrificing Liberty* (Oxford: Oxford University Press).
Chevigny, Paul (1999), 'Police Accountability in Hemispheric Perspective', in Errol Mendes, Joaquin Zuckerberg, Susan Lecorre, Anne Gabriel, and Jeffrey Clark (eds), *Democratic policing and accountability: global perspectives* (Aldershot: Ashgate), 69–87.
CIA Inspector General (2004), 'Counterterrorism, detention and interrogation activities: September 2001–October 2003', Special Report, 2003-7123-IG, 7 May 2004.
Clark, Ian (2005), *Legitimacy in international society* (Oxford: Oxford University Press).
Clarke, Richard (2004), *Against all Enemies: Inside America's War on Terror* (New York: Free Press).
CNN (2009a), 'Italy convicts "U.S. agents" in CIA kidnap trial', 4 November.
——(2009b), 'Lithuania denies report it hosted secret CIA prisons', 23 December.
——(2009c), 'State of the Union with John King: Interview With Dick Cheney', 15 March 2009.
Cobain, Ian (2009a), 'How UK's torture policy was traced back up political ladder', *Guardian*, 18 June.
——(2009b), 'Blair knew of secret policy on torture of terror suspects', *Guardian*, 18 June.
Colombani, Jean-Marie (2001), 'Nous sommes tous Américains', *Le Monde*, 13 September 2001.
Commission of the European Communities [Commission] (2011a), 'Progress Report on the development of the second generation Schengen Information System (SIS II), July 2010–December 2010', Report from the Commission to the European Parliament and the Council, Doc. COM(2011) 391 final, Brussels, 29 June 2011.
——(2011b), 'Proposal for a Council Decision on the conclusion of the Agreement between the United States of America and the European Union on the use and transfer of Passenger Name Records to the United States Department of Homeland Security', Doc. COM(2011) 807 final, Brussels, 23 November 2011.
——(2011c), 'A European terrorist finance tracking system: available options', Communication from the Commission to the European Parliament and the Council, Doc. COM(2011) 429 final, Brussels, 13 July 2011.
——(2010a), 'The EU Internal Security Strategy in Action: Five steps towards a more secure Europe', Communication from the Commission to the European Parliament and the Council, Doc. COM(2010) 673 final, Brussels, 22 November 2010.
——(2010b), 'Amended Proposal for a Regulation of the European Parliament and of the Council concerning the establishment of "EURODAC" for the comparison of fingerprints for the effective application of Regulation (EC) No [.../...] [establishing the criteria and mechanisms for determining the Member State responsible for examining an application for international protection lodged in one of the Member States by a third-country national or a stateless person concerning Eurodac', October 2010.
——(2010c), 'Delivering an area of freedom, security and justice for Europe's citizens: Action Plan Implementing the Stockholm Programme', Communication from the Commission to the European Parliament, the Council, the European Economic and

Social Committee and the Committee of the Regions, Doc. COM(2010) 171 final, Brussels, 20 April 2010.
——(2009a), 'Awareness of key-policies in the area of Freedom, Security and Justice', *Flash Eurobarometer Series* 252, conducted by The Gallup Organization, Hungary, January.
——(2009b), 'The setting up of an Agency for the operational management of large-scale IT systems proposed by the Commission', Doc. MEMO/09/290, 24 June, Brussels.
——(2009c), 'European Commission Report Visa Information System: Report from the Commission to the European Parliament and the Council on the development of the Visa Information System (VIS) in 2008 (submitted in response to the obligation under Article 6 of Council Decision 2004/512/EC)', Doc. COM(2009) 473 final, 15 September, Brussels.
——(2009d), 'Commission Decision of 5 May adopting implementing measures for the consultation mechanism and the other procedures referred to in Article 16 of Regulation (EC) No 767/2008 of the European Parliament and of the Council concerning the Visa Information System (VIS) and the exchange of data between Member States on short-stay visas (VIS Regulation)', Doc. C(2009) 2359, Brussels.
——(2009e), 'Amended proposal for a Regulation of the European Parliament and of the Council concerning the establishment of "EURODAC" for the comparison of fingerprints for the effective application of Regulation (EC) No [.../...] [establishing the criteria and mechanisms for determining the Member State responsible for examining an application for international protection lodged in one of the Member States by a third-country national or a stateless person]', Recast version, Doc. COM(2009) 342 final, 10 September, Brussels.
——(2009f), 'Problems relating to cross-border law enforcement cooperation cannot be effectively dealt with at a national level or on the basis of bilateral arrangements between Member States. Only coordinated action at an EU level can ensure such cooperation', Doc. IP/09/1295, 10 September, Brussels.
——(2007a), 'Prevention of and fight against crime: Annual Work Programme 2008', adopted by the Commission on 4 December, Brussels.
——(2007b), 'Proposal for a Council Framework Decision on the use of Passenger Name Records (PNR) for law enforcement purposes', Doc. COM(2007)654 final, 6 November, Brussels.
——(2006), 'Proposal for a Council Decision establishing the European Police Office (EUROPOL)', Doc. COM (2006) 817 final, 20 December, Brussels.
——(2005a), 'Proposal for a Council framework decision on the exchange of information under the principle of availability', Doc. COM(2005) 490 final, 12 October, Brussels.
——(2005b), 'Communication from the Commission to the Council and the European Parliament: The Hague Programme: Ten Priorities for the next five years—The Partnership for European renewal in the field of Freedom, Security and Justice', Doc. COM(2005) 184 final, 10 May 2005, Brussels.
——(2005c), 'Proposal for a Council Framework Decision on the protection of personal data processed in the framework of police and judicial cooperation in criminal matters', Doc. COM(2005) 475 final, Brussels.

——(2005d), 'Council Decision concerning access for consultation of the Visa Information System (VIS) by the authorities of Member States responsible for internal security and by Europol for the purposes of the prevention, detection and investigation of terrorist offences and of other serious criminal offence', Brussels.

——(2005e), 'Communication on Improved Effectiveness, Enhanced Interoperability and Synergies among European Databases in the Area of Justice and Home Affairs', Doc. COM(2005) 597 final, 24 November, Brussels.

——(2005f), 'Proposal for a Council decision on the improvement of police cooperation between the Member States of the European Union, especially at the internal borders and amending the Convention implementing the Schengen Agreement', Doc. COM(2005) 317, 18 July, Brussels.

——(2005g), 'Communication to the Council and the European Parliament on improved effectiveness, enhanced interoperability and synergies among European databases in the area of Justice and Home Affairs', Doc. COM(2005) 597 final, 24 November, Brussels.

——(2004), 'Communication from the Commission to the Council and the European Parliament—Towards enhancing access to information by law enforcement agencies', Doc. COM/2004/0429 final, 16 June 2004, Brussels.

——(2003), 'Communication from the Commission to the Council, the European Parliament and the European Economic and Social Committee—On a comprehensive EU policy against corruption', Doc. COM/2003/0317 final, Brussels.

Conference of Community and European Affairs Committees of Parliaments of the European Union (COSAC) (2008), 'Ninth bi-annual Report: Developments in European Union Procedures and Practices Relevant to Parliamentary Scrutiny', prepared by the COSAC Secretariat, May, Brussels.

——(COSAC) (2007), 'Eighth bi-annual Report: Developments in European Union Procedures and Practices Relevant to Parliamentary Scrutiny', prepared by the COSAC Secretariat, November, Brussels.

——(COSAC) (2005), 'Third bi-annual Report: Developments in European Union Procedures and Practices Relevant to Parliamentary Scrutiny', prepared by the COSAC Secretariat, May, Brussels.

Coolsaet, Rik (2010), 'EU counterterrorism strategy: value added or chimera?', *International Affairs* 86/4, 857–73.

Council of Europe Parliamentary Assembly [PACE] (2008a), 'Recommendation 1824 (2008) on United Nations and European Union blacklists' adopted by the Assembly on 23 January 2008, Strasbourg.

——(2008b), 'Resolution 1597 (2008) on United Nations and European Union blacklists', adopted by the Assembly on 23 January 2008, Strasbourg.

——(2005), 'Lawfulness of detentions by the United States in Guantánamo Bay', Resolution 1433 (2005), adopted by the Assembly on 26 April 2005, Strasbourg.

——(2004), 'Resolution 1400 (2004): Challenge of terrorism in Council of Europe member states', adopted by the Assembly on 6 October 2004, Strasbourg.

Council of Europe (2002), 'Guidelines on human rights and the fight against terrorism', DG General of Human Rights, adopted by the Committee of Ministers on 11 July, Strasbourg.

Council of Europe (2001), 'European Code of Police Ethics', Strasbourg.
——(1987), 'Recommendation No. R (87) 15 of the Committee of Ministers to Member States regulating the use of personal data in the police sector', 17 September, Strasbourg.
——(1981), 'Convention for the Protection of Individuals with regard to Automatic Processing of Personal Data', 28 January, Strasbourg.
——(1950), 'Convention for the Protection of Human Rights and Fundamental Freedoms' as amended by Protocol No 11, 4 November 1950, Rome.
Council of the European Union (2011a), 'EU Counter-Terrorism Strategy—Discussion paper', Note from EU Counter-Terrorism Coordinator to Council/European Council, Doc. 10622/1/11, Brussels, 7 June 2011.
——(2011b), 'Council Conclusion on Counter-Terrorism', 3109th General Affairs Council meeting, Brussels, 12 September 2011.
——(2011c), 'Council Implementing Regulation (EU) No 1375/2011 of 22 December 2011 implementing Article 2(3) of Regulation (EC) No 2580/2001 on specific restrictive measures directed against certain persons and entities with a view to combating terrorism and repealing Implementing Regulation (EU) No 687/2011'.
——(2010a), 'Draft Internal Security Strategy for the European Union: "Towards a European Security Model"', Doc. 7120/10, Brussels, 8 March 2010.
——(2010b), 'EU-US Summit: Joint statement', Presse 315, Doc. 16726/10, 20 November 2010, Lisbon.
——(2010c), 'EU Counter-Terrorism Strategy—Discussion paper', Note from EU Counter-Terrorism Coordinator to Council/European Council, Doc. 9685/10, Brussels, 10 May 2010.
——(2010d), 'Framework Agreement on relations between the European Parliament and the Commission', Doc. 15018/10, 18 October 2010, Brussels.
——(2009a), 'Council Decision of 6 April 2009 establishing the European Police Office (Europol)', OJ L 121/37, 15 May 2009, Brussels.
——(2009b), 'Council Common Position 2009/468/CFSP of 15 June 2009 updating Common Position 2001/931/CFSP on the application of specific measures to combat terrorism and repealing Common Position 2009/67/CFSP', 16 June 2009, Brussels.
——(2009c), 'Proposal for a Council Framework Decision on the use of Passenger Name Record (PNR) for law enforcement purposes', Doc. 618/2/09 REV 2 LIMITE, 29 June, Brussels.
——(2009d), 'Implementation of the Action Plan on Enhancing the Security of Explosives', Note from Council Secretariat to Delegations, Doc. 11056/09, 18 June, Brussels.
——(2009e), 'EU-US Joint Statement on Enhancing Transatlantic Cooperation in the Area of Justice, Freedom and Security of 28 October 2009'. Online access at <http://register.consilium.europa.eu/pdf/en/09/st15/st15184.en09.pdf>.
——(2009f), 'The Stockholm Programme—An open and secure Europe serving the citizen', Draft Multiannual programme for an area of Freedom, Security and Justice serving the citizen (The Stockholm Programme), Presidency Draft, Doc. 14449/09, 16 October.
——(2009g), 'Council Decision 2009/935/JHA determining the list of third States and organisations with which Europol shall conclude agreements', 29 June.

——(2009h), 'Press Release of the 2936th Council meeting Justice and Home Affairs', Luxembourg, 6 April, Doc. 8478/09 (Presse 83), Provisional Version, Brussels.

——(2009i), 'Draft Fiche on possible implications of the Treaty of Lisbon provisions for the JHA working structures', Presidency, 8 September, Brussels. Available via Statewatch: <http://www.statewatch.org/news/2009/sep/eu-jha-working-structures.pdf>.

——(2008a), 'Note from the Counter-Terrorism Coordinator on the EU Counter-Terrorism Strategy—Discussion Paper', Doc. 15983/08, 19 November, Brussels.

——(2008b), 'Europol to become EU agency in 2010', Press Release, IP/08/610, 18 April, Brussels.

——(2008c), 'Justice and Home Affairs Ministers adopt EU Action Plan on Enhancing the Security of Explosives', Press Release, IP/08/611, 18 April, Brussels.

——(2008d), 'Cooperation between Europol and Eurojust', Note from Presidency to Article 36 Committee', Doc. 7191/08, 3 March, Brussels.

——(2008e), 'Council Decision 2008/617/JHA of 23 June 2008 on the improvement of cooperation between the special intervention units of the Member States of the European Union in crisis situations', OJ L 201/73.

——(2008f), 'Council Framework Decision 2008/977/JHA of 27 November 2008 on the protection of personal data processed in the framework of police and judicial cooperation in criminal matters', Brussels.

——(2008g), 'Council Conclusions on possible cooperation mechanisms between civilian ESDP Missions and Europol as regards the mutual exchange of information', JHA Council meeting, 5–6 June, Luxembourg.

——(2008h), 'EU US Summit, 12 June 2008—Final report by EU-US High Level Contact Group on information sharing and privacy and personal data protection', Note from Presidency to COREPER Brussels, 28 May 2008, Doc. 9831/08 LIMITE. Access via: <http://www.statewatch.org/news/2008/jun/eu-usa-data-sharing-privacy-hlg-9831-08.pdf>.

——(2008i), 'Council Decision 2008/615/JHA of 23 June 2008 on the stepping up of cross-border cooperation, particularly in combating terrorism and cross-border crime', Brussels.

——(2008j), 'Council Decision 2008/616/JHA of 23 June 2008 on the implementation of Decision 2008/615/JHA on the stepping up of cross-border cooperation, particularly in combating terrorism and cross-border crime', Brussels.

——(2008k), 'Europol Work Programme 2009', Doc. 7801/08, 27 March, Brussels.

——(2007a), 'The EU Strategy for Combating Radicalisation and Recruitment—Implementation report', Note from Counter-terrorism Co-ordinator to COREPER/Council, Doc. 15443/07, 23 November, Brussels.

——(2007b), 'Council decision on the implementation of Decision 2007/JHA on the stepping up of cross-border co-operation, particularly in combating terrorism and cross-border crime', Doc. 11045/2007, Brussels.

——(2007c), 'Factsheet: The European Union and the fight against terrorism', EU Council Secretariat, Press Release, 9 March, Brussels.

——(2007d), 'Schlussfolgerungen des Rates zur Zusammenarbeit gegen die terroristische Nutzung des Internets ('check the web')', JHA Council, Press Release, 12–13 June, Luxembourg.

——(2007e), 'Council Conclusions on cooperation to combat terrorist use of the Internet ("Check the Web")', Note from Working Party on Terrorism to Article 36 Committee/COREPER/Council, Doc. 8457/2/07 REV 2, 16 May, Brussels.

Council of the European Union (2007f), 'Comprehensive Operational Strategic Planning for the Police (COSPOL)', Note from Presidency to Delegations, Doc. 13412/07, 2 October, Brussels.
——(2007g), 'Council Decision 2007/551/CFSP/JHA of 23 July 2007 on the signing, on behalf of the European Union, of an Agreement between the European Union and the United States of America on the processing and transfer of Passenger Name Record (PNR) data by air carriers to the United States Department of Homeland Security (DHS) (2007 PNR Agreement)', Brussels.
——(2007h), 'Note from the Counter-Terrorism Coordinator on the Implementation of the Strategy and Action Plan to Combat Terrorism', Doc. 15411/07, 23 November, Brussels. Access via Statewatch: <http://www.statewatch.org/news/2007/nov/eu-terr-action-impl-coord.pdf>.
——(2007i), 'Contribution of the Legal Service concerning the Proposal for a Council Framework Decision on the use of Passenger Name Record (PNR) for law enforcement purposes', Doc. 16614/07, 18 December, Brussels.
——(2007j), 'Implementation of the EU Counter-terrorism strategy—Discussion paper', Note from the Counter-Terrorism Coordinator to COREPER/Council/European Council, Doc. 15448/07, 23 November, Brussels.
——(2006a), 'Initiative of the Republic of Austria with a view to adopting a Council Decision on the improvement of cooperation between the special intervention units of the Member States of the European Union in crisis situations', Doc. 2006/C 321/15, Brussels.
——(2006b), 'Policy Document Concerning Access to Eurodac by Member States' Police and Law Enforcement Authorities', Doc. 16982/06, Brussels.
——(2006c), 'Council Framework Decision 2006/960/JHA on simplifying the exchange of information and intelligence between law enforcement authorities of the Member States of the European Union', Doc. 2006/960/JHA, Brussels.
——(2006d), Justice and Home Affairs Presse 341, Doc. 15801/06, 4–5 December.
——(2005a), 'Council Decision 2005/511/JHA of 12 July 2005 on protecting the euro against counterfeiting, by designating Europol as the Central Office for combating euro counterfeiting', Doc. 2005/511/JHA, Brussels.
——(2005b), 'The European Union Counter-Terrorism Strategy', Note from Presidency and CT Co-ordinator to Council/European Council, Doc. 14469/4/05 REV 4, 30 November, Brussels.
——(2005c), 'Council Act of 29 May 2000 establishing in accordance with Article 34 of the Treaty on European Union the Convention on Mutual Assistance in Criminal Matters between the Member States of the European Union', Brussels.
——(2005d), 'Council Decision 2005/211/JHA of 24 February 2005 concerning the introduction of some new functions for the Schengen Information System, including in the fight against terrorism', Brussels.
——(2005e), 'The European Union Strategy for Combating Radicalization and Recruitment to Terrorism', Doc. 14781/1/05, 24 November, Brussels.
——(2005f), 'A Strategy for the External Dimension of JHA: Global Freedom, Security and Justice', Doc. 14366/3/05, Brussels, 30 November 2005.
——(2005g), 'Mutual evaluation of the cooperation agreements Europol—United States, from Europol to Article 36 Committee', Doc. 11502/05, Brussels, 27 July 2005. Available via Statewatch at <http://www.statewatch.org/news/2006/jun/europol-usa-11502-05.pdf>.

——(2005h), 'Council Decision 2005/671/JHA of 20 September 2005 on the exchange of information and cooperation concerning terrorist offences', Brussels.
——(2005i), 'Replies to questionnaire on Framework Decision on simplifying the exchange of information and intelligence between law enforcement authorities of the Member States of the EU, in particular as regards serious offences including terrorist acts', Doc. 5815/1/05 REV1 LIMITE, 2 February, Brussels. Available via Statewatch at <http://www.statewatch.org/news/2005/feb/5815-rev-1-05.pdf>.
——(2005j), 'Prüm Convention', Doc. 10900/05 LIMITE, 7 July, Brussels.
——(2004a), 'Council Act of 27 November 2003 drawing up, on the basis of Article 43 (1) of the Convention on the establishment of a European Police Office (Europol Convention), a Protocol amending that Convention)' [Danish Protocol], Brussels.
——(2004b), 'Declaration on Combating Terrorism', 25 March, Brussels.
——(2004c), 'The Hague Programme: strengthening freedom, security and justice in the European Union', Note from General Secretariat to Delegations, 13 December, Brussels.
——(2004d), 'Strengthening the EU operational police co-operation', Doc. 13075/1/04 REV 17 October, Brussels.
——(2004e), 'Council Regulation (EC) No 871/2004 of 29 April 2004 concerning the introduction of some new functions for the Schengen Information System, including in the fight against terrorism', Brussels.
——(2004f), 'Initiative of the Kingdom of Sweden with a view to adopting a Framework Decision on simplifying the exchange of information and intelligence between law enforcement authorities of the Member States of the European Union, in particular as regards serious offences including terrorist acts', Brussels.
——(2004g), 'Council Decision of 17 May 2004 on the conclusion of an Agreement between the European Community and the United States of America on the processing and transfer of PNR data by Air Carriers to the United States Department of Homeland Security, Bureau of Customs and Border Protection', Doc. 2004/496/EC, Brussels.
——(2003a), 'Council Decision 2003/170/JHA on the common use of liaison officers posted abroad by the law enforcement agencies of the Member States', 12 March, Brussels.
——(2003b), 'Council Decision 2003/48/JHA on the implementation of specific measures for police and judicial cooperation to combat terrorism', Brussels.
——(2003c), 'Annual report from the Council to the European Parliament on the main aspects and basic choices of CFSP, including the financial implications for the general budget of the European Communities (point H, paragraph 40, of the Interinstitutional Agreement of 6 May 1999) -2002', Doc. 7038/03, 29 April 2003, Brussels.
——(2003d), 'A secure Europe in a better world: European Security Strategy', 12 December, Brussels.
——(2002a), 'Council Framework Decision of 13 June 2002 on combating terrorism', Doc. 2002/475/JHA, Brussels.
——(2002b), 'Council Framework Decision of 13 June 2002 on the European Arrest Warrant and the surrender procedures between Member States', Doc. 2002/584/JHA, Brussels.

Council of the European Union (2002c), 'Council Regulation (EC) No 881/2002 of 27 May 2002 imposing certain specific restrictive measures directed against certain persons and entities associated with Usama bin Laden, the Al-Qaeda network and the Taliban, and repealing Council Regulation (EC) No 467/2001', Brussels.

——(2002d), 'Council Act of 28 February 2002 amending the Council Act of 12 March 1999 adopting the rules governing the transmission of personal data by Europol to third States and third bodies', Doc. 2002/C 76/01, Brussels.

——(2002e), 'Initiative of the Kingdom of Denmark with a view to adopting a Council Act drawing up, on the basis of Article 43(1) of the Convention on the Establishment of a European Police Office (Europol Convention), of a protocol amending that Convention', Doc. 10307/02, 2 July, Brussels.

——(2002f), 'Council Framework Decision of 13 June 2002 on joint investigation teams', Doc. 2002/465/JHA, Brussels.

——(2002g), 'Council Act of 28 November 2002 drawing up a Protocol amending the Convention on the establishment of a European Police Office (Europol Convention) and the Protocol on the privileges and immunities of Europol, the members of its organs, the deputy directors and the employees of Europol' [JIT Protocol], Doc. 2002/C 312/01, Brussels.

——(2002h), 'Access by Europol to the Schengen Information System', Doc. 5970/02, Brussels.

——(2001a), 'Conclusions adopted by the Council (Justice and Home Affairs)', Doc. SN 3926/6/01, 20 September, Brussels.

——(2001b), 'Council Regulation (EC) No 2424/2001 of 6 December 2001 on the development of the second generation Schengen Information System (SIS II)', Brussels.

——(2001c), 'Council Decision of 6 December 2001 on the development of the second generation Schengen Information System (SIS II)', Doc. 2001/886/JHA, Brussels.

——(2001d), 'Council Common Position of 27 December 2001 on the application of specific measures to combat terrorism', Doc. 2001/931/CFSP, Brussels.

——(2001e), 'Council Regulation (EC) No 2580/2001 of 27 December 2001 on specific restrictive measures directed against certain persons and entities with a view to combating terrorism', Brussels.

——(2000a), 'Council Act of 30 November 2000 drawing up, on the basis of Article 43 (1) of the Convention on the establishment of a European Police Office (Europol Convention), a Protocol amending Article 2 and the Annex to that Convention' [Money Laundering Protocol], Doc. 2000/C 358/01, Brussels.

——(2000b), 'Council Act of 29 May 2000 establishing in accordance with Article 34 of the Treaty on European Union the Convention on Mutual Assistance in Criminal Matters between the Member States of the European Union', Doc. 2000/C197/01, Brussels.

——(1999a), 'Council Act of 12 March 1999 adopting the rules governing the transmission of personal data by Europol to third States and bodies', Brussels.

——(1999b), 'Presidency Conclusion—Tampere European Council 15 and 16 October 1999', Brussels.

——(1999c), 'First reflections concerning the Tampere Conclusions as far as they relate to Europol', 25 November 1999, Doc 13370/99, Brussels.

——(1998), 'Council Decision of 3 December 1998 instructing Europol to deal with crimes committed or likely to be committed in the course of terrorist activities against life, limb, personal freedom or property', Doc. 1999/C 26/06, Brussels.

——(1997), 'Protocol of 19 June 1997 on the privileges and immunities of Europol, the members of its organs, the deputy directors and employees of Europol', Brussels.

——(1996), 'Council Act of 23 July 1996 drawing up, on the basis of Article K.3 of the TEU, the Protocol on the interpretation, by way of preliminary rulings, by the Court of Justice of the European Communities of the Convention on the establishment of a European Police Office', Brussels.

——(1995a), 'Council Act of 26 July 1995 drawing up the Convention based on Article K.3 of the Treaty on European Union, on the establishment of a European Police Office (Europol Convention)', Brussels.

——(1995b), 'Joint Action of 10 March 1995 adopted by the Council on the basis of Article K.3 of the Treaty on European Union concerning the Europol Drugs Unit', Doc. 95/73/JHA, Brussels.

——(1995c), 'Directive 95/46/EC on the protection of individuals with regard to the processing of personal data and on the free movement of such data', Brussels.

Court of Justice of the European Communities (2008), 'The Court annuls the Council Regulation freezing Mr Kadi and Al Barakaat's Funds', Judgment of the Court of Justice in Joined Cases C-402/05 P and C-415/05 P, Press Release No 60/08, 3 September, Brussels.

Craig, Paul (1999), 'The Nature of the Community: Integration, Democracy, and Legitimacy', in Paul Craig and Gráinne de Búrca (eds), *The Evolution of EU Law* (Oxford: Oxford University Press), 1–54.

Cronin, David (2009), 'Police Cooperation With Israel Challenged', *Inter Press Service News Agency*, 5 February, Brussels.

Crown Prosecution Service (2012), 'Joint Statement by the Director of Public Prosecutions and the Metropolitan Police Service', Press Statement, London, 12 January 2012.

Curtin, Deirdre (2011), 'Top Secret Europe', Inaugural lecture, University of Amsterdam, 20 October 2011. The text is available at <http://www.jur.uva.nl/acelg-news/news.cfm/79CDFCB7-D34E-43C5-82E327BAC76BF3F4>.

——(2007), 'Holding (Quasi-)Autonomous EU Administrative Actors to Public Account', *European Law Journal* 13/4, 523–41.

Dahl, Robert (2000), *On Democracy* (Yale: Yale Nota Bene).

——(1999), 'Can international organizations be democratic? A skeptic's view', in Ian Shapiro and Casiano Hacker-Cordón (eds), *Democracy's Edges* (Cambridge, MA: Cambridge University Press), 19–36.

Dalgaard-Nielsen, Anja (2006), 'Transatlantic homeland security: Why, what, and how?', in Anja Dalgaard-Nielsen and Daniel Hamilton (ed), *Transatlantic Homeland Security: Protecting Society in the Age of Catastrophic Terrorism* (Abingdon: Routledge), 1–17.

D'Appollonia, Chebel and Reich, Simon (2008), 'The Securitzation of Immigration: Multiple Countries, Multiple Dimensions', in Ariane Chebel d'Appollonia and Simon Reich (ed), *Immigration, Integration,* and *Security: America and Europe in Comparative Perspective* (Pittsburgh: University of Pittsburgh Press), 1–22.

Davis Cross, Mai'a (2007), 'An EU Homeland Security? Sovereignty vs. Supranational Order', *European Security* 16/1, 79–97.

De Buck, Bart (2007), 'Joint Investigation Teams: The participation of Europol officials', *ERA Forum* 8, 253–64.

De Búrca, Gráinne (2009), 'The European Court of Justice and the International Legal Order after *Kadi*', Jean Monnet Working Paper 01/09, NYU School of Law, New York.

Deflem, Mathieu (2010), *The Policing of Terrorism: Organizational and Global Perspectives* (New York: Routledge).

——(2009), 'Interpol', in Alison Wakefield and Jenny Fleming (ed), *The Sage Dictionary of Policing* (London: Sage), 179–81.

——(2006a), 'Europol and the Policing of International Terrorism', *Justice Quarterly* 23/3, 336–59.

——(2006b), 'Global Rule of Law or Global Rule of Law Enforcement? International Police Cooperation and Counter-Terrorism', *The Annals of the American Academy of Political and Social Science,* 603, 240–51.

——(2002), *Policing World Society* (Oxford: Oxford University Press).

De Goede, Marieke (2011), 'The SWIFT Affair and the Global Politics of European Security', *Journal of Common Market Studies* 50/2 (online access as of 8 November 2011), 1–17.

De Greiff, Pablo (1999), 'Drugs, National Sovereignty, and Democratic Legitimacy', in Pablo de Greiff (ed), *Drugs and the limits of liberalism: moral and legal issues* (Cornell: Cornell University Press), 156–72.

De Hert, Paul (2005), 'Balancing security and liberty within the European human rights framework. A critical reading of the Court's case law in the light of surveillance and criminal law enforcement strategies after 9/11', *Utrecht Law Review* 1/1, 68–96.

——(2004), 'Division of Competencies between National and European Levels with regard to Justice and Home Affairs', in Joanna Apap (ed), *Justice and Home Affairs in the EU: Liberty and Security Issues after Enlargement* (Cheltenham: Edward Elgar), 55–99.

——and Gutwirth, Serge (2006), 'Interoperability of Police Databases within the EU: An Accountable Political Choice?' *International Review of Law Computers* 20/1–2, 21–35.

De Laat, Paul (1999), 'Dangerous liaisons: sharing knowledge within research and development alliances', in Anna Grandori (ed), *Interfirm Networks: Organization and industrial competitiveness* (London: Routledge), 208–33.

Den Boer, Monica (2003), 'The EU Counter-Terrorism Wave: Window of Opportunity or Profound Policy Transformation?', in Marianne van Leeuwen (ed), *Confronting Terrorism: European Experiences, Threat Perceptions and Policies* (The Hague: Kluwer Law International), 185–206.

——(2002), 'Towards an Accountability Regime for an Emerging European Policing Governance', *Policing and Society* 12/4, 275–90.

——and Fernhout, Roel (2008), 'Policing Police: Police Oversight Mechanisms in Europe: Towards a Comparative Overview of Ombudsmen and Their Competences, Background Report for the Asia-Europe Foundation, December 2008. Online access at: <http://www.asef.org/images/docs/1270-Police_Oversight_Mechanisms_in_Europe.pdf>.

—— Hillebrand, Claudia, and Nölke, Andreas (2008), 'Legitimacy under Pressure: The European Web of Counter-Terrorism Networks', *Journal of Common Market Studies* 46, 1, 101–24.

——and Monar, Jörg (2002), '11 September and Global Terrorism as a Challenge to the EU as a Security Actor', *Journal of Common Market Studies* 40, Annual Review, 11–28.

Der Spiegel (2009), 'BND-Untersuchungsausschuss Union wirft Steinmeier "doppeltes Spiel" vor', 19 June 2009.

De Smet, Peter (2008), 'Confidence is fine, control is better?', Excerpt of the speech held at Community of Interest on the Practice and Organisation of Intelligence, Belgian Standing Intelligence Agencies Review Committee, December 2008, Belgium. Online access at <http://www.comiteri.be/images/pdf/engels/speechbelgium.pdf>.

Deutscher Bundestag (2009), 'Beschlussempfehlung und Bericht des 1. Untersuchungsausschusses nach Artikel 44 des Grundgesetzes', Berlin, 18 June 2009.

——(2005), 'Vertrag zwischen der Bundesrepublik Deutschland und dem Königreich der Niederlande über die grenzüberschreitende polizeiliche Zusammenarbeit und die Zusammenarbeit in strafrechtlichen Angelegenheiten', Bundestag Drucksache 16/57, 2 March 2005.

Deutscher Bundestag, Wissenschaftliche Dienste (2008), 'Aktueller Begriff: "Gefährder"'. Online access: <http://www.bundestag.de/dokumente/analysen/ 2008/Gefaehrder.pdf>.

De Villepin, Dominique (2006), 'Prevailing Terrorism: White Paper on Domestic Security Against Terrorism' (Paris: La Documentation Francaise).

De Vries, Gijs (2008), 'The Nexus Between EU Crisis Management and Counter-Terrorism', in Steven Blockmans (ed), *The European Union and Crisis Management* (The Hague: T.M.C. Asser Press), 355–72.

——(2006), 'The Fight Against Terrorism: Five Years After 9/11'. Presentation at the Annual European Foreign Policy Conference London School of Economics & King's College London, 30 June 2006.

——(2003), 'Debating Europe's Future: The Political Setting of the European Convention', in *Debating Europe's Future: The Political Setting of the European Convention*, Conference Report of 22 November 2002, published in March 2003 (The Hague: Clingendael Institute), 13–20.

De Witte, Lode (1993), 'The Belgian Perspective on the Internationalization of Police Cooperation in Western Europe', in Cyrille Fijnaut (ed), *The Internationalization of Police Cooperation in Western Europe* (Deventer: Kluwer), 85–99.

Donohue, Laura (2008), *The Cost of Counterterrorism: Power, Politics, and Liberty* (Cambridge: Cambridge University Press).

Douglas-Scott, Sionaidh (2008), 'Fundamental rights in EU justice and home affairs', in Martin Maik (ed), *Crime, rights and the EU: the future of police and judicial cooperation* (London: Justice), 14–33.

Dupont, Benoît (2004), 'Security in the age of networks', *Policing & Society* 14/1, 76–91.

DW World (2011), 'US, EU seek consensus on securing cargo shipments from terrorists', 24 June 2011.

Eder, Klaus and Trenz, Hans-Jürgen (2003), 'The Making of a European Public Space: An Inquiry into Relating Supranational Politics and Transnational Spaces of Communication: The Case of Justice and Home Affairs', in Beate Kohler-Koch (ed), *Linking EU and National Governance* (Oxford: Oxford University Press), 51–68.

Edwards, Charles (2005), *Changing Policing Theories for 21st Century Society* (Sydney: Federation Press).

Eijkman, Quirine (2006), 'To be Held Accountable: Police Accountability in Costa Rica', *Police Practice and Research* 7/5, 411–30.

Eilstrup-Sangiovanni, Mette (2009), 'Varieties of Cooperation: Government Networks in International Security', in Miles Kahler (ed), *Networked Politics: Agency, Power, and Governance* (Ithaca, NY: Cornell University Press), 194–227.

Ericson, Richard (1994), 'The Division of Expert Knowledge in Policing and Security', *British Journal of Sociology* 45, 149–75.

Erlanger, Steven (2008), '14 arrested in Belgium for links to terrorism', *New York Times*, 11 December.

EU Institute for Security Studies (2010), 'Crisis response to the Haiti earthquake—an EU SITCEN perspective', CSDP Newsletter, Issue 10 (Summer).

EU Network of Independent Experts on Fundamental Rights (CFR-CDF) (2006), 'The Human Rights responsibilities of the EU member states in the context of the C.I.A. activities in Europe ("extraordinary renditions")', Opinion no 3-2006, 25 May 2006.

——(2003), 'The Balance between freedom and security in the response by the European Union and its Member States to the terrorist threats', Thematic Comment, 31 March 2003.

Eurojust (2011), *Annual Report 2010*, The Hague.

——(2008), *Annual Report 2008*, The Hague.

——(2008), *Annual Report 2007*, The Hague.

Europa (2007), 'The Passenger Name Record (PNR): Frequently Asked Questions', Memo MEMO/07/294, Brussels, 13 July 2007.

——(2006), 'Rapid reaction teams of border guards', Press Release, Memo MEMO/06/297, Brussels, 19 July 2006.

European Center for Constitutional and Human Rights (2010), 'Blacklisted: Targeted Sanctions, Preemptive security and fundamental rights', by Gavin Sullivan and Ben Hayes, Berlin.

European Commission for Democracy Through Law [Venice Commission] (2007), *Report on the Democratic Oversight of the Security Services*, Adopted by the Venice Commission at its 71st Plenary Session, Strasbourg, 11 June 2007, Study no 388/2006.

European Council (2010), 'The Stockholm Programme—An Open and Secure Europe Serving and Protecting Citizens', Doc. 2010/C 115/01, Brussels.

——(1999), 'Tampere European Council 15 and 16 October 1999: Presidency Conclusions'.

European Data Protection Supervisor (2008), 'EDPS sees adoption of Data Protection Framework for police and judicial cooperation only as a first step', Press Release Brussels, 28 November.

——(2007a), 'Opinion of the European Data Protection Supervisor on the Proposal for a Council Decision establishing the European Police Office (Europol)—COM (2006) 817 final', Doc. 2007/C 255/02, 16 February.

——(2007b), 'Third opinion of the European Data Protection Supervisor on the Proposal for a Council Framework Decision on the protection of personal data processed in the framework of police and judicial co-operation in criminal matters', Doc. 2007/C 139/01, 27 April, Brussels.

European Economic and Social Committee (2008), 'Opinion of the European Economic and Social Committee on the 'Prevention of Terrorism and Violent Radicalisation"', Doc. 2008/C 211/17.

European Parliament (2007a), 'European Parliament resolution of 12 July 2007 on the PNR agreement with the United States of America', Doc. P6_TA(2007)0347, 12 July.

——(2007b), 'Prüm Treaty: cross-border cooperation in combating terrorism and cross-border crime', European Parliament legislative resolution of 7 June 2007 on the initiative by the Kingdom of Belgium, the Republic of Bulgaria, the Federal Republic of Germany, the Kingdom of Spain, the French Republic, the Grand Duchy of Luxembourg, the Kingdom of the Netherlands, the Republic of Austria, the Republic of Slovenia, the Slovak Republic, the Italian Republic, the Republic of Finland, the Portuguese Republic, Romania and the Kingdom of Sweden on the stepping up of cross-border cooperation, particularly in combating terrorism and cross-border crime (6566/2007—C6-0079/2007—2007/0804 (CNS)), 7 June.

——(2007c), 'Opinion of the Committee on Civil Liberties, Justice and Home Affairs for the Committee on Constitutional Affairs on the Treaty amending the Treaty on European Union and the Treaty establishing the European Community (Lisbon Treaty)', Doc. 2007/2286(INI), 18 December.

——(2007d), 'Resolution of 11 July 2007 on the convening of the Intergovernmental Conference (IGC): the European Parliament's opinion (Article 48 of the EU Treaty)', P6_TA-PROV(2007)0328.

——(2006a), 'Proposal for a recommendation to the Council on the content of the Agreement with the United States of America on the use of Passenger Name Records (PNR) data to prevent and combat terrorism and transnational crime, including organised crime', by Sophie in't Veld, Doc. B6-0382/2006, 3 July.

——(2006b), 'European Parliament recommendation to the Council on the negotiations for an agreement with the United States of America on the use of passenger name records (PNR) data to prevent and combat terrorism and transnational crime, including organised crime (2006/2193(INI))', Doc. P6_TA(2006)0354, Strasbourg, 7 September 2006.

——(2003), 'European Parliament recommendation to the Council on the future development of Europol (2003/2070(INI))' [Resolution of 10 April 2003], Doc. P5_TA(2003)0186, 10 April.

——(2001), 'Motion for a resolution on EU judicial cooperation with the United States in combating terrorism', Doc. B5-0813/2001, 11 December.

——(2000), 'Subsidiarity', fact sheet 1.2.1, 16 November.

European Parliament, Committee on Civil Liberties, Justice and Home Affairs (LIBE Committee) (2008), 'Working document on problem of profiling, notably on the basis of ethnicity and race, in counter-terrorism, law enforcement, immigration, customs and border control', Rapporteur: Sarah Ludford, Doc. PE413.954v02-00, 30 September.

——(2001), 'Report on the role of the European Union in combating terrorism (2001/2016(INI))', Rapporteur: Graham R. Watson, Doc. A5-0273/2001 Final, 12 July.

European Parliament, Directorate General Internal Policies, Policy Department C—Citizens' Rights and Constitutional Affairs (2009a), 'Exchange of information and data between law enforcement authorities within the European Union', Study by Leon Hempel, Michael Carius, and Carla Ilten, Doc. PE 419.590, April.

European Parliament (2009b), 'Overview of European and international legislation on terrorist financing', Study by Henri Labayle and Nadja Long, Doc. PE 410.695, April.
European Parliament, Temporary Committee on the alleged use of European countries by the CIA for the transportation and illegal detention of prisoners (TDIP) (2007), 'Report on the alleged use of European countries by the CIA for the transportation and illegal detention of prisoners', Rapporteur: Giovanni Claudio Fava, Doc. A6-9999/2007.
European Parliament and Council of the European Union (2007), 'Regulation (EC) No 863/2007 of the European Parliament and of the Council of 11 July 2007 establishing a mechanism for the creation of Rapid Border Intervention Teams and amending Council Regulation (EC) No 2007/2004 as regards that mechanism and regulating the tasks and powers of guest officers', Doc. 863/2007.
——(1995), 'Directive 95/46/EC of the European Parliament and of the Council of 24 October 1995 on the protection of individuals with regard to the processing of personal data and on the free movement of such data', Doc. 95/46/EC, Brussels.
European Union, Delegation of the European Commission to the State of Israel (2007), 'The European Neighbourhood Policy and Israel', *EU Focus* 4 November.
European Union and the United States of America (2007), 'Agreement between the European Union and the United States of America on the processing and transfer of Passenger Name Record (PNR) data by air carriers to the United States Department of Homeland Security (DHS) (2007 PNR Agreement)', OJ L204/18, 4 August.
Europol (2011a), *The European Investigator*, The Hague.
——(2011b), *Europol Review: General Report on Europol Activities*, The Hague.
——(2011c), *TE-SAT 2011: EU Terrorism Situation and Trend Report*, The Hague.
——(2011d), 'Europol responds to attacks in Norway by mobilising the EU First Response Network', 27 July 2011, The Hague.
——(2011e), 'Democratic accountability of the ISS and the role of Europol', Speech by Rob Wainwright at the Interparliamentary Committee Meeting, Brussels, 5 October 2011.
——(2011f), 'Cybercrime presents a major challenge for law enforcement', Europol Press Release, The Hague, 3 January 2011.N.
——(2009a), *TE-SAT 2009: EU Terrorism Situation and Trend Report*, The Hague.
——(2009b), *Annual Report 2008*, The Hague.
——(2009c), 'Strong support from EU ministers to Europol', The Hague, 1 October 2009.
——(2008a), *EU Terrorism Situation And Trend Report 2008* (TE-SAT), The Hague.
——(2008b), *Annual Report 2007*, The Hague.
——(2008c), 'Europol supports the development of the European Network of Advisory Teams (EuNAT)', Press Release, 28 February, The Hague.
——(2007a), *EU Organised Crime Threat Assessment 2007* (OCTA), The Hague.
——(2007b), 'Signing of Cooperation agreement between Europol and CEPOL', Press Release, 19 October, The Hague.
——(2007c), *Annual Report 2006*, The Hague.
——(2007d), *Code of Conduct*, The Hague.
——(2006), 'Europol Work Programme 2007', 31 March, The Hague.
——(2005), 'Mutual evaluation of the cooperation agreements Europol—United States', Letter from the Chairman of the Europol Management Board, Rob Wainwright, to the

Secretary-General of the Council of the European Union, Doc. MBS 070.2005/# 128051, The Hague, 13 July 2005. Unpublished document, available via Statewatch: <http://www.statewatch.org/news/2006/jun/europol-usa-11502-05.pdf> (Annex I).

——(2004a), *Annual Report 2003*, The Hague.

——(2004b), 'Agreement between Eurojust and Europol', The Hague, 9 June 2004.

——(2002), *Annual Report 2001*, The Hague.

Evans, Jonathan (2009), 'Defending the realm', Speech by the Director General of the Security Service at Bristol University, 15 October 2009.

Evans, Michael (2009), 'MI6 faces torture investigation after reporting its own officer', *The Times*, 12 September 2009.

Fijnaut, Cyrille (2004), 'The attacks on 11 September 2001, and the immediate response of the European Union and the United States', in Cyrille Fijnaut, Jan Wouters, and Frederik Naert (eds), *Legal instruments in the fight against international terrorism: A transatlantic dialogue* (Leiden: Martinus Nijhoff Publishers), 15–36.

——(2002), 'Europol and the parliaments of the member states of the European Union', in Dutch Parliament (ed), *From Europol to Parlopol: interparliamentary conference on democratic control of Europol* (Amsterdam: Boom), 15–19.

——(1993), 'The Internationalization of Police Cooperation in Western Europe', in Cyrille Fijnaut (ed), *The Internationalization of Police Cooperation in Western Europe* (Deventer: Kluwer), 9–17.

Finnemore, Martha (2005), 'Fighting about rules: the role of efficacy and power in changing multilateralism', *Review of International Studies* 31/S1, 187–206.

Fleming, Jenny and Wood, Jennifer (eds) (2006a), *Fighting Crime Together: The Challenges of Policing and Security Networks* (Sydney: University of New South Wales Press).

——(2006b), 'Introduction: New ways of doing business Networks of policing and security', in Jenny Fleming and Jennifer Wood (eds), *Fighting Crime Together: The Challenges of Policing and Security Networks* (Sydney: University of New South Wales Press), 1–14.

Foley, Frank (2009), 'Reforming Counterterrorism: Institutions and Organizational Routines in Britain and France', *Security Studies* 18/3, 435–78.

Føllesdal, Andreas (2005), 'Survey Article: The Legitimacy Deficits of the European Union', *The Journal of Political Philosophy* 14/4, 441–68.

——and Hix, Simon (2006), 'Why there is a Democratic Deficit in the EU: A Response to Majone and Moravcsik', *Journal of Common Market Studies* 44/3, 533–62.

Foreign & Commonwealth Office, Counter Terrorism Department (2008), Letter to MP Andrew Tyrie, Reference 0442/08, 2 September, London.

Friedrichs, Jörg (2007), *Fighting Terrorism and Drugs: Europe and International Police Cooperation* (London: Routledge).

FRONTEX (2007), 'Agelaus—Minors arriving to the EU', 20 September 2007. Online access: <http://frontex.europa.eu/operations/archive-of-accomplished-operations/13>.

Geiger, Hansjörg (2007), 'Wie viel Kontrolle ist möglich und nötig? Rechtliche Grundlagen und politische Praxis in Deutschland', in Wolbert Smidt et al (eds), *Geheimhaltung und Transparenz: Demokratische Kontrolle der Geheimdienste im internationalen Vergleich* (Berlin: Lit), 33–45.

Gerspacher, Nadia and Dupont, Benoît (2007), 'The nodal structure of international police co-operation: an exploration of transnational security networks', *Global Governance* 13/3, 347–64.

Gibson, Stevyn (2009), 'Future roles of the UK intelligence system', *Review of International Studies* 35/4, 917–28.
Gill, Peter (2009), 'Security Intelligence and Human Rights: Illuminating the "Heart of Darkness"?', *Intelligence and National Security* 24/1, 78–102.
——(2006), 'Not Just Joining the Dots But Crossing the Borders and Bridging the Voids: Constructing Security Networks after 11 September 2001', *Policing & Society* 16/1, 27–49.
——and Phythian, Mark (2006), *Intelligence in an Insecure World* (London: Polity Press).
Glaeßner, Gert-Joachim and Lorenz, Astrid (2005a), 'Europa und die Politik der inneren Sicherheit', in Gert-Joachim Glaeßner and Astrid Lorenz (eds), *Europäisierung der inneren Sicherheit: Eine vergleichende Untersuchung am Beispiel von organisierter Kriminalität und Terrorismus* (Wiesbaden: VS Verlag für Sozialwissenschaften), 21–41.
—— and —— (eds) (2005b), *Europäisierung der inneren Sicherheit: Eine vergleichende Untersuchung am Beispiel von organisierter Kriminalität und Terrorismus* (Wiesbaden: VS Verlag für Sozialwissenschaften).
Glees, Anthony and Davies, Philip (2006), 'Intelligence, Iraq and the Limits of Legislative Accountability during Political Crisis', *Intelligence and National Security* 21/5, 848–83.
——(2004), *Spinning the Spies* (London: The Social Affairs Unit).
Goetz, John and Sandberg, Britta (2009), 'Milan Trial Could Expose Italian Role in CIA Kidnapping', *Der Spiegel Online*, 28 October.
Goldenberg, Suzanne (2009a), 'Obama shuts network of CIA "ghost prisons"', *Guardian*, 23 January.
——(2009b), 'New Chapter begins with end to Guantánamo and torture', *Guardian*, 23 January.
Goldsmith, Andrew (1999), 'Better Policing, More Human Rights: Lessons from Civilian Oversight', in Errol Mendes, Joaquin Zuckerberg, Susan Lecorre, Anne Gabriel, and Jeffrey Clark (eds), *Democratic policing and accountability: global perspectives* (Aldershot: Ashgate), 33–67.
Goldsmith, Stephen and Eggers, William D (2004), *Governing by Network: The New Shape of the Public Sector* (Washington, DC: Brookings Institution Press).
Gordon, Philip (2003), 'Bridging the Atlantic Divide', *Foreign Affairs* 82/1, 70–83.
Grey, Stephen (2006), *Ghost Plane: The True Story of the CIA Torture Program* (New York: St. Martin's).
Griffith, Gareth (2005), 'Parliament and Accountability: The Role of Parliamentary Oversight Committees', Briefing Paper 12/05, NSW Parliamentary Library Research Service, November, Sydney.
Guild, Elspeth (2008), 'The Uses and Abuses of Counter-Terrorism Policies in Europe: The Case of the "Terrorist Lists"', *Journal of Common Market Studies* 46/1, 173–93.
——(2007), 'Inquiry into the EU-US Passenger Name Record Agreement', CEPS Policy Brief No 125, March.
——and Geyer, Florian (2007), 'Getting local: Schengen, Prüm and the dancing procession of Echternach—Three paces forward and two back for EU police and judicial cooperation in criminal matters', Brussels: CEPS.
——and Carrera, Sergio (2005), 'No Constitutional Treaty? Implications for the Area of Freedom, Security and Justice', CEPS Working Document No. 231, Brussels.

Guillaume, Gilbert (2004), 'Terrorism and International Law', *International and Comparative Law Quarterly* 53/3, 537–48.

Gunaratna, Rohan (2002), *Inside Al Qaeda: Global Network of Terror* (London: Hurst and Co Publishers).

Gutwirth, Serge (2002), *Privacy and the Information Age* (Lanham, MD, Rowman & Littlefield).

Haas, Peter (1992), 'Introduction: epistemic communities and international policy coordination', in Peter Haas (ed), *Knowledge, Power, and International Policy Coordination* (Columbia, SC: University of South Carolina Press), 1–36.

Halperin, Morton and Hoffman, Daniel (1977), *Top secret: national security and the right to know* (Washington, DC: New Republic Books).

Hanning, August (2008), 'German and European Security Interests in the Federally Administrated Tribal Areas (FATA)', Speech by State Secretary August Hanning at the FATA Workshop of the World Security Network Foundations, 28 May 2008.

Harden, Ian (1996), 'Democracy and the European Union', in Paul Hirst and Sunil Khilnani (eds), *Reinventing Democracy* (Cambridge, MA: Blackwell Publishers), 132–43.

Harlow, Carol (2002), *Accountability in the European Union* (Oxford: Oxford University Press).

Haubrich, Dirk (2003), 'September 11, Anti-Terror Laws and Civil Liberties: Britain, France and Germany Compared', *Government & Opposition* 38/1, 3–28.

Hayman, Andy (2009), *The Terrorist Hunters* (London: Bantam Press).

Heath, Joseph (2006), 'The Benefits of Cooperation', *Philosophy & Public Affairs* 34/4, 313–51.

Held, David (2004), 'Democratic Accountability and Political Effectiveness from a Cosmopolitan Perspective', *Government and Opposition* 39/2, 364–91.

——(1996), *Models of Democracy*, 2nd edn (Stanford: Stanford University Press).

——(1995), *Democracy and the Global Order: From the Modern State to Cosmopolitan Governance* (Cambridge: Polity Press).

Helsingin Sanomat (2004), 'Head of Parliamentary committee wants tighter controls on Security Police', International edn, 6 September 2004.

Henderson, Karen (2005), 'Perceptions of Internal Security Issues in the New Member States', in Karen Henderson (ed), *The Area of Freedom, Security and Justice in the Enlarged Europe, Palgrave Macmillan* (Basingstoke: Palgrave Macmillan), 1–24.

Hendricks, Steve (2010), *A Kidnapping in Milan: The CIA on Trial* (New York: W.W. Norton & Co.).

Heng, Yee-Kuang and McDonagh, Kenneth (2011), 'After the "War on Terror": Regulatory States, Risk Bureaucracies and the Risk-Based Governance of Terror', *International Relations* 25/3, 313–29.

Hennessy, Peter (2007), 'From Secret State to Protective State', in Peter Hennessy (ed), *The New Protective State: Government, Intelligence and Terrorism* (London: Continuum), 1–41.

Herman, Michael (2004), 'Ethics and Intelligence after September 2001', in Len Scott and Peter Jackson (eds), *Understanding Intelligence in the Twenty-First Century: Journeys in shadows* (London: Routledge), 180–94.

——(2002), *Intelligence Power in Peace and War* (Cambridge: Cambridge University Press).

Hillebrand, Claudia (2010), 'Written Evidence on the EU's Internal Security Strategy to the House of Lords EU Sub-Committee F (Home Affairs)', December 2010.

Hillebrand, Claudia (2009), 'The CIA's extraordinary rendition and secret detention programme: European reactions and the challenges of future international intelligence co-operation', Policy Paper, March 2009 (The Hague: Clingendael Institute).

Hobbing, Peter (2008), 'Uniforms without Uniformity: A Critical Look at European Standards in Policing', in Elspeth Guild and Florian Geyer (eds), *Security versus Justice?: Police and Judicial Cooperation in the European Union* (Aldershot: Ashgate), 243–64.

Hoffman, Bruce (1999), 'Is Europe Soft on Terrorism?', *Foreign Policy*, No 115, 62–76.

Højbjerg, Jens Henrik (2004), 'Building Trust and Developing More Efficient Sharing of Intelligence in Response to and Prevention of Terrorist Acts: The Europol perspective', in EULEC (ed), *European Cooperation against Terrorism: Conference*, (Nijmegen: Wolf Legal Publishers), 49–57.

House of Commons (1997), 'Draft European Communities (Immunities and Privileges of the European Police Office) Order 1997', 9th Standing Committee on Delegated Legislation, Session 1997–98, 4 December 1997.

——(1996), 'Written Answers to Questions', by Home Department, House of Commons Hansard Written Answers, Thursday 11 January 1996, Column 276.

House of Commons, Foreign Affairs Committee (2009), 'Human Rights Annual Report 2008', Seventh Report, London, 21 July.

——(2008), 'Human Rights Annual Report 2007', Ninth Report of Session 2007–08, London, 20 July 2008.

House of Commons, Home Affairs Committee (2007), 'Justice and Home Affairs Issues at European Union Level', 3rd Report of Session 2006–07, Report, together with formal minutes and evidence, 5 June, London.

——(2005), 'Terrorism and Community Relations', Sixth Report of Session 2004–05, Volume I, Report, together with formal minutes and appendix, 22 March.

House of Lords (2009), Debate on 'Civil Liberties: Electronic Surveillance', Lords Hansard text for 23 April 2009, Column 1646–73.

House of Lords, Select Committee on European Union (2011), 'The EU Internal Security Strategy', 17th Report of Session 2010–12, London, 24 May 2011.

——(2008), 'The Passenger Name Record (PNR) Framework Decision', 15th Report of Session 2007–08, Report with Evidence, London, 11 June 2008.

——(2007a), *The EU/US Passenger Name Record (PNR) Agreement*, 21st Report of Session 2006–07, Report with Evidence, 5 June, London.

——(2007b), 'Prüm: an effective weapon against terrorism and crime', 18th Report of Session 2006–07, Report with Evidence, 9 May, London.

——(2007c), 'Schengen Information System II (SIS II)', Report with Evidence, Report of Session 2006–07, 2 March, London.

——(2003), 'Europol's role in fighting crime', 5th Report of Session 2002–03, Report with Evidence, London, HL Paper 43, 28 January.

House of Lords/House of Commons Joint Committee on Human Rights (JCHR) (2009a), 'Demonstrating respect for rights? A human rights approach to policing protest', 7th Report of Session 2008–09, Vol I (Report, together with formal minutes and written evidence), HL Paper 47-I/HC 320-I, 23 March (London: The Stationery Office).

——(2009b), 'Allegations of UK Complicity in Torture', 23rd Report of Session 2008–09, Report, together with formal minutes and oral and written evidence, HL Paper 152/HC 230, 4 August (London: The Stationery Office).

Howorth, Jolyon (2008), 'European Security and Counter-Terrorism', in Ariane Chebel d'Appollonia and Simon Reich (eds), *Immigration, Integration,* and *Security: America and Europe in Comparative Perspective* (Pittsburgh: University of Pittsburgh Press), 95–110.

Hulnick, Arthur (1999), 'Openness: Being Public About Secret Intelligence', *International Journal of Intelligence and Counterintelligence* 12/4, 463–83.

Huysmans, Jef (2006), *The Politics of Insecurity: Fear, migration and asylum in the EU* (London/New York: Routledge).

Independent Police Complaints Commission (2009), 'Commissioner's report following the IPCC independent investigation into a complaint that officers used excessive force against a woman during the G20 protests', London.

—— (2006a), 'Stockwell One: Investigation into the shooting of Jean Charles de Menezes at Stockwell underground station on 22 July 2005', London.

—— (2006b), 'Stockwell Two: An investigation into complaints about the Metropolitan Police Service's handling of public statements following the shooting of Jean Charles de Menezes on 22 July 2005', London.

Ingleton, Roy (1994), *Mission Incomprehensible* (Clevedon: Multilingual Matters Ltd).

Intelligence and Security Committee (2009), 'Could 7/7 Have Been Prevented? Review of the Intelligence on the London Terrorist Attacks on 7 July 2005', Report, May, London.

—— (2007), 'Report into Rendition', July, London.

International Commission of Jurists, Eminent Jurists Panel (2009), 'Assessing Damage, Urging Action: Report of the Eminent Jurists Panel on Terrorism, Counter-Terrorism and Human Rights', Geneva.

International Commission of Jurists (2004), 'The Berlin Declaration: The ICJ Declaration on Upholding Human Rights and the Rule of Law in Combating Terrorism', adopted on 28 August.

International Committee of the Red Cross (2007), 'Report on the treatment of Fourteen "High Value Detainees" in CIA Custody' (Washington, 14 February 2007).

International Herald Tribune (2008), 'Italian judge suspends trial of CIA agents', 3 December.

Interview A, Interview with a senior official of Europol, 2008.

Interview B, Interview with a senior official in the field of EU data protection, 2008.

Interview C, Interview with a senior official of Europol, 2008.

Interview D, Interview with two liaison officers of a European bilateral border police office, 2007.

Interview E, Interview with the head of a national liaison office at Europol's headquarters, 2008.

Interview F, Interview with a European senior liaison officer in the field of law enforcement, 2009.

Interview G, Interview with a senior national police official who works in the field of international police coordination, 2008.

Interview H, Interview with a senior official of Europol's Counter-terrorism Unit, 2009.

Interview I, Interview with MEP, 2008.

Interview J, Interview with MEP, 2008.

Interview K, Interview with a senior official of the US intelligence community, 2009.

Interview L, Interview with a senior official and two national representatives at the General Secretariat of the Council of the European Union, DG H, 2008.

Interview M, Interview with a senior official of European Commission, 2008.
Interview N, Interview with a senior official of Europol's Counter-Terrorism Unit, 2008.
Interview O, Interview with a senior policy advisor of a European national police unit, 2008.
Interview P, Interview with officials of the European Commission, DG Justice, Freedom and Security, 2008.
Interview Q, Interview with a senior official of a European national counter-terrorism body, 2009.
Interview R, Interview with a European senior liaison officer seconded to the US, 2009.
Interview S, Interview with a senior official at Eurojust, 2008.
Interview T, Interview with a senior official of the General Secretariat of the Council of the European Union, DG H, 2008.
Interview U, Interview with a legal scholar, 2008.
Interview V, Interview with a senior official at Europol, 2008.
Interview W, Interview with a senior official at Europol, 2008.
Interview X, Interview with a senior official at the European Commission, DG Justice, Freedom and Security, 2008.
Interview Y, Interview with an official based at a national desk at Eurojust, 2008.
Interview Z, Interview with a senior official of a European Ministry of Interior, involved in counter-terrorism, 2008.
In't Veld, Sophie (2010), 'Dirty Harry Meets Hercule Poirot: Transatlantic Cooperation in the Fight Against Crime and Terrorism', *European Affairs*, October 2010 (Washington, D.C.: The European Institute).
Jeffreys-Jones, Rhodri (2007), 'The idea of a European FBI', in Loch Johnson (ed), *Counterintelligence and Counterterrorism* (New York: Praeger), 73–97.
Jenkins, Brian (2010), 'Would-Be Warriors: Incidents of Jihadist Terrorist Radicalization in the United States Since September 11, 2001', *Occasional Papers* OP-292-RC (Santa Monica, CA: RAND Corporation).
Johnson, Alan and Miliband, David (2009), 'We firmly oppose torture—but it is impossible to eradicate all risk', Comment, *The Telegraph*, 8 August 2009.
Johnston, Les (2006), 'Transnational security governance', in Jennifer Wood and Benoît Dupont (eds), *Democracy, Society and the Governance of Security* (Cambridge: Cambridge University Press), 33–51.
——and Shearing, Clifford (2003), *Governing Security: Explorations in Policing and Justice* (London: Routledge).
Joint Supervisory Body of Europol [JSB] (2008), 'The fourth activity report of the Joint Supervisory Body of Europol', November 2006–November 2008, The Hague.
——(2007), 'The Third Activity Report of the Joint Supervisory Body of Europol: November 2004–October 2006', 18 December 2007.
Jozwiak, Rikard (2008), 'Brussels police thwart "imminent" terrorist attack', *European Voice*, 11 December.
Kahler, Miles (ed) (2009), *Networked Politics: Agency, Power, and Governance* (Ithaca, NY: Cornell University Press).
Kahlke, Svenja (2004), *Eurojust—Auf dem Weg zu einer Europäischen Staatsanwaltschaft?: Die Justizielle Zusammenarbeit in Strafsachen innerhalb der Europäischen Union* (Berlin: Logos).

Kaiafa-Gbandi, Maria (2001), 'The Development towards Harmonization within Criminal Law in the European Union—A Citizen's Perspective', *European Journal of Crime, Criminal Law and Criminal Justice* 9/4, 239–63.

Kaiser, Karl (1971), 'Transnational Relations as a Threat to the Democratic Process', *International Organization* 25/4, 706–20.

Kaldor, Mary (1999), *New and Old Wars: Organised Violence in a Global Era* (Cambridge: Polity Press).

Kantner, Cathleen and Liberatore, Angela (2006), 'Security and Democracy in the European Union: An Introductory Framework', *European Security* 15/4, 363–83.

Katzenstein, Peter (2005), *A World of Regions: Asia and Europe in the American Imperium* (Ithaca, NY: Cornell University Press).

Kaunert, Christian (2010a), 'Europol and EU Counterterrorism: International Security Actorness in the External Dimension', *Studies in Conflict & Terrorism* 33/7, 652–71.

——(2010b), 'The External Dimension of EU Counter-Terrorism: Competences, Interests and institutions', *Terrorism and Political Violence* 22/1, 41–61.

——(2006), *The European Commission: an 'engine' in the area of freedom, security and justice?*, PhD thesis, Department of International Politics, Aberystwyth University.

Kehaulani Goo, Sara (2004), 'Sen. Kennedy Flagged by No-Fly List', *Washington Post*, 20 August.

Keller, Helen and Stone Sweet, Alec (eds) (2008), *A Europe of Rights: The Impact of the ECHR on National Legal Systems* (Oxford: Oxford University Press).

Kenney, Michael (2007), *From Pablo to Osama: Trafficking and Terrorist Networks, Government Bureaucracies, and Competitive Adaptation* (University Park, PA: Pennsylvania State University Press).

——(2005), 'Drug Traffickers, Terrorist Networks, and Ill-Fated Government Strategies', in Elke Krahmann (ed), *New Threats and New Actors in International Security* (New York: Palgrave Macmillan), 69–90.

Kent Police (2009), 'N135 Briefing and Debriefing'. Online access: <http://www.kent.police.uk/about_us/policies/n/n135.html>.

Keohane, Daniel (2008), 'The absent friend: EU foreign policy and counter-terrorism', *Journal of Common Market Studies* 46/1, 125–46.

——(2005), *The EU and counter-terrorism*, CER Working Paper, London.

Kohler-Koch, Beate and Rittberger Berthold (eds) (2007), *Debating the Democratic Legitimacy of the European Union* (Lanham: Bowman & Littlefield).

König, Marco (2005), *Trennung und Zusammenarbeit von Polizei und Nachrichtendiensten*, Schriften zum Recht der Inneren Sicherheit—Band 7 (Stuttgart: Boorberg).

Koslowski, Rey (2006), 'Immigration Reforms and Border Security Technologies' (New York: Social Science Research Council), <http://borderbattles.ssrc.org/Koslowski/printable.html>.

Krahmann, Elke (ed) (2005), *New Threats and New Actors in International Security* (New York: Palgrave Macmillan).

Laurence, Jonathan (2010), 'The US-EU Counter-Terrorism Conversation: Acknowledging a Two-Way Threat', US-Europe Analysis Series No 44, Center on the United States and Europe at Brookings, 24 February 2010.

Lavranos, Nikolaos (2003), 'Europol and the Fight Against Terrorism', *European Foreign Affairs Review* 8/2, 259–75.

Lefebvre, Stéphane (2003), 'The Difficulties and Dilemmas of International Intelligence Cooperation', *International Journal of Intelligence and CounterIntelligence* 16/4, 527–42.

Leigh, Ian (2005), 'More Closely Watching the Spies: Three Decades of Experiences', in Hans Born, Loch K. Johnson, and Ian Leigh (eds), *Who's Watching the Spies? Establishing Intelligence Service Accountability* (Dulles: Potomac Books), 3–11.

Lemmens, Paul (2004), 'Respecting Human Rights in the Fight against Terrorism', in Cyrille Fijnaut, Jan Wouters, and Frederik Naert (eds), *Legal instruments in the fight against terrorism: a transatlantic dialogue* (Leiden: Martinus Nijhoff Publishers), 223–49.

Lepri, Charlotte (2011), 'France', in Aidan Wills et al (eds), 'Parliamentary Oversight of Security and Intelligence Agencies in the European Union', Study for the European Parliament, Directorate General for Internal Policies, Policy Department C, Doc. PE 315.238, 20 June 2011, 205–17.

Lerner, Craig (2003), 'The USA Patriot Act: Promoting the cooperation of foreign intelligence gathering and law enforcement', *George Mason Law Review* 11/3, 493–526.

Liberty et al (2003), 'Casualty of War: 8 weeks of counter-terrorism in rural England', Report by Liberty, Gloucestershire Weapons Inspectors and Berkshire Citizens Inspections Agency, July. Online access at <http://www.liberty-human-rights.org.uk/policy/reports/casualty-of-war-counter-terror-legislation-in-rural-england-2003.pdf>.

Lilleker, Darren (2003), 'Interviewing the Political Elite: Navigating a Potential Minefield', *Politics* 23/3, 207–14.

Lippert, Randy and O'Connor, Daniel (2006), 'Security Intelligence Networks and the Transformation of Contract Private Security', *Policing & Society* 16/1, 50–66.

Liu, Edward C. (2009), 'The State Secrets Privilege and Other Limits on Litigation Involving Classified Information', Congressional Research Service Report R41741, 28 May.

Loader, Ian (2002), 'Governing European Policing: some problems and prospects', *Policing and Society* 12/4, 291–306.

——and Walker, Neil (2007), *Civilizing Security* (Cambridge: Cambridge University Press).

Lodge, Juliet (2007), 'The (non)Role of National Parliaments in the EU's AFSJ and the Security Policies on New Technologies', Paper prepared for the CEPS Conference on 'Democratic Control and Judicial Accountability in an Area of Freedom, Security and Justice', 4–6 July 2007, Brussels.

Lord, Christopher (1998), *Democracy in the European Union* (Sheffield: Sheffield Academic Press).

Ludford, Sarah (2008), 'Conservatives and Socialists block search for rendition truth', Press Release, 11 December 2008.

——(2004), 'An EU JHA Policy: What should it Comprise?', in Joanna Apap (ed), *Justice and Home Affairs in the EU: Liberty and Security Issues after Enlargement* (Cheltenham: Edward Elgar Publishing), 27–35.

Lummer, Benjamin (2008a), '50 years of Interparliamentary Cooperation: Disaggregating parliamentary participation: an analysis of different policy fields', Conference Proceedings: 'Fifty Years of Interparliamentary Cooperation: Progressing towards Effective Cross-Level Parliamentarism?' (Berlin: Stiftung Wissenschaft und Politik).

——(2008b), '50 years of Interparliamentary Cooperation: Early Warning Mechanism', Conference Proceedings: 'Fifty Years of Interparliamentary Cooperation: Progressing towards Effective Cross-Level Parliamentarism?' (Berlin: Stiftung Wissenschaft und Politik).

Lustgarten, Laurence (2003), 'National Security and Political Policing: Some Thoughts on Values, Ends and Law', in Jean-Paul Brodeur, Peter Gill, and Dennis Töllberg (eds), *Democracy, Law and Security: Internal security services in contemporary Europe* (Aldershot: Ashgate), 319–34.

Lyon, David (2003), *Surveillance after September 11* (Cambridge: Polity).

Maddrell, Paul (2009), 'Failing Intelligence: U.S. Intelligence in the Age of Transnational Threats', *International Journal of Intelligence and CounterIntelligence* 22/2, 195–220.

Magee, Ian (2008), 'The Review of Criminality Information (ROCI)', Doc. HO_01033_G, London: Home Office.

Marty, Dick (2007a), 'UN Security Council black lists: introductory memorandum', Council of Europe Parliamentary Assembly, Committee on Legal Affairs and Human Rights, Memorandum by Rapporteur, Doc. AS/Jur (2007) 14, 19 March 2007, Strasbourg.

——(2007b), 'Report on UN Security Council and European Union blacklists', Council of Europe Parliamentary Assembly, Committee on Legal Affairs and Human Rights, Report by Rapporteur, Doc. 11454, 16 November 2007, Strasbourg.

——(2007c), 'Secret detentions and illegal transfers of detainees involving Council of Europe member states: second report', Council of Europe Parliamentary Assembly, Committee on Legal Affairs and Human Rights, Report by Rapporteur, Doc. AS/Jur (2007) 36, 7 June 2007.

——(2006), 'Alleged secret detentions and unlawful inter-state transfers of detainees involving Council of Europe member states', Council of Europe Parliamentary Assembly, Committee on Legal Affairs and Human Rights, Report by Rapporteur, Doc. 10957, 12 June 2006, Strasbourg.

Marx, Gary (1988), *Undercover: Police Surveillance in America* (Berkeley: University of California Press).

McCulloch, Jude and Pickering, Sharon (2009), 'Pre-crime and counter-terrorism: imagining future crime in the "war on terror"', *British Journal of Criminology* 49/5, 628–45.

McDonald, Henry (2009), 'Covert army unit played role in Menezes killing', *The Observer*, 8 March.

Mendes, Errol (1999), 'Raising the Social Capital of Policing and Nations: How Can Professional Policing and Civilian Oversight Weaken the Circle of Violence?', in Errol Mendes, Joaquin Zuckerberg, Susan Lecorre, Anne Gabriel, and Jeffrey Clark (eds), *Democratic policing and accountability: global perspectives* (Aldershot: Ashgate), 13–32.

Miller, Greg (2009), 'CIA says it gets its money's worth from Pakistani spy agency', *Los Angeles Times*, 15 November.

Miller, Seumas and Blackler, John (2005), *Ethical Issues in Policing* (Aldershot: Ashgate).

Mitsilegas, Valsamis and Baldaccini, Anneliese (2007), 'Interdependence of the various initiatives and legislative proposals in the fields of counter-terrorism and police cooperation at the European level', Briefing Note, European Parliament, DG Ipol, Policy Department C—Citizens Rights and Constitutional Affairs, Doc. PE 393.257, Brussels, October 2007.

Mohamed, Binyam (2009), 'Statement: I don't want vengeance; only the truth', *Guardian*, 24 February 2009.

Monar, Jörg (2010), 'The Rejection of the EU-US SWIFT Interim Agreement by the European Parliament: A Historic Vote and Its Implications', *European Foreign Affairs Review* 15, 143–51.

——(2009), 'Justice and Home Affairs', *Journal of Common Market Studies* 47/S1, 151–70.

——(2008), 'Justice and Home Affairs', *Journal of Common Market Studies* 46/S1, 109–26.

——(2007), 'Common Threat and Common Response? The European Union's Counter-Terrorism Strategy and its Problems', *Government and Opposition* 42/3, 292–313.

——(2006), 'Cooperation in the Justice and Home Affairs Domain: Characteristics, Constraints and Progress', *European Integration* 28/5, 495–509.

——(2005a), 'Anti-terrorism law and policy: the case of the European Union', in Victor V. Ramraj, Michael Hor, and Kent Roach (eds), *Global Anti-Terrorism Law and Policy* (Cambridge: Cambridge University Press), 425–52.

——(2005b), 'Transparency in the exercise of power in the "constitutionalized" Union: the problem of diffused leadership and responsibility', in Deidre Curtin, A.E. Kellermann, and S. Blockmans (eds), *The EU Constitution: The Best Way Forward?* (The Hague: TMC Asser Instituut), 209–20.

——(2004), 'The EU as an International Actor in the Domain of Justice and Home Affairs', *European Foreign Affairs Review* 9, 395–415.

Moravcsik, Andreas (2002), 'In Defence of the "Democratic Deficit": Reassessing Legitimacy in the European Union', *Journal of Common Market Studies* 40/4, 603–24.

Morgan, Rod and Newburn, Tim (1997), *The Future of Policing* (Oxford: Clarendon Press).

Mueller, John and Stewart Mark, 'Terror, Security, and Money: Balancing the Risks, Benefits, and Costs of Homeland Security', Paper at the Annual Convention of the Midwest Political Science Association, Chicago, 1 April, 2011.

Müller-Wille, Björn (2008), 'The Effect of International Terrorism on EU Intelligence Co-operation', *Journal of Common Market Studies* 46/1, 49–73.

——(2006), 'Intelligence and Democratic Accountability: A Blessing Not a Curse', *European Security* 15/4, 491–506.

——(2002), 'EU Intelligence Co-operation: A Critical Analysis', *Contemporary Security Policy* 23/2, 61–86.

Münkler, Herfried (2002), *Die neuen Kriege* (Berlin: Rowohlt).

Murray, Craig (2007), *Murder in Samarkand: A British Ambassador's Controversial Defiance of Tyranny in the War on Terror* (Edinburgh: Mainstream).

Nadelmann, Ethan (1993a), *Cops Across Borders: The Internationalization of U.S. Criminal Law Enforcement* (University Park, PA: Pennsylvania State University Press).

——(1993b), 'U.S. Police Activities in Europe', in Cyrille Fijnaut (ed), *The Internationalization of Police Cooperation in Western Europe* (Deventer: Kluwer), 135–54.

National Commission on Terrorist Attacks upon the United States (2004), '9–11 Commission Report', online access: <http://www.9-11commission.gov/>.

Naumann, Michael (2009), 'Jeder ist verdächtig', *Die Zeit*, 23 April 2009.
Neumann, Peter (2009), *Old and New Terrorism: Late Modernity, Globalization and the Transformation of Political Violence* (Cambridge: Polity).
Neumann, Volker (2007), 'Das parlamentarische Kontrollgremium', in Wolbert Smidt et al (eds), *Geheimhaltung und Transparenz: Demokratische Kontrolle der Geheimdienste im internationalen Vergleich* (Münster: Lit), 46–9.
Neve, Rudie, Vervoorn, Lisette, Leeuw, Frans, and Bogaerts, Stefan (2006), 'First inventory of policy on counterterrorism: Germany, France, Italy, Spain, the United Kingdom and the United States—"research in progress"', Cahier 2006-3a, The Hague: Wetenschappelijk Onderzoek- en Documentatiecentrum (WODC).
Neyroud, Peter and Beckley, Alan (2007), *Policing Ethics and Human Rights* (Ufculme, Devon: Willan).
——and Disley, Emma (2008), 'Technology and Policing: Implications for Fairness and Legitimacy', *Policing* 2/2, 1–7.
Nilsson, Hans (2004), 'Judicial Cooperation in the European Union', in EULEC (ed), *European Cooperation against Terrorism: Conference* (Nijmegen: Wolf Legal Publishers), 15–22.
Nomikos, John (2005), 'A European Union Intelligence Service for Confronting Terrorism', *International Journal of Intelligence and CounterIntelligence* 18/2, 191–203.
Norheim-Martinsen, Per and Ravndal, Jacob Aasland (2011), 'Towards Intelligence-Driven Peace Operations? The Evolution of UN and EU Intelligence Structures', *International Peacekeeping* 18/4, 454–67.
Norman, Paul (2005), 'The evolution of European policing strategies in response to transnational crime', in John Sheptycki and Ali Wardak (eds), *Transnational and comparative criminology* (London: GlassHouse), 317–34.
Norton-Taylor, Richard (2009), 'The secret servants', *The Guardian Weekend*, 11 July 2009.
——(2005), 'Documents reveal hidden EU cooperation with US', *The Guardian*, 1 September 2005.
Nowak, Manfred (2009), 'Fact-Finding on Torture and Ill-Treatment and Conditions of Detention', *Journal of Human Rights Practice* 1/1, 101–19.
Nye, Joseph and Keohane, Robert (1971), 'Transnational Relations and World Politics: An Introduction', in Robert Keohane and Joseph Nye (eds), *Transnational Relations and World Politics* (Cambridge, MA: Harvard University Press), ix–xxiv.
Occhipinti, John (2010), 'Parallel paths and productive partners: the EU and US on counter-terrorism', in Frédéric Lemieux (ed), *International Police Co-operation: Emerging issues, theory and practice* (Cullompton: Willan), 167–85.
——(2003), *The Politics of EU Police Cooperation: Toward a European FBI?* (Boulder, CO: Lynne Rienner Publishers).
O'Donnell, Guillermo (2004), 'Why the Rule of Law Matters', *Journal of Democracy* 15/4, 32–46.
Omand, David (2009), 'The National Security Strategy: Implications for the UK intelligence community', Discussion Paper for the IPPR Commission on National Security for the 21st Century, February 2009 (London: Institute for Public Policy Research).
——(2007), 'The Dilemmas of Using Secret Intelligence for Public Security', in Peter Hennessy (ed), *The New Protective State: Government, Intelligence and Terrorism* (London: Continuum), 142–69.
O'Neill, Maria (2012), *The Evolving EU Counter-Terrorism Legal Framework* (Abingdon: Routledge).

OSCE (2009), *Guidebook on Democratic Policing*. Online version: <http://polis.osce.org/library/f/2505/113/OSCE-AUS-EVT-2505-EN-Background.pdf>.

O'Toole, Laurence J. Jr. (1997), 'The Implications for Democracy in a Networked Bureaucratic World', *Journal of Public Administration Research and Theory* 7/3, 443–59.

Papadopoulos, Yannis (2007), 'Problems of Democratic Accountability in Network and Multilevel Governance', *European Law Journal* 13/4, 469–86.

Parliament of Ireland, Joint Committee on European Scrutiny (2007), Draft Council Decision: Discussion with Department of Justice, Equality and Law Reform on 13 December 2007, 30JeuS 1, No. 3, Official Report—Revised (Dublin: The Stationery Office).

Pavia, Will (2008), 'Miliband apologises over US rendition flights that did land on British soil', *Times Online*, 21 February.

Pawlak, Patryk (2010), 'Transatlantic homeland security cooperation: the promise of new modes of governance in global affairs', *Journal of Transatlantic Studies* 8/2, 139–57.

——(2009), 'Made in the USA? The Influence of the US on the EU's Data Protection Regime', CEPS Liberty and Security in Europe Series, Brussels, November 2009. Peers, Steve (2005), 'Operational Collaboration On Justice, Security and Policing in the Constitutional Framework', in Deidre Curtin, A.E. Kellermann, and S. Blockmans (eds), *The EU Constitution: The Best Way Forward?* (The Hague: T.M.C. Asser Press), 201–7.

Peirce, Gareth (2009), 'Make sure you say that you were treated properly', *London Review of Books* 31/9, 9–14.

Peterson, John (2004), 'America as a European Power: The End of Empire by Integration?', *International Affairs* 80/4, 613–29.

Pillar, Paul (2006), 'Jihadist Terrorism: The State of the Threat', Presentation at 'Jihadi Terrorism—Where Do We Stand?' Second IRRI Conference on International terrorism, Brussels, 13 February 2006.

Pincus, Walter (2009), '1,600 are suggested daily for FBI's list: Number of names on terrorist watch list at 400,000, agency says', *Washington Post*, 1 November 2009.

Pitschas, Rainer (2005), 'Kulturelle Integration in der europäischen inneren Sicherheit: Die interkulturelle Zusammenarbeit nationaler Polizeikräfte im Kontext des Europäischen Polizeirechts', in Peter-Christian Müller-Graff (ed), *Der Raum der Freiheit, der Sicherheit und des Rechts* (Baden-Baden: Nomos), 149–63.

Pollack, Mark (2005), 'The New Transatlantic Agenda at Ten: Reflections on an Experiment in International Governance', *Journal of Common Market Studies* 43/5, 899–919.

——(2003), *The Engines of the European Integration* (Oxford: Oxford University Press).

Presidency of the Council of the European Union (2009), 'Developing synergies between Internal and External Security', Informal Meeting of the Ministers of the Interior on the Future of Europol and EU Law Enforcement Cooperation', Working document No 3. Online access: <http://www.statewatch.org/news/2009/sep/eu-council-presidency-no-3-internal-external.pdf>.

——(2008), 'EU Interior Ministers Reach Political Consensus on Europol and Enhancing the Security of Explosives and Approve the Commission's Mandate to Negotiate with the USA', Press Release, 18 April 2008.

——(2001a), 'Conclusions and Plan of Action of the Presidency', Extraordinary informal meeting of the European Council', Presidency, Brussels, 21 September 2001.

——(2001b), 'Presidency Conclusions of the Laeken European Council (14 and 15 December 2001): Annex I: Laeken Declaration on the future of the European Union', in *Bulletin of the European Union* 2001, No 12, 19–23.

Priest, Dana (2005a), 'CIA Holds Terror Suspects in Secret Prisons', *Washington Post*, 2 November 2005.

——(2005b), 'Secret Anti-Terrorism Unit Pairs CIA, Europeans', *Washington Post*, 7 April 2005.

——(2005c), 'Help From France Key In Covert Operations', *Washington Post*, 3 July 2005.

——and Arkin, William (2011), *Top Secret America: The Rise of the New American Security State* (New York: Little, Brown, and Company).

Privy Counsellor Review Committee (2003), 'Anti-terrorism, Crime and Security Act 2001 Review Report', Presented to Parliament pursuant to Section 122(5) of the Anti-terrorism, Crime and Security Act 2001, HC 100 (London: The Stationery Office).

Puntscher Riekmann, Sonja (2008), 'Security, Freedom and Accountability: Europol and Frontex', in Elspeth Guild and Florian Geyer (eds), *Security versus Justice?: Police and Judicial Cooperation in the European Union* (Aldershot: Ashgate), 19–34.

Raab, Jörg and Milward, H. Brinton (2003), 'Dark Networks as Problems', *Journal of Public Administration Research and Theory* 13/4, 413–39.

Ratcliffe, Jerry (2008), *Intelligence-Led Policing* (Ufculme, Devon: Willan Publishing).

——and Guidetti, Ray (2007), 'State police investigative structure and the adoption of intelligence-led policing', *Policing* 31/1, 109–28.

Rees, Wyn (2011), *The US-EU Security Relationship* (Basingstoke: Palgrave Macmillan).

——(2006), *Transatlantic Counter-terrorism Cooperation: Drugs, Crime and Terrorism in the Twenty-First Century* (London: Routledge).

——(2003), 'Transnational organized crime, security and the European Union', in Felia Allum and Renate Siebert (eds), *Organized Crime and the Challenge to Democracy* (London: Routledge), 112–26.

Reeve, Simon (2006), *One Day in September: The Full Story of the 1972 Munich Olympics Massacre and the Israeli Revenge Operation 'Wrath of God'* (New York: Arcade Publishing).

Reiner, Robert (2000), *The Politics of the Police* (Oxford: Oxford University Press).

Rettman, Andrew (2011), 'EU intelligence bureau sent officers to Libya', *EU Observer*, 12 April 2011.

Rhodes, R.A.W. (1990), 'Policy Networks: a British Perspective', *Journal of Theoretical Politics* 2/3, 293–317.

Rijken, Conny (2006), 'Joint Investigation Teams: Principles, Practice, and Problems Lessons Learnt from the First Efforts to Establish a JIT', *Utrecht Law Review* 2/2, 99–118.

——and Vermeulen, Gert (2006), *Joint Investigation Teams in the European Union: From Theory to Practice* (The Hague: TMC Asser Press).

Riksdagens ombudsmän [Sweden's Parliamentary Ombudsman] (2005), 'A review of the enforcement by the Security Police of a Government decision to expel two Egyptian citizens', Report, 22 March 2005.

Rimington, Stella (2002), *Open Secret: The Autobiography of the Former Director-General of MI5* (London: Arrow Books).

Roberts, Alasdair (2006), *Blacked Out: Government Secrecy in the Information Age* (New York: Cambridge University Press).

Robertson, Kenneth G. (1999), *Secrecy and Open Government: Why Governments Want you to Know* (Basingstoke: Palgrave, 1999).

Robertson, Simon (1997), 'Intelligence-Led Policing: a European Union View', in Angus Smith (ed), *Intelligence Led Policing: International Perspectives on Policing in the 21st Century* (Lawrenceville (NJ): International Association of Law Enforcement Intelligence Analysts, Inc.), 21–3.

Ross, Mike (2009), 'Pakistan: A Test of Transatlantic Co-operation', NATO Parliamentary Assembly, 2009 Annual Session, 181 PCTR 09 E, Rapporteur of the US. Online access: <http://www.nato-pa.int/default.asp?SHORTCUT = 1775>.

Rupprecht, Reinhard (1993), 'Internationalization of Police Cooperation in Western Europe: the German Perspective', in Cyrille Fijnaut (ed), *The Internationalization of Police Cooperation in Western Europe* (Deventer: Kluwer), 41–8.

Salgó, Lásyló (2009), 'Priorities of Europol in Western Balkans', Speaking Points, European Parliament, Brussels, 01 April 2009.

——(2004), 'Police Co-operation from the Perspective of a new EU Member State', in ICLN and EULEC (eds), *European Co-operation against Terrorism* (Nijmegen: Wolf Publishers), 83–9.

Salter, Mark (2008), 'Imagining Numbers: Risk, Quantification and Aviation Security', *Security Dialogue*, 39/2–3, 243–66.

Sanfrutos Cano, Eulalia (2008), 'The Third Pillar and the Court of Justice: A "Praetorian Communitarization" of Police and Judicial Cooperation in Criminal Matters?', in Elspeth Guild and Florian Geyer (eds), *Security versus Justice? Police and Judicial Cooperation in the European Union* (Aldershot: Ashgate), 51–69.

Santiago, Michael (2000), *Europol and Police Cooperation in Europe* (Lewiston: The Edwin Mellen Press).

Scharpf, Fritz W. (1999), *Governing in Europe: effective and democratic?* (Oxford: Oxford University Press).

——(1998), 'Demokratie in der transnationalen Politik', in Wolfgang Streeck (ed), *Internationale Wirtschaft, nationale Demokratie. Herausforderungen für die Demokratietheorie* (Frankfurt a.M.: Campus Verlag), 151–74.

Scheinin, Martin (2009), 'Report of the Special Rapporteur on the promotion and protection of human rights and fundamental freedoms while countering terrorism', UN General Assembly, Human Rights Council, Doc. A/HRC/10/3, 4 February 2009.

——(2007), 'Access to Justice before International Human Rights Bodies: Reflections on the Practice of the UN Human Rights Committee and the European Court of Human Rights', in Francesco Francioni (ed), *Access to Justice as a Human Right* (Oxford: Oxford University Press), 135–52.

Schmid, Gerhard (2009), 'Die Kontrolle von EU-Intelligence durch das Europäische Parlament', in Thomas Jäger and Anna Daun (eds), *Geheimdienste in Europa: Transformation, Kooperation und Kontrolle* (Wiesbaden: VS Verlag), 333–47.

Schmid, Alex and Jongman, Albert (1988), *Political Terrorism* (Edison, NJ: Transaction Publishers).

Schmidt-Radefeldt, Roman (2005), *Parlamentarische Kontrolle der internationalen Streit kräfteintegration* (Berlin: Duncker und Humblot).

Schmitt, Eric and Shanker, Tom (2011), *Counterstrike: The Untold Story of America's Secret Campaign Against Al Qaeda'* (New York: Henry Holt and Company).

Schmitter, Philippe (2000), *How to Democratize the European Union... and Why Bother?* (Lanham, MD: Rowman & Littlefield Publishers).

Schröder, Gerhard (2001), Regierungserklärung des Bundeskanzlers Gerhard Schröder zu den Anschlägen in den Vereinigten Staaten von Amerika vom 12. September 2001'. Online access: <http://www.documentarchiv.de/brd/2001/rede_schroeder_terror-usa.html>.

Schulte, Rainer (2001), 'A German Perspective on Future European Security Needs', in Daniel J. Koenig and Dilip K. Das (eds), *International Police Cooperation: A World Perspective* (Boston: Lexington Books), 141–58.

Sheptycki, James (2007), 'High Policing in the Security Control Society', *Policing* 1/1, 70–9.

——(2002), *In Search of Transnational Policing: Towards a Sociology of Global Policing* (Aldershot: Ashgate).

——(2001), 'Patrolling the New European (In)Security Field: Organisational Dilemmas and Operational Solutions for Policing the Internal Borders of Europe', *European Journal of Crime, Criminal Law and Criminal Justice* 9/2, 144–60.

——(ed) (2000), *Issues in transnational policing* (London: Routledge).

Shapiro, Jeremy and Byman, Daniel (2006), 'Bridging the Transatlantic Counterterrorism Gap', *The Washington Quarterly* 29/4, 33–50.

Simmons, A. John (1999), 'Justification and Legitimacy', *Ethics* 109/4, 739–771.

Slaughter, Anne-Marie (2009), 'America's edge', *Foreign Affairs* 88/1, 94–113.

——(2004a), *A New World Order* (Princeton, NJ: Princeton University Press).

——(2004b), 'Disaggregated Sovereignty: Towards the Public Accountability of Global Government Networks', *Government and Opposition* 39/2, 159–90.

Smidt, Wolbert (2007), 'Systeme parlamentarischer Kontrolle von Geheimdiensten—Versuch eines Vergleichs', in Wolbert Smidt et al (eds), *Geheimhaltung und Transparenz: Demokratische Kontrolle der Geheimdienste im internationalen Vergleich* (Berlin: Lit), 235–56.

Smith, Angus (1997), 'Editor's Introduction', in Angus Smith (ed), *Intelligence Led Policing: International Perspectives on Policing in the 21st Century* (Lawrenceville (NJ): International Association of Law Enforcement Intelligence Analysts, Inc.), 3–4.

Sørensen, Eva and Torfing, Jacob (2005), 'The Democratic Anchorage of Governance Networks', *Scandinavian Political Studies* 28/3, 195–218.

Sottiaux, Stefan (2008), *Terrorism and the Limitation of Rights: The ECHR and the US Constitution* (Oxford and Portland, Oregon: Hart Publishing).

Spence, David (ed) (2007a), *The European Union and Terrorism* (London: John Harper Publishing).

——(2007b), 'Introduction: International Terrorism—the Quest for a Coherent EU Response', in David Spence (ed), *The European Union and Terrorism* (London: John Harper Publishing), 1–29.

Statewatch (2007), 'Terror Lists—monitoring proscription, designation and asset freezing: EU case-law'; available at <http://www.statewatch.org/terrorlists/listschallenges.html>.

——(2001), 'US letter from Bush to EU, 16.10.01', Statewatch analysis No 2; available at <http://www.statewatch.org/analyses/no-2-useu.pdf>.

Stegmaier, Peter and Feltes, Thomas (2007), '"Vernetzung" als neuer Effektivitätsmythos für die "innere Sicherheit"', *Aus Politik und Zeitgeschichte*, 12, 18–25.

Steinberg, Guido (2009), 'Terrorismusbekämpfung', in Stiftung Wissenschaft und Politik (ed), *Deutsche Nah-, Mittelost- und Nordafrikapolitik* (Berlin, 16–23 May).

Stevenson, Jonathan (2005), 'Transatlantic Counter-Terrorism Cooperation after 11 September 2001', in Karin von Hippel (ed), *Europe Confronts Terrorism* (Houndmills: Palgrave Macmillan), 208–31.

Stevenson, Richard (2005), 'President Makes It Clear: Phrase Is "War on Terror"', *New York Times*, 4 August 2005.

Stewart, Phil (2009), 'U.S. invokes jurisdiction in CIA kidnap case', *Reuters*, 23 September 2009.

Storbeck, Jürgen (2009), 'Ansätze und Entwicklungsmöglichkeiten europäischer Intelligencestrukturen', in Thomas Jäger and Anna Daun (eds), *Geheimdienste in Europa: Transformation, Kooperation und Kontrolle* (Wiesbaden: Verlag für Sozialwissenschaften), 155–67.

Strange, Hannah (2005), 'United Nations Orders Guantanamo Abuse Inquiry', UPI, London, 18 November 2005.

Süddeutsche Zeitung (2008), '"Zu viele Eingriffe zu Lasten der Freiheit": Wolfgang Hoffmann-Riem zur Zukunft der Medien und zur hektischen Politik der inneren Sicherheit', Interview, 12/13 April 2008.

Sullivan, John (2008), 'Global Terrorism and the Police', Paper presented at 49th Annual ISA Convention, San Francisco, CA, 29 March, 2008.

Svendsen, Adam (2008), 'The Globalization of Intelligence Since 9/11: The Optimization of Intelligence Liaison Arrangements', *International Journal of Intelligence and CounterIntelligence* 21/4, 661–78.

Szyszkowitz, Tessa (2005), 'The European Union', in Karin von Hippel (ed), *Europe Confronts Terrorism* (Houndmills: Palgrave Macmillan), 171–90.

Tanchev, Evgeni (2005), 'Wine-bottling legitimacy or EU legitimacy by a written Constitution', in Deidre Curtin, A. E. Kellermann and S. Blockmans (eds), *The EU Constitution: The Best Way Forward?* (The Hague: TMC Asser Instituut), 105–44.

Tenet, George (2007), *At the Center of the Storm: My Years at the CIA* (New York: HarperLuxe).

Thwaites, Nadine (2003), 'Mutual Trust in Criminal Matters: the European Court of Justice gives a first interpretation of a provision of the Convention implementing the Schengen Agreement', *German Law Journal* 4/3, 254–62.

Torda, Péter (2007), 'European arrangements for co-operation and mutual assistance between law enforcement agencies during consequence management of terrorism: The Hungarian perspective', 15 June 2007. Online access: <http://ukinhungary-stage.fco.gov.uk/resources/en/pdf/pdf1/posthu_wpcbrnabridged>.

Tran, Mark (2008), 'EU rebukes Poland and Romania over rendition role', *The Guardian*, 22 February 2008.

Travis, Alan (2009), 'Police increased stop and searches for 'racial balance', *The Guardian*, 18 June 2009.

Tremlett, Giles and Black, Ian (2004), 'Explosives theft linked to Madrid bomb', *The Guardian*, 23 March 2004.

Treverton, Gregory (2009), *Intelligence for an Age of Terror* (Cambridge: Cambridge University Press).

Tsakatika, Myrto (2007), 'A Parliamentary Dimension for EU Soft Governance', *European Integration* 29/5, 549–64.

Tsoukala, Anastassia (2004), 'Democracy against Security: the debates about Counter Terrorism in the European Parliament, September 2001–June 2003', *Alternatives* 29, August-October, 417–39.

UK Chief Inspector of Constabulary (2009), 'Adapting to Protest—Nurturing the British model of policing,' November, London.
UK Home Office (2009), 'Pursue Prevent Protect Prepare: The United Kingdom's Strategy for Countering International Terrorism', Presented to Parliament by the Prime Minister and the Secretary of State for the Home Department by Command of Her Majesty, Doc. CM 7547, March, London.
UK Prime Minister's Office (2005), 'PM's Press Conference—5 August 2005'. Online access: <http://webarchive.nationalarchives.gov.uk/20061004051823/number10.gov.uk/page8041>.
United Nations Economic and Social Council, Commission on Human Rights (2002), 'Report of the United Nations High Commissioner for Human Rights and follow-up to the World Conference on Human Rights', Report of the High Commissioner submitted pursuant to General Assembly resolution 48/141, Doc. E/CN.4/2002/18, 27 February 2002.
United Nations General Assembly (2009), 'Report of the Committee against Torture: Forty-first session (3–21 November 2008) and Forty second session (27 April–15 May 2009)', Doc. A/64/44.
——(2006), 'Resolution 60/288 of 8 September 2006: The UN Global Counter-Terrorism Strategy', 20 September 2006, Doc. A/RES/60/898.
United Nations Security Council (2003), 'All must work together to counter terrorism, prevent spread of weapons of mass destruction, Secretary-General says', Press Release, Doc. SG/SM8624, SC/7680, 6 March 2003.
——(2001), 'Resolution 1373 (2001)', adopted by the Security Council at its 4385th meeting on 28 September 2001, Doc. S/RES/1373 (2001), New York.
——(1999), 'Resolution 1267 on sanctions against the Taliban regime in Afghanistan', New York.
US Department of Homeland Security (2010), 'U.S.-EU Joint Declaration on Aviation Security', Press Release, 21 January 2010.
——(2007), *National Strategy for Aviation Security*, Washington, DC, 26 March 2007.
——(2002), *National Strategy for Homeland Security*, Washington, DC, July 2002.
US Department of Justice, Office of the Inspector General, Audit Division (OIG) (2009), 'The Federal Bureau of Investigation's Terrorist Watchlist Nomination Practices', Audit Report 09-25, May 2009. Online access: <http://www.usdoj.gov/oig/reports/FBI/a0925/final.pdf>.
US Department of Justice (DOJ), Office of Justice Programs, Bureau of Justice Assistance, in collaboration with DOJ's Global Justice Information Sharing Initiative and the U.S. Department of Homeland Security (n.d.), 'Fusion Center Guidelines: Developing and Sharing Information and Intelligence in a New Era'. Online access: <http://www.it.ojp.gov/documents/fusion_center_guidelines_law_enforcement.pdf>.
US Department of Justice, Office of Legal Counsel (2005), 'Re: Application of 18 U.S.C. §§ 2340–2340A to [*redacted*] That May Be Used in the Interrogation of a High Value al Qaeda Detainee', Memorandum for John A. Rizzo, Senior Deputy General Counsel, Central Intelligence Agency, by Steven G. Bradbury, Principal Deputy Assistant Attorney General, Washington, D.C., 10 May 2005. Online access: http://luxmedia.vo.llnwd.net/o10/clients/aclu/olc_05102005_bradbury46pg.pdf.
US General Accounting Office (2009), 'Firearm and Explosives Background Checks Involving Terrorist Watch List Records', GAO-09-125R, 21 May 2009.

United States Secret Service (2010), 'United States Secret Service signs partnership agreement with United Kingdom officials establishing the second European Electronic Crimes Task Force', Press Release, 9 August 2010.

United States Senate Committee on Homeland Security and Governmental Affairs, 'Violent islamist extremism, the internet, and the homegrown terrorist threat', Majority & Minority Staff Report, 8 May 2008.

Van den Wyngaert, Christine (1997), 'Organized Crime, Proactive Policing and International Cooperation in Criminal Matters: Who Controls the Police in a Transnational Context?', in Monica den Boer (ed), *Undercover Policing and Accountability from an International Perspective* (Maastricht: European Institute of Public Administration), 163–77.

Vande Walle, Gérald (2008), Paper presented at the international congress on accountability of international intelligence cooperation (Norway), Belgian Standing Intelligence Services Review Committee, October 2008. Online access: <http://www.comiteri.be/images/pdf/engels/norwaypaper.pdf>.

Van Kersbergen, Kees and Van Waarden, Frans (2004), '"Governance" as a Bridge Between Disciplines: Cross-Disciplinary Inspiration Regarding Shifts in Governance and Problems of Governability, Accountability and Legitimacy', *European Journal of Political Research* 43/2, 143–71.

Van Leeuwen, Marianne (ed) (2003), *Confronting Terrorism: European Experiences, Threat Perceptions and Policies* (The Hague: Kluwer Law International).

Van Sluis, Arie and Cachet, Lex (2007), 'Police, Policing and Governance in the Netherlands and in the United Kingdom', in Victor Bekkers et al (ed), *Governance and the Democratic Deficit: Assessing the Democratic Legitimacy of Governance Practices* (Aldershot: Ashgate), 107–24.

Van Waarden, Frans (2003), 'Regulating across borders: the power of international expert communities in international regulation and enforcement', Paper presented at the Robert Schuman Centre, EUI, Florence.

Verbruggen, Frank (2004), 'Bull's-eye? Two Remarkable EU Framework Decisions in the Fight Against Terrorism', in Cyrille Fijnaut, Jan Wouters, and Frederik Naert (eds), *Legal instruments in the fight against terrorism: a transatlantic dialogue* (Leiden: Martinus Nijhoff Publishers), 299–341.

Verfaillie, Kristof and Vander Beken, Tom (2008), 'Proactive Policing and the Assessment of Organised Crime', *Policing: An International Journal of Police Strategies & Management* 31/4, 534–55.

Vervaele, John A. E. (2005), 'Terrorism and information sharing between the intelligence and law enforcement communities in the US and the Netherlands: emergency criminal law?', *Utrecht Law Review* 1/1, 1–27.

Wagner, Wolfgang (2004), '"Halt, Europol!" Probleme der europäischen Polizeikooperation für parlamentarische Kontrolle und Grundrechtsschutz', HSFK-Report Nr. 15/2004 (Frankfurt am Main: HSFK).

Walker, Neil (2004), 'In Search of the Area of Freedom, Security and Justice: A Constitutional Odyssey', in Neil Walker (ed), *Europe's Area of Freedom, Security and Justice* (Oxford: Oxford University Press), 1–37.

Walsh, James (2010), *The International Politics of Intelligence Sharing* (New York: Columbia University Press).

Walters, William (2002), 'Mapping Schengenland: denaturalizing the border', *Society and Space* 20/5, 561–80.

Weick, Karl (1995), *Sensemaking in Organizations* (London: Sage).

Weiler, Joseph (1995), 'Does Europe Need a Constitution? Reflections on Demos, Telos and the German Maastricht Decision', *European Law Journal*, 1/3, 219–58.

Wensink, Wim, Van de Velde, Michael, and Boer, Lianne (2011), 'Estimated Costs of EU Counterterrorism Measures', Note, European Parliament, Directorate General for Internal Policies, Policy Department C, Doc. PE 453.181, May 2011.

White House (2011), *National Strategy for Counterterrorism*, Washington, DC, June 2011.

——(2010), 'Remarks by Vice President Biden to the European Parliament', Brussels, 6 May 2010.

——(2002), 'The National Security Strategy of the United States of America', September 2002, Washington DC.

——Office of the Press Secretary (2004), 'Text of U.S.—EU Declaration on Combating Terrorism', Shannon, 26 June 2004.

Whitlock, Craig (2009), 'Lithuanian resignation tied to CIA inquiry', *Washington Post*, 15 December.

——(2005), 'CIA Ruse Is Said to Have Damaged Probe in Milan', *Washington Post*, 6 December.

Whitman, James (2004), 'The Two Western Cultures of Privacy: Dignity versus Liberty', *Yale Law Journal* 113/6, 1151–221.

Wiegand, Irina (2008), *The Protection of Human Rights and Fundamental Freedoms in the Fight Against Terrorism: The Case of the European Union after September 11, 2001* (Stuttgart: ibidem).

Wilkinson, Paul (ed) (2007), *Homeland Security in the UK: future preparedness for terrorist attack since 9/11* (Abingdon: Routledge).

——(2011), *Terrorism versus democracy: the liberal state response*, 3rd edn (Abingdon: Routledge).

Wills, Aidan et al (2011), 'Parliamentary Oversight of Security and Intelligence Agencies in the European Union', Study for the European Parliament, Directorate General for Internal Policies, Policy Department C, Doc. PE 315.238, 20 June 2011.

Wilson, Scott and Kamen, Al (2009), '"Global War on Terror" is given new name', *Washington Post*, 25 March 2009.

Wimmel, Andreas (2008), 'Die demokratische Legitimität europäischen Regierens: ein Labyrinth ohne Ausgang?', *Integration* 31/1, 48–64.

Wincott, Daniel (2002), 'National States, European Union and Changing Dynamics in the Quest for Legitimacy', in Anthony Arnull and Daniel Wincott (ed), *Accountability and Legitimacy in the European Union* (Oxford: Oxford University Press), 487–96.

Wood, Jennifer and Dupont, Benoît (eds) (2006), *Democracy, Society and the Governance of Security* (Cambridge: Cambridge University Press).

——and Shearing, Clifford (2007), *Imagining Security* (Devon: Willan).

Zegart, Amy (2007), *Spying blind: the CIA, the FBI, and the origins of 9/11* (Princeton: Princeton University Press).

Zürn, Michael (2005), 'Global Governance and Legitimacy Problems', in *Government and Opposition* 39/2, 260–87.

Zweifel, Thomas (2006), *International Organizations & Democracy: Accountability, Politics, and Power* (Boulder, CO: Lynne Rienner Publishers).

International Treaties and Agreements

Agreement between the United States of America and the European Police Office, signed by the Ambassador of the United States of America to the European Union and the Director of Europol, Brussels, 6 December 2001. Online access: <https://www.europol.europa.eu/sites/default/files/flags/united_states_of_america.pdf>.

Consolidated Version of the Treaty on the functioning of the European Union (TFEU). Online access: <http://eur-lex.europa.eu/LexUriServ/LexUriServ.do?uri=OJ:C:2010:083:0047:0200:en:PDF>.

Joint EU-US Action Plan, 3 December 1995. Online access: <http://eurunion.org>.

Supplemental agreement between the Europol Police Office and the United States of America on the exchange of personal data and related information, signed by the Representative of the United States of America to the European Union and the Director of Europol, Copenhagen, 20 December 2002. Online access: <https://www.europol.europa.eu/sites/default/files/flags/supplemental_agreement_between_europol_and_the_usa_on_exchange_of_personal_data_and_related_information.pdf>.

Treaty of Lisbon amending the Treaty on European Union and the Treaty establishing the European Community, Doc. 2007/C 306/0, Lisbon, 13 December 2007. Online access: <http://europa.eu/lisbon_treaty/full_text/index_en.htm>.

Treaty on European Union (TEU, often referred to as Maastricht Treaty), 7 February 1992. Online access: <http://eur-lex.europa.eu/en/treaties/dat/11992M/htm/11992M.html>.

Websites

American Civil Liberties Union (ACLU)—No Fly List: <http://www.aclu.org/national-security/aclu-challenges-government-no-fly-list>.

Belgian Standing Intelligence Agencies Review Committee: <http://www.comiteri.be/>.

City of New York Police Department: <http://www.nyc.gov/html/nypd/html/home/home.shtml>.

Conference of Community and European Affairs Committees of Parliaments of the European Union (COSAC): <http://www.cosac.eu>.

Council of Europe—Conventions: <http://conventions.coe.int>.

Council of Europe—Country profiles on counter-terrorist capacity: <http://www.coe.int/t/dlapil/codexter/4_theme_files/country_profiles/default_en.asp>.

Der Bundesbeauftragte für den Datenschutz und die Informationsfreiheit (BfDI) [The Federal Commissioner for Data Protection and Freedom of Information]: <http://www.bfdi.bund.de>.

Detainee Inquiry: <http://www.detaineeinquiry.org.uk/>.

EU/EC basic legal texts (founding treaties, etc.): <http://eur-lex.europa.eu/en/treaties/index.htm#founding>.

Eurojust: <http://eurojust.europa.eu/>.

EUR-Lex—Access to European Union law: <http://eur-lex.europa.eu>.

European Commission for Democracy Through Law [Venice Commission]: <http://www.venice.coe.int>.

European Commission—Justice—Protection of personal data: <http://ec.europa.eu/justice/data-protection/index_en.htm>.

European Data Protection Supervisor: <http://www.edps.europa.eu>.

European External Action Service—EU-US Cooperation by Sector: <http://eeas.europa.eu/us/sector_en.htm>.

European Parliament—Relations with National Parliaments: <http://www.europarl.europa.eu/webnp/cms/lang/en/pid/1>.

European Parliament, Committee on Civil Liberties, Justice and Home Affairs (LIBE Committee): <http://www.europarl.europa.eu/committees/en/LIBE/home.html>.

European Parliament—Relations with National Parliaments: <http://www.europarl.europa.eu/webnp/cms/pid/1;jsessionid=B79C7632C640B9A1B40514581B96D0B0?matrix = 1221051954573>.

Europol: <https://www.europol.europa.eu/>.

Europol Joint Supervisory Body: <http://europoljsb.consilium.europa.eu/about.aspx>.

FBI website: <http://www.fbi.gov/>.

Frontex: <http://www.frontex.europa.eu/>.

German Presidency of the EU 2007: <http://www.eu2007.de/de/index.html>.

House of Commons, Home Affairs Committee: 'Project CONTEST—The Government's Counter-Terrorism Strategy', Online access: <http://www.publications.parliament.uk/pa/cm200809/cmselect/cmhaff/212/21205.htm>.

ICPO-Interpol: <http://www.interpol.int>.

Information Commissioner's Office: <http://www.ico.gov.uk/>.

Institute for Criminal Justice Ethics, Overview on Police Codes: <http://www.lib.jjay.cuny.edu/cje/html/codes.html>.

Slovenian Presidency of the EU 2008: <http://www.eu2008.si>.

Southeast European Cooperative Initiative—Regional Center for combating transborder crime (SECI): <http://www.secicenter.org/>.

Statewatch: <http://www.statewatch.org>.

The Charter of Fundamental Rights of the European Union: <http://www.europarl.europa.eu/charter/default_en.htm>.

The Egmont Group of Financial Intelligence Units: http://www.egmontgroup.org/.

UN Action to Counter Terrorism: <http://www.un.org/terrorism/>.

UN Counter-Terrorism Online Handbook: <http://www.un.org/terrorism/cthandbook/index.html>.

UN Security Council Counter-Terrorism Committee: <http://www.un.org/en/sc/ctc/>.

US Bureau of Customs and Border Protection (CBP): <http://www.cbp.gov/>.

US Department of Homeland Security: <http://www.dhs.gov>.

Index

The manufacturer's authorised representative in the EU for product safety is Oxford University Press España S.A. of el Parque Empresarial San Fernando de Henares, Avenida de Castilla, 2 – 28830 Madrid (www.oup.es/en or product.safety@oup.com). OUP España S.A. also acts as importer into Spain of products made by the manufacturer.

www.ingramcontent.com/pod-product-compliance
Ingram Content Group UK Ltd.
Pitfield, Milton Keynes, MK11 3LW, UK
UKHW020924170926
475595UK00031B/51
9780199655052